OUTSOURCING
THE POLITY

OUTSOURCING THE POLITY

Non-State Welfare, Inequality, and Resistance in Myanmar

Gerard McCarthy

SOUTHEAST ASIA PROGRAM PUBLICATIONS

AN IMPRINT OF CORNELL UNIVERSITY PRESS   ITHACA AND LONDON

Publication of this book was made possible by a grant from the Asia Research Institute, National University of Singapore.

First published 2023 by Cornell University Press

Library of Congress Cataloging-in-Publication Data

Names: McCarthy, Gerard (Gerard T. J.), author.
Title: Outsourcing the polity : non-state welfare, inequality, and resistance in Myanmar / Gerard McCarthy.
Description: Ithaca : Southeast Asia Program Publications, an imprint of Cornell University Press, 2023. | Includes bibliographical references and index.
Identifiers: LCCN 2022017829 (print) | LCCN 2022017830 (ebook) | ISBN 9781501767968 (hardcover) | ISBN 9781501767975 (paperback) | ISBN 9781501767999 (pdf) | ISBN 9781501767982 (epub)
Subjects: LCSH: Public welfare—Contracting out—Burma. | Social service—Contracting out—Burma. | Burma—Social policy. | Burma—Social conditions—20th century. | Burma—Social conditions —21st century. | Burma—Economic conditions—20th century. | Burma—Economic conditions—21st century.
Classification: LCC HC422 .M39 2023 (print) | LCC HC422 (ebook) | DDC 338.9591—dc23/eng/20220912
LC record available at https://lccn.loc.gov/2022017829
LC ebook record available at https://lccn.loc.gov/2022017830

Contents

Preface   vii

Acknowledgments   ix

Note on Language, Usage, and Currency   xi

Introduction: Social Outsourcing and Inequality   1

1. Distributive Politics since Colonization   24

Part 1 AUTOCRATIC WELFARE CAPITALISM

2. Post-Socialist Welfare Outsourcing   59

3. Disasters and the Polity   94

Part 2 DEMOCRATIC WELFARE CAPITALISM

4. Democracy, Freedom, and Morality   123

5. Philanthropy and Wealth Defense   148

6. Self-Reliance and Entitlement   178

Conclusion: Path-Dependence and Welfare Regime Change   200

Notes   211

References   237

Index   255

Preface

This book would not have been possible without the support and insight of countless individuals and institutions. Over seven years, hundreds of people gave their time and energy to help me grasp the complexities of non-state welfare in Myanmar. Given the vexed moment in which the country finds itself, I have kept most of my closest interlocutors anonymous. Yet more than anyone else, this book is for them.

The bulk of research for this book was conducted before the February 2021 coup, which came after the harrowing first year of the COVID-19 pandemic. Since the return to military rule, many of the non-state welfare actors at the core of this book have been at the vanguard of the struggle against dictatorship, bravely finding creative ways to support the civil disobedience movement and sustain resistance efforts. At the time of writing, the prospects for a more progressive political order emerging in the near term in Myanmar appear bleak. The military continues to brutally suppress dissent and refuse negotiations while advancing reforms to the electoral system to benefit its political allies. Yet in the face of regime recalcitrance, the terms of Myanmar's political and social order are being contested and reimagined in ways unseen since the struggle for independence. Though this critical juncture has opened new political possibilities, the fracture of existing systems of governance following the coup has also deepened the reliance of everyday people on many of the non-state actors described in this book—private and communally focused—both to survive and to sustain the fight for a more equitable political future.

Amid this fractious and ambiguous moment, I hope the chapters that follow offer some perspective and inspiration for the millions of people seeking to make possible a more equitable and democratic future in Myanmar.

Acknowledgments

I am tremendously grateful to the National University of Singapore (NUS) Asia Research Institute (ARI), Australian National University (ANU), and the University of Yangon for providing the fertile intellectual environments from which this book has sprung. At ANU, Nicholas Farrelly, Nick Cheesman, Paul Kenny, and Caroline Schuster were a constant source of intellectual encouragement, mentorship, and practical advice. At NUS, numerous colleagues gave in-depth input on chapters; they include Naoko Shimazu, Yang Yang, Matthew Reeder, Maitrii Aung-Thwin, Tim Bunnell, Carola Lorea, Neena Mahadev, Andrew Ong, Elliot Prasse-Freeman, James Crabtree, James Sidaway, Matt Wade, Eve Warburton, and the entire ARI Inter-Asian Engagements Cluster. My colleagues in the ANU Department of Political and Social Change—especially Edward Aspinall, Paul Hutchcroft, Tamara Jacka, Marcus Mietzner, Andrew Walker, and Meredith Weiss—similarly offered insightful feedback on conceptual frameworks early in the research. Within the ANU Myanmar Research Centre community—Jane Ferguson, Charlotte Galloway, Helen James, Philip Taylor, and Ben Hillman all gave practical and analytically clear-eyed advice. Special thanks go to David Oakeshott for his meticulous eye for detail and to Justine Chambers for her insight and support during the dissertation. Karina Pelling at the ANU College of Asia and the Pacific CartoGIS unit spent many hours working on my complex map requests. I am especially gratefully for the countless hours spent discussing key concepts and dynamics with staff at the University of Yangon Department of International Relations, where I was Visiting Fellow throughout 2015 and 2016.

Special thanks go to the wider world of Burma scholars, especially Stephen Campbell, Mike Griffiths, and Matt Walton, whose insights and ideas helped me navigate complex empirical, historical, and technical conundrums. Ardeth Maung Thawnghmung, Phyo Win Latt, Mee Mee Zaw, Benedicte Brac de La Perriere, David Brenner, Mary Callahan, Luke Corbin, James Davies, Michael Edwards, Renaud Egreteau, Htwe Htwe Thein, Stephen Huard, Pia Jolliffe, Marie Lall, Jennifer Leehey, Shona Loong, Helene Maria Kyed, Paul Minoletti, Geoff Myint, Richard Batchelor, Elizabeth Rhoads, Jayde Roberts, Richard Roewer, Mandy Sadan, Matthew Schissler, Martin Smith, Ashley South, Ikuko Okamato, Andrew Selth, Robert Taylor, Moe Thuzar, Thant Myint-U, Tin Maung Maung Thant, Alicia Turner, Courtney Wittekind, and Tamas Wells have all been sources of wisdom, feedback, and critique, especially on early versions of chapters. I am grateful for their intellectual generosity.

Vanessa Van Den Boogaard and Max Gallien offered thoughtful feedback on the manuscript in the crucial final stages. I am also grateful to the two anonymous reviewers of the book for their encouragement and productive suggestions.

The research on which the book is based was supported by the generous funding of the Australian government and people in the form of a Research Training Scholarship and an Endeavour Award that supported eighteen months in Myanmar in 2015–2016. My fieldwork would not have been possible without two anonymous research assistants who thoughtfully and patiently humored my curious questions in and out of countless interviews. I am grateful for the direction of my many formal and informal Burmese-language *sayamas* and *sayas* in Myanmar, along with Burmese teachers both at the University of Wisconsin Madison and ANU, especially Yuri Takahashi. The survey was made possible by a grant from the International Growth Centre Myanmar and conducted by staff and enumerators from the Yangon School of Political Science who patiently implemented the complex survey instrument in often treacherous conditions. I am grateful to them along with Fabrizio Santoro and Andrea Smurra for their detailed feedback and methodological assistance on the survey.

Earlier versions of chapters appeared in "Democratic Deservingness and Self-Reliance in Contemporary Myanmar," *Sojourn: Journal of Social Issues in Southeast Asia* 34, no. 2 (2019), and "Bounded Duty: Disasters, Moral Citizenship and Exclusion in Myanmar," *South East Asia Research* 28, no. 1 (2020).

Thanks to Sarah Grossman at Cornell University Press for her support and stewardship.

My parents John and Christine have been the source of unwavering faith and love throughout my life and especially during this book. Their patient and steadfast commitment to the holistic welfare of others has deeply shaped my path of personal and scholarly development. My siblings, especially Helena and James, offered moral support and assistance while many friends gave encouragement, pro bono proofing and sustenance, including Joss Engebretsen, Sarah Bornstein, Corinne Shalala, Eloise Nigro, Meg Madden, Pat Schneider and Nussi Khalil, Andrew Swanson, Tim Kennedy, Louisa Macdonald Hall, Nuala Bethel and Jack Frail, Lauren Hendry-Parsons and Will Betts, Tom Westbrook, Paul Lemaistre and Elena Fanjul-Debnam, Jemma Lampkin, Laura-Liisa Laving, Sarah Liu and Michael Mitchell, and Jane and Adrian Baskerville. Buddy and Luna motivated me with copious encouraging licks. Finally, my deepest appreciation to Jenny Baskerville, who encouraged and kept me grounded, shared immense joy and silliness, and lent her sharp editorial eye in the final throes.

I share the credit for any insights herein with all these people along with the many Burmese colleagues I cannot name here. All errors are, of course, my own.

Names of People, Country, Towns, and Ethnicity

Readers will note that names for cities and the country of Myanmar change slightly depending on the period to which the text or maps are referring. For the pre-1989 period, I use colonial-era terms and thus refer to the country as "Burma," the capital as "Rangoon," and my primary site of research as "Toungoo." In referring to the period after 1989, when the military government changed the name of the country from "Burma" to "Myanmar" without public approval, I use the most commonly transliterated versions of the Burmese terms used by my interlocutors—"Myanmar" for the country, "Taungoo" for my primary field site, and "Yangon" for the former capital. Throughout the text, I also use "Burmese" to refer to citizens of the state as well as the majority language and "Bamar" to refer to the majority ethnic group. When referring to ethnic Karen people or the contemporary administrative territory of Karen State, I prefer to use "Karen" rather than the officially used "Kayin" because this was the strongly stated preference of many of my Karen interlocutors. Throughout the text, I use honorifics when referring to historical personalities whose names are rarely cited without them (e.g., U Nu) or when it was appropriate to include an honorary title in the pseudonym of an interlocutor.

Translation and Transliteration

The bulk of in-depth interviews, speeches, and sermons quoted verbatim in the text were conducted with research assistants present or were translated with their assistance later to clarify ambiguities in interpretation. All remaining errors and ambiguities are my own. In some cases, I have relied on English-language translations of original Burmese sources provided by government departments or media agencies.

When transliterating Burmese, in most cases I have followed the convention of John Okell's *Guide to Romanization*, although in a few instances I have chosen to use the transliterations commonly cited by other scholars or those who most sensibly reflected the phrasing of my interlocutors. In the case of some complex phrases or metaphors, I have cited the Burmese-language text as well as transliteration to reduce the chance of interpretive ambiguities.

Anonymization

To limit any risk to interlocutors, I have given pseudonyms to people with whom I spent considerable time and have flagged this the first time I mention them in the text. I have also anonymized most organizations and associations with the exception of those with national prominence.

Exchange Rates

Throughout the book, I quote Myanmar kyats in US dollars to allow non-Myanmar specialists to compare the magnitude and value of the amounts cited. For post-2011 amounts, the rate has been calculated at the average market rate during the bulk of my fieldwork between 2015 and late 2016: 1,250 kyats to US$1. Unless otherwise noted, historical rates during the 1990s and 2000s dictatorship are quoted as the official junta rate until the early 2000s of six kyats to US$1. However, the black-market rate throughout this period appreciated from around 100 kyats to US$1 in 1996 to over 1,000 kyats to US$1 after 2002 and was thus far weaker than the official rate suggested (Kubo 2007, 290). Amounts cited must therefore be assessed alongside the black-market value.

OUTSOURCING
THE POLITY

SOCIAL OUTSOURCING AND INEQUALITY

In the early hours of 13 February 2014, a devastating fire broke out inside the downtown market of Taungoo in central Myanmar. One of the primary trading hubs in the northern Bago Region, the market housed more than a thousand shops and informal sellers. The under-resourced local fire brigade could not contain the blaze, and by dawn, the entire market had been reduced to ashes. All that remained when I visited months later was a pile of rubble the size of a football field surrounded by scorched brick walls—a visual and economic wound in the heart of the town.

The destruction of the market loomed large throughout my fieldwork in Taungoo after 2014. Some of my interlocutors ran shops in or near the market. Others worked for the municipal authority that owned the land where the market stood. Several were closely linked to businesspeople vying to build a replacement complex. Shopkeepers, property developers, and the municipal authority could not reach a consensus about the market's reconstruction, creating an impasse that had already endured for a year when I commenced fieldwork.

Two options dominated this debate. Many shopkeepers supported reconstruction of a simple single-story building, as they hoped it would be completed within six months. Others, especially those linked to prominent businesspeople hoping to invest in the market, called for the market to be replaced by a multistory shopping mall, cinema, and condominium complex that would take years to build. For the municipal authority, these contending visions for the future of the market and of the town were not easy to reconcile. Many people expressed hope that the victory of Myanmar's opposition National League for Democracy (NLD) in the November 2015 election might help resolve the local impasse and deliver a trading space that would meet the needs of shopkeepers and the town as a whole.

In early 2016, soon after the NLD took charge of the national and regional governments, the newly appointed chief minister of Bago Region, U Win Thein, made his move. Alongside local legislators, he called a town-hall meeting in Taungoo in May 2016 to try and reach consensus.

Hundreds of shopkeepers, together with dozens of businesspeople and representatives of various local welfare groups, were packed into the municipal hall overlooking Taungoo's historical moat.[1] The chief minister opened the event by urging "unity" in order for the reconstruction to be successful. He then introduced Dr. Kyaw Tu, one of Taungoo's preeminent businessmen and a protégé of the nationally prominent tycoon Khin Maung Aye.[2]

Dr. Kyaw Tu stepped to the microphone with his hands shaking nervously. Unveiling a large vinyl poster, he began to explain in painstaking detail the specifications for an eight-story shopping center and condominium complex that he hoped to build on the public land where the market once stood. He described the "visionary" planning committee he had formed for the project, claiming that it "represented" the town because it included "all people like engineers, social workers, shopkeepers, and citizens." He promised that if the project was approved, he would provide "free" shops for all former shopkeepers, and he claimed to be willing to make sacrifices for the "public benefit" as a backer of the NLD:

> I don't care what the cost to me is, or [about] the accusations and attacks. If the people can get benefits, I am ready to serve for them. The [NLD] government says it is time for change, so if they approve the new market I will build it!

He concluded somberly: "If the shopkeepers continue to fight each other, 'crony companies'"—meaning tycoons with links to the military—"will come and take advantage of the people."

The speech, especially its threatening tone, fell flat with the group assembled on the opposite side of the hall. A market trader stepped to the microphone to denounce the idea of a modern, multilevel shopping complex. All the town needed, he declared, was a simple single-story market; anything more would delay reconstruction and further disrupt the livelihoods of shopkeepers. Another attendee then criticized Dr. Kyaw Tu and the committee of associates that he had formed to push for redevelopment of the market:

> Even though the government is different now [after the November 2015 election], that market committee includes the same "big men/women"

from the old regime. If Myanmar is democratic, we need a more representative committee!

For the next ninety minutes, attendees continued to debate the proposed shopping center, the appropriate use of public land, and the lack of insurance payouts to those who had lost property in the fire. Once the debate had begun to peter out, the chief minister returned to the microphone and made his own preference clear. Blaming all parties for the discord, he urged everyone to "stop fighting and start coordinating." He then enthusiastically described the gigantic shopping centers he had seen on travels to Thailand and concluded, "I want Taungoo to have a big shopping center like Junction Centre and City Mart in Yangon. . . . There should be parking for motorbikes *and* cars!" If the shopkeepers and businesspeople could not come to an agreement, however, he would make what he called "difficult choices":

> In Buddhism, the government has always been one of the five enemies of the people. We are trying not to be [the enemy], but if you continue to fight, I will invite a Japanese company to come and build the market, and you won't be able to afford shops here at all!

The event that night exposed the local tensions between skeptical shopkeepers and an aspiring tycoon who they doubted was acting in the "public" interest, despite his high-level political backers and promises of free shops for victims of the blaze. Yet most contributions to the debate that day shared a common assumption and ideal: that non-state actors—businesspeople, charities, and community groups—are crucial to providing support to the poor, delivering "development," and achieving social justice. None of the parties—the chief minister, the aspiring tycoon, or the shopkeepers left destitute by the fire—viewed the newly elected government as chiefly responsible for aiding the destitute, whether rendered so by market fires, economic downturns, or otherwise. Instead, attendees framed the role of government agencies and elected officials as *enabling* non-state actors to provide welfare and deliver development by giving rhetorical or organizational support and offers of special concessions, like free use of public land.

Beyond the provincial context of Taungoo, the assumption of state social absence underpinning the town-hall meeting points to a logic of social outsourcing that has become a go-to strategy of governance both in Myanmar and across numerous autocratic and democratic contexts in recent decades. Since the 1980s, states considered both "weak" and "strong"—from Botswana and Chile to Italy, Lebanon, and the United States—have empowered non-state and private actors to perform diverse redistributive and social welfare tasks. Although frequently justified on ideological as well as practical grounds, shifting social responsibility from state to non-state and market actors has delivered unequal social and economic outcomes that have mired the poor in precarity and encouraged wealth to trickle up to the already affluent.

The enduring appeal of outsourcing as a strategy of social governance runs contrary to classic theories of redistributive politics, which assume that representative regimes tend to force states to expand their social footprint. Faced with elections, the theory goes, political candidates are encouraged to address the vulnerabilities experienced by the "median voter" by promising to expand state social programs through redistribution of wealth (Meltzer and Richard 1981; Boix 2003; Acemoglu and Robinson 2006). Redistributive theories of political transition have been increasingly questioned in recent years because of the persistence of dire inequality in democracies across the globe and in light of the diversity of state-led social initiatives rolled out by autocratic and hybrid regimes seeking to co-opt their critics and maintain the loyalty of their backers (Eibl 2020). Scholars have highlighted that state capacity to raise revenue and implement social initiatives, rather than regime type alone, are critical determinants of whether governments deliver social initiatives in response to popular or electoral pressures for redistribution (Soifer 2013; Slater and Soifer 2020). Yet little research has examined why political elites rely on state social outsourcing over time, even despite changes in political regimes that are meant to make state officials more accountable to the citizenry. This book advances the debate by focusing on why practices and ideals of social outsourcing, assumed as the basis for social justice by attendees at Taungoo's town-hall meeting, find persistent appeal over time, even though they often deliver poor social outcomes and erode state capacity to address injustice and drive development.

Myanmar as Research Site

Myanmar is a fruitful site for studying state social outsourcing and its long-run implications for welfare outcomes and political culture. Following successive socialist (1962–1988) and capitalist (1988–2010) dictatorships, an election in 2010 boycotted by the democratic opposition led to the formation of a reformist government in 2011 (Farrelly 2013; Bogais 2015; Bünte 2016). The new administration, comprised mostly of civilianized former military leaders, then led social, economic, and political reforms that partly liberalized the country after decades of direct military rule. Elections in late 2015 then led to the transfer of partial executive power to a popularly elected civilian government in 2016 headed by Nobel Peace Prize laureate Aung San Suu Kyi and her NLD party. Between 2011 and the military coup of February 2021, elected officials had only partial control over the state apparatus: The 2008 Constitution drafted during the dictatorship of the 1990s and 2000s gave the military 25 percent of parliamentary seats, control of three ministries (Defense, Home Affairs, and Border Affairs), and veto power over constitutional reform. Despite these constraints, elected civilians were able to lead and implement reforms to key agencies of service delivery and economic regulation across a range of areas including health, education, welfare, taxation, and foreign investment.

Despite elected officials having some scope to make policy change, demands for the state to expand its role in welfare provision and wealth redistribution were rare in the years between the transition to partial civilian rule in 2011 and the military's ousting of civilian leaders and seizure of power in February 2021.[3] Amending the military's 2008 Constitution was a major priority of the NLD and other key parties for a decade. Yet there was little attempt to expand government commitment to socioeconomic justice and development through any constitutional amendments or major policy reforms. The Union of Myanmar government did spend more on social sectors over this period relative to the dire autocratic austerity of the 1990s and 2000s.[4] However, it allocated markedly less to social sectors than regional neighbors while giving the Ministry of Defence the same amount earmarked for health, education, and welfare *combined*.[5] The lion's share of additional social budget after 2011 went to health and education while social welfare spending grew far slower, receiving less than 0.4 percent of the Union budget prior to COVID-19.[6]

Instead of expanding the meager government welfare budgets, many political leaders and grassroots activists encouraged and supported diverse non-state actors to fill gaps in social welfare and public goods provision. During the COVID-19 downturn, which drove millions of people into dire food insecurity and debt, the elected government urged individuals and businesses to contribute to response efforts, including to the government's procurement of vaccines.[7] Meanwhile, the social and economic stimulus package only partly implemented prior to the February 2021 coup was directed largely at formal businesses—which comprise less than half of Myanmar's economy—and social aid was provided on an explicitly one-off basis to the poor to deter expectations of ongoing entitlement to state support.[8]

In February 2021, the Myanmar military seized direct power once again—provoking an extraordinary civilian mobilization against dictatorship and rupturing the government pandemic response, including the planned state social aid package. Since then, ordinary people have relied more than ever on non-state networks and practices of reciprocity both to survive economic collapse and the worsening pandemic as well as sustain their resistance to the renewed dictatorship.[9]

The reluctance of successive generations of Myanmar's political elites to address dire socioeconomic vulnerability may not be surprising, given institutional constraints. For decades, the Myanmar state has collected some of the lowest tax revenues relative to its gross domestic product (GDP) of any country in the world, restraining the financing of new state social initiatives. Still, focusing solely on the *absence* of direct state social action misses a large part of the picture and also clouds the understanding of why state fiscal and social capacity has remained persistently low for so long: that for decades government officials have encouraged and at times mandated non-state actors to fulfill social responsibilities, which the state refuses to assume or perform itself, often granting tax remissions or exemptions in exchange. Grasping this puzzling dynamic of state officials across regimes evading direct government social involvement and instead outsourcing and privatizing it to charities, volunteers, philanthropists, and private providers (who at times contest the government's authority) requires a reassessment of how institutional inheritances, including ideals of social justice, evolve in ways that shape the trajectory of welfare politics over time.

Key Arguments of This Book

By expanding the understanding of path dependence and policy feedback, this book probes how earlier patterns of state welfare outsourcing can shape the policy options imagined and pursued by political leaders in later regimes. Informed by the experience of Myanmar, the book argues that social outsourcing can deliver aid to the needy, but it comes with short-term and long-run trade-offs—including regressive outcomes for the poor and the erosion of popular faith in the state as an agent of social justice and development.[10] Despite these repercussions, state officials across regimes may continue to outsource redistributive and social welfare responsibilities to non-state charitable, philanthropic, and private providers over time—by choice and by happenstance—as it can partly satisfy the *material interests* and *distributive ideals* of diverse political and economic constituencies.

Recipients of aid, for instance, often view charitable and philanthropic provision of social support and public goods as generous, virtuous, and practically necessary in the absence of substantive state initiatives—even if the support provided is frequently patchy and insufficient for basic needs. Volunteers and activists who lead non-state welfare efforts also tend to view their work as both practically necessary and, especially in liberalized autocratic contexts, civically and even religiously virtuous, given state clampdown on more overt political mobilization. Corporate leaders for their part often use philanthropic generosity as a way to make themselves indispensable to the public good and thereby undermine the capacity and desire of state officials to regulate their businesses, fairly resolve economic injustices, or directly tax them to deliver fairer public welfare outcomes.

Finally, political actors—including state officials and elected representatives from across the partisan spectrum—may encourage non-state welfare as it coheres with ideologies of civic or religious duty while allowing them to avoid taxing constituents, especially the wealthy, to fund more expansive and effective public welfare systems.

The combination of these *material* and *ideational factors*—especially when inherited from earlier regimes—can undermine capacity for, and commitment to, state social action and hollow out the ideas, discourses, and systems that form the basis of national political community.[11] What emerges from these processes is a *privatized form of polity*: Non-state and market actors become so crucial to achieving social justice and the collective good that interventions by government agencies and elected officials to address inequities are framed by diverse interests as ineffective, undesirable, and even corrosive of civic norms. Inversely, for communities and networks that oppose ruling regimes, the adaptability of non-state welfare practices and ideals makes them useful for sustaining solidarity and resistance in the face of state repression.

Balancing a focus on political economy and ideology, the chapters that follow trace ideals and practices of non-state welfare and redistribution as they have evolved throughout Myanmar's modern political history. To deepen an understanding of path dependency, the book offers a new account of social outsourcing through market reform in Myanmar and traces the consequences of these processes for distributive politics since independence in 1948. It shows how successive regimes—reluctant to expand state social initiatives for fear of ongoing fiscal commitment—instead deliberately and inadvertently outsourced the achievement of social justice to private and non-state actors at critical moments of institutional development through processes of "social licensing." Following chapter 1's analysis of the colonial legacies that shaped welfare politics from independence to 1988, the chapters of part 1 draw on oral history, archival sources, and ethnography to show how the post-socialist dictatorship mediated market reform and regulated civil society throughout the 1990s and 2000s in ways that transferred social responsibility from the state and entrenched ideals and practices of non-state social action at the heart of popular and political culture. Informed by extensive interviews, ethnographic fieldwork, and survey research during Myanmar's decade of partial civilian rule, the chapters of part 2 then examine the way non-state welfare shapes how elites and grassroots activists framed issues of social justice, rights, and democratic struggle. By spotlighting non-state welfare ideas and practices throughout Myanmar's modern political development, the book demonstrates how pragmatic concerns can blend with normative ideals of moral and political community in ways that ensure social outsourcing remains an enduring feature of autocratic, hybrid, and democratic regimes alike.

During the most recent period of partial civilian rule between 2011 and 2021, for instance, State Counselor Aung San Suu Kyi praised the virtue of economic elites, charitable groups, and local communities that responded to floods, displacement of refugees, and the COVID-19 pandemic. She also encouraged foreign governments to lift economic sanctions on Myanmar's tycoons and urged military-linked "cronies" to make tax-deductible charitable donations and volunteer services to social initiatives she personally led. As successive civilian-led governments, including the NLD, continued to rely on non-state welfare actors and elite philanthropy to bolster Myanmar's welfare regime, they limited their own capacity to use state agencies to redress the inequities generated by decades of crony dictatorship and social austerity. Yet the same ideals and practices of non-state welfare have also proved crucial both to everyday survival along with the resistance efforts of democratic forces in the wake of Myanmar's return to dictatorship in 2021: Neighborhood groups have organized support for families of civil servants dismissed for opposing the coup; charitable clinics have delivered critical health care services following the collapse of the government's pandemic response; service providers allied with non-state armed groups have helped deliver education to children displaced by Myanmar military attacks.

Given the pernicious effects of social outsourcing, do ideals and practices of private, non-state welfare endure only out of such necessity? On the contrary, this book argues that the persistence of precarious welfare regimes in diverse contexts—developed and developing; autocratic, hybrid, and democratic—is best explained by the way non-state welfare provision satisfies the interests and ideals of diverse constituencies. The remainder of this introduction frames out concepts and approaches used throughout the book to situate Myanmar's experience in cross-national dynamics of state social retrenchment and inequality.

Welfare Regimes and Non-State Providers

The persistent role of non-state social actors over many decades is not unique to Myanmar. In both developing and developed countries, families, charities, for-profit organizations, and other non-state providers often perform major social welfare and redistributive roles. Studies of social protection in late-developing countries, for instance, have argued that "meaningful rights and correlative duties" are frequently found "through *informal* community arrangements" rather than the state (Wood and Gough 2006, 1700, 1702, emphasis in original). Some of these non-state mechanisms of social support, such as nongovernmental organizations (NGOs), are formally institutionalized in law; others are based on personal, clientelist, and reciprocal relations among people in highly unequal social and economic positions of power. In addition to providing a source of social protection, these relations, as Wood (2003) highlights, can reinforce "adverse incorporation" defined by contingent or "problematic inclusion" rather than absolute social exclusion of the poor and vulnerable. In other words, welfare regimes that entrench the role of non-state and private providers or intermediaries often deliver a measure of social protection to the poor while systematically benefiting the more affluent and powerful—a dynamic evident in Myanmar over decades.

On the basis of these empirical realities, sociologists Geof Wood and Ian Gough (2006, 1700) conceive of a broad universe of welfare *regimes* that they define as "repeated systematic arrangements through which people seek livelihood security both for their own lives and for those of their children, descendants and elders." The ideal-types in this universe differ in both the degree to which they protect against the commodification of labor and the extent to which brokerage and clientelism are essential features of the regime. Welfare regimes, plotted on these axes, vary substantially: from arrangements where households receive patchy and precarious support from kin, community, and religious or private sources, often in exchange for favors (insecure welfare regimes), to more expansive regimes in which government agencies provide fairly consistent support for health care, unemployment, disaster relief, aged care, retirement, or disability assistance (welfare states).

This book adopts a broad concept of non-state social providers and enlists the analytical framework of welfare regimes to understand the path dependency of these actors and their roles over time. Derived from historical institutional theory, the notions of path dependence and policy feedback posit that political arrangements, once established, tend to stabilize and reproduce themselves over time as a consequence of the way they empower some groups and restrict the influence of others.[12] Applied to welfare regimes, especially to the role played by non-state social providers, path dependency theory offers a useful framework through which to examine the puzzling endurance of welfare regimes that outsource social roles to non-state providers, even despite transitions in political regime. Existing theoretical and empirical research on regime change and welfare outsourcing provides conceptual and analytical tools relevant to studying these dynamics in Myanmar.

Political Transitions and Welfare States

How does social outsourcing shape the politics of welfare and redistribution across successive regimes? Theories of inequality and political transition have long held that representative forms of governance lead to greater state role in redistribution and social spending. In one of the earliest expressions of this expectation, Aristotle argued that the incentive to appeal to the masses by redistributing wealth from rich to poor could result in the downfall of democracy as elites would seek to protect their wealth by eroding representative institutions (Slater, Smith, and Nair 2014, 355). The Meltzer-Richard model (1981) systemized the redistributive expectations of democracy by theorizing that democratic elections incentivize politicians to advocate policies that redistribute wealth from the rich to the far poorer "median" voter.[13] More recent models (Boix 2003; Acemoglu and Robinson 2006) emphasize how economic inequality prior to political transition can distort the incentives of elected officials. Where the concentration of wealth during the old regime undermines elite support for democracy, these models predict two outcomes: capitalists usurp representative institutions by supporting military coups, or they "rig" regimes to protect their economic interests.[14] The redistributive stakes of democratization are further restricted in contexts where state capacity to actually deliver social initiatives is weak to begin with, as the limits of governmental efficacy tie the hands of political elites.[15] The dynamics of outsourcing that entrench inequality would, following these expectations, be more likely to persist in contexts such as Myanmar, where the state has limited capacity to tax populations and deliver social initiatives and where formal laws protect the interests of old elites. However, welfare regimes can also evolve and markedly change over time—especially when new alliances are formed between interest groups.

Empirical studies of welfare state development in democratic and autocratic regimes alike emphasize that political coalitions—electoral and otherwise—can transform the social role of the state across decades. Focusing on developed countries within the Organization for Economic Cooperation and Development (OECD), Gøsta Esping-Andersen's *Three Worlds of Welfare Capitalism* traced the changes in the extent to which "individuals, or families, can uphold a socially acceptable standard of living independently of market participation" (1990, 37). He identified three welfare state regimes—liberal, conservative, and social democratic—between which the role played by state, market, and household varied considerably. Building on earlier work on the determinant impacts of labor unions and left-wing parties on welfare state development (Stephens 1979; Korpi 1983), Esping-Andersen argued that these differences derived from the varying strength of labor-based political parties, employers, and the state during key moments of institutional negotiation. These moments of confrontation, or critical juncture, often gave rise to new state interventions and social schemes for de-commodifying labor that endured and evolved over time to form more expansive and generous welfare states.

Subsequent work on social policy in autocratic and post-authoritarian contexts highlight how interest-group politics can shape the welfare mix across regimes.

Autocratic leaders often use state-mediated or mandated social policy to ensure the political stability or economic viability of their regimes (Mares and Carnes 2009; Eibl 2020). Studies from Africa, Asia, Eastern Europe, and Latin America also highlight that authoritarian regimes can enlist non-state actors as partners in service delivery in ways that undermine or stifle their capacity to mobilize for political change.[16] The logics and systems of redistribution and social service delivery institutionalized during one regime often shape the trajectory of welfare reform after subsequent political transitions. Stephan Haggard and Robert Kaufman (2008) explore how earlier autocracies shaped the trajectory of social policy after regime change in East Asia, Latin America, and Eastern Europe and argue that the welfare mix that emerged after transitions to democracy in each context was shaped by two factors: *political coalitions* (formed between elites, labor and peasant organizations, and mass political parties) and the *industrialization strategy* of earlier regimes. Welfare regimes in East and Southeast Asia offer particularly fruitful parallels to Myanmar given geographic and cultural proximity. In a coalition similar to that seen in Myanmar after the end of socialism in 1988, autocratic elites across the region tended to ally themselves with industrial capitalists in order to distribute the rents associated with export-led industrialization. As labor and popular movements were largely suppressed in these contexts, there was little popular pressure on political leaders to expand systems of state-led social welfare and redistribution. Social policy in these "productivist welfare capitalist" regimes thus tended to serve the interests of industrialists; government expenditure focused largely on education and human resource sectors in order to boost formal-sector productivity (Holliday 2000). Meanwhile, schemes of social insurance—such as unemployment support—relied on co-contribution by employees and employers, while more protective areas of social policy (e.g., support for the destitute, aged care, pensions, and health insurance) largely remained the domain of family, market, and charitable providers (Cook and Pincus 2014, 8).

Democratization in East and Southeast Asia challenged path dependence by encouraging politicians to expand the government's social footprint to win the support of the median voter. In some cases, the government's social role expanded dramatically as elected governments sought to secure voter support by extending state-led schemes to sectors previously left largely to the family and the market (Wong 2006; Nam 2014). However, the shape of democratic social policy often bore the imprint of autocratic-era elite coalitions and the logics embedded in social schemes developed before the political transition (London 2018, chap. 6). As trade unions were largely suppressed in Asia's authoritarian capitalist regimes, for instance, leftist groups had little chance to mobilize popular support once elections were introduced. Consequentially democratically elected conservative governments allied themselves with business owners and expanded state-mediated schemes of welfare and redistribution in ways that maximized the benefit for companies while reducing the fiscal burden on the state. The evolving welfare mix in these contexts thus tended to rely on co-contributions from employees as well as employers and tended to benefit middle-income households employed in more formal arrangements than less politically mobilized working-class and informal-sector workers.[17]

Elite coalitions during autocratic rule, and the resulting state capacities for social service provision, can feed back after political transition via the logics embedded in government social and taxation policies. Research from Latin America highlights how transitionary elites often "game" democracy in ways that "complicate the ability of democratic politicians to orient public spending priorities toward the poor majority" (Albertus and Menaldo 2013, 576–577). Elite dominance prior to political transitions across Latin America produced legal constitutions that formally entrenched their economic interests through mechanisms such as military veto powers over policy—a pattern of reserved power familiar to Myanmar. If those constitutions endured political change, the social schemes that emerged tended to have limited coverage and benefits. Meanwhile, fiscal sustainability was often eroded by tax concessions linked to the creation of these social schemes, which imposed tight fiscal constraints on state revenue and minimized the financial threat of redistribution to economic elites (Fairfield and Garay 2017). Only in contexts where democracy came about through revolution or uprising, sidelining established interests, did subsequent elected governments take a more proactive approach to social protection and taxation. The logics underpinning formal political institutions and policies of earlier authoritarian regimes can thus hem in the options of later regimes to expand state-led redistributive action.

Policy Feedback and Informal Institutions

Normative path dependence can similarly complicate substantial reform or evolution of political structures by shaping popular expectations and demands on the state. Beyond constraints imposed by "rigged" laws, government welfare initiatives can shape popular expectations of the state's appropriate role in welfare and social aid. Mixed-methods research from West Africa suggests that people expect greater state social leadership in sectors where government agencies have previously been a significant provider of support than in areas policymakers have historically left to local community or private providers (L. MacLean 2011b). Studies of Latin American welfare states describe how expectations generated by government welfare policies can constrain later attempts to retrench the state's social role (Segura-Ubiergo 2007). Government social initiatives may thus cultivate not just functional but also *normative* support for the ideals embedded within them as they directly or indirectly fulfill community- or individual-level needs, functions that begin to be seen as social "rights" to which citizens are entitled. Indeed, examples of distributive ideals embedded in state social policies enduring over time abound in literature from democratic and autocratic contexts alike.[18] State welfare schemes, by laying the ground for path dependence or a gradual shift in policy trajectory, can thus set the rules of the distributive game in ways that markedly shape the social role of the state and popular conceptions of who is entitled to receive aid from the government (Béland 2005). Informed by dynamics of normative path dependence, this book conceives of the distributive ideals that underpin welfare regimes as *informal* institutions that are "socially shared rules, usually unwritten, that are created, communicated, and enforced outside of officially sanctioned channels" (Helmke and Levitsky 2004, 727), even though they may not be formally enshrined in law or official policy.

One of the major limits of existing scholarship on social policy feedbacks is its focus on *formal* state policies, such as subsidies for consumer goods or government support to specific demographics (Béland 2010). Meanwhile, analysis of how regime change influences redistribution has largely focused on how preexisting laws or schemes affect the magnitude of direct state social expenditure. Yet, as the growing literature on inequality in industrialized welfare states highlights, a full picture of social spending must include the expenditures made by private, charitable, and philanthropic actors, focusing both on direct state social delivery and roles that may be outsourced to non-state providers often in exchange for tax concessions. Although the social objective of both state and non-state welfare modalities may be similar, a wide literature highlights the regressive distributive outcomes produced by outsourcing and privatization, even though it may comprise a large proportion or even a majority of overall social outlays, both state and non-state (Adema 1999; Martin and Prasad 2014; Hacker 2016a). Given the major role played by non-state social actors in Myanmar, especially since the end of socialism in 1988, it is necessary to look beyond the legacies of state social schemes or the constraints imposed by "rigged" laws to understand why social outsourcing to non-state providers has persisted across successive regimes.

Non-State Social Provision and Welfare Regime Development

The feedbacks created by outsourcing can distort later incentives for redistribution and policy reform, especially when ideals of privatization are embedded in state social policies. The experience of the United States highlights how ideals enshrined in state welfare schemes can embed conditions on who receives basic social protection and how this protection is provided decades down the line. For example, New Deal welfare initiatives established in the wake of the Great Depression and the tax system that funded them were the product of compromises made between Progressive idealists and industrial capitalists about who should be eligible to receive state social aid (Thorndike 2009). Economic elites feared that social benefits not linked to work would promote laziness among poor Americans, thinning out the supply of cheap labor on which they relied while draining government budgets (Orloff 1988). The social initiatives subsequently introduced by President Franklin D. Roosevelt thus made access to health care and a range of state social schemes conditional on recipients' employment status (Quadagno 1984; Béland and Hacker 2004, 52). Instead of the state being responsible for the direct provision of health care, laws passed during this period required employers to take out private health insurance for their employees as a way of encouraging labor market participation. The ideal that work should determine access to (privately provided) health care subsequently constrained later attempts to address deep disparities in access to health care, especially among the underemployed and unemployed who could not find work but were not provided with health care. The outcome is that, despite repeated reform efforts, including the Affordable Care Act, signed into law by President Barack Obama in 2010, the vast majority of Americans still receive health care through private insurance policies taken out by their employers on their behalf, in contrast to most European industrialized democracies where basic health care is considered a "social right" best provided to citizens by a state-managed system (Hacker 2016a). Imposing an employment condition on access to health care has produced a costly welfare mix that mires many people in debt, constrains upward social mobility of the working class, and delivers comparatively poorer health outcomes.[19] So why has this approach endured over time, despite electoral incentives?

Providing social protection and income redistribution through private and charitable arrangements, or imposing stringent conditions on access to state aid, is often viewed as *practically* preferable by elites and ordinary people alike. In both the United States and Myanmar, many middle-class voters and political elites question the efficiency of state initiatives relative to non-state provision or private contracting, under the belief that government provision often involves considerable waste. Importantly, these practical preferences are bolstered by a *normative* outlook that frames hard work, self-reliance, social obligations to the family and community, and donations to charitable non-state welfare providers as morally and civically superior to paying taxes that fund government social initiatives (Block 2009, 78). Implementation of this ideology can entrench the vulnerability of the poor by making upward mobility conditional on meeting eligibility criteria of various kinds or by incentivizing accrual of debt that further constrains life choices. Yet in contexts where the likelihood of voting increases by income level and educational attainment, it can be electorally popular to reduce taxes, cut state social spending, and outsource social roles to community, charity, and market-based welfare providers (Jacobs and Skocpol 2007).

Practical and normative preferences for non-state welfare and development can also shape how government officials expend state funds toward social justice ends. For instance, politicians in the United States have recalibrated state spending in recent decades to expand funding for private, non-state social initiatives while putting increasingly stringent conditions on individuals and households receiving state social aid. Reflecting these shifts, and challenging the common characterization of the United States as an "underdeveloped and stingy welfare state" relative to its European counterparts, studies of fiscal outlays have highlighted that the United States is not a welfare laggard, at least in terms of the amounts the government commits to ostensibly social objectives (Hacker 2002; Martin, Mehrotra, and Prasad 2009, 15; Hacker 2016a). Instead, the more "visible" or direct social schemes of the American state must be assessed alongside the ubiquitous provision of tax *concessions* by American policymakers to achieve social policy objectives. Indirect or "hidden" forms of social spending are crucial fiscal mechanisms in larger processes whereby government officials recalibrate and retrench the role of the state in achieving social outcomes (Howard 1999; Hacker 2002). In the United States, these forms of indirect state expenditures are as diverse as tax offsets for homeowners, deductions for health insurance premiums, concessional treatment of pension contributions, along with tax credits for families with dependent children and deductions for charitable donations.

There are often distributive consequences to the outsourcing of state social spending and service delivery. Granting tax concessions for private donations, for instance, can disproportionately benefit the middle and upper classes, especially economic elites whose donations to charities, foundations, and endowments often advance and protect their ideological and material interests. As a result, scholars and activists have begun to question whether allowing private donors to make major tax-deductible donations to organizations that advance their policy or social agenda is "repugnant to the whole idea of 'democracy'" (Reich 2016; Reich 2018; Giridharadas 2019). Giving public tax concessions for private social expenditures that heighten the sway of economic elites over the democratic process may be politically controversial, at least in its most extreme forms. Yet bipartisan support for tax expenditures in the United States shows how granting tax remissions in exchange for private social spending can appeal to actors from across the political spectrum, thus ensuring the logic and practice endure changes in administration, despite the long-term costs to state fiscal and thus redistributive capacity (Block 2009; Newman and O'Brien 2011; Prasad 2018).[20] The appeal of norms or ideals of non-state welfare across the political spectrum can in this way entrench indirect tax expenditures that reward non-state welfare provision, even when ruling coalitions and regimes may change over time.[21]

Formal state policies that outsource welfare and development initiatives to charities, philanthropists, and private companies can reshape popular ideas of state social obligations. Drawing on historical research and ethnographic fieldwork with charitable welfare groups in northern Italy, anthropologist Andrea Muehlebach (2012, 17) exposes how major cuts to state social spending have been justified by a "crisis of loneliness," which politicians and some activists argued could only be addressed through the relational labor of volunteers. Despite the diverse political and ideological leanings of the welfare groups that responded to this crisis—from conservative Catholic volunteer groups to socialist trade unionists highly skeptical of state retrenchment—Muehlebach recounts seeing "many a citizen disagreeing ideologically with the prevailing order [of austerity] while signing on, either consciously or inadvertently, to its discourses and practices in ontological terms" (12). She further highlights how the embrace of non-state welfare practices and ideals by diverse constituencies has made concepts of "society" and "citizenship" slippery and conditional, writing that "the social now usually comes as an addendum and descriptor rather than as an object sui generis. It is a relation produced, step by step, by participatory citizens rather an *a priori* domain into which the state interjects" (43).

The entitlement of worker-oriented social citizenship on which many European welfare states were erected has been replaced by a deeply contingent and relational "ethical citizenship" that "encloses citizens within the intimate space of the 'welfare community' or 'welfare society'" (Muehlebach 2012, 43). Across contexts—from India, Indonesia, and Thailand to Myanmar, Europe, and the United States—ideologies legitimizing state social outsourcing amid market reform have similarly uprooted notions that a secure welfare regime is "a matter of entitlement," often feeding conceptions that such supports are generous "gifts" from authorities or patrons (Nickel 2018, 63).[22] State policies aimed at outsourcing social services to charitable, philanthropic, and nongovernmental providers or that privilege private and market actors can thus over time shape popular perceptions of entitlement and citizenship in ways that legitimize inequality and establish the influence of wealthy donors. Treating ideals and practices of non-state welfare as path dependent (the same as formal laws and state social schemes) opens up new ways of understanding how social outsourcing can affect the trajectory of distributive politics and can entrench inequality over time (Béland and Hacker 2004, 53).

Gaps in Literature and Approach to Research

By examining how distributive ideals and practices can evolve and shape the trajectory of welfare regimes, this book opens up new theoretical and methodological directions in the study of inequality. Much existing literature on the endurance of inequality across regimes focuses on the constraints on state redistributive capacity—for example, through "rigged" laws and constitutions that protect the interests of economic elites, from the path dependence of old state social policies or the distortionary impact of political patronage and vote-buying on redistributive politics.[23] Most of the literature, however, focuses on the mediation of state social programs rather than the entrenchment of non-state actors in the welfare mix or in net social spending (state and non-state).[24] In order to understand the persistence of dire inequality and the absence of substantive direct state action over time, it is crucial to bring into the picture how the outsourcing of social justice to non-state actors has formed a core logic of successive political regimes.

Methodologically, existing historical research on path dependence of social policy and distributive ideals is predominantly post hoc, based largely on secondary sources and archives. As these studies tend not to rely on in-depth fieldwork with ordinary people and elites during periods of political contingency, they offer little insight into how ideals and practices of non-state welfare and development, especially the legacies of past social outsourcing, shape decision making during periods of potential political change.[25] In field-based ethnographic research, on the other hand, the skew toward the contemporary moment means these studies may have difficulty accounting for the historical origins and evolution of distributive ideals or policies encountered at the time of fieldwork. This book seeks to bridge these approaches by coupling historical examination of the origins, evolution, and continuity of Myanmar's insecure welfare regime with extensive fieldwork on the social ideals and practices of grassroots democrats, tycoons, and ordinary people during the decade-long period of partial civilian rule.

The Scene and Approach

This book is informed by mixed-methods research in provincial central-east Myanmar since 2013, especially sixteen months of in-depth fieldwork conducted during 2015 and 2016. Most of the analysis throughout the chapters focuses predominantly on lowland areas that have been under government control since soon after independence in 1948. However, frequent comparisons are made throughout the book with northern Karen State, a region that did not experience the same form of capitalist dictatorship because of conflict throughout the 1990s and 2000s.

Fieldwork was predominantly concentrated in Taungoo, a town in the eastern plains of central Myanmar around 115 kilometers south of Naypyidaw, the new administrative capital. Taungoo is historically notable as the seat of "probably the largest empire in the history of Southeast Asia" between the fourteenth and sixteenth centuries (Lieberman 2003, 152). Although no field site in Myanmar could be nationally "representative," Taungoo and the broader region of central-east Myanmar provide a fruitful prism through which to view the evolution of welfare politics for three reasons.

First, Taungoo township offers an insight into the lowland plains where the bulk of Myanmar's ethnic Bamar and Buddhist majority reside. The area was a major trade hub for agricultural and forestry goods during the colonial period, when it was directly ruled by the British. It has been under almost constant control of the Burmese state since independence and is a major regional node of regime control since it plays host to a range of Myanmar military installations, including army engineers corps, artillery and infantry units, and an air base (ANU 2014).[26] The 2014 census registered a population of 262,056 people in the township, of which 41 percent lived in urban wards and 59 percent lived in rural villages—a proportion roughly reflecting Myanmar's growing urbanization, which was estimated at 35 percent in 2015 by the World Bank.[27] Importantly, Taungoo's sizable urban population and growing tourism sector during the early 2010s meant that my long-term presence did not attract undue suspicion from authorities or compromise my research agenda or access to interlocutors.

Second, central-east Myanmar is a demographic microcosm of the country as a whole. Taungoo's location at the crossroads of lowland and upland trade and government administration has bequeathed the township an ethnic Bamar Buddhist majority and large numbers of Karen Christians, Muslims, Hindus, along with Shan and Chinese Buddhists and other minorities.[28] In this sense, while it is not nationally "representative," Taungoo's demographic composition broadly reflects the breakdown of Myanmar's population estimated at around 68 percent ethnic Bamar and 88 percent Buddhist.[29] Taungoo did not experience communal violence in the decade of partial civilian rule (2011 and 2021) as many towns around the country did, but it was the site of religious conflict in May 2001 (HRW 2002 7–8; Cheesman 2017b).[30]

Third, Taungoo's proximity to mountainous regions in the east enables comparison of lowland dynamics with those of upland regions that had not experienced autocratic capitalism and social outsourcing in the same way throughout the 1990s and 2000s. The eastern administrative limits of Taungoo township directly borders Thandaungyi township in northern Karen State, a mountainous and densely forested region that has been the site of ongoing conflict between the Karen National Union (KNU) and the state military since independence in 1948. The conflict continued throughout the 1990s and 2000s, until the KNU signed a bilateral preliminary ceasefire in 2012 and the Nationwide Ceasefire Agreement in 2015—both of which frayed in the years after 2016 and especially after the return to dictatorship in 2021.[31] Figure 0.1 depicts the topography and administrative boundaries of the largely flat Taungoo and the more mountainous Thandaungyi township.

Although some less elevated regions of northern Karen State came under government control in the 1990s, much of the region was under mixed KNU-government administration or sole KNU administration throughout the research period and remained so at the time of writing. According to the 2014 census, conducted only in government and mixed-administered areas of the township, the region has a population of 96,000 people of which 22 percent live in three small urban areas and 78 percent in rural, mountainous villages. Central-east Myanmar's place at the crossroads of various commercial, administrative, and political flows, coupled with its viability as a relatively open and accessible field site during the 2010s, made it an ideal place to conduct fieldwork.

Fieldwork Phases

To understand the way that ideals and practices of non-state welfare evolved and endured during Myanmar's decade of partial civilian rule, research was conducted in an iterative, mixed-method manner that privileged the way interlocutors understood and evaluated their social reality. For logistic, linguistic, and authorization reasons, long-term fieldwork was predominantly conducted in lowland areas. However, interviews, oral histories, archival research, and the household socio-economic survey were conducted in both upland and lowland areas.[32]

Rather than viewing non-state welfare provision as the outcome of "traditions" or the consequence of formal institutional design, I placed the origins, functions, and meaning of non-state social aid at the center of analytical inquiry. Political ethnography was conducive to iterative hypothesis testing because it allowed ideals and practices of non-state welfare to be studied "as products of the complex sets of associations and experiences which composed them" (Marcus 1998, 63–66). As studies of post-socialism in Eastern Europe have demonstrated, long-term ethnographic research in a specific site or with a particular group can expose how macro-level political changes connect to "micro worlds" that influence those larger structures and processes (Burawoy and Verdery 1999, 3).[33] Developing deep relationships with interlocutors over time allows tracking of change, continuity, and

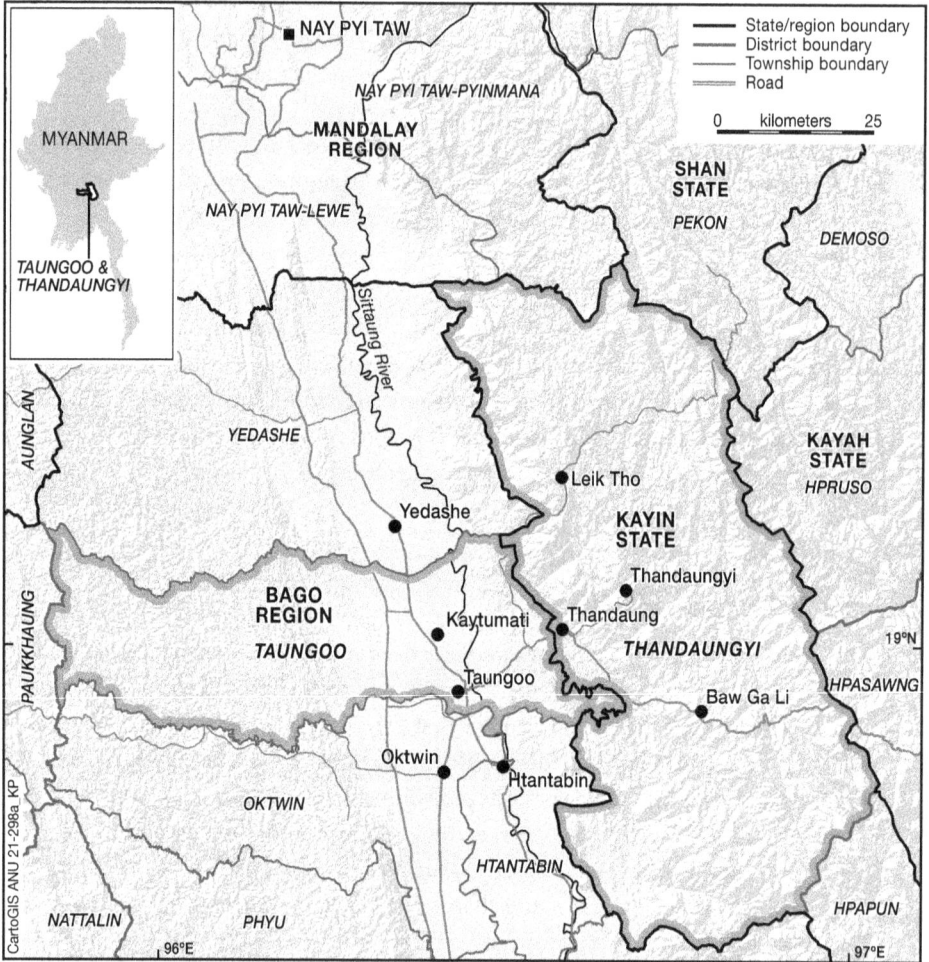

FIGURE 0.1. Topographical map of lowland Taungoo (main field site) and mountainous Thandaungyi (secondary field site). *Source:* Map courtesy of Australian National University CartoGIS Services.

contradiction at an individual or institutional level in ways that one-off interviews and snapshot surveys cannot reliably provide (Trickett and Oliveri 1997, 149). Ethnography thus opened up opportunities to see people, institutions, and processes from new vantage points, uncovering how macro-level developments or processes—such as practices of commercial licensing during the 1990s that form a central focus of part 1—shaped the contemporary behaviors of traders or attitudes of individuals regarding the social role of the state. For these reasons an interpretive, ethnographic approach was uniquely well suited to expose how logics, processes, and ideals endured and evolved at various levels during a period of heightened political contingency (Wedeen 2010, 261).

Participant observation was conducted in two phases. Phase one (March through June 2015) focused on five predominantly Buddhist social and welfare groups based in lowland Taungoo. These groups were selected on the basis of their time of establishment, pre- or post-2011, and their operation area (township, ward/village, and place of worship). In addition to working with these groups, I studied the donations records of several key groups and initiatives, which offered important insights into the authoritarian origins of non-state welfare when juxtaposed with oral histories from managers or donors of these welfare groups. In the second phase (July 2015 through June 2016), I shifted focus from organizations to the larger networks and practices of which they formed a part, especially the ties that connected welfare groups to business and political party elites. I complemented this network ethnography with focused fieldwork in three urban wards and six rural villages selected to gain insight into grassroots ideals and practices of non-state welfare and how these varied according to the degree of state presence and social support in a specific area.[34] I returned to these neighborhoods fortnightly to meet with interlocutors, allowing me to track small shifts in sentiment as events occurred over time.

Throughout my fieldwork, I also made fortnightly visits to interlocutors in the administrative towns of Thandaung, Thandaungyi, and Leiktho in northern Karen State. I conducted interviews with representatives of Karen political parties, Christian pastors, Myanmar government officials, and civilian representatives of the KNU. These contacts and networks helped to shed light on government service delivery following the 2012 bilateral ceasefire between the KNU and Myanmar military, the role of nongovernmental providers of welfare in the lives of ordinary people, and elite and grassroots aspirations of the more federalized political system promised by the 2015 Nationwide Ceasefire Agreement. They also exposed distributive ideals and practices that appeared to produce expectations of the state quite different from those I encountered in lowland areas.

After more than a year of qualitative research and hypothesis testing, in March 2016, I conducted a household sociopolitical survey in central-east Myanmar.

One thousand (1,000) households were included in the survey, split equally between Taungoo and Thandaungyi townships (500 each).[35] Respondents were recruited in a systematically randomized fashion across fourteen villages and seven urban wards in each township. Interviews were conducted in Burmese and Sgaw Karen by a group of twenty-eight survey enumerators recruited and managed by the Yangon School of Political Science with support from a Karen community organization. There were numerous intriguing quantitative patterns exposed in the initial April 2016 data analysis (G. McCarthy 2016), and I followed up these findings with further qualitative fieldwork between May and June 2016.

In addition to field-based interviews and ethnography, the book draws regularly on public and private Facebook posts made by my interlocutors. Images, articles, and personal opinions shared over social media offered an essential insight into personal and public opinion in the rapidly digitizing context of post-2011 Myanmar, where Facebook quickly became the most significant source of media and information in the country following telecommunications liberalization (McCarthy 2018b). To secure informed consent, I discussed private and public posts directly in person with interlocutors and used pseudonyms when citing their posts.[36] Coupling in-person ethnography with digital research, even after I had physically left "the field," helped reveal how practices and ideals encountered during fieldwork evolved over time—including during COVID-19 and in the wake of the military coup in February 2021.

Structure of the Book

Chapter 1 traces the genealogy of distributive politics in Burma since the colonial period and uncovers how institutional inheritances shaped welfare regime development in the decades following independence. The chapters that follow are structured in two parts.

Part 1 has two chapters that examine how state social responsibility was outsourced after the end of the socialist dictatorship in 1988. Chapter 2 exposes the way post-socialist junta officials shifted social obligations and functions to non-state actors throughout the 1990s and 2000s by coupling commercial and tax incentives with Buddhist propaganda and selective encouragement of civil society. Chapter 3 then explores how ideals and practices of non-state welfare were entrenched and stretched during natural disasters in 2008 and 2015, popularizing expansive notions of political and social duty beyond direct kinship that implicitly exclude ethnic and religious minorities.

Part 2 has three chapters that assess how ideals and practices of non-state welfare proved path dependent during the decade of partial civilian rule between

2011 and 2020. Chapter 4 explores the role of charity and philanthropy in conceptions of freedom and democracy enacted by grassroots activists, arguing that their work delivered crucial aid to the needy and yet also contribute to the normative and material exclusion of minorities—particularly Muslims—from assistance and notions of political community. Chapter 5 examines how tycoons who accrued wealth by assuming social responsibility during junta rule rendered themselves essential to collective identity and shielded their assets and power from redistribution or scrutiny in a more democratic context. Chapter 6 explores how logics of social outsourcing can render slippery and conditional ideas of social rights and entitlement from the state, even at times when government agencies are expanding their social footprint. It focuses on how ideals and practices of self-reliance became a basis for claiming government social support, encouraging communities to compete with each other for basic "rights," legitimizing the vicious exclusion of the "unworthy," and entrenching a pernicious ideal of "co-produced" development.

The book concludes by examining the practical and ideational appeal of state social outsourcing and how it can ensure the endurance of non-state social provision, even with often inequitable impacts and corrosive civic consequences. Despite regressive outcomes, the book considers how the legacies of social outsourcing have also paradoxically sustained democratic struggle—noting the role of non-state social providers in supporting resistance efforts against dictatorship after the Myanmar military seized power in February 2021. Exploring how social outsourcing can shape both the desirability and fiscal potential for greater state role in the welfare mix, the book concludes by theorizing the implications of this study for comparative research on welfare and inequality more broadly.

1

DISTRIBUTIVE POLITICS SINCE COLONIZATION

During the rule of socialist dictator General Ne Win, the central bank of Burma issued a variety of odd-denominational currencies featuring heroes of class struggle. The banknotes sought to place the autarkic regime, which held power between 1962 and 1988, in the lineage of late colonial anti-capitalist, anti-imperialist movements.

One of the most widespread uprisings of that period followed the economic devastation of the Great Depression. It was led by peasant activist and traditional healer Saya San against the exploitative colonial agricultural economy (his image was later emblazoned on the ninety kyat banknote).[1] Between the 1890s and the 1920s, Burmese farmers had migrated in droves to the Irrawaddy Delta and other regions chasing the promise of British laws that would give them titles after twelve years of cultivation. The human energy this incentive unleashed transformed the delta from a largely vacant marshland in the mid-nineteenth century into one the most agriculturally productive regions in the world. Yet, in the absence of any legal protections or social insurance schemes for Burmese farmers, when the price of rice halved between 1929 and 1931, hundreds of thousands of peasants were unable to repay loans they had taken to fund the conversion of marshy wetlands into fertile rice fields.[2] Amid widespread debt defaults, non-peasant creditors seized land that farmers had spent years improving. By 1937, more than half of the delta was owned by nonagricultural interests, up from less than 20 percent before the Great Depression (Adas 1974, 188).

The dispossession of the peasantry fed the Burma Rebellion, as it was dubbed by British administrators. Led by Saya San, farmers across the country took up arms against colonial authorities, blaming their destitution on British laws and policies that structured the extractive imperial economy. The insurgency commenced in Saya San's native town of Tharrawaddy in Bago Region after British administrators, deaf to demands for remission in light of the hardship many faced, began collecting land and head taxes. Within weeks the rebellion spread throughout the delta, to Rangoon and north into central Burma and the Shan States, eventually encompassing twelve of Burma's twenty colonial districts (Brown 1999a, 143). Saya San was arrested, trialed, and promptly executed in mid-1931, following the deployment of hundreds of additional troops from India (Aung-Thwin 2010, 6–8). The rebellion continued for more than two years, and by then colonial forces had killed between 1,300 and 10,000 rebels while another 9,000 or so surrendered (Cady 1958, 316; Maung Htin Aung 1967, 292; Aung-Thwin 2010, 8).

British colonial rulers succeeded in violently suppressing the rebellion. Yet an independence movement was spawned aimed at dismantling the colonial economy by ending both foreign economic dominance and practices of unfair taxation. Debates about how to balance the people's welfare concerns with capitalism, especially the place of foreign investment in Burma's postindependence economy, defined the late colonial and subsequent parliamentary period from 1948 to 1962 (Badgley 1974, 244). Prime Minister U Nu's Pyidawtha Plan attempted to address these concerns by requiring industrial enterprises to contribute to a state-run social security scheme for their employees (Brown 2013, 136). Yet many civilian and military leaders viewed the plan as overly reliant on foreign investment and capitalist enterprise. General Ne Win later justified his 1962 coup and nationalization of all large and small businesses on the basis that, by embracing foreign capital, civilian leaders had betrayed the vision of a fairer, welfare-oriented economy for which independence-era heroes like Saya San had fought and died.

Postcolonial concerns about economic injustice were enlisted by state officials to justify an autarkic socialist dictatorship between 1962 and 1988. Following the dissolution of socialism in 1988, however, military state officials in the 1990s and 2000s reconfigured the relation between state, market and society, returning to a welfare capitalist ideal in which the achievement of social justice was outsourced largely to private and non-state actors. To understand the entrenched role of non-state actors in social and redistributive functions, both during the period of partial civilian rule between 2011 and 2020 and following the return to dictatorship in 2021, it is crucial to understand how state officials sought to configure capitalism, state interventionism, and public welfare between the colonial period and the dissolution of socialism in 1988.

This chapter explores this evolution by examining four institutional inheritances that markedly shaped the postindependence welfare regime: an elite and popular Burmese Buddhist consensus that unregulated capitalism threatens the welfare of ordinary people; the ethnic and ideological fragmentation of state elites, especially within the military; an economy based largely on raw agricultural commodity export; and a weak state apparatus of coercion and taxation, particularly in the upland periphery. Successive regimes since 1948 have recalibrated the role of state, market, and society in the welfare mix as they attempted to come to terms with, and at times challenge, these competing institutional inheritances. Yet, as subsequent chapters show, these factors combined to hem in successive elite coalitions, leading to a reliance on a paradoxical strategy of redistribution without taxation. This approach limited the viability, generosity, and breadth of state welfare action and led to an embrace of social outsourcing as a core tool of governance. This chapter traces these competing priorities from their origins in the colonial period through to the dissolution of socialist dictatorship in 1988. It then briefly examines how the post-socialist junta abandoned a direct role in welfare provision after 1988 while using market reform to expand state coercive control in the upland periphery. The chapter concludes by noting a major gap in existing narratives about the 1990s and 2000s, which the chapters in part 1 subsequently address: how post-socialist junta officials dramatically reconfigured Myanmar's welfare regime by outsourcing state social functions to market and community actors after 1988.

Colonial Rule and the Consensus against "Free Market" Capitalism

British colonial exploitation led Burma's independence leaders to embrace a highly interventionist vision for the postindependence state. The opportunist manner in which colonial administrators governed commodity extraction throughout the country seeded deep grievances with imperial capitalism. In fertile lowland areas, especially the Ayeyarwaddy Delta, the British encouraged the development of an intensive system of cultivation. The frontier nature of the deltaic plain formed by the Ayeyarwaddy and Sittang Rivers enabled the rapid conversion of an area that was "sparsely populated and largely abandoned to nature" until the mid-nineteenth century annexation of Lower Burma by the British (Brown 2013, 44). Subsequent colonial land legislation and administration provided strong incentives for Burmese pioneer agriculturalists to clear tracts of vacant land and then cultivate, occupy, and pay revenue on it; doing so for twelve years would allow them to acquire a title to the land (Brown 2013, 37). During that twelve-year period, British regulations allowed land investment by permitting squatters to use the land they cleared as collateral for credit to pay for improvements. These regulations and practices resulted in a massive expansion in the area under cultivation by the late nineteenth century as both cultivators as well as creditors moved into the delta and expanded arable land (Adas 1974, 128, 131). The promise that tenancy would lead to ownership and land accumulation lured many Burmese cultivators to the region, where some accrued modest fortunes by claiming land and using it as collateral to establish expansive holdings (Brown 2013, 46; Adas 1974, chap. 6).

There were inherent tensions in the credit system that underpinned the lowland agricultural economy. Unlike in Malaysia, where the British had imposed restrictions on alienation of agricultural land to foreign interests, moneylending in Burma was dominated by mostly South Indian merchants (*chettiars*) who were legally permitted to seize land if cultivators defaulted on their loans (Brown 2013, 38–40). The result was the gradual transfer of land to nonagricultural interests by the early years of the twentieth century, which generated popular misgivings about the colonial economy (Brown 2013, 38). As the frontier became crowded with cultivators and competition for increasingly poor quality yet high-priced land intensified, the material circumstances of both tenant-cultivators and landless laborers deteriorated markedly—the price of land in the delta increased more than fivefold, from 20 rupees (Rs) per acre around 1900 to 70 Rs in 1910 and 105 Rs in the early 1930s (Adas 1974, 79, 148). The price of land rental rose accordingly, with the amount of output paid by tenants to landowners increasing from 10 percent in the late 1880s to up to 50 percent in the most fertile areas and 20 percent in less fertile areas by the 1920s (Brown 2013, 47). Paths of upward mobility began to evaporate at the same time that many lost land to creditors, dynamics that fed grievances about the colonial economy and British rule more broadly.

Meanwhile, colonial administrators extracted commodities from Burma's mountainous periphery and borderlands by governing upland areas indirectly. A degree of recognition and trade autonomy was granted to ethnic elites in hilly areas in exchange for them recognizing British dominion over natural resources such as teak, gemstones, and precious metals (Thant Myint-U 2001, 216–217). After extraction, these commodities were quickly transported to lowland areas for processing and trade. Felled teak logs, for instance, would be dragged by elephants and buffalo and then dispatched by raft to Rangoon or Moulmein down the Ayeyarwaddy, Sittang, and Salween Rivers for cutting and sale (Brown 2013, 11–12). Although the bulk of workers in the sawmill industry—as with oil refineries and ricemills—were Indian, local populations were often engaged as manual laborers in the forests and on the rivers (Brown 2013, 12). Some hereditary rulers, regional elites, and their clients were also able to act as intermediaries in logging, harvesting, or transportation, forming the basis of an emergent commercial class in upland areas. Combined with British railroad construction projects and other infrastructure initiatives that employed local laborers, some upland elites and populations supported colonial administration because it offered them a share in the spoils of imperial resource extraction (Thant Myint-U 2001, 222–227).

Differential experiences of colonial authority produced divergent upland and lowland political aspirations and grievances. The British granted significant autonomy to some ethnic authorities in upland regions where resources could be extracted without the kind of labor-intensive apparatus needed in the lowland delta. In a form of governance best conceptualized as hybrid rule, the British acknowledged selected chiefs and tribal councils in hilly ethnic areas and empowered them to administer populations with the primary aim of enabling resource extraction.[3] Following the colonial suppression of insurgency, for instance, a number of hereditary Shan dynasties (*sawbwa*) submitted to British authority by recognizing the colonial state's right to extract forests and mineral resources in these areas (Thant Myint-U 2001, 216–217). In return, they were granted legal status as indirect rulers able to maintain royal courts and engage in trade. Other ethnic minorities from borderland regions categorized by the British as Frontier or Excluded areas also remained under the nominal authority of their traditional rulers, often retaining considerable power to manage social and political affairs according to tradition and custom (Smith 2007, 9; R. Taylor 2009, 80). As the struggle for independence from Britain began to intensify in lowland areas, the variation between upland and lowland modes of colonization effectively mapped populations in the Frontier borderland areas "out of the political struggles and imaginations of the center" (Callahan 2004, 107). As political scientist Mary Callahan (2005, 107, 109) observed, "The center was where politics happened, full citizens lived, and Burmese was the currency of public life; in the margins . . . lesser citizens lived out 'primitive' existences and language was not a public activity, since the public had been territorially limited to the center."

This strategy of direct rule in lowland areas and varying forms of indirect rule in the periphery (see figure 1.1) placed upland native territories on radically different paths of political development compared with lowland areas that were directly ruled. These divergent experiences of colonial authority shaped attitudes toward imperial capitalism and established alternative non-state structures of administration and coercion in hilly periphery areas. Both these formal and informal institutional dynamics shaped trajectories of state-building, taxation, and welfare regime development for decades to follow.

In fertile lowland areas, British administrators imposed an entirely new order rather than adopting existing social structures. These regions were governed directly from Calcutta via Rangoon, creating an appearance, if not reality, of colonial legal and administrative order down to the village level.[4] Following escalating agitation for greater autonomy in the 1920s, Burmese voices were granted some input into noncritical areas such as agriculture, education, forestry, and local government.[5] However, all major organs of civil service and law enforcement in Ministerial Burma or Burma Proper, defined as areas ruled directly by

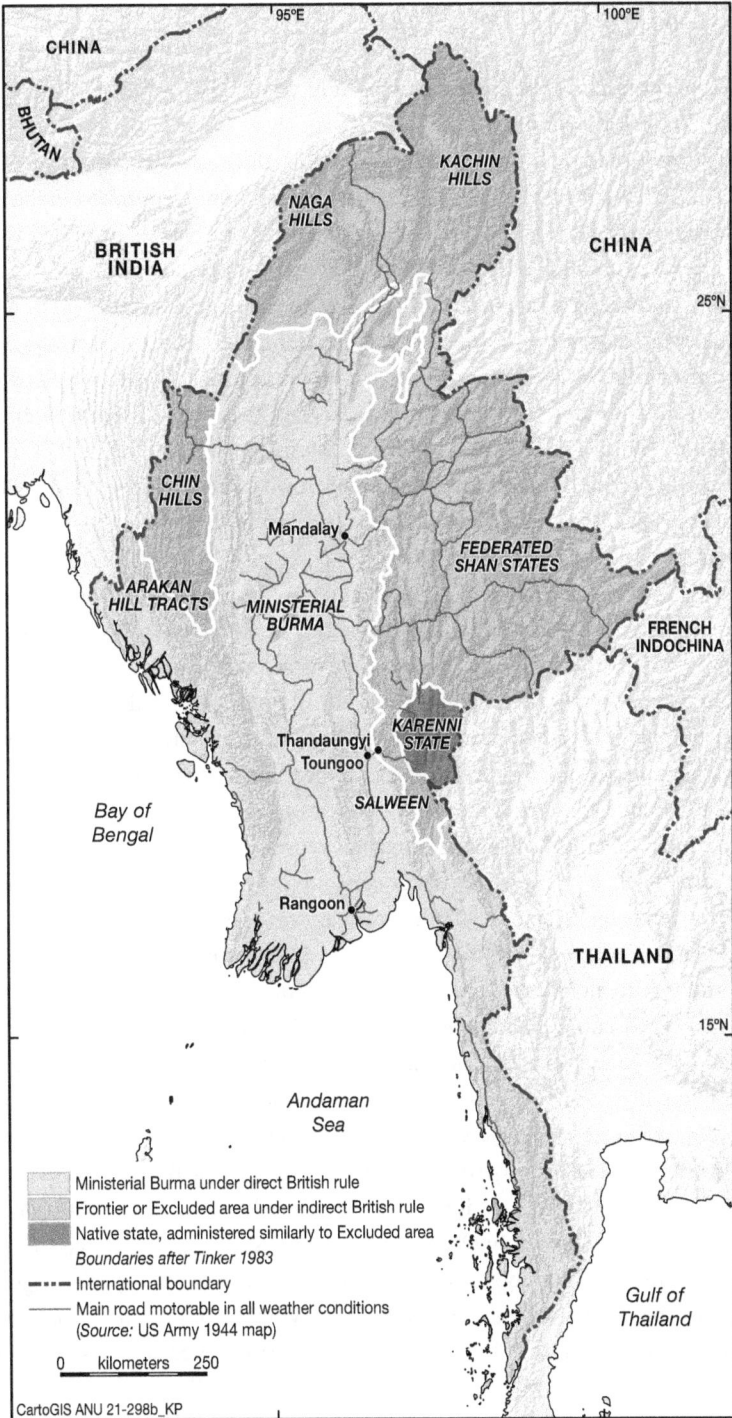

FIGURE 1.1. Administrative and infrastructure limits of colonial Burma. *Source*: Adapted from Tinker 1984, with addition of all-weather roads from 1944 US Army map.

Rangoon, continued to be staffed at upper ranks by British officers (Thant Myint-U 2001, 208). The bulk of administrative work at the lower levels of the colonial state was managed by Indian civil servants, with Burmese township and village heads mostly overseen by European deputy commissioners stationed in the largest towns (Saha 2013, 47–50). A colonial legal system, which extended to the local level, was established.[6] Populations that resisted British rules and laws were violently pacified by garrisons of British and Indian soldiers stationed in major urban centers. Quotidian order, especially in the increasingly fractious delta, where armed robbery became more common by the 1920s, was enforced by predominantly Indian soldiers along with largely Burmese, Karen, and Indian civil police (R. Taylor 2009, 99–103; Thant Myint-U 2001, 208). The role of foreigners and perceived ethnic outsiders in coercive law enforcement fed lowland discontent with British rule, especially as the cost of deploying troops and police was recouped through local taxes.[7]

Perceptions of colonial tax as regressive and unfair compounded anger at colonial repression in the lowland. Land taxes, the largest single source of financial receipts, were in theory levied progressively as colonial officers recalculated the amount due from a household annually, adjusting for soil fertility, water conditions, and proportion of acreage under cultivation.[8] They often gave remissions if cultivators lost one-third or more of a crop because of flood or other exigency.[9] However, despite these progressive dimensions to revenue collection, animosity toward taxation, fueled by having to pay for repression, was compounded by the regressive and rigidly imposed head or capitation tax. Comprising only 6 percent of total revenue in 1926 and 1927, the head tax was massively unpopular as it was levied at the same rate for all males aged 18 to 60: five rupees a year for a married man and two to eight rupees for a bachelor (Brown 1999b, 386–387). Given the head tax was asset blind and thus regressive, it "bore particularly hard on tenants and laborers" in the wake of crop failure, a fall in wages, or periods of unemployment (Scott 1976, 99).[10] A flat-rate tax was not levied in any other part of British India but appealed to Burmese administrators because it was relatively easy to implement. However, it proved deeply unpopular among Burmese taxpayers—and some British officials—as it obviously burdened the poor disproportionately more than the rich (Brown 1999b, 387, fn12). Animosity caused by the administration of colonial taxation intensified throughout the 1920s, with special anger reserved for the regressive head tax that became symbolic of British exploitation of Burmese land and labor in return for scant welfare-oriented services and public goods and weak regulation of creditors.

The dominance of foreign interests at higher rungs of the colonial economy was another source of discontent, especially among Burmese peasant and student groups. A commercial class mostly composed of preexisting elites or hereditary rulers emerged in some parts of the country.[11] A path to modest commercial success for Burmese cultivators had existed through to the turn of the twentieth century, creating a small group of indigenous landholders in the delta. However, in key sectors of the economy, British administrators discriminated against Burmese businesspeople in favor of Western-owned companies (Aung Tun Thet 1989, 64–65). The teak industry, for instance, was dominated by five British companies that were issued licenses on a long-term, renewable basis (Thant Myint-U 2001, 227). Meanwhile, the British-owned Irrawaddy Flotilla Company was permitted to maintain a near monopoly in transport services and received substantial subsidies from the colonial state (Aung Tun Thet 1989, 65, 78–79). British administrators similarly permitted Indian *chettiar* moneylenders to play increasingly dominant roles in the provision of credit in both the lowland delta and upland Frontier trading and mining towns.[12] The gradual result was widespread indebtedness among Burmese and ethnic minority populations to mostly Indian bankers, who increasingly turned to the British colonial legal system to recover defaulted loans (Thant Myint-U 2001, 224). Meanwhile, Indian laborers were favored above Burmese workers for skilled roles in rice milling and the teak and oil industries (Brown 2013, 19). Although the imbalances of the colonial economy meant that substantive Burmese participation in the market was effectively foreclosed, British administrators largely maintained a rigid "belief in the efficiency and effectiveness of the market" and avoided interventions to redress imbalances (Brown 2013, 19).

Lowland economic grievances were exacerbated by cultural insensitivities. The British failure to maintain the Buddhist order as earlier regents had, and their refusal to require colonial officers remove shoes at pagodas, came to be viewed as assaults on the moral order from which many Burmese saw sovereignty and nationhood as emerging (Thant Myint-U 2001, 127, 209–210; Brown 1999a, 144; Turner 2014, chaps. 5 and 6). Despite the introduction of legislative elections at the district and township level in the early 1920s, protests and strikes both against the colonial economy and Burmese subordination within the colonial education system intensified (R. Taylor 2009, 184–188). The leaders of prominent Buddhist organizations subsequently formed a General Council of Burmese Associations, with the goal of unifying the largely Buddhist patriotic groups (*wunthanu athins*) that were proliferating in mostly rural areas of the country (Turner 2014, 138; Walton 2016, 20). These grievances exploded when the Great Depression dispossessed much of the lowland peasantry and the colonial state did little to support people rendered destitute.

The Great Depression Intensified Anger at Colonial Taxation

The Great Depression delivered a major shock to the already-fractious colonial economy. The price of rice almost halved in value in 1930 and did not begin to return to earlier levels until 1935.[13] As Burmese cultivators defaulted on loans taken out to finance their land reclamation and cultivation efforts, *chettiar* and nonagriculturalist moneylenders foreclosed on debts and repossessed land. In the absence of colonial regulations restricting the alienation of land to foreign interests, by 1937 Indian *chettiars* owned 25 percent of the delta while nonagriculturalists controlled 50 percent, a dramatic increase from 6 and 19 percent in 1930 respectively (Adas 1974, 188).

Anger toward the colonial economy, especially moneylending and unfair taxation, became a defining feature of emergent Burmese political movements. As political anthropologist James C. Scott (1976, 99) notes, the burden of colonial revenue collection on cultivators had already made taxation and the head tax in particular the "central issue of popular nationalist agitation from 1915." Despite the rapid decline in rice prices and a subsequent wave of defaults and dispossession following the Great Depression, colonial administrators continued to collect land dues as well as the regressive head tax in lowland regions. The anger generated by British administration in rural areas resonated with the growing frustration with the colonial economy in urban areas. In early 1930, riots broke out in Rangoon between Indian and Burmese dockworkers following a pay dispute with dock managers. Then, in December 1930, the Saya San Rebellion commenced in Tharrawaddy district after colonial administrators rejected petitions from thousands of landowners, cultivators, rice millers and moneylenders for "drastic cuts" to, or postponement of, both land and head taxes (Brown 1999b, 389). Saya San, earlier a traditional healer and fortune-teller, drew people to the rebellion by combining anti-tax rhetoric with Buddhist prophecies.[14] The uprising quickly spread as dispossessed farmers and disaffected laborers raided weapons from police stations and attacked government representatives. Emergency powers were granted from India, and a Special Rebellion Commission was appointed by colonial authorities to assist in command of additional troops (Aung-Thwin 2010, 6–8). Once Saya San was executed, colonial administrators were ordered to exercise "careful discretion" in levying the regressive head tax from 1931 and gave remissions on land taxes until 1935.[15] Despite these belated concessions, abolishing unfair taxation and redressing the injustices of the colonial economy through state welfare interventions became articles of faith for emergent Burmese nationalist leaders.

The Saya San Rebellion and nationalist groups (*wunthanu athins*) that had proliferated throughout rural areas of the country during the 1920s shaped the development of the more urban-centric independence organization *Dobama Asiayone* (Our Burma). Officially founded in 1933, it quickly became the primary political vehicle of largely middle-class student leaders, including Aung San, who later led the country to independence (Khin Yi 1988; R. Taylor 2009, 216–217). Leaders similarly critiqued the colonial economy but sought reform rather than revolution of colonial institutions, distancing themselves from the tax revolt campaigns that *wunthanu* groups had led prior to and following the Great Depression. The Dobama movement instead focused on organizing factory workers and oil field laborers with the aim of making demands from existing colonial state institutions (R. Taylor 2009, 215–217). Strikes became a favored tool of the Dobama movement's leadership, with walkouts in major cities and towns often escalating into riots that British and ethnic Karen troops violently suppressed.[16] Animosity began to develop between lowland political leaders, who viewed colonial rule as exploitative and inequitable, and the ethnic minority populations that were viewed as collaborationists for serving as police and soldiers under British command.

As anti-colonial sentiment escalated in India and Burma, the British extended greater political autonomy to Burma. By 1937, Burma was entirely separated from India and a new constitution, which established a parliamentary form of government, was imposed (R. Taylor 2009, 121–124). Notwithstanding these reforms, revolutionary and especially Marxist thought found increasing traction among elite Burmese activists because it offered a potent critique of the colonial capitalist economy (Thompson 1959, 19; R. Taylor 2009, chap. 3; Walton 2016, 27). The independence movement increasingly converged around a broad leftist ideology, especially after the translation of Marx's writings into Burmese in 1937 (Walton 2016, 26–27). The terminologies of socialism, Marxism, and communism were used interchangeably by many in the movement, with activists often explaining these concepts to colleagues and the general population using Buddhist terminology (Walton 2016, 27–28). The main parties that emerged from the Dobama movement varied in their opinion of existing legal institutions but largely converged around a paradoxical anti-capitalist vision of a redistributive state that simultaneously collected minimal tax. The outbreak of the Second World War and mobilization of nationalist leaders in Japan subsequently laid the ground for full independence while also entrenching socio-institutional fractures and center-periphery divides that later undermined the possibilities for building a state-led welfare regime.

Second World War Further Fractured Society and State

The Second World War pitted lowland populations against upland minorities while decimating the infrastructure, administration, and taxation capacities of

the colonial state. Early in the war, leaders of the Burmese independence movement, popularly termed the Thirty Comrades, sought out and received military
training from Japan. The group, led by Aung San, subsequently established the
Burma Independence Army, which participated in the Japanese invasion of Burma
in 1942. Subsequent military campaigns brought ethnic Burmese forces into conflict with British troops, predominantly comprised of ethnic minority soldiers recruited from upland areas.[17] After British forces abandoned Rangoon and the
Japanese occupation commenced, Burmese administrators took control of non-
military organs of the colonial state. However, there were minimal funds for state
spending, and the bureaucratic separation of lowland Burma from most upland
areas continued (Guyot 1966, 215). Despite the ambitious social plans of Burmese
politicians who were collaborating with Japanese imperial forces, government expenditure dropped precipitously, and a pattern of minimal taxation and austere
public service provision commenced and recurred for decades to follow.[18]

The relationship between independence leaders and the Japanese became increasingly strained as both Burmese resistance and Allied advances intensified in
1942. Both communists and nationalists had been disseminating anti-Japanese
propaganda and organizing peasants in rural areas throughout the war, and
these efforts received increasingly formal support from the British from late 1943
(Guyot 1966, chap. 10; Callahan 2003, 72–82). In August 1944, the Anti-Fascist
Organisation (AFO) was established, reunifying senior members of the Burma
National Army (the reformulated Burma Independence Army) with the Communist Party of Burma and the Socialist Party under the banner of national liberation. In March 1945, Supreme Allied Commander Admiral Louis Mountbatten
decided to arm the AFO in an attempt to control the Burmese nationalists and
ease the path of Allied forces into Burma (Callahan 2003, 83). Later that month,
Aung San marched the Burma National Army (BNA) with British troops against
the Japanese who then agreed to withdraw (R. Taylor 2009, 237). By May 1945,
a compromise was reached between Burmese nationalist leaders and British officers to permit a British military administration and integrate the BNA into the
British-led Burma Army (R. Taylor 2009, 237–238). A standing army of 12,000
men, divided by ethnicity, was established. Senior command of Burman-majority
battalions was jointly granted to later dictator Ne Win and two other members of
the Thirty Comrades. However, ethnic Karen, Kachin, and Chin soldiers—who
were viewed by many of their Burman counterparts as collaborationists—
remained the core of the Burma Army (Callahan 2003, 96–99). Ethnic and ideological fractures between upland and lowland elites were thus embedded at the
heart of the armed forces.

After negotiating these reforms, Aung San commenced a campaign for full
independence from the British. In August 1945, he reorganized the AFO into the

Anti-Fascist People's Freedom League (AFPFL), a catchall mass organization he coled aimed at unifying a "motley assembly of young left-wing politicians and the old guard" (Maung Maung 1989, 182). The group included representatives from diverse party, business, ethnic, and religious groups, including civil servants and public figures previously aligned with both the British and Japanese.[19] The organization attracted widespread support, with the first public meeting in Rangoon on 19 August 1945 attended by an estimated 300,000 people from across the political spectrum, including traders and trade unionists (Maung Maung 1989, 181).

The terms of the May 1945 military compromise also permitted Aung San to establish the People's Volunteer Organisation (PVO), a militia whose local leaders would later play a central role in postindependence state-building outside Rangoon. The PVO quickly began to work closely with the AFPFL, and a subsequent attempt by the British to partially disband it in May 1946 led to clashes with police and the arrest of hundreds of PVO volunteers. AFPFL demands for independence for the entirety of Burma, including both lowland Ministerial Burma and the upland Frontier areas, began to intensify (Callahan 2003, 110–111). Growing anger about escalating inflation and insufficient pay from British administrators to Burmese state employees prompted strikes by clerks and police officers in June and July 1946 (Callahan 2003, 107). Enlisting its close links with labor unions and the Communist and Socialist Parties while maintaining ties with Indian and Chinese businesspeople, in August 1946 the AFPFL encouraged a nationwide general strike at all ports, roads, and trade routes (Slater 2010, 267; Maung Maung 1989, 188). Threatening further mass demonstrations and labor unrest if the AFPFL did not form government, Aung San subsequently reached an agreement with British Prime Minister Clement Attlee in January 1947 for independence within a year.

The Aung San–Attlee Agreement required Burmese politicians to secure the assent of elites from indirectly ruled upland areas to join a Union of Burma based in Rangoon (R. Taylor 2009, 228). Decades of autonomy, militarization, and earlier promises of self-determination made by British officers during the war led some ethnic elites to question whether Burmese politicians would, after independence, respect and maintain the administrative status granted to them and their communities during colonial rule. As cleavages between lowland Burmese politicians and upland ethnic minority populations deepened, leaders of several ethnic groups boycotted the February 1947 Panglong Conference. For instance, a group of Karen leaders instead met to form the Karen National Union, a political organization aimed at safeguarding the interests of Karen people at independence (Callahan 2003, 120). Other ethnic groups—including those located in lowland Burma Proper such as the Mon and the Arakanese, along with more remote groups such as the Wa, Naga, and smaller ethnicities—were excluded entirely (Walton 2008, 901–903). In their absence, Aung San, along with his AFPFL colleagues and other

Shan, Kachin, and Chin elites, agreed to include principles of federalism within the 1947 Constitution—specifically, autonomy in internal affairs as well as revenue sharing and a right to secession (see Tinker 1984, 404–405). After ratification of the agreement by a British House of Commons special committee in April 1947, the British treated the issue of the Frontier areas as sufficiently resolved, clearing the path to the end of colonial rule (R. Taylor 2009, 229; Walton 2008, 897).

Months later, in July 1947, Aung San and part of his cabinet were assassinated by a political rival. Despite practically eliminating a generation of nationalist leaders less than half a year before independence in January 1948, their ideological commitment to ending colonial economic exploitation through a redistributive welfare state endured and was enshrined in postcolonial political institutions. Reflecting a consensus expressed publicly by Aung San before his assassination, the constitution drafted by non-Communist factions within the AFPFL and ratified by a constituent assembly in Rangoon called for the establishment of a "socialist and egalitarian society" (R. Taylor 2009, 229–230). The socialist objectives enshrined in the constitution departed radically from the laissez-faire market ideology of British rule, reflecting the commitment made by Aung San in a June 1947 speech "to bring to an end the 'colonial economy' based on the export of raw materials" through a form of socialism focused on nationalization and industrialization (Tinker 1967, 93). However, the centralized federal structure created by the constitution granted also considerable colonial-era autonomy to upland ethnic elites to manage their own tax regimes, budgets, and police forces, albeit for only five groups: the Federated Shan States, Kachin State, Karen State (also known as Kaw-thulay), Karenni State, and the Special Division of the Chins (R. Taylor 2009, 230). Varying lowland and upland experiences of colonial rule thus markedly shaped the design of independence political institutions. Elite attempts to balance competing ideas about the role of market forces and state interventionism, along with the central state's febrile administrative and coercive capacity after the war, produced a post-colonial regime with minimal capacity to deliver welfare and public goods and little willingness to tax populations.

Almost a century of British governance geared toward agricultural and commodity extraction, followed by a destructive period of conflict and Japanese occupation, came to a close, leaving four paradoxical institutional inheritances confronting the independence government. The first was a consensus among lowland political and military elite, embedded in the 1947 Constitution, in favor of an actively redistributive welfare state. The second was an economy reliant on commodity export, especially agricultural goods, around which a fair system of taxation was yet to be developed. The third was a central military organization riven by disputes over ideology, personal loyalty, and ethnicity. Last, and relatedly, was an apparatus of state coercion and administration with little capacity to impose order, raise revenue, and effectively deliver governance or public goods outside of Rangoon, especially in the upland periphery where minority elites retained considerable autonomy. Successive regimes attempted to accommodate and challenge these formal and informal institutional inheritances for decades, repeatedly revising the envisioned role of state and market in achieving collective welfare and social justice.

The Rise and Fall of Interventionist Welfare Capitalism (1948–1962)

With independence, civilian leaders sought to satisfy diverse electoral constituencies, including commercial elites and communists, by embracing an ideology that fused rural socialism with urban welfare capitalism. In lowland regions, the government tentatively planned redistribution of farmland while simultaneously passing laws requiring private companies based mainly in Rangoon to assume significant social obligations for their formal-sector employees. Although the government avoided making major budgetary outlays for welfare, it still claimed to be advancing a modern welfare state by coupling industrial welfare capitalism with rural land redistribution. As army leaders crafted themselves increasing autonomy from civilian oversight and coalesced the rank and file around a potent blend of nationalism and socialism, they framed U Nu's partial embrace of capitalism and foreign investment as a threat to both the territorial integrity of the postcolonial state and the vision of state-mediated public welfare enshrined in the 1947 Constitution.

Postindependence Leaders Embraced Interventionist Welfare Capitalism

The postindependence government sought to advance industrialization through state interventions into a partially market-based economy. The 1947 Constitution of the Union of Burma gave significant power to the state to own and control resources and regulate economic life (Mya Maung 1970, 535). Bequeathed with these powers, Prime Minister U Nu attempted to balance the competing interests of local business and trading constituencies within the AFPFL. Demands for land nationalization were vocally expressed by the left of the AFPFL along with the White Flag faction of the Communist Party, which briefly aligned itself with the AFPFL after independence.[20] U Nu's vision of modernization and industrialization, referred to in Burmese as the Pyidawtha Plan, attempted to parry these seemingly contradictory demands into a cohesive strategy. Launched in August 1952, the more technical English version and the Burmese folk version championed by Prime Minister U Nu differed greatly in their rhetorical emphasis (Tharaphi Than 2013). However, both plans shared the same measures and focus aimed at reducing Burma's economic reliance on raw commodity export—especially rice, oil, and teak—and encouraging and regulating industrialization so as to deliver "modern" welfare to Burmese workers (Brown 2013, 106). Pyidawtha was translated into English as the welfare plan, but literally it means "Happy Royal Land," signaling U Nu's simultaneous desires "to embrace tradition and promise development to the country" (Tharaphi Than 2013, 647).

Formulated with the assistance of foreign consultants, the Pyidawtha Plan comprised ten key schemes aimed at achieving economic modernization. They included nationalization and redistribution of cultivable lands, predominantly in lowland areas, to create small land holders; schemes to provide health and welfare services; improvements in education and infrastructure; and transfer of power to regional governments (Tharaphi Than 2013, 646). Central to these objectives was the creation of state industrial enterprises and public corporations ranging from steel and sugar mills to pharmaceuticals and brick and tea factories (Brown 2013, 106). All were to operate according to "business principles" and were to be financed initially through the sale of rice, which boomed in the early 1950s with the outbreak of the Korean War (Khin Maung Kyi 1966, 96; Brown 2013, 106). A statutory monopoly in the export of rice was granted to the newly created State Agricultural Marketing Board (SAMB), continuing a practice established during the British wartime administration (Brown 2013, 104; Khin Maung Kyi 1966, 96). SAMB decided on the purchase price for rice at a set rate and then sold at fluctuating international export prices, justifying the practice on the basis of protecting farmers from extreme fluctuations in commodity prices. The scheme netted considerable profits, and SAMB quickly became an essential source of state revenue, partly supplementing the collapse in land tax revenues that had not been collected since the outbreak of the Second World War.[21] A State Agricultural Bank was established to provide loans to cultivators and replace the credit functions performed by chettiars, many of whom had fled either during the war or in the early years of independence (Turnell 2009, 174–202).[22]

Despite state intervention into the rural economy, the Pyidawtha Plan stopped short of socializing all ownership and production. Rather, it aimed for a "mixed" economy in which 65 percent of capital would be held by the private sector (Tin Maung Maung Than 2007, 54). Even with measures aimed at redistributing land, private property ownership remained a key principle of U Nu's government. Land nationalization legislated initially in 1948 and again in 1954 effectively served to shift legal ownership of agricultural land from foreign and indigenous landlords to sitting tenants, with compensation provided for their loss, albeit with plenty of conditions (R. Taylor 2009, 278–280). Profits from state control over the profitable agricultural economy, meanwhile, were intended to finance a form of industrialization that required companies and employees to co-contribute to a social security scheme for formal-sector workers managed by the government.

The blending of market and social concerns in the Pyidawtha Plan bore striking similarity to the American ideology of welfare capitalism, which had been dominant in the decades before the Great Depression. The philosophy idealized an "associative" state in which companies would voluntarily provide welfare to both their workers and the broader community through privatized or local charity, without state laws or mandates (Hawley 1974; Orloff 1988, 62–63). Advocates argued that corporate measures to improve the welfare of workers, such as eight-hour days and enterprise-level collective bargaining, were in the economic interests of industrialists as they boosted worker productivity and strengthened loyalty to employers (Zieger 1977, 178–179). Although rarely enacted on any consistent basis, welfare capitalism as a cultural ideal appealed to "Progressive" reformers and political leaders in the United States who feared that state mandates or public provision of social support, such as universal health care, would discourage the working class from seeking industrial employment (Brandes 1976; Brody 1980, 61). One of the major advocates of welfare capitalism in the 1920s was then secretary of commerce (and later US president) Herbert Hoover. In a series of writings in the early twentieth century, he developed a philosophy of collaborative industrial democracy in which he argued that businesses should cooperate with each other, with the government, and with their employees through self-governing organizations to deliver "desired outcomes for society" (Himmelberg 2001, 34–35). Hoover and other Progressive leaders viewed government regulation requiring these outcomes as both unnecessary and undesirable and proselytized the merits of welfare capitalism throughout the 1920s. [23] They argued that the productivity benefits of corporate social action should be naturally evident to all, making their adoption inevitable, and thus requiring their implementation through regulation was unnecessary and immoral as social contributions from wealthy industrialists were far more virtuous if given voluntarily rather than being compelled by law. In the first decades of the twentieth century, Hoover's own Burma Corporation had enacted a form of welfare capitalism at a mining concession in upland areas of Shan State near the current border with China and Thailand.[24] As US president, Hoover responded to the economic downturn of the Great Depression by encouraging private philanthropic efforts while giving little government support to those rendered destitute (Wilson 1975, chap. 4). The blatant failure of voluntary employer-based and charitable initiatives in the United States to alleviate dire need in the wake of mass layoffs discredited Hoover's ideology of voluntary welfare capitalism and drove increasing "demands for federal action to cope with the economic crisis" from across the social and political spectrum (Orloff 1988, 65). Thus, the Depression laid the path for President Franklin D. Roosevelt's later New Deal program, which mandated employers to provide old-age and unemployment insurances in ways that continue to define the character of America's contemporary welfare regime.

Despite it being discredited in the United States, a form of welfare capitalism appealed to U Nu and other middle-class AFPFL politicians as it allowed them to chart a course ideologically between a regulated form of capitalism, on the one hand, and the anti-tax sentiment and redistributive demands of the Communist Party of Burma, on the other.[25] The initiatives of the Pyidawtha Plan thus sought to couple redistribution of land and a state monopoly over rice export with a market-based industrial economy that encouraged private enterprise and foreign investment and required employer provision of social protection for workers. Companies formally registered in Burma were legally required to enroll their workers in a state-run Social Security Board (SSB) that was charged with providing workers with medical treatment, maternity and injury benefits, a survivor's pension, and funeral assistance. The scheme was drawn up with the assistance of Cornell-trained economist and consultant Louis Walinsky (Tharaphi Than 2013, 641). It was to be financed by a set percentage contribution of monthly salaries to the SSB by employers and employees, with capital contributions for clinics and other buildings made by the government (Walinsky 1962; Tin Maung Maung Than 2007, 85). People who were unemployed, employed in small businesses, or worked outside of state-owned, private, foreign, and joint ventures were excluded from the scheme. These design features reflected US Progressive-era aims—earlier embedded in the health care and social insurance programs of Roosevelt's New Deal (Quadagno 1984)—of minimizing government costs for social welfare while using basic health care as a way to encourage workers to participate in the industrial economy and ensure low wages in the labor market.[26]

U Nu's domestic campaign to support the mixed welfare regime envisaged in the Pyidawtha Plan promised a "morally rich" capitalist society while actively downplaying the role of foreign interests and investors in the development and execution of the plan. U Nu promised a developmental future achieved through a combination of state economic intervention and the hard work, moral conduct, and participation of ordinary citizens with future-oriented schemes of national development (Aung 2019). In widely circulated Burmese language speeches and writings, he argued that "poverty brought corrupt morality" and warned of the "dangers of not uniting or working hard or having loose morals" (Tharaphi Than 2013, 648).[27] The plan, and the propaganda that accompanied it, urged "public co-operation" among charitable welfare groups and encouraged the formation of local Community Chests to raise funds "for the use of voluntary social welfare agencies" (Union of Burma 1954, 125). Drawing heavily on Buddhist cosmology along with Burmese legends, U Nu encouraged Buddhists to view their contributions and sacrifices to the various schemes and components of the Pyidawtha Plan as meritorious donations (*dana*) and promised that their collective effort would make them "as healthy and strong as the legendary heroes" of Burmese history (Tharaphi Than 2013, 648).

U Nu's attempted reframing of Buddhist giving was significant. Anthropological research during the early independence period suggested that many people preferred to make charitable donations to monks, monasteries, and pagodas rather than to the poor or state institutions. Melford Spiro noted that in the 1950s Buddhists, who comprised the majority of the population in lowland areas, viewed donations and the patronage of Buddhist structures and monks as attracting the highest form of spiritual merit (*kutho*). These contributions would thus improve the chance of ending the cycle of rebirth and reaching Nibbana (*neikban*) while contributing to more socially oriented causes, in contrast, attracted little or no merit (Spiro [1970] 1982, 463). To help justify the disproportionate burden born by rural cultivators, who were forced to sell their produce to state agencies that bought at a fixed rate and sold at the international market rate, U Nu appealed directly to the "strong Burmese tradition of charity (*a-hlu*)" in an effort "to persuade the people that merit can be acquired through devoting their resources and their energies to the building of works of social benefit" (Tinker 1957, 129). Analysts at the time noted that if "Buddhism and socialism could be conjugated to the extent of making social service a part of the acquisition of merit," it would have significant implications for the "whole nature of Burmese society" (Mendelson 1975).

Ideologically, the postcolonial futurism enshrined in Pyidawtha "modernism" (Aung 2019) attempted to balance the elite consensus favoring a low-tax yet redistributive state with U Nu's personal commitment to rejuvenate Buddhist customs and morality that appealed to many Burmese people. He sought to fulfill the independence-era commitment to public welfare by promising land, improved infrastructure, and support for community associations in rural areas while providing health care and support (in the event of layoff or injury) to formal-sector workers. Importantly, he sought to do this without increasing direct taxation through land or head taxes and instead envisaged funding through indirect means: first, by forcing rural cultivators to sell their produce to a government trading monopoly at a price significantly below the international market rate and using sale by a state monopoly as a major source of revenue; and second, by requiring formal-sector companies and employees, including foreign enterprises, to co-contribute to the government's social security scheme for formal-sector workers.

Functionally, by the mid-1950s it became clear that the administrative and economic assumptions underpinning the Pyidawtha Plan, reliant as it was on indirect taxation of agricultural commodity exports, were overly optimistic. The rising global price of rice, which drove sizable budget surpluses in 1951 and 1952 and underpinned the finances of the plan, subsequently slumped, resulting in sizable deficits from 1953 to 1955 (Brown 2013, 106). Newly established state corporations struggled to manage both industrial production and the distribution of goods. As their commercial performance was relatively poor and government revenue had become scarce, no additional state-run enterprises were created after 1952 (Brown 2013, 106–109). With the AFPFL increasingly fractured over whether to continue to accept foreign investment or aid, international companies such as Unilever were reluctant to invest in new facilities or in joint ventures with state enterprises for fear that the state may later nationalize these assets (Brown 2013, 111). Private-sector manufacturing did begin to expand and diversify during the 1950s and pay into the Social Security Board, although on a relatively modest scale.[28] Yet the fiscal constraints and limited administrative capacity of the state, especially beyond Rangoon, meant the government's social footprint and welfare role did not expand as envisaged. In addition to internal AFPFL divisions and budgetary impediments, by the mid-1950s, the tensions within Burma's postindependence military and its evolution began to pose the biggest threat to U Nu's vision of welfare capitalism.

Consolidation of the Military-Laid Path to Socialist Dictatorship

Colonial rule and the struggle for independence left the Burmese army (Tatmadaw) organizationally and ideologically fractured as the period had pitted ethnic Bamar soldiers and armed leaders against their mostly British and Karen commanding officers. The 1945 merger of BNA forces with the British Burma Army further entrenched ethnicity as an organizing principle for military affairs, since it placed ethnic Karen soldiers into senior command positions at independence (Callahan 2003, 119–120). This arrangement proved debilitating for the postindependence army, exacerbating anxieties among recently integrated soldiers that their commanding officers were conspiring against U Nu's government (Callahan 2003, 118–119). While anger at what was perceived as a continuation of British rule generated a degree of unity among senior Burmese officers and soldiers, they were also deeply divided along ideological lines. In March 1948, the Communist Party of Burma insurgency intensified its insurrection against the government with the shifting allegiances of the White Flag faction previously aligned with the AFPFL (Smith 1999, 105–106). The ethnic Karen leaders of the military subsequently adopted the same "ruthless scorched-earth policy" taken by the British against Communist insurgents in the immediate postwar period, razing villages and executing those suspected of sympathizing with or harboring

Communist Party rebels (Callahan 2003, 123). Many soldiers merged or recruited into the military after the 1945 agreement associated capitalism with imperialism and thus sympathized with communism themselves. As a consequence, many viewed the brutal approach adopted by the British, Burmese loyalist, and Karen superiors to the Communist insurgency as denying their legitimate political grievances. Violent suppression thus only served to confirm Communist Party propaganda that was circulating that framed AFPFL leaders as "tools of the imperialists who cared nothing for Burmese villagers" (Callahan 2003, 123–124). Tensions over the commitment of the elected government to public welfare were playing out along ethnic cleavages within the armed forces.

In the wake of the counterinsurgency campaigns, a large number of mostly ethnic Bamar soldiers deserted the army to join local PVO militias that had increasingly aligned themselves with the Communist Party insurgency (Callahan 2003, 122–123). In May and June 1948, the AFPFL government and senior Burmese officers, viewing Karen loyalists as a far greater threat to independent Burma than the Communist rebels, offered them amnesty and sought to forge an alliance in an effort to counter Karen dominance within the army (Callahan 2003, 124, 129). After the power-sharing plan failed, the AFPFL government began to expand resourcing for a new paramilitary force, the Sitwundan, under the control of the AFPFL-aligned minister of home affairs. Earlier support provided by U Nu to the armed wing of the Karen National Union, the Karen National Defense Organization (KNDO), was also withdrawn (Callahan 2003, 127). Karen militia leaders quickly recognized that Burmese politicians and army officers were moving against them. Karen police and Sitwundan mutineers, as well as KNDO units and some defectors from the army, took control of major towns and strategic assets outside of Rangoon in the final months of 1948 (Callahan 2003, 131–132). Despite a peace deal brokered by the British between U Nu and the Karen rebels in November 1948, within a month local Sitwundan units began slaughtering Karen civilians (Callahan 2003, 132). The massacres prompted a further mutiny of Karen army units previously deployed against Communist Party rebels, many of whom promptly joined forces with the KNDO. By early January 1949, these units took control of Karen-majority neighborhoods of Rangoon. The insurgency then spread throughout central Burma as a Karen army unit mutinied in Toungoo before proceeding northward to Pyu and Maymyo (Callahan 2003, 133). The KNDO was promptly outlawed by U Nu, and in early February 1949, General Ne Win, one of the few senior Burmese army officers remaining in the military, deposed ethnic Karen General Smith Dun as Supreme Commander of All Defence and Police Forces (Callahan 2003, 134).

After taking control of the army, Commander in Chief Ne Win deployed several strategies aimed at unifying an army deeply fractured by mutinies. By

February 1949, fewer than 2,000 men remained in the uniform of the Union of Burma army, a fraction of the 12,000 soldiers at the time of the 1945 agreement between Aung San and the British (Callahan 2003, 114, 98). In order to bring a semblance of order to restive regions outside Rangoon, U Nu deployed Socialist Party politicians to strike alliances of convenience with local PVO, Sitwundan, and other militia leaders in provincial areas (Callahan 2003, 138). Their contingent loyalty and assistance in counterinsurgency campaigns were secured through dispersion of state spoils such as weapons, commercial licenses, land, loans, subsidies, and grants from the Pyidawtha Plan, as well as "unofficial promises" to ignore their smuggling of teak, rice, gold, and other commodities (Callahan 2003, 141–142).[29] PVO, Sitwundan, and other irregular forces were also integrated into the military, and by 1950 major insurrections began to lose steam as locally raised militias assisted state forces to recapture strategic towns (Callahan 2003, 149).

Ne Win simultaneously set out to transform the army's organization and distance it from civilian oversight.[30] Fear of the growing presence of the Kuomintang (KMT) in the Shan states bordering China in the early 1950s was a primary driver of these organizational reforms.[31] Following the Tatmadaw's repeated defeat at the hands of the better-trained KMT military leaders between 1950 and 1953, Ne Win and military leaders began arrogating for themselves expansive planning and budgetary powers autonomous of civilians (Callahan 2003, 150). Ne Win and other military leaders had earlier begun to see U Nu and his civilian government as naïve and overly trusting of British and Karen officers, openly criticizing them for being willing to cede central authority to armed leaders for political benefit. Fearing that U Nu was willing to make political concessions with armed leaders they saw as threatening the state, Ne Win and senior ranking officers demanded a sizable increase in the army's budget in 1951 to 40 percent of the civilian government's expenditures (Callahan 2003, 150). Backed by expanded civilian financing, reforms were also implemented to military doctrine and command structures along with training and logistics with the aim of cultivating a distinct organizational esprit de corps in the fractured military.

Newly developed military doctrine positioned Communist China as the most likely external threat to Burma. Meanwhile, the Psychological Warfare Unit established in 1952 developed a vernacular ideology combining nationalism and socialism that resonated with the political and economic grievances of soldiers and officers while unifying them against Burma's own Communist Party threat (Callahan 2003, 182–184; Maung Aung Myoe 2009, chap. 2). Military doctrines and ideologies emphasizing the importance of preserving the army and the socialist state at all costs were instilled into the officer corps at the West Point–style Defence Services Academy, also established in 1952 (R. Taylor 1985). Nonprofit, tax-exempt enterprises created initially to provide food and supplies for field units quickly expanded into other sectors (Callahan 2003, 168–169). By the late 1950s, a degree of organizational unity and self-confidence, relative to civilian politicians, had developed among both military staff and field commanders. When a 1958 split within the AFPFL prompted rumors that U Nu would integrate communist guerrillas into the government and the army, senior military officers including Ne Win responded by demanding a period of military "caretaker" rule (Callahan 2003, 185).

Army leaders in the military administration between 1958 and 1960 further institutionalized their organizational dominance, exacerbating their preexisting skepticism of civilian politicians. Army officers were embedded throughout the bureaucracy while brigade commanders were appointed to head regional "security councils." Charged with disarming civilian-controlled police and militias at a local level, they took control of mass organizations and led efforts to register populations in areas under their command (Callahan 2003, 192). Meanwhile, military-owned business conglomerates, such as the Defence Services Institute (DSI) and Burma Economic Development Corporation, diversified rapidly.[32] By 1960 the tax-exempt, ostensibly nonprofit enterprises managed by the DSI had expanded and now included banks, shipping companies, hotels, manufacturers, fisheries, and poultry distributors along with a construction firm, a bus line, and the biggest department store in the country (Mya Maung 1970, 538; Tin Maung Maung Than 2007, 57; Callahan 2003, 191). Although supportive of a socialist trajectory for the country, the military was also openly critical of the 1947 Constitution and of civilians. The Psychological Warfare Directorate released papers criticizing liberal aspects of the constitution along with U Nu's conciliatory approach to anti-government forces.

Despite increasing public critiques of civilian rule, the Union of Burma Parliament extended the mandate of the caretaker administration until general elections were held in February 1960. Power was then returned to U Nu, whose party won a decisive victory, notwithstanding the apparent attempts by some military field commanders to rig the poll against his party (Callahan 2003, 197; Nakanishi 2013, 89). Although U Nu renewed his commitment to advancing a "modern welfare state," the low international price of rice and the limited will to increase direct taxation, especially on rural populations, deprived the state of revenue necessary to implement it. Meanwhile, the lack of foreign investment in local industry and the rapid expansion of the military into new sectors of the economy meant that targets for private-sector ownership central to the Pyidawtha Plan went unmet. By the end of 1960, the state's share of capital remained at 56 percent relative to less than 44 percent for the private sector, well below the 65 percent private-sector objective in the original Pyidawtha Plan (Mya

Maung 1970, 537). The shortfall prompted the passage of a new "Four Year Plan" in 1960 and a law that sought to provide further incentives for foreign investment (Mya Maung 1970, 537; Tin Maung Maung Than 2007, 58). In August 1961, the Parliament declared Buddhism the state religion, fulfilling a promise made by U Nu during the election campaign but angering many Christian Kachin and Karen leaders (Brown 2013, 133). U Nu also appeared to be considering granting more extensive autonomy to Shan and Kayah leaders, who had been given a right to secede from the Union of Burma by Aung San in the Panglong Agreement of 1947. The military viewed these moves as chaotic and blundering, reinforcing a growing disdain for civilians among both officers and enlisted personnel. Following further consolidation after the caretaker administration, by 1962 the Tatmadaw had entrenched itself as the largest and most cohesive institution in lowland areas of the country, boasting fifty-seven infantry battalions and more than 100,000 soldiers (Callahan 2003, 173). Its growing institutional capability and self-confidence, combined with the unification of personnel around an ideology of nationalist socialism, granted Ne Win the heft and confidence to seize power and abandon the path of interventionist welfare capitalism chartered by Burma's postcolonial civilian leaders.

The Rise and Fall of Military Socialism (1962–1988)

The Revolutionary Council (RC) chaired by Ne Win justified its March 1962 coup against U Nu's democratically elected government in explicitly redistributive terms, blending socialist, Buddhist, and nationalist discourses (Nakanishi 2013, chap. 3). Contrary to dominant theoretical explanations for military coups against democratic governments, Burma's military in 1962 did not seize power to protect commercial elites from democratic demands for economic redistribution (Slater, Smith, and Nair 2014). Drawing heavily on propaganda formulated in the 1950s by the military's Psychological Warfare Directorate, the coup leaders articulated their social and economic goals in the texts *The Burmese Way to Socialism* (April 1962) and *System of Correlation of Man and His Environment* (January 1963). Both emphasized the need for military intervention to put an end to the ongoing exploitation of Burmese people by commercially motivated "feudalists" and "imperialists." Referencing the role of foreign advisers and the government's plans to attract foreign investment and encourage private capital, the new junta claimed U Nu had collaborated with foreign profiteers to return "landlords and capitalists" to positions of dominance within the economy (quoted in Mya Maung 1970, 538). *The Burmese Way to Socialism* provided scope for some profit-oriented businesses to function, stating that "national private enterprises" that had been "steadfastly contributing to the general well-being of the people" would be permitted to "occupy a worthy place in the new society" (cited in Brown 2013, 135). However, profit-seeking enterprises were declared to be "social evils" as they relied on "exploitation of man by man" (quoted in Brown 2013, 134). The RC's July 1962 *Constitution of the Burma Socialist Programme Party* also repeated concerns about the "general apathy of the electorate" earlier expressed during the caretaker administration (Callahan 2003, 189). These concerns were used to justify the dominance of military officials, especially General Ne Win, over the pyramidal structure of the socialist order that became the Burma Socialist Programme Party (BSPP) (Kyi May Kaung 1995).[33] The more philosophical *System of Correlation of Man and His Environment* reinforced the regime's commitment to a top-down Marxist-Leninist one-party state with a Buddhist inflection (Brown 2013, 135; Campbell 2014). Civilian leaders who embraced welfare capitalism in an attempt to satisfy the colonial-era ideological consensus of a redistributive yet low-taxing state were declared "guilty of having betrayed socialism by perpetuating capitalism and infecting the masses with a bourgeois mentality" (Mya Maung 1970, 538). In their stead, the Revolutionary Council resolved itself "to march unswervingly and arm-in-arm with the people of the Union of Burma towards the goal of socialism" (quoted in Brown 2013, 134).

The industrialization strategy adopted by the RC aimed to create a redistributive, highly interventionist state. Ne Win and his officials sought to proactively root out what it considered the "moral degeneracy" of capitalist enterprise and foreign interests, themes central to earlier nationalist and independence struggles. In 1963, Ne Win committed the state to take over production, distribution, import, and export of all major commodities and commenced nationalizing the assets of local and foreign traders and capitalists. In early 1963, Western companies such as the Burma Corporation, Bombay Burmah Trading Corporation, and subsidiaries of Unilever and other multinationals were nationalized and integrated into the newly formed Socialist Economy Construction Committee. All of Burma's private commercial banks, around half of which were Indian owned, were nationalized and reconstituted as People's Banks (Brown 2013, 135; Turnell 2009, 224–228). Then, in late 1963, the Revolutionary Council banned private imports and clearly broke away from the AFPFL's more accommodating approach to the private sector to nationalize the export trade along with all wholesale and retail outlets, including more than 15,000 small private shops (Turnell 2009, 229). Combined with the seizure of most Indian-owned banks, these nationalizations prompted the exodus of perhaps 300,000 subcontinental traders and financiers from 1963 to 1964, leaving behind mostly the stateless and poor (Brown 2013, 136, fn11). In a further measure aimed at rooting out the commercial class, in

May 1964 the RC demonetized all 100 and 50 kyat notes in an attempt to strip funds away from "foreign capitalists" and the wealthy, claiming that they were using the currency "to attack the construction of the socialist economy" (Mya Maung 1970, 542). However, loopholes enabled most well-connected businesspeople to exchange their currency into new denominations.[34]

The BSPP used control over trade and distribution to pursue an import-substitution industrialization (ISI) economic strategy. The 1960s and 1970s effectively saw almost all private enterprise, including military-owned companies, displaced by governmental trade corporations consistent with the RC's vision of socialist order (Mya Maung 1970, 548). Though Ne Win pursued nationalization more aggressively than U Nu, his economic strategy largely relied on the same mechanisms of state economic intervention enlisted during the AFPFL government. The state enterprises that had achieved minimal success in the 1950s were expanded and driven harder through the appointment of military officers (most of whom had no prior industry experience) to positions as factory and enterprise managers (Brown 2013, 145). However, welfare capitalist initiatives established as part of the 1950s Pyidawtha Plan also endured into the BSPP period. The state-mediated Social Security Board was extended to industrial workers in provincial towns, its scope expanded to include establishments with five or more workers and, later, broadened further to respond to worker needs. However, even with these efforts to expand the number of enrolled participants, the SSB was never a major part of the BSPP welfare regime. Despite significant state investment in industrial enterprises, the number of enrolled workers in the scheme only increased from 296,000 in 1962 to a high of 365,000 in 1973, reducing thereafter due to a tightening of membership criteria.[35] Rather than a co-contributory model of welfare provision that theoretically offered formal-sector workers more advanced health and social insurance than the rural population, the BSPP instead promised to deliver "welfare" to all citizens by providing quotas and rations of food and basic goods.

Despite the BSPP's philosophical commitment to the welfare of the peasantry, state-led industrialization was financed by expansive demands on the country's rural population. The private agricultural market, which had functioned during the colonial and early independence periods, was superseded by a system of co-operatives, quotas, and food stores. Retaining the state rice trading monopoly model established by the British and continued by U Nu, the BSPP set quotas for the sale of agricultural produce, with farmers forced to sell at a fixed price to the state enterprise (Brown 2013, 140). Rice and other staple goods were then sold at a floating international market rate or disbursed domestically through government shops, known as People's Stores, which were generally under-resourced.[36] The BSPP organized cooperatives (along with other mass organizations) to ensure at

least ritualistic adherence of their members to the language, symbols, and ceremonies of the socialist state (R. Taylor 2009, 373). These cooperatives were often
established through confiscation of land, an approach legitimized by the state's
claim to ownership of all agricultural plots (Kyaw Yin Hlaing 2007b, 252).

Cooperatives, like smallholder farmers more broadly, received state support
through agricultural loans. However, it was short-term credit and generally insufficient to finance long-term improvements in agriculture.[37] Cooperative-based
land ownership certainly increased cultivator access to land and achieved a degree of equity. Yet, in the absence of viable access to credit, [38] most of these plots
were too small to produce the economies of scale crucial to the agricultural surpluses necessary to supply government food rations (Myat Thein 2004, 89). As
farmers could not shop around for the best market price for their goods and were
constrained from investing in their land, their capacity to repay loans taken out
from state agencies led many into worsening cycles of debt (Mya Maung 1970,
544–545). Even though many farmers who participated in cooperatives found
themselves indebted to the state, politically speaking the cooperative movement
was crucial to the BSPPs domination of the lowland peasantry (Mya Maung 1970,
546). Many community or civil society groups independent of BSPP mass organizations were shut down or integrated into the local party, leaving the cooperative movement as the primary vehicle of mass mobilization for the party-state
and for communication with it (Steinberg 1999).

The cooperative movement, and BSPP local structures more broadly, barely expanded beyond the lowland boundaries of directly governed Ministerial Burma
inherited after colonial rule. Ethnic minority areas, especially mountainous regions, were mostly excluded from struggles over control of the state or political
community headquartered in Rangoon, where Burmese was the lingua franca of
postindependence administration and government. Consequentially, the map of
political contestation remained tightly constrained to lowland Burman-majority
areas throughout BSPP rule. Although the party-state did make policies that applied to the ethnic minority or Frontier regions, political scientist Mary Callahan
argues that few AFPFL or BSPP politicians sought to "[deliver] on the goods of citizenship to these territorially and linguistically distinct populations" with whom
they had little contact or means of communication (Callahan 2004, 107). Instead,
in the absence of marked industrial expansion in the periphery, BSPP initiatives in
upland areas largely comprised "programs aimed at teaching 'backward' peoples
how to think correctly" as BSPP socialists, rather than attempting to deliver the
haphazard system of redistribution it operated in lowland areas (Callahan 2004,
104). These problematic ideological and linguistic programs, coupled with differential material experiences of the "socialist" state, compounded feelings of mar-
ginalization among ethnic and religious minorities (Lehman 1967, 104). These

sentiments were reinforced when the BSPP revised the citizenship laws in 1982 and effectively rendered minority peoples inferior to the ethnic Bamar majority.[39] Widespread minority perceptions of political exclusion by the state provided fertile ground for insurgent elites to extend and expand their resistance to the socialist state following the promises of autonomy made by earlier independence politicians and embedded in the 1947 Constitution (Smith 1999, 98–99, 283). By the mid-1970s, more than a dozen ethnic-based armed groups had launched or intensified rebellions against the state, including the Communist Party of Burma active both in mountainous central regions and on the border with China. In some cases, armed elites and their societal partners developed health and education systems to cultivate popular support, financing social governance through their control of licit and illicit smuggling routes that crisscrossed Burma's borderlands with Thailand, China, and India in order to plug the supply gaps in the autarkic lowland BSPP economy (Smith 2007, 19; Oh 2013, 8). The blossoming of the borderland black market on which much of central Burma relied gradually began to be viewed as a threat to the BSPP promise of equitable food rations and industrialization as it sat outside the state's regulatory and taxation regime.

BSPP Attempts to Resolve the Contradictions of Its Economic Strategy

The mechanisms of price setting and food quotas at the core of the BSPP's welfare regime proved irreconcilable with its broader ISI policies. In addition to border smuggling, a sizable black market began to flourish for goods that were often in scarce supply in the lowland command-and-control economy. In rural areas, many farmers sold excess rice to black marketeers who offered higher prices than official food stores. This gave peasants an alternative source of (technically illicit) income, while many of them collected their official quotas of rice and other food stuff as well, depleting already limited state supplies (Mya Maung 1970, 543). The role of the informal economy, both as a coping mechanism and a perceived threat to BSPP rule, was reinforced in the mid-1960s when severe food shortages in parts of the country resulted in riots in Rangoon in 1967. The state responded by temporarily allowing consumers to purchase directly from farmers, effectively encouraging commercial transactions to occur outside official processes (Stifel 1971, 805).

In addition to helping to solve distribution problems, the black market became central to local BSPP officials hosting state spectacles and official visits by senior members of the regime. In many cases, these illicit enterprises were run by the same local bosses who had formed alliances of convenience with Socialist Party politicians during the early independence period (Kyaw Yin Hlaing

2003, 45–54, 57–58). In addition to fulfilling essential supply functions for the local state, political scientist Kyaw Yin Hlaing (2003, 51) recounts that many illegal traders (*hmaung-kho*) also maintained good relations with BSPP officials at a local level through regular donations to government initiatives. In this context of implicit and sometimes explicit tolerance of non-state commercial transactions, by the mid-1980s the black market was estimated at up to 75 percent of Myanmar's officially recorded international trade.[40] In addition to signaling the structural problems of supply inherent in BSPP autarky, these non-state flows of trade also deprived the government of taxation revenue and the foreign currency it sorely needed to finance its envisioned welfare regime.

Low agricultural productivity and the ubiquity of the black market compounded another contradiction within the BSPP's economic strategy: that distribution of rice quotas to mostly industrial workers depleted the available stock of rice for the state monopoly to export.[41] This deprived the BSPP of the foreign currency it needed to import machinery and grow its manufacturing sector as its ISI strategy demanded (Kudo 2005, 11). Because of these constraints—coupled with the deployment of inexperienced military personnel into industrial management positions—manufacturing-sector output grew by a total of less than 10 percent throughout the entire 1960s and 1970s (Myat Thein 2004, 61), in spite of the sector receiving almost 25 percent of state investment by the mid-1970s. Although the BSPP attempted to use the coercive apparatus of the military state to achieve its welfare regime through an autarkic ISI strategy, the contradictions inherent to it forced a significant proportion of economic activity underground.[42]

At least in lowland areas, non-state actors played a minimal role in the welfare mix throughout this period. Although further research on local reciprocity practices during the BSPP period is needed, existing accounts suggest that BSPP attempts to control food supply and suppress capitalist activity while requiring civil society, including at a village level, to be run through the party limited the financial and organizational possibilities for informal reciprocity to extend beyond the confines of immediate kin relations. The sparse ethnographic fieldwork that was conducted in lowland areas during BSPP rule suggests these constraints limited the scope of Buddhist charity (*dana*) and the ritualized giving to monks or monastic institutions, especially for the purposes of religious celebrations (Schober 1989; Schober 1996, 197). Illegal traders (*hmaung-kho*) often made big donations at these events along with local BSPP initiatives more broadly, highlighting the codependence that developed between lowland state officials and technically illicit commercial elites who traded with upland smugglers and emergent armed groups during this period.[43] Yet it appears that while officials sought to stamp out private enterprise and deliver basic food and supplies to all, at least in lowland areas, they gave little encouragement to Buddhist ideals[44] and left little space for practices of communal welfare provision and risk-sharing to develop beyond immediate family networks (Walton 2016, 152). A spatially varied welfare regime was thus entrenched. In lowland areas, the BSPP promised welfare through state economic control and provision of rations, forcing many to rely on a combination of kin-based reciprocity and illicit trade. Meanwhile, in upland areas, armed groups intensified their ethno-nationalist struggles for autonomy, often through state-like social service provision funded by their role in brokering the borderland black-market economy.

A Partial Embrace of the Market Hastened BSPP Collapse

Faced with recurrent social uprisings brought on by contradictions inherent in the BSPP's economic strategy, its officials made attempts to reform the economic system. Yet they were constrained by the inheritances of the colonial period, especially the commitment to a redistributive welfare state that engaged in as little direct taxation as possible. In order to finance productivity improvements, especially in agriculture, BSPP officials began to welcome foreign aid and technical assistance beginning in the 1970s. By the end of the 1980s, Ne Win's regime had taken more than US$2 billion in loans from the Asian Development Bank, the World Bank, International Monetary Fund, and others (Kyaw Yin Hlaing 2003, 23). Private capital was also given some minimal role in the economy through laws restricting nationalization of businesses and market-based incentives for agriculture and state enterprises (Cook 1994, 131; Brown 2013, 172). Along with significant investment in rural productivity, the 1970s reforms boosted rice and other crop yields and led to rapid growth in production and export of oil, natural gas, and raw metals (Brown 2013, 152). However, contradictions between the new measures and the BSPP's twenty-year economic plan meant they did little to stoke private domestic investment (Cook 1994, 131). Constraints in financing, input sourcing, and foreign trade for small and medium enterprises endured while the regime continued to suppress market-based activities and reject foreign direct investment apart from in offshore oil extraction (Tin Maung Maung Than 2007, 275; Brown 2013, 163, 172). Meanwhile, state-led import-substitution industrialization remained the driver of BSPP economic strategy, with state economic enterprises claiming over one-third of government expenditures between 1978 and 1985 (Brown 2013, 152). Consequentially, contrary to the objectives of reforms, private manufacturing declined markedly during this period.[45] Meanwhile, large private enterprises employing more than 100 workers were virtually wiped out, dropping from twenty-six in 1974 to four in 1988. With the decline in sizable employers came a corresponding drop in the number of workers covered by formal social insurance schemes, further eroding the formal role played by market actors in the BSPP welfare regime.[46]

The unprofitability of industrial enterprises and the limited export of rice, along with the proliferation of the formally untaxed black market, combined to hollow out the BSPP's revenue capacity. British administrators had used tax revenue to finance the colonial apparatus of lowland control and commodity extraction while providing minimal protection to farmers from the vagaries of the market. In contrast, the BSPP's apparatus of taxation sought to fund lowland industrialization and a state-dominated welfare regime by requiring farmers to sell their goods below market rate to the regime—effectively substituting formal for informal taxation. The result was that even excluding the sizable informal and untaxed economy[47] the country's declared formal tax revenue as a percentage of gross domestic product (GDP) was well below its more export-oriented regional neighbors during this period, averaging around 9 percent between 1974 and 1987, compared with 13 percent in Thailand and 17 percent in Indonesia (Brown 2013, 161). Meanwhile, informal taxes, such as the requirement for farmers to sell produce to state monopolies below market rate, were barely converted into revenue because most was domestically redistributed and only a fraction sold on the international market. The vast bulk of state revenue, collected throughout the 1980s in predominantly lowland areas, instead came from commodities and services taxes (around 60 percent), customs duties (around 20 percent), and a smaller portion (around 5 percent) from profit and income taxes (Brown 2013, 161).

Having assumed considerable debts to international lenders during the 1970s, the BSPP's revenue problems meant it quickly began running a ballooning budget deficit. By 1986 and 1987, the dollar cost of servicing Burma's almost US\$4 billion of external debt had grown to 80 percent of overall export values. The state was approaching major debt default and looming bankruptcy while printing large volumes of new money (Brown 2013, 165). The financial crisis led Ne Win to impose reforms and demonetize currency aimed at formalizing and taxing the black-market economy while weakening ethnic armed groups. The first demonetization occurred in November 1985 and permitted a per-head quota of kyat to be converted into new currency, a loophole that allowed friends and clients of illegal traders to exchange notes on their behalf (Kyaw Yin Hlaing 2003, 53). After that measure failed, in August 1987 Ne Win called an extraordinary meeting of the BSPP central committee and announced further economic reforms. A month later the state monopoly on rice procurement was abolished and restrictions on domestic trade in agricultural commodities, including rice, were lifted, prompting rapid inflation in the urban price of rice (Brown 2003, 157). Five days later Ne Win imposed a more punitive demonetization of almost 80 percent of all currency, with no loophole for transfer into the new denominations. The blunt measure effectively decimated the networks of illegal trade that had provided an alternative to the state's command and control in the economy while wiping out the currency-based savings of most ordinary people (Kyaw Yin Hlaing 2003, 52–54; Brown 2013, 155).

The economic and social grievances generated by these measures, combined with the military's brutal response to subsequent protests, led to an escalating cycle of demonstrations against the regime. General Aung San's daughter, Aung San Suu Kyi, emerged as a key leader of the protest movement along with senior military leaders purged by Ne Win, students, monks, civil servants, industrial workers, and later, commercial elites (Kyaw Yin Hlaing 2003, 56–57). Despite Ne Win's resignation in July 1988, in August people went on strike for weeks marching through towns and cities across the country demanding an end to BSPP rule. Military leaders brutally suppressed the protests, killing several thousand people.[48] After protests continued when Ne Win's civilian successor resolved to hold multiparty elections in 1990, in September 1988 a faction within the army dissolved the BSPP, initially forming the State Law and Order Restoration Council (SLORC) and then in 1997 reorganizing into a more hierarchical structure it termed the State Peace and Development Council (SPDC) (R. Taylor 2009, 393–395). Ne Win's attempt to navigate postcolonial inheritances while delivering a redistributive but low-taxing state-led welfare regime had brought the country to the brink of bankruptcy and provoked increasingly violent cycles of political repression. The junta officials of the SLORC/SPDC who seized power subsequently used market reform and selective suppression of civil society to outsource welfare functions to non-state and private actors while rapidly expanding the coercive state into the periphery.

The Afterlives of Colonial Inheritances

Between independence and 1988, the politics of postcolonial Burma was constrained by a series of formal and informal legacies inherited from British rule. Successive regimes grappled with how best to deliver a redistributive welfare regime across a territory where state administrative and coercive capacity varied greatly, while at the same time taxing citizens as little as possible.

After independence in 1948, civilian leaders led by U Nu attempted to enact this consensus while broaching the interests and demands of the AFPFL's coalition of commercial elites along with Socialist Party politicians and Community Party representatives and rebels. As the military transformed itself during the 1950s into the largest and most cohesive institution in lowland areas of the country, a rigidly nationalistic socialism was placed at the core of army ideology.

U Nu's path of interventionist welfare capitalism, which required the private sector and its employees to shoulder much of the burden for formal social security, was subsequently abandoned with the 1962 coup in favor of aggressive import-substitution industrialization. Confident of the military's capacity to coercively deliver social change and public welfare, Ne Win's BSPP nationalized all private and foreign businesses and attempted to manage domestic trade and distribution to deliver a welfare regime primarily defined as state provision of basic food security to citizens. As the territorial and ideological boundaries of state and nation inherited at independence remained fairly rigid between 1948 and 1988, the geographic scope of BSPP rule and welfare provision was predominantly limited to lowland areas of the country. With supply gaps in the lowland socialist economy creating strong demand for scarce goods, ethnic and communist insurgents in upland areas brokered borderland smuggling routes and used the windfalls to fund armed struggles for independence and autonomy from the socialist state.

The new capitalist junta that took power following the 1987 economic crisis and 1988 uprising in lowland areas challenged the economic, administrative, and ideological inheritances that had set the parameters of the BSPP welfare regime. They attempted to wrest control over the black market and the restive borderlands while retrenching the role of the state in welfare. Dominant narratives of post-socialism suggest that the social role of the state that had defined independent Burma until that point largely evaporated with the demise of Ne Win's BSPP. Existing accounts of the post-1988 dictatorship suggests that "the 'sons of Ne Win' completely abandoned socialism" (Skidmore 2004, 85), instead justifying themselves as economic reformers who would bring "peace" to the restive borderlands and "revive good old traditions, promote Buddhism" (Kyaw Yin Hlaing 2001, 72). Concerns about the distributive inequities generated by capitalism, which for decades had shaped the role of the state and capitalism in the welfare regime, were seen by many scholars as evaporating and being replaced by a rigid commitment to transforming borderlands into partially governable spaces of economic extraction.

This portrayal gives only a fragment of the picture because it fails to convincingly account for how and why non-state welfare actors came to play such dominant roles in the insecure welfare regime that emerged after 1988. Drawing on in-depth archival and interview research focused on this period in lowland areas of provincial central Myanmar, part 1 (encompassing chapters 2 and 3) reveals how post-socialist junta officials used market reform to dramatically reconfigure the role of non-state actors in the welfare mix. Informed by the concept of the hidden welfare state (Howard 1999), part 1 recounts how subnational officials outsourced distributive obligations previously ideologically promised by the BSPP state to businesspeople, communities, and households, including during natural disasters using economic incentives, tax concessions, and ideological persuasion. In so doing, it exposes how the new junta substituted direct tax revenue for an autocratic form of welfare capitalism, outsourcing state social functions deliberately and haphazardly to non-state actors in ways that would shape the trajectory of distributive politics for decades to follow.

Part 1

AUTOCRATIC WELFARE CAPITALISM

POST-SOCIALIST WELFARE OUTSOURCING

In April 2016, on the final morning of Thingyan, the water festival that marks the Burmese New Year, a charitable aged home in Taungoo in central-east Myanmar was bustling with activity. I had met a few residents from here earlier in my fieldwork, so when friends mentioned that people often pay homage to the elderly during the New Year, I stopped by for an impromptu visit.

Riding into the compound, I encountered far more hustle-bustle than on any previous visits. Three dark green military pickup trucks were parked in the dusty yard, along with several four-wheel drives. A group of men wearing white shirts, holstered sidearms, and red-and-white striped military police helmets chatted casually in the shade of trees beside the dining room that was doubling as a meditation hall. As I parked my motorbike nearby, one of the officers caught my eye. He smiled and nodded, seemingly unperturbed by a foreigner entering the compound during whatever was about to occur.

Glancing inside the hall, I saw boxes of cooking oil and sacks of rice stacked up along one side of the room. A group of people in formal *lungyis* (Burmese sarongs) and shirts, including a prominent local entrepreneur, buzzed around preparing for the event. The manager of the home for the aged came out to greet me. He was followed a few minutes later by another entrepreneur, a rice miller, who was introduced as a town elder (*myo mi myo pah*) and a member of the facility management committee. We chatted and joked for a few minutes about the antics and heat of the past few days of New Year celebrations, when young and old throw water, drink heavily, and dance freely. I explained that I was researching welfare and charity in Myanmar and had heard there might be a ritual of giving (*a-hlubwe*) today to celebrate Thingyan. The entrepreneur grabbed my arm and smiled widely. Gesturing to the military vehicles parked beside the hall, he explained that a donation celebration was about to be held by personnel from the local military garrison to mark the New Year.

A few minutes later, plumes of dust engulfed the car park as a convoy of seven dark green four-wheel drives and pickup trucks arrived. The entire compound leaped into action. As a military police officer opened the door to the vehicle in the middle of the convoy, the more senior of the two entrepreneurs rushed to the front steps of the building. He thrust his hand out and enthusiastically greeted the top brass from the largest military installation in central-east Myanmar and their wives. They walked together to the prayer hall, and after a few minutes, with a wink and tilt of the head from the rice miller, I found myself attending the local military's formal Thingyan giving ceremony for 2016.

Inside the hall the elderly members of the village proceeded to a platform at the front of the room slightly elevated from the officers, their families, and the local entrepreneurs who all sat cross-legged on the floor. After some short remarks from the manager of the facility and a speech by a representative of the assembled military officers, the event culminated with the handing of a stack of 5,000 kyat notes (around US$4 each) from the local commander to the oldest resident, an elderly woman in her eighties whose long gray hair was pinned up gracefully. She closed her eyes and slowly recited a ritual blessing of recognition for the various gifts of rice, oil, and snacks that flanked her. She concluded by chanting the words "*Thadu Thadu Thadu*," a Pali-derived phrase uttered by monks and laity in appreciation of gifts meritoriously given by donors, which roughly translates as "Well done, well done, well done."

The spectacle of military officials donating to a charitable aged care facility managed by local commercial elites offered a glimpse into the dynamics of social outsourcing during the 1990s and 2000s that markedly remade the role of the state in Myanmar's post-socialist welfare regime. The enthusiasm of traders and entrepreneurs to mediate between military personnel and local charitable organizations especially hinted at a configuration of market, society, and state that has privileged non-state and private social actors in Myanmar's welfare mix for decades. Yet existing literature on the 1990s and 2000s offers little insight into post-1988 provincial processes of market reform that allowed this form of social outsourcing. The literature focuses largely on businesspeople who were nationally prominent by the 2000s and on the quid pro quo of the commercial deals they struck with junta officials to sustain the State Law and Order Restoration Council which was rebadged after 1997 as the State Peace and Development Council (hereafter SLORC/SPDC) (Jones 2014, 151; Ford, Gillan, and Htwe Htwe Thein 2016). The paucity of research in provincial areas throughout this period thus blinds us to how the political economy of the 1990s and 2000s generated ideals and practices of non-state welfare provision that shaped distributive politics and enabled resistance in the hybrid and autocratic regimes that followed. A new account is needed if the enduring appeal of social outsourcing to diverse political and economic actors over time is to be fully understood.

Drawing on primary archival, oral history and ethnographic and survey data collected in provincial central-east Myanmar, this chapter uncovers the informal institutions generated by welfare outsourcing after 1988 and offers a new vantage point for thinking about the impact of post-socialist market reform for distributive politics across regimes.

Post-1988 Capitalist State-Building

On seizing power, suppressing protests, and dissolving the Burma Socialist Programme Party (BSPP), the new post-socialist junta was faced with a host of socioeconomic crises. After decades of autarkic socialism, the regime was financially bankrupt and territorially fragmented, having little coercive or administrative presence in much of the borderlands. Meanwhile, the justification for BSPP socialism—delivering a fair and redistributive welfare regime—was widely and publicly contested in the face of rampant inflation, shortages of basic supplies, and repeated demonetizations. In response, senior members of the junta tentatively commenced market liberalization and, under pressure from the international community following the brutal suppression of the 1988 protests, committed to holding popular elections in 1990. As economic reforms proceeded apace, they disregarded the poll results when a party led by Aung San Suu Kyi, the daughter of General Aung San, won 392 out of 425 seats in the new parliament—including the bulk of the vote in ethnic minority areas.[1] Accepting that popular will was against it, the junta instead embraced a form of crony capitalism aimed at challenging the territorial, economic, and ideological legacies it had inherited while retrenching the state from the welfare mix by outsourcing social functions to market and private providers. The informal institutions of non-state welfare generated amid this post-socialist period have proved to be durable features of Myanmar political economy and culture for decades, being entrenched even further during the decade of partial civilian rule and since the return to military dictatorship in 2021. In an attempt to recover Myanmar's dire financial situation, in late 1988, military officials initiated a series of economic reforms that sought to diversify their personal income and that of the regime. Following the adoption of new economic laws,[2] junta officials began to permit market trade in commodities while encouraging foreign investment in a swathe of industries, including agriculture, timber, fisheries, oil and gas exploration and extraction, hotels, manufacturing, and real estate and construction while privatizing a range of state enterprises (Brown 2013, 177; Kudo 2005, 11; Ford, Gillan, and Htwe Htwe Thein 2016). Private credit was permitted for the first time since 1963 with the establishment of domestic commercial banks. Meanwhile, a chunk of revenue from Myanmar's extensive illicit economy was routed through government banks so that military officials could capture a greater share of the profits (Turnell 2009, 258–260; Meehan 2011, 391). Military enterprises, previously nationalized after 1963, were also reestablished and quickly entered into joint ventures with foreign firms across diverse sectors, including extractive industries (oil, gas, and mining), manufacturing, and hospitality sectors (Brown 2013, 193; G. McCarthy 2019, 10, 13).

Over the next decade, substantial growth in trade, extractive industries, construction, finance, and manufacturing reshaped Myanmar's economy. Driven by post–Cold War demand for natural resources from neighbors, especially China and Thailand, junta officials reported foreign investment totaling more than US$7.2 billion between 1989 and 1998 (Steinberg 2001, 169; Jones 2016, 99). By 1998 to 1999 financial year, the junta claimed that the "private sector" accounted for 85 percent of manufacturing output and almost three-quarters of gross domestic product (GDP), although these figures counted the Tatmadaw commercial interests as private rather than state-owned (Myat Thein 2004, 125, 200–251).

While making structural economic changes, junta officials also reallocated a huge proportion of government funds from social to military portfolios. Government-declared budget for health and education fell as a percentage of GDP from 2.6 percent and 1 percent, respectively, in 1990 to 0.64 percent and 0.18 percent in 1998. Meanwhile, the Ministry of Social Welfare, Relief, and Resettlement (MoSWRR) received less than 0.003 percent of GDP throughout this period. These social allocations combined were less than half of the 6 percent GDP received by the military, which accounted for 40 percent of on-budget spending throughout the 1990s and early 2000s.[3]

Instead of spending on human development, the junta used revenue and foreign currency reaped from market reform to extend the coercive apparatus of the state in the upland periphery. Tatmadaw units grew in size from around 200,000 personnel in 1988 to more than 400,000 by the late 1990s, making it the eighteenth largest military in the world (Selth 2002, 253). Military officials also purchased large quantities of Chinese arms through Singaporean banks and prioritized infrastructure projects such as highways, bridges, dams, and reservoirs that were "easily visible by the populace" (Myat Thein and Khin Maung Nyo 1999, 403; Steinberg 2005, 110). In addition to constructing the new administrative capital Naypyitaw in the plains of central Myanmar and a north-south highway connecting Mandalay and Yangon, significant state funds were expended on the renovation and construction of Buddhist pagodas and monasteries and hosting of Buddhist festivals, all of which military officials personally claimed credit for.[4]

The reinvigoration of the military, coupled with shifting geopolitics across Asia, meant that insurgent elites in the periphery faced triple pressures: an increasingly well-armed and assertive Tatmadaw; the evaporation of revenue they previously collected from brokering the socialist smuggling economy; and weakening external support from China and Thailand (Meehan 2011, 385–386; Jones 2016, 98). Under mounting territorial and financial pressure, seventeen of twenty-one ethnic armed groups signed (tentative) agreements with the Tatmadaw in the early 1990s.[5] These ceasefires were lubricated by commercial incentives that encouraged elites to demobilize forces or retreat to agreed territories in return for nonbinding "advisory" roles and business concessions that largely benefited rebel leaders and their families (Steinberg 2006; Callahan 2007; Jones 2016, 101–102). These "extraction pacts" (Snyder 2006) permitted the state to roll out Border Areas Development programs on which ethnic elites were permitted to "advise" but had no formal veto over (Meehan 2011, 382). Some larger groups such as the Kachin Independence Army (KIA), which signed an agreement in 1994, also retained the right to tax goods—licit and illicit—that passed through borderland checkpoints, ensuring they retained some revenue (Callahan 2007, 24; Jones 2016, 100–101).

Termed "ceasefire capitalism" by scholars, these market reforms were devised by the junta to support military state-building. The elite commercial fixes reached during this period did succeed in delivering a degree of stability to borderland areas while enabling coercive expansion of the junta into the periphery. [6] Informal agreements tied ethnic armed elites to the Myanmar military-state through joint ventures, taxation regimes, and money-laundering schemes (Meehan 2011, 391; Woods 2011; Jones 2016). The state then used its commercial leverage to expand military, administrative, and economic reach "into areas of the country where it previously had little or none" (K. MacLean 2008, 143). The parameters of central administration following this period of military expansion and ceasefires in the periphery, depicted in figure 2.1, contrast starkly with the boundaries of the lowland state inherited at independence, as depicted in chapter 1.

The junta's strategy of military state-building funded through social austerity had pernicious consequences. In borderland areas, the absence of genuine political autonomy for minority populations, the plunder of natural resources such as jade and gems, and the proliferation of the drug trade that came with peace gradually re-radicalized the insurgent grassroots (Brenner 2015, 2018 2019). Some ethnic elites redistributed a portion of profits garnered from ceasefire capitalism to local civil society, though beneficiaries narrowed as many armed groups lost revenue in the years after striking these extraction pacts.[7] Numerous ceasefires subsequently collapsed in the years after their agreement.[8] Meanwhile junta-mediated market

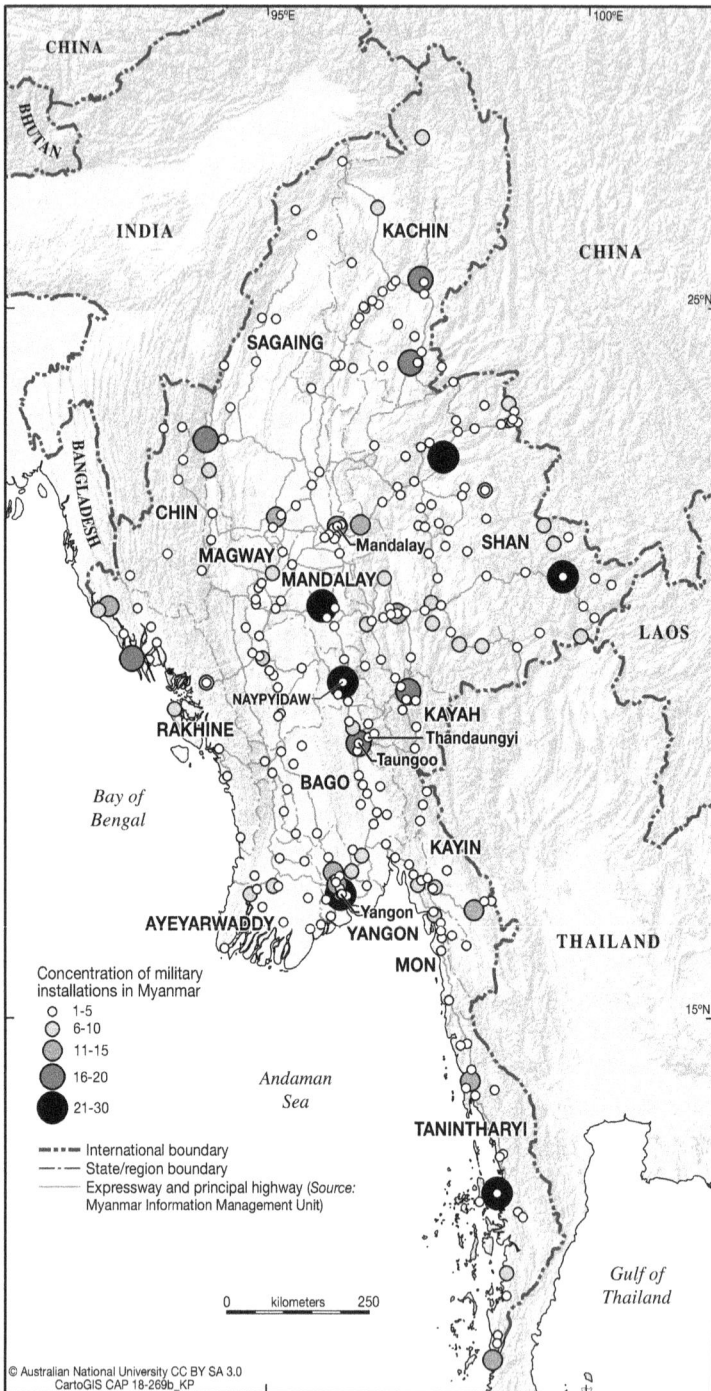

FIGURE 2.1. Military installations and roads around Myanmar by 2012. *Source*: Australian National University Myanmar Military Power Index and Myanmar Information Management Unit. Map courtesy of Australian National University CartoGIS Services.

reforms and retrenchment of state social spending had dire human and fiscal impacts, including on state capacity. At the family level, many households were
forced to accrue catastrophic debts as they tried to make ends meet to cover the
escalating out-of-pocket costs of medical care, schooling, and basic survival.[9]
Families that managed to survive often did so through a combination of favors
from well-connected patrons (Brac de la Perriere 2014) and diversified livelihood
strategies which commonly relied on remittances from family members sent
abroad to work (Thawnghmung 2019). Even within the comparatively well-funded
Tatmadaw, provincial military officials were told to "find external income" to finance regimental welfare activities and supplement the meager pay of troops
rather than rely on central budget allocations (Maung Aung Myoe 2009, 189;
G. McCarthy 2019, 17–18). In this context, provincial military officers and officials
declared plots across the country "vacant, fallow, and virgin" as part of regime
agricultural reform policies, often trading land titles for profit or favors from businesspeople (U San Thein et al. 2018). By 2016, more than 2 million hectares had
been allocated for large-scale agribusiness concessions alone, totaling more than
17 percent of Myanmar's total land sown.[10] In the process, titles to plots cultivated
for decades by millions of rural people were legally granted to agribusiness interests, laying the seeds of what remains an intractable land-grab crisis today.

Attempts to expand government tax revenue after 1988 largely failed because
of haphazard implementation and the widespread practice of granting tax exemptions or reductions to businesspeople in return for favors and support for local junta initiatives or officials (Myat Thein 2004, 145–146). Government-declared
revenue as a percentage of GDP fell from 12 percent in 1988 to less than 7 percent
in 1998.[11] Reported tax revenue itself dropped from 6 percent in 1988 to 4 percent
of GDP by the end of the 1990s and fell further to 2 percent in 2002—one of the
smallest tax takes anywhere in the world (Mya Than and Myat Thein 2000, 10–11;
Myat Thein 2004, 145–146). With revenue dwindling and most of the formal budget funding military expansion and infrastructure, the junta instead printed money
to pay off compounding deficits, driving further inflation in basic household goods
(Brown 2013, 199).

These factors meant that post-1988 social austerity and market reform drove
more households into dire poverty. Aggregate human development outcomes in
Myanmar mildly improved, according to official data during the 1990s and 2000s,
alongside counterparts such as Cambodia, Laos, and Nepal (see figure 2.2), even
though those countries spent far more, proportionally, on social sectors such as
health throughout this period (see figure 2.3).[12]

There are good reasons to be skeptical of this data, given both the weakness of
Myanmar government survey capacity, the major subnational variations in social
outcomes, and the propaganda functions that reporting social improvements

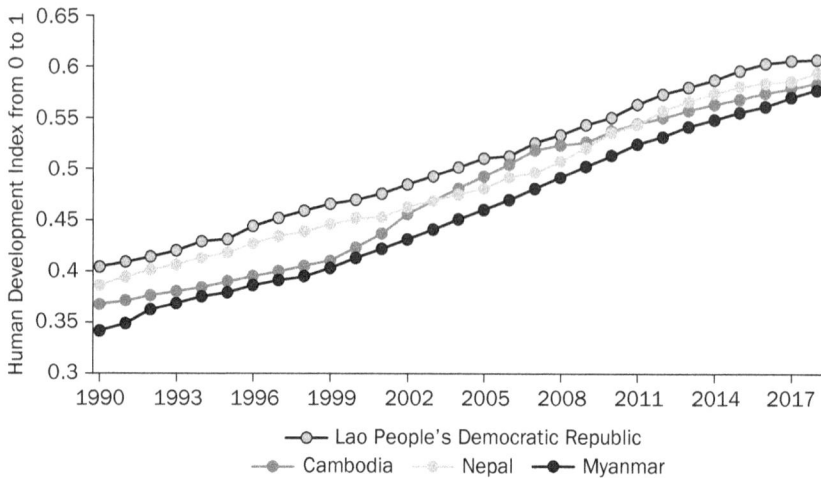

FIGURE 2.2. In the aggregate, human development outcomes (life expectancy, schooling years, and income per capita) show improvement in Myanmar and its regional counterparts. *Source*: United Nations Development Programme.

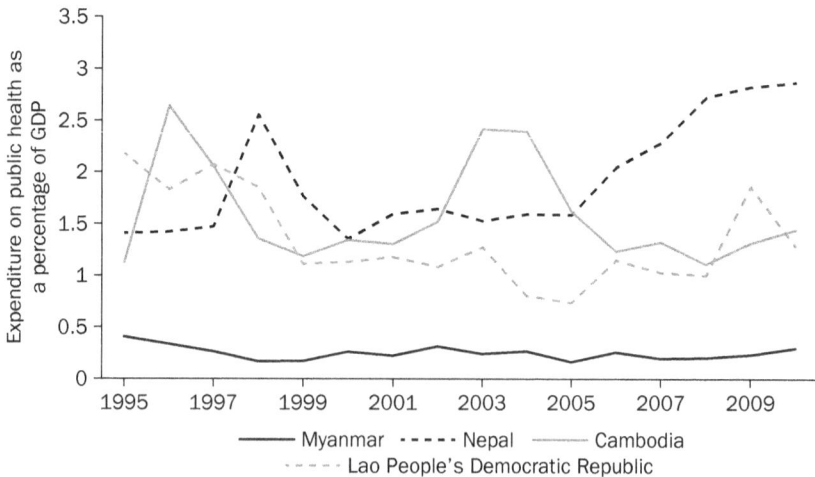

FIGURE 2.3. Public health expenditure as percentage of GDP shows that Myanmar government health spending lagged considerably behind regional counterparts through the 1990s and 2000s. *Source*: World Bank.

would have served domestically and internationally for the junta.[13] Yet these trends of aggregate improvement raise a larger question about the welfare mix after 1988. As junta officials retrenched the state from social sectors, how did families, businesspeople, and communities cope in the face of extreme precarity? What kind of welfare mix emerged as the junta combined social austerity with regime-mediated market reform?

Existing narratives of state social retrenchment after 1988 offer a fragmented account of the welfare regime that emerged during the 1990s and 2000s. Apart from some "in-kind" social expenditures made by the government, current literature suggests that the non-state sector assumed many of these obligations.[14] Research on civil society during junta rule, for instance, found thousands of local community risk-sharing and charitable groups operating in all corners of the country across every conceivable sector, from maternal health to water infrastructure.[15] Few have examined the political economy of outsourcing which characterized this period. [16] Instead, scholars have largely framed the growth of these "horizontal solidarity" groups as the consequence of "community leaders, Buddhist monks, retirees and businesspeople . . . witnessing the difficulties of the ordinary people" (Kyaw Yin Hlaing 2007a, 162–163) and recognizing the need for them to take action given the junta's "failure (or unwillingness) to alleviate the poverty of most Myanmar people" (Seekins 2009, 730). Yet fieldwork in central-east Myanmar on market reform and welfare provision after 1988 suggests that military commanders directly *encouraged* nongovernmental actors to assume responsibility for delivering welfare and public goods in the wake of the central state's social withdrawal, generating ideals and practices of non-state social provision that have durably shaped state-business relations and distributive politics across subsequent regimes.

Market Reform and Welfare Outsourcing

Non-state institutions and actors assumed a crucial role in addressing dire vulnerabilities generated by market reform and state retrenchment after 1988. Following the dissolution of the BSPP, the junta mediated the transition to capitalism in a way that empowered military officials to support or stymie the commercial success of civilians. Most of the day-to-day of market reform, including commercial licensing, taxation, and administration, was devolved to the twelve regional military commanders who had de facto control over local affairs in lowland and ceasefire areas throughout the 1990s and 2000s.[17] Tatmadaw commanders and their subordinates used influence over the issuance of licenses, permits, leases, contracts, and tax remissions to enlist commercial elites and their assets to implement local junta objectives and projects (Cook 1994, 132, citing World Bank 1990). These administrative powers included the ability to decide on annual renewal of licenses to operate heavy machinery, such as rice mill and mining equipment; to approve new construction projects or commercial initiatives; and to issue tenders to perform key functions for state economic enterprises (Kudo 2001, 12). Provincial military officials also decided how much formal tax would be levied on businesspeople and their commercial activities (Cook 1994, 132). Those who did not hold appropriate permits, or who ran afoul of local junta officials, could have agricultural goods, gems, and machinery seized; they could also be subject to fines and jail terms or might be selectively prosecuted for corruption or money laundering (Jones 2014, 150; Cook 1994, 132 citing World Bank 1990; Kyaw Yin Hlaing 2007b, 222). Previous studies of the logic underpinning junta-era patronage relationships have highlighted dynamics of licensing, profit-sharing, and favor-trading between nationally prominent businesspeople and military officials (Jones 2014, 151). However, provincial dynamics of market reform during the SLORC/SPDC period reveal how marketization went hand in hand with the explicit outsourcing of state social and redistributive functions to emergent businesspeople.

The enlistment of the commercial classes into social functions was enabled by a shift in the logic of battalion and civilian administration after the BSPP period.[18] Military life during the BSPP period was organized around a rigid notion of distributive justice that was achieved through state control of all supply and distribution along with mass mobilization only through state-controlled organizations. Economic and social activity seen to pose a threat to the socialist regime could be legally suppressed.[19] After 1988, however, regional commanders began to adopt an explicit attitude of practicality and "doing what is necessary" to achieve objectives, capitalist or otherwise. A civil servant familiar with military administration recounted that Tatmadaw officials adopted a highly practical approach to management of both battalion and civilian life, often telling their subordinates that "it doesn't matter what the vessel is, all I want is water!" (interview, 6 September 2016). From the early 1990s, both internal military social life as well as public "mobilizing" (siiyoneye) by soldiers and their families were increasingly directed toward activities that created functional bonds between battalion personnel and civilians. Junta officials particularly encouraged military families to engage in merit-making and meditation as well as social work with local children and the elderly (interview, 6 September 2016).

Despite the administrative and ideological shifts of the 1990s, many military officials remained concerned about potential self-interested profiteering of the emergent business class.[20] As often occurs following revolution and upheaval,[21] SLORC/SPDC officials in Myanmar "recombined and reconfigured" previously dominant redistributive ideals in ways that attempted to outsource some of the previous social commitments of the state to non-state actors (R. Lieberman 2002, 704). At a provincial level, entrepreneurs who received licenses and permits to operate businesses also took on roles governing and reporting back to military officials about the local situation garnered through their role in welfare groups. Willingly engaging in both transactional and redistributive functions could earn entrepreneurs what I term a "social license" in the eyes of influential provincial commanders, which differentiated them from other businesspeople and cleared a path to further capital accumulation and commercial success. As entrepreneurs assumed these roles, often at the explicit urging of provincial military officials, a new welfare regime highly reliant on private and charitable actors began to emerge in lowland areas under junta control.

Transactional and Redistributive Dimensions of Social Licensing

Social licensing, and through it the outsourcing of state social obligations to private business and societal actors, became a crucial path to commercial success in post-socialist Myanmar. Emergent businesspeople helped regional commanders achieve either their personal or regional command priorities by performing three functions: (i) providing resources or labor for junta initiatives; (ii) helping deliver welfare and support social initiatives that ameliorated dire need in the wake of austerity and market reform; and (iii) collecting information on local social and political dynamics and reporting back to provincial military handlers.

Existing research highlights that commercial aspirants played a major role in constructing national infrastructure, including bus terminals, highways, and the new capital in Naypyitaw, along with funding junta-initiated Buddhist structures and festivals (Kyaw Yin Hlaing 2001; R. Taylor 2009, 456–457; Jones 2014, 151). Although military officials clearly held the dominant positions in these relationships of patronage, scholars have noted that these dynamics were often "not entirely one-sided but rather symbiotic" (Jones 2014, 151). Kyaw Yin Hlaing's (2001, 261–262) study of state-business relations in the late 1990s, for instance, highlighted how financial or in-kind support provided by commercial actors in many cases was reciprocated with material support, such as the allocation of plots of land in rural areas.[22]

In lowland central Myanmar, local junta officials developed relations of unequal transactional reciprocity with traders, entrepreneurs, and bureaucrats who had been awarded commercial tenders, licenses, and permits. These transactions sometimes flowed one way, relying on the threat of coercion levied by military officials, the "peer pressure" wielded by groups such as the Union Solidarity and Development Association (USDA) or the Myanmar Maternal and Child Welfare

Association (MMCWA), or blunt claims of state dominion over all "private" property (Turnell 2011, 142). Indeed, old BSPP attitudes of state entitlement died hard. Throughout the 1990s and 2000s military officials continued to claim "state prerogative" as they seized the land and produce of rural people throughout provincial Myanmar. Land in particular was often sold for battalion or personal benefit, creating a land-grab crisis that plagued governance throughout the subsequent decade of partial civilian rule (2011–2021). However, in urban areas, junta representatives often felt obliged after 1988 to compensate traders and entrepreneurs for contributions they made to local initiatives.[23] As a township official said to Kyaw Yin Hlaing in 1998:

> We can order peasants to sell their rice to us but we cannot *order* businessmen to donate their money. We have to *request* them to donate. We had to return their favor in ways we could, so that we would be able to solicit more donations from them whenever we needed to raise funds for state functions. (Kyaw Yin Hlaing 2007b, 253, emphasis in original)

Businesspeople were often informally taxed by local officials in these ways when senior SLORC/SPDC ministers visited provincial areas to "inspect" the progress made in implementing central directives. These visits often prompted regional commanders and their subordinates to enlist the material and logistic support of local businesspeople. The typical visit would be managed by military officers embedded throughout local government agencies such as the Ministry of Health or the Ministry of Agriculture, Livestock, and Fisheries. However, the regional military commander bore ultimate responsibility for coordinating the visit, including the "extracurricular" activities that ministers would often indulge in. At the end of each trip, the visiting minister or general would usually make a "donation" in recognition of the efforts of their subordinates in coordinating logistics, banquets, and ceremonies on their behalf (Farrelly 2008). The amount of these donations would vary depending on how well the visit was managed, an incentive that encouraged considerable one-upmanship among regional military commanders and their subordinate officers and bureaucrats. Failing to provide adequate transportation, lodging, or entertainment for visiting junta officials could result in reprimand or demotion. The battalion or region may also receive fewer central resources and patronage in the future and may receive a minuscule donation or none at all. This would worsen their individual and collective economic standing and deprive the region of central state resources (Mya Maung 1991; Farrelly 2008). Inversely, hosting a successful ministerial tour could elevate the status and reputation of local bureaucrats or military officials, ensure a large "donation" from the visiting delegation, and prompt more favorable treatment for the region or office in the future in the form of additional funds or material resources.

Given that so much was at stake in these visits, regional commanders and their subordinates relied heavily on support from local entrepreneurs to ensure their success. Businesspeople who complied willingly with requests for material aid from military officials were often immediately compensated: For instance, traders with cars or trucks were often enlisted (*chaw swe*) by civil servants to help with logistics for a local inspection visit, with their assistance often repaid in the form of a roughly equal favor, such as a full tank of petrol from military supply in return for a week using their vehicle. According to businesspeople who were asked to meet such demands during the 1990s and 2000s, for more significant aid such as construction of a road or school, military officials might provide them with an official letter supporting their commercial license or permit application to central ministries; in some cases, a military official might even publicly recognize their contributions in the presence of a senior minister or general whose influence could be crucial to business success (interview with trader, 3 August 2015). By gatekeeping the commercial expansion of businesspeople in this manner, junta officials were able to outsource the social obligations of the state at a provincial level, generating a post-socialist welfare regime increasingly reliant on contributions from private and non-state social actors.

Ideological Dimensions of Welfare Outsourcing

SLORC/SPDC officials used ideology as well as transactional incentives to encourage businesspeople, religious authorities, and ordinary people to assume expansive social and redistributive responsibilities during the 1990s and 2000s. State propaganda after 1988 popularized a "nationalist interpretation of Buddhist ethics" that rendered businesspeople and ordinary folks responsible for the needy while shrinking the social obligations of the state (Schober 1997, 238). One book, disseminated widely during the 1990s by the Department for Promotion and Propagation of the Sasana in Burmese and English and used in training for the regime-linked USDA social welfare group, connected Buddhist notions of charity (*dana*) to the "building of an ideal state" (Kyaw Htut 1994, xi). Emphasizing the duties of "good citizens," it specifically examined the Mangala Sutta, one of the sermons the Buddha delivered after enlightenment that contains the Thirty-Eight Blessings seen as essential to realizing Nibbana (*neikban*), which included paying respect to elders and practicing a "pure life."[24] The official state guide depicted the Mangala Sutta as the Buddha's attempt to translate "signs and omens" into "modes of conduct, family responsibilities, social obligations and training of self" (Kyaw Htut 1994, x–xi). According to this interpretation, "any gift or donation given for the welfare of the country is *dana mangala*, an act of charity" that will bring "peace, prosperity and well-being to all mankind" (Kyaw Htut 1994,

36, 85). The guide is a striking echo of the interventionist welfare capitalism of U Nu's Pyidawtha Plan during the 1950s, urging Buddhists to "do business which is free from complications and . . . if there is still some surplus of what you have earned, do not consume or use up all by yourself" (Kyaw Htut 1994, 35). The training guide then reflects nostalgically on the earlier reign of kings when "the people" followed the obligations of the Mangala Sutta and "built monasteries, dug wells and tanks, built roads and bridges on their own initiative and at their own expense . . . out of their own free will and generosity" so that "government had to spend very little on such works" (Kyaw Htut 1994, 35–36). During the time of kings, the tract claims, "there were no poor people" because they "would be given the necessary help out of the treasury of the king" (Kyaw Htut 1994, 35).

The junta established government-organized, nongovernmental organizations (GONGOs) that actively spread this welfare capitalist interpretation of Buddhist social teaching. Groups such as the USDA and the MMCWA led by wives of senior generals delivered a narrow range of health and education services to "trusted" populations while serving regime functions of surveillance and mass mobilization (Schober 1997; Steinberg 1997; James 2005). Their work was infused with Buddhist idioms that encouraged members, especially local businesspeople, to assume roles in social aid and welfare within their communities both through and beyond these organizations. The junta and its GONGOs also gave out awards for contributions to various religious and social causes, conferring titles on prominent businesspeople that directly referenced similar recognition issued during the time of Burmese kings (Jordt 2007, 135). Echoing the vision of an "associative state" that underpinned U Nu's earlier Pyidawtha Plan, state-endorsed Buddhist ideology during the 1990s and 2000s framed moral and political order as deriving from "the aggregate and held-in-common views and practices of its citizens," fusing Buddhist virtues, welfare work, and ideas of the "nation" (Jordt 2007, 106). Capitalism, meritorious donations, and the moral state of the polity were thus intimately intertwined in the philosophy of welfare capitalism embraced by the post-socialist junta.

Military officials encouraged businesspeople to embrace these expansive social and moral responsibilities by rewarding those who proactively complied with the expectations of philanthropy and charity, especially through GONGOs. A prominent rice merchant described how one would accrue and maintain capital during this period by willingly assuming responsibility for local social affairs, at the explicit or implicit urging of military patrons:

> If you wanted to get permission to run a rice mill or another business, then you needed to be involved in the community. . . . If you had a good name/reputation, then the military would be more likely to cooperate

with you. . . . Why? Because wealthier people in the community must
provide for those who are suffering. If you did this kind of [welfare/re-
ligious] work, then you and the government would have a good reputation. (Interview with trader, 6 May 2016)

"Donating" an "appropriate" proportion of profits to support GONGOs and
other junta initiatives was particularly important as it served as a pathway to
commercial success. Images of businesspeople making "donations" to junta officials at public ceremonies for various SLORC initiatives and schemes would
feature in daily state newspapers and TV broadcasts. Researchers at Mandalay
University collated data on these ceremonies reported in government newspapers, finding that more than 1 billion kyat was contributed between 1988 and
1998, equivalent to US$167 million at the official exchange rate, or between
US$1 million and $10 million at the black-market rate in the late 1990s (Kyaw Yin
Hlaing 2007b, 221).[25] Anthropologist Ingrid Jordt (2007, 132) analyzed these ceremonies as part of a donation "pyramid." Contributions from civilians would be
pooled by more senior government and military officials who would be listed as
the "foremost" donors regardless of the amount they personally donated. Total
amounts were then directed to specific initiatives, such as the renovation of Buddhist sacred sites, a favorite project of senior junta officials during the post-1988
period and again since the return to direct dictatorship in 2021.[26]

During the 1990s and 2000s, the structure of donation pyramids allowed individual military officials to claim spiritual merit for donations extracted semi-
coercively from their subordinates while simultaneously presenting the junta
collectively as a "charismatic magnet capable of drawing together people and resources" (Jordt 2007, 132–133; Schober 1997, 230–231). As the SLORC retrenched
the state from direct redistribution and moved toward encouraging non-state
welfare provision, businesspeople were required to assume the vast majority of
the financial burden for "socially" oriented initiatives, including care for the needy.[27]
Data collected by Mandalay University on reported donation ceremonies records a significant skew in junta donations toward religious initiatives: businesspeople gave between 80 percent and 90 percent of the funds for welfare, cultural,
and sports initiatives between 1988 and 1998, compared with religious activities,
for which they constituted around 60 percent, with the junta making up the
40 percent difference (Kyaw Yin Hlaing 2007b, 221).

Businesspeople who enthusiastically assumed their subordinate yet crucial
place in these donation pyramids were far more likely to receive the patronage
of military commanders and senior members of the junta crucial to their commercial success. Yet some entrepreneurs were reluctant to participate in these
spectacles because they saw the solicitation of compelled donations "as a form

of taxation" or had doubts about "how the donations [would] be used" (Schober 1997, 240). Despite these misgivings, most businesspeople seeking commercial expansion contributed at least some funds to state initiatives, since failure to do so could be viewed by military officials as not cooperating with the junta or, worse, an indicator of directly supporting the democratic resistance. As a result, many entrepreneurs who were privately critical of the regime during the 1990s and 2000s would still make "perfunctory donations" and then avoid participating in public gifting ceremonies. Some would then make more generous offerings to "sources of merit that reflect[ed] a personal choice" (Schober 1997, 240). Yet even these quiet donations to non-state welfare mechanisms less directly controlled by state officials helped to establish a welfare regime in which the state allowed, encouraged, and at times explicitly required private and non-state actors to fill marked gaps in social aid and public goods provision.

Buddhist Welfare Groups Emerged from Local Coalitions

Because of the poor reputation of GONGOs and state initiatives, many local entrepreneurs and bureaucrats linked to military officials also founded, managed, and partly financed their own welfare groups with the support of religious authorities and other influential civilians during the SLORC/SPDC period.[28] In central-east Myanmar, many of these groups emerged amid the failure of family-based practices of reciprocity in times of "wellbeing and sickness" (*tha yay na yay*) to materially and ritually provide for the massive need in the wake of state social retrenchment. Founders of these groups often solicited contributions both from military patrons and other civilians, especially at the early stages of group formation. Yet the patronage of Buddhist monks, Christian pastors, and other religious authorities also often proved crucial to ensuring support from ordinary people, since it allowed these groups to craft administrative distance from junta officials. In contrast with the coercively given contributions to GONGOs, the involvement of religious actors in soliciting donations strengthened the expectation that these groups would actually improve local social affairs. Contributing to these initiatives was thus intended to be seen as drawing good spiritual merit to donors.

The ballooning cost of funerals during the 1990s laid the ground for rapid expansion of non-state social groups into a range of health, education, and local community services. Formation of the earliest non-GONGO township welfare group at the ward, village, and township level in central-east Myanmar, for instance, was driven by price-gouging by alleged funeral racketeers. Committee members of several groups formed during the 1990s and 2000s claimed that local businesspeople were inflating the cost of funerals and burial beyond the reach of many poor households. In Myanmar's tropical climate, failure to properly bury corpses could result in pollution of groundwater, driving the outbreak of epidemics (Lorch 2008b, 32). Unaffordable funerals thus posed a serious public health risk. Responding to what they termed the "selfish" (*atta seit*) behavior of people who ran for-profit funeral and car rental businesses, junta officials, entrepreneurs, and local monks came together in 2002 to form a local chapter of *Byama-so*, a funeral organization that had earlier been established by monks in Mandalay in 1998 (Tosa 2018, Hsu 2019). An abbot (*sayadaw*) of an urban monastery in the southern part of Taungoo was instrumental in establishing the local chapter, which was the case with many of the groups that emerged in other government-controlled areas during the 1990s and 2000s.[29] The *sayadaw* provided a small plot of land adjacent to a meditation hall to house the office, store supplies, and safely park ambulances and funeral vans. However, founding committee members recounted that the abbot rarely played an active role in the day-to-day administration of the group because of monastic rules about the renunciation of worldly affairs, including a reticence to handle and manage money. Instead, donation records from the early 2000s list the "who's who" of important businesspeople and local civil servants involved in managing the group. Blackboards prominently posted on the walls of the office and organized according to hierarchies of social rank listed the names, occupations, and amounts donated to the 2002 formation of the group and construction of the crematorium. Two military generals top the list with donations of 100,000 kyats each (around US$16,666 at the official exchange rate or between US$100 to $1,000 on the black market). The largest contribution of 1,000,000 kyats (US$166,666 at the official exchange rate and US$1,000 to $10,000 on the black market) from Khin Maung Aye, a Taungoo native and the chairman of CB Bank, appears in bold letters. However, even though his contribution was ten times the amount of the regional commanders, his donation is listed third, a demonstration of the donation "pyramid" logic discussed earlier. Other noteworthy individuals and industry groups such as the Rice Traders Association made cash or in-kind contributions to support the purchase of vans, employ drivers, and construct the crematorium on the fringe of the township. Despite the dominance of Buddhists within the organization, prominent local Karen Baptist leaders also contributed funds to support the purchase of the funeral van, highlighting the role such welfare groups may have played in interethnic socialization during junta rule.[30]

Within months of establishing the local chapter of Byama-so, the cost of basic funeral services dropped from US$100 (or as high as $150) to US$20, with the families of the deceased paying some small expenses, including fuel and a processing fee.[31] In 2006, the organization established an offshoot chapter adjacent to the local public hospital with the support of an elderly cigar manufacturer. This endowment allowed the group to expand into local and intercity ambulance services and establish a township-level blood bank with over 4,000 registered donors. By the time my fieldwork commenced in 2015, hundreds of volunteers were working with the group every week to deliver a suite of support services, including funeral and ambulance transportation, assistance with paperwork for the sick or deceased, along with coordination of blood donations and discounted oxygen tanks for patients at the Taungoo General Hospital needing oxygen supplementation.

Smaller ward and village associations were also established in the late 1990s and 2000s at the same time more formal organizations proliferated around the country. Many of these local teams were linked to local religious patrons, most commonly monks. However, junta representatives also made small recurrent contributions to support the work of some neighborhood welfare groups. For instance, though the elderly home that featured in the opening vignette to this chapter was largely funded from donations by local entrepreneurs and civil servants. since the 1990s the facility had also received a small monthly grant as well as in-kind assistance in the form of rice and cooking oil from the MoSWRR, which was run until 2011 by military officers (interview, 22 January 2016). Additionally, regional military commanders hosted *a-hlu bwe* or donation celebrations at the center two or three times a year of the kind described in the opening vignette, where they and their battalion entourage gave cooking oil, rice, and money from military supplies to the facility.[32] However, beyond these occasional "gifts," the day-to-day management of welfare groups (which included ensuring their financial viability through fundraising) ultimately fell to local businesspeople—a dynamic that endured well beyond their establishment in the 1990s and 2000s. As the secretary of a township funeral group explained, "We do not have regular donations or a large group of donors. But if we are low on funds we let the town elder [the chairman of the organization] know, and he gets donations from the big men/women (*lu gyi*) to make sure there is enough" (interview, 2 May 2015).

Probed about who "big people" were, he named the local Tatmadaw commander and several male businesspeople, highlighting both the gendered nature of local elite administration and the coproduced logic of "social affairs" (*lu-mu-yay*) that characterized this period. Among civilians, the responsibility of "big men/women" did not end at care for the elderly, sick, or deceased but also extended to providing and maintaining local infrastructure. Interviewees in a downtown area of Taungoo described the construction of roads in the 1990s as the outcome of cooperation between local entrepreneurs, state administrators, social or religious authorities, and residents. According to participants in one of these urban road construction projects, the military administrator for the ward met with a group of local traders and shopkeepers and directed them to lead the resurfacing of a number of degraded arterial roads in the ward (interview with ward elders, 20 February 2016). Specific roles such as chairperson and treasurer were allocated by the military administrator to entrepreneurs and civil servants who lived in the area, with military trucks provided for transporting materials. The project committee then coordinated a ward fundraising and construction campaign with employees of businesspeople expected to "volunteer" their labor alongside members of neighborhood religious and welfare teams. In return for facilitating the road construction, committee members were able to solicit endorsement letters from the military commander and his officers in bids for licenses or permits from other parts of the Myanmar state apparatus. By combining transactional incentives and ideological persuasion, regional military commanders thus encouraged businesspeople and the community groups they patronized to assume greater responsibility for local improvement initiatives along with welfare for the needy.

A "Social License" Brought Commercial Success, Minimized Taxes

Military officials were far more likely to renew licenses and issue lucrative contracts to businesspeople who actively fundraised and assumed administrative responsibility for local social affairs. Accruing what I term a *social license* in the eyes of junta officials by proactively assuming responsibility for local social governance became essential to business success during the 1990s and 2000s.[33] It also reduced how much formal tax officials sought to collect from businesspeople. Social criteria thus stood alongside legality, rent-seeking, and other objectives as a factor that shaped how junta officials regulated the behavior and taxed the commercial enterprises of emergent business elites.

Many who entered into initial patron-client relations with regional military commanders and founded welfare groups in the early 1990s were gradually requested to take on positions as village, ward, or town "elders" (*myo mi myo pah*). This informal role did not technically exist within the administrative system that was the local basis of junta rule. However, becoming a local elder allowed businesspeople to act as liaisons with regional military commanders on how subnational and township-level junta objectives and schemes would be implemented. Both the businessmen described in the opening vignette of this chapter mediated regularly between military commanders and the local populace throughout the 1990s and 2000s. According to other local commercial elites active during this period, in return they were given considerable freedom to run social and religious organizations independent of direct junta oversight because the military officials trusted them to report back on social issues or mounting discontent. In return, many "town elders" were also able to secure local monopolies over the production or sale of popular and essential products and services, operate unlicensed or illegal businesses with bureaucratic impunity, or purchase large land plots at concessionary rates during the 1990s and 2000s, often in areas officially designated as "virgin" but long cultivated by farming families (Kudo 2005; Kyaw Yin Hlaing 2007b; Woods 2015, 8).

The wealth that emergent commercial elites could accrue, the power they wielded through informal administration, and their ability to lend capital to smaller commercial aspirants, meant that becoming an "elder" during junta rule offered a path to rapid upward mobility. Many of Myanmar's now nationally prominent tycoons accrued their wealth and social standing through artful navigation of these provincial commercial and social licensing expectations. However, even emergent "cronies," as they came to be known, ultimately relied on the patronage of their regional—or in some cases national—junta patrons to ensure their continued commercial success and social prestige. These hierarchies of power and obligation can be conceived as a pyramid of patronage in which national and regional junta commanders used processes of legal and social licensing to ensure that civilian businesspeople with whom they had cultivated clientelistic relations assumed responsibility for the social governance of the broader community. Some examples of the career trajectories and varied fortunes of businesspeople from provincial Myanmar demonstrate how these patterns of patronage, especially assuming welfare and social roles from the state, determined the commercial success of entrepreneurs during post-socialist junta rule.

Philanthropy as a Path to Capital Accumulation

The commercial ascendancy of Khin Maung Aye clarifies the links between social outsourcing and business expansion during post-socialist junta rule. Born in Taungoo in 1964, Khin Maung Aye attended a local state high school and then the University of Yangon as a mathematics student, graduating in 1985.[34] Interlocutors recounted how he then became actively involved in the 1988 protests against Ne Win's regime back in Taungoo and was appointed local treasurer of the student movement protesting the mismanagement of the BSPP. During this period, Khin Maung Aye coordinated fundraising and donations for the protesters who had set up camp in late July and early August 1988 around the entrance to the largest pagoda in Taungoo, Shwe San Daw, and two other locations. In early August, these camps were attacked by military police, who refused to negotiate with protesters. Between ten and twenty people were killed on the steps of the pagoda, and hundreds more were injured. It is not clear if Khin Maung

Aye was arrested during this time or if he was personally wounded when the protests were suppressed by authorities.

In the years after 1988, Khin Maung Aye formed his own company, Kaung Myanmar Aung (KMA) Group, and he began to bid for licenses from local representatives of the new military regime.[35] The nature of Khin Maung Aye's early dealings with the government are difficult to ascertain. Yet it is clear that Khin Maung Aye's operations increasingly shifted away from Taungoo as he established new patrons in more senior ranks of the junta. With the privatization of the banking sector in 1992, Khin Maung Aye became involved in the management of Cooperative Bank (CB), the financial arm of the Ministry of Cooperatives that provided loans to farmers during the Ne Win period. In 1997, he became chairman and chief executive of CB Bank, and in 2002 he was appointed vice chairman of the Central Cooperative Society. Throughout the 1990s and 2000s he contributed to major national strategic projects, including the financing and construction of parts of the new administrative capital Naypyitaw. He also received various licenses and permissions to expand the KMA Group into mining, logging, construction, hotels, aviation, and shipping.[36] During his rise to national prominence he built close ties with members of the regime, including with Thein Sein. In late 2010, competition between Khin Maung Aye, Asia World's Steven Law, and Kanbawza Bank's Aung Ko Win over government contracts and the privatization of national carrier Myanmar Airways International reportedly provoked a dispute between senior junta officials and their respective civilian clients. According to news reports by *The Irrawaddy* at the time, the dispute prompted panicked customers to withdraw their cash deposits from accounts in CB Bank.[37] The run brought the bank to the brink of bankruptcy until then-prime minister Thein Sein personally intervened on behalf of Khin Maung Aye.[38] Thein Sein soon thereafter ascended to the presidency and later appointed Khin Maung Aye to a series of advisory roles in the civilianized government that held power until early 2016. Reflecting his close ties with President Thein Sein, Khin Maung Aye was a major financier of the USDA's reinvention as a political vehicle, the Union Solidarity and Development Party (USDP), ahead of the November 2010 elections. In 2015, however, he definitively supported the election campaign of the National League for Democracy (NLD), a shift in political allegiance examined in greater depth in chapter 5.

Throughout his rise from provincial businessman to protégé of Myanmar's top junta officials, Khin Maung Aye maintained extensive practices of philanthropy around the country but especially in his hometown. Donations records from various Buddhist religious sites from the early 1990s show his donations to the construction of major monasteries in Taungoo. He was the donor listed third in donation records for the 2002 formation of the local chapter of the funeral and welfare association Byama-So and contributed to its 2007 expansion. He also made symbolic attempts to rejuvenate the local memory of the Taungoo dynasty throughout junta rule. The Taungoo kingdom conquered parts of Myanmar and Southeast Asia between the fourteenth and sixteenth centuries and formed a key element of the SLORC/SPDC's nationalist education in state schools during the 1990s and 2000s. To commemorate the historic lineage of the town and demonstrate his commitment to the shared political mythology of the junta, Khin Maung Aye donated large golden gates alongside two towering twenty-foot statues of kings of the Taungoo dynasty, Tabinshwehti and Bayinnaung, to place at the entrance to the city. His patronage of the junta's historic imaginary provides an insight into post-socialist Burmese "philanthronationalism," a form of business praxis previously theorized in Sri Lanka under Mahinda Rajapaksa where state-sanctioned nationalist rhetoric and ideology were extended and diffused by commercial elites aligned with the government (see Widger 2016). In the context of 1990s Myanmar, these kinds of philanthropic practices gave Khin Maung Aye a reputation for generosity among officials that ensured their support for his various plans to expand his commercial empire. Donations that helped spread the junta's nationalist ideology and initiatives could in this way open up a fruitful path to commercial dominance of specific sectors and private capital accumulation.

Avoiding Junta Welfare Groups, Maintaining Modest Wealth

Not all businesspeople were willing to assume the social obligations of the SLORC/SPDC's autocratic welfare capitalism. Some commercial operators who were more circumspect of the junta often refused to contribute more than was strictly necessary to state appeals. Those who were able to resist or avoid symbiotic relations with military commanders tended to be independently wealthy, in many cases inheriting capital or land from their parents or in-laws. As failure to obtain and maintain a social license from junta officials meant that they received far fewer business concessions throughout the 1990s and 2000s than "cronies" did, but they tended to have less bullish commercial aspirations, too. The pathways of two individuals—the relatively modest entrepreneur Dr. Than Zin (pseudonym), and actor turned social worker Kyaw Thu—show how lack of effort or interest in earning a social license through partnership with military officials constrained their commercial expansion during junta rule.

Dr. Than Zin inherited land from his father, who had engaged in trade during the late socialist period. After winning a prestigious position in medical school and practicing as a doctor, he then left medicine to open a small guesthouse with existing family capital. A degree of interaction with junta officials was inevitable in order to receive and annually renew the required legal licenses to host foreigners. Yet his reliance on inherited wealth and his seeming contentment with a business that was largely locally oriented meant that he had little incentive to join committees and contribute more than was strictly necessary to GONGOs and welfare groups managed by "cronies." He still felt an obligation to render aid to others by providing free medical treatment directly to the villages he occasionally visited with local and foreign tourists to the region. This approach allowed him to bypass the intermediation of assistance by welfare groups patronized by regime-aligned businesspeople while still fulfilling what he said he felt were his moral obligations as a comparatively wealthy man. Other members of the local commercial class such as Khin Maung Aye founded or administered welfare groups while accruing considerable landholdings and commercial interests across sectors such as agriculture, mining, construction, hospitality, and transport. Dr. Than Zin's business, in contrast, remained fairly humble and largely focused on central-east Myanmar, apart from the acquisition of a few small plots of land elsewhere in the country.

Some people who had accrued capital and fame with the endorsement of the regime also strove to engage in social work independent of junta GONGOs. Actor Kyaw Thu became one of these social activists. Kyaw Thu starred in a number of well-known films in the 1980s, winning the acclaim of the SLORC in 1994 with a "Myanmar Academy Award" from the Ministry of Culture. Known for his roguish, abrupt demeanor, and for his alcoholism, he largely eschewed public activism for much of the 1990s and 2000s. In 2001, however, inspired by similar organizations in Mandalay and Yangon formed in the late 1990s, he founded the Free Funeral Service Society with film director Thukha, reportedly after encountering a hospitalized woman whose family had abandoned her fearing they would not be able to afford her funeral if she passed away.[39] Branches of the charity subsequently sprang up around Myanmar. After providing aid to monks and other protesters involved in a 2007 uprising against the government, however, Kyaw Thu was subsequently banned by the junta from acting and directing films.[40] Despite these restrictions, Kyaw Thu expanded into ambulance, hospital, disaster relief, and education provision, funded by donations from the public as well as contributions from his significant fortune—a pattern of expanding service provision that occurred in local welfare groups across the country.[41] As he had already accrued financial and reputational capital, the regime's effective suspension of his film career was not financially catastrophic. Kyaw Thu continued to engage in social work independent of regime-linked groups, notwithstanding the restrictions placed on his profitable industry roles during military rule.

Examination of provincial state-business relations during the 1990s and 2000s highlights how junta officials in post-socialist Myanmar encouraged business-people, welfare groups, and society at large to take on significant responsibility to support the community in which they operated or originated. Businesspeople who found ways to redistribute wealth and deliver social support to the needy and demonstrate these contributions to junta officials paved their path to commercial success. The organizational autonomy and financial resources that non-state wel-fare groups received from these regime-linked businesspeople allowed them to popularize an expansive notion of social obligation and duty, which in turn pro-vided the ideological basis for ordinary people to engage in ostensibly apolitical reciprocity activities amid dictatorship.

The Reimagining of Social Obligations and Rise of "Parahita"

The proliferation of welfare groups after 1988 prompted major shifts in how people got by and the way they understood obligations to the needy beyond their imme-diate family. These material and ideological shifts were driven by the suspicion many lay Buddhists, especially emergent entrepreneurs, had toward junta de-mands for donations to GONGOs and state initiatives. Participants in state-coordinated donation rituals became the focus of intense moral scrutiny: Many questioned whether these "donations" addressed real needs in the community and if donors contributed with the detached, volitional, and compassionate intentions (*cedana*) necessary for them to accrue good merit within a Buddhist framework.[42] The perception that regime-linked "charities" were actually mass organizations for the regime was confirmed when the USDA was transformed into a junta-aligned political party and enlisted its networks of material aid and reliance to influence and coerce voters ahead of the 2010 elections. As disdain for the junta's extraction of "donations" for such groups intensified, by the mid-1990s welfare group managers and volunteers in neighborhoods, villages, and townships sought organizational and symbolic distance from state authorities. By virtue of respond-ing to more specific and localized needs in the community, and their rhetorical use of Buddhist idioms in rituals linked to the provision of social aid, these groups were able to convince ordinary people more easily than GONGOs were to con-tribute their money, time, and resources "quasi-voluntarily" (Levi 1988). The ex-panding social scope of "charity" thus coincided with and enabled a dramatic flourishing of non-state mechanisms of welfare and redistribution.

Monks and Political Elites Reinterpreted the Scope of "Charity"

Monastic authorities and political elites, including democratic leaders, led an expansion and reimagining of the social role of charitable giving throughout the 1990s and 2000s. *Dana* or charity is considered one of the central mundane practices through which lay Buddhists can seek to achieve Nibbana (*neikban*), the end of cycles of rebirth and suffering (Jordt 2007, 100; Schober 1997). Research on charitable practices among Burmese Buddhists in the 1950s and 1960s previously suggested that the scope of meritorious giving (*dana*) was tightly bound to the metaphysical "religious" rather than the social or "this worldly" domain. In an interpretation still held by many Burmese Buddhists, anthropologist Milford Spiro concluded from fieldwork in the 1950s and 1960s that "merit [accrued] is proportional to the sanctity of the recipient" (Spiro [1970] 1982, 463). Consequently, constructing religious buildings such as pagodas as well as donating food or other material support to monks was seen by many Burmese people to be the most meritorious actions a person can take (Spiro [1970] 1982, 104). After 1988, as monks began to establish or patronize civilian-run welfare-oriented organizations, the social boundaries of Buddhist charity began to expand rapidly.

Soon after the dissolution of the BSPP and the commencement of market reforms, monks around Myanmar began to challenge these ideas by consciously positioning themselves "as both recipients and distributors of donations" (Walton 2016, 154). The most prominent abbots to enlist monastic hierarchy to serve religious and socially redistributive outcomes were the Sitagu and Thamanya Sayadaws. Sitagu Sayadaw, also known as U Nyanissara, gained particular renown across Myanmar after speaking in support of the 1988 protests. When he returned to Myanmar from exile, he promptly began to establish a network of charitable health facilities and educational institutions in Sagaing and Yangon in the mid-1990s (Walton 2016, 33, 142). Laypeople from around the country, including entrepreneurs and senior members of the junta, increasingly came to offer money and time at Sitagu's facilities, where his staff and volunteers often delivered free treatment for the sick that was of higher quality than in government-run hospitals.[43] Thamanya Sayadaw developed a similarly autonomous compound in the mid-1990s in an area outside Hpa-an in Karen State to which millions of people, including Aung San Suu Kyi, flocked from across Myanmar (Rozenberg 2010, chap. 4).

Sitagu and other prominent monks increasingly began to refer to their social projects and interventions using the Pali-derived concept of *parahita* (social work).[44] The concept previously had a fairly strict religious scope, having been enlisted most prominently by Burmese nationalists in the decades before independence to encourage lay involvement in the nationwide propagation of Buddhism through religious instruction or *thathana* (Pali: *sasana*).[45] From the mid-1990s, however, prominent monks endorsed *parahita* as a form of *byama-so taya*, or meritorious practices of moral conduct or truth that bridge the mundane (*lawki*) and supra-mundane (*lawkouttara*) realms (Houtman 1999, 308). Sitagu and other abbots often dedicated lengthy public sermons to detailing their parahita activities and encouraging welfare work by the laity (Walton 2016, 153). By lending their support to local social initiatives that responded to suffering, misfortune, or inequality within the community, monks challenged the logic that merit was accrued proportional to the moral status of the beneficiary; instead, they argued that it was also "in part contingent on the *need* of the recipient" (Walton 2016, 60, emphasis in original).

Critics of the junta endorsed a similarly expansive interpretation of charity as a way to sustain democratic ideals in the face of repression. Democracy activists including Aung San Suu Kyi condemned the junta's coerced solicitation of "donations" from businesspeople and ordinary people to fund GONGOs and state projects. Enlisting similar Buddhist moral discourse as the prominent monks did, Suu Kyi instead encouraged supporters of "democracy" to engage in voluntary charitable work and exercise *myitta* (loving kindness), contrasting their actions with the ruthless and selfish governing approach of junta officials.[46] She encouraged people to "concentrate on cultivating loving kindness and compassion" by engaging in charity work separate from the regime, arguing it would lead to "the emergence of feelings of solidarity and the formation of a society" necessary to achieve political freedom and individual liberation from cycles of rebirth (Suu Kyi quoted in Houtman 1999, 314, 322). Aforementioned actor, director, and social worker Kyaw Thu was one of the most prominent lay activists to enact these broader notions of social work. He appeared in public and in the media driving ambulances for the sick and funeral hearses for the deceased, including after the 2007 uprising. He quickly became a paragon of humanitarian and democratic virtue that other celebrities and many ordinary Buddhist people sought to emulate, with chapters of the Free Funeral Service Society subsequently opening in Mandalay and provincial areas across Myanmar in the mid to late 2000s (San San Oo 2018).[47] The expanding scope for Buddhist "charity" in the context of state retrenchment allowed new notions of social obligation and kinship to take social root. Categorical distinctions between meritorious charity (*dana*) and the more familial, obligatory, and less meritorious sphere of "social affairs" (*lu-mu-yay*) became increasingly blurred as local welfare practices and groups began to demand more of the "community."

Welfare Capitalism Remade Social Obligations

The provision of material aid at times of crisis and need by Buddhist monks, welfare activists, and businesspeople reshaped popular understandings of relatedness and social duty. Decades of anthropological research across contexts of conflict, displacement, scarcity, and insecurity highlights that a sense of obligation to others emerges not simply from biological kinship but from "long processes of building social ties and reciprocal obligation" through aid that is publicly and privately recognized or compelled (Ferguson 2015, 108). Idioms of kinship and relatedness are "aspirational and negotiable" (McGovern 2012, 739) modes through which hosts and strangers, wealthy and poor cooperate and reciprocate at times of scarcity (Englund 2008, Stasch 2009). Kinship or relatedness, from this perspective, is "not really something you *have*—it is something you *do*" by enacting, and responding to, distributive claims on finite resources (Ferguson 2015, 134, emphasis added). The magnitude of material obligation that welfare groups claim from donors must be carefully bounded in the context of extreme scarcity such as that experienced during junta rule in Myanmar. Despite generating a degree of intimacy by including the needy within the vision of a supposedly equitable "community," as Erica Bornstein notes in her ethnography of humanitarianism in New Delhi, a careful social distance must be maintained between donor and recipient to prevent opening the giver "up to unlimited demand[s]" on already scarce household resources (Bornstein 2012, 150).

The activists who partnered with businesspeople to establish welfare and neighborhood groups throughout the 1990s and 2000s became skilled at making materially limited requests for aid framed in Buddhist concepts of obligation. Echoing the expanding social interpretation of charity endorsed by religious and democratic leaders, these groups often drew on idioms of *parahita* (work for others), *myitta* (loving kindness), *karuna* (charity), and *cedana* (compassion) to encourage "quasi-voluntary compliance" with their material demands (Levi 1988). In many cases these notions became the "organizing 'idea'" of welfare groups, lending moral legitimacy to their solicitation of funds, labor, or in-kind contributions from community members (Griffiths 2017, 8). For instance, the aforementioned welfare and funeral organization Byama-so, founded in Mandalay in 1998 and in Taungoo in 2002, references the *byama-so taya* "this worldly" spiritual truths widely seen by democracy activists and ordinary Buddhists alike as "[helping to] bridge the mundane and the supra-mundane . . . collective and personal aspirations . . . permit[ing] vision of the unconditioned emptiness of *nibbana* upon which can be projected ultimate ideals of freedom and [fulfillment]" (Houtman 1999, 308, 311).

Drawing on these ideas, volunteers and donors that I encountered throughout my fieldwork often made grand claims about charitable action transforming the individual and society. Managers and volunteers carefully intermediated transactions of money, time, or other aid in order to emphasize the larger spiritual and collective stakes of charitable giving. A fine balance was struck between encouraging donations and ensuring that the aid provided was perceived as freely given. The art of bounded solicitation was evident in June 2015, when I followed an entourage of local university students to the blood bank at the Taungoo General Hospital. In the donation room, we were joined by a volunteer from Byama-so who had coordinated blood donations from a range of networks, including university student groups since the mid-2000s. During the forty-five-minute blood donation procedure, I asked one of the students, "What does it feel like to give blood?" The volunteer, who was a commercial trader who took the morning off work to meet the students and provide encouragement, quickly interjected: "It feels fantastic! It is essential that they give blood. . . . People need blood to continue their lives. By giving blood, your happiness is limitless because you save lives!"

The students donating nodded weakly as 450 milliliters of their rare AB blood slowly trickled into bags propped up on wooden blocks on the floor. Similar encouragement came from another student who donated the week before and sat beaming at the foot of the bed, loading photos of the students to their group's newly formed Facebook page. The volunteer from Byama-So pulled me to the side of the room and quietly explained the importance of his role. "If they come alone," he told me, "they get a bit scared and decide not to donate." He then returned to encouraging them, stressing the contribution they were making not just to patients in need of their blood but also to spreading what he and many other volunteers referred to as *parahita seit*, or "mind for others," or more figuratively "social consciousness."[48] Volunteers and coordinators of welfare groups often sought to use charitable transactions to cultivate the moral imagination of the donors in this manner, encouraging them to view their actions as reducing suffering not just for recipients but also across society more broadly. Buddhist idioms form a central part of the "gifting" process, reinforcing the meritorious nature of the act of giving while cultivating a sense of shared collective identity between donor and recipient. By framing and intermediating transactions of physical or monetary aid in this way, volunteers and managers of welfare groups lead donors to see their contribution of blood as generative of a compassionate and empathetic community or society.

A retired nurse, Daw Khin Nwe (pseudonym), evoked similar social stakes when recounting her provision of free treatment to impoverished villagers during the 1990s. After we met during the visit of Aung San Suu Kyi to Taungoo in

August 2015, she later described her charitable work as simultaneously improving the lives of the needy, transforming herself and catalyzing social and political transformation:

> It is important to balance working for my family and friends, working for others, and meditating for myself. I used to work in a free clinic in a village, giving blood tests and vaccinations. There were patients who could not afford even the trishaw ride to the clinic. When I saw that people were not equal, I wanted them to live to some standard. . . . Just like Aung San Suu Kyi said at the rally: "Everything you do is somehow connected with politics." . . . So, doing *parahita* is politics as well as social work. This kind of work can start something much bigger, be the catalyst or the seed for something that is a force for democracy. (Interview, 17 August 2015).

Other donors and welfare volunteers framed their charitable work in similarly spiritual and civic terms. Risk-pooling groups, which proliferated at the neighborhood and village level after 1988, were particularly skilled at using richly symbolic language to mobilize donors and volunteers and encourage beneficiaries to view themselves as future contributors to a cycle of reciprocity. By the time I commenced fieldwork, the most common relief organizations that I encountered in central-east Myanmar were neighborhood and village welfare teams for whom such framing and redistributive functions were crucial parts of their work. They were often formed with initial donations from monks, local businesspeople, and remittances from migrant teams, and they played a major role around Myanmar in alleviating significant out-of-pocket expenses associated with family deaths, medical emergencies, aged care, education, and other regular and unexpected social expenses.[49]

There were various models as to how funds were collected and redistributed. Some of these groups would collect contributions from local residents only when an accident or medical emergency occurred. Others gathered an agreed amount of funds on a monthly basis regardless of need and drew down on their principal fund when crises struck. In addition to dispensing funds for emergencies and unexpected misfortunes, these groups also raised funds to host ceremonies to honor the elderly with cash and in-kind support.[50] In urban neighborhoods, welfare groups often had several hundred members comprising around 30 to 50 percent of households from within the ward. Each household that participated in funeral groups, for instance, donated an average of 300 and 500 kyats (approximately US 20 to 40 cents) when a death occurred within the ward, with contributions varying by both the affluence and generosity of the donor household. Higher rates of participation of around 80 percent of households were encountered in rural welfare groups, although smaller monetary donations of 100 to 200 kyats per household were often supplemented by the donation of a cup of dry rice to the group's emergency granary. In the majority of contexts encountered, donors received a customized receipt for their contributions inscribing the details of the organization, name of the donor, and the amount given. In the case of funerals, the name of the deceased was also recorded alongside venerations emphasizing the meritorious nature of the donations. The invocation of Buddhist concepts by these groups, along with the common involvement of welfare group volunteers in Buddhist rituals such as funeral chanting for the deceased, helps strengthen the perception that donations to these initiatives are karmically beneficial.[51]

Depending on the size and affluence of the neighborhood or village, between 70,000 kyat (US$50) and 150,000 kyat (US$120) was typically raised from residents for a specific funeral or emergency.[52] These contributions would then be aggregated by a representative of the rotating scheme, often a local businessperson but in some cases the ward or village administrator. These funds would then be given to the family experiencing the crisis to defray a portion of the cost of hospitalization or funeral rituals.[53] These contributions from the community supplemented donations from more intimate family and friends, who generally made larger monetary donations directly on the behalf of their family in the case of a death or medical emergency, in addition to giving through formal relief groups.[54]

Not all recipients of support from welfare groups contributed regularly to the schemes from which they benefited. Need and residency within the community determined eligibility to receive aid. A member of a neighborhood funeral group explained the flexibility of the mechanism in his ward regardless of the background of the household: "If we hear about a death, we alert the network and then we all come together to raise money." He suggested that some residents complained about including nonmembers, recent migrants to the neighborhood, or non-Buddhists in risk-pooling mechanisms. In these cases the managers of welfare groups would appeal for a shared communal identity based on Buddhist concepts such as "loving kindness" (*myitta*) and "work for others" (*parahita*).[55] As scholars of kinship, relatedness, and obligation in other contexts have observed, elevating points of similarity between residents in this way serves to incorporate as "sources of power and potential" people and groups whose mutuality may be materially and relationally beneficial in the future, especially local businesspeople who had access to far more resources than most average people (Goldfarb and Schuster 2016, 9). The abstract and materially limited demands made on people by welfare groups proved highly flexible and adaptable to diverse contexts, allowing the ideals and practices underpinning these teams to spread organically as local communities around the country responded to the magnitude of need. In the process, ordinary people and businesspeople alike in lowland areas of the country came to view "donations" to non-state welfare mechanisms as both materially and karmically beneficial, providing the political economy and ideational backdrop for the emergence of a resilient welfare capitalist regime.

Groups that extended kin-like care to non-intimate community members often observed the patchiness of support provided by charities and philanthropists. For example, a Buddhist nun who ran an orphanage for abandoned girls noted that it was difficult to support the needs of the young women from donations alone as these contributions were often given irregularly and commonly on days considered auspicious by donors. She was grateful for the generosity provided by donors but added that the girls were "lucky." Most of the costs for their lodging was financed by the sale of timber logs stored in a yard beside the main building, the legacy of a logging license apparently granted to the orphanage by a minister in U Nu's government in the 1950s. The animating logic of meritorious charity and service for others (*parahita*), based on ostensibly free and intentional acts of generosity, can help bridge social distance between donor and recipient. Yet the underlying logic of giving bounded aid to non-state welfare groups is that the giver is shielded from addressing the needs of the destitute or the community. The result is that the needy often remained structurally vulnerable. What emerged during the 1990s and 2000s was an autocratic form of welfare capitalism in which state social obligations were outsourced to emergent businesspeople who delivered often suboptimal social aid to the needy. Meanwhile, the capacity of the state to directly support social development itself was structurally undermined by the provision of tax deductions and exemptions for contributions made to non-state social mechanisms.

Hidden Welfare Regime Relied on Indirect Tax Expenditure

Businesspeople and ordinary households made significant contributions to non-state social institutions during junta rule. Quantifying the proportional size of donations for different households is difficult because few surveys of this kind were conducted in the 1990s and 2000s. What is clear, however, is that many national, regional, township, and neighborhood welfare associations established after 1988 relied heavily on community contributions. A survey of 1,000 households that I conducted in March 2016 in central-east Myanmar gave a quantitative insight into these dynamics (G. McCarthy 2016a). The survey found that "donations" to religious and social institutions comprised a significant portion of annual household spending, adding up to a sizable and mildly progressive financial burden for households: an average of 7 percent total expenditure for families in the poorest two quintiles and 10 percent for those in the top two wealth quintiles.[56] More affluent households reported donating slightly more in *amounts* on a daily basis, an average of 770 kyats (around US$0.62) compared with around 500 kyats (US$0.4) for poorer households. The survey was conducted during the period of partial civilian rule, so it does not measure the true informal contributions made to the "hidden welfare state" of the 1990s and 2000s (see Howard 1999). What these findings do suggest, though, is that the welfare regime that emerged amid post-socialist market reform endured the transition from direct dictatorship, highlighting the appeal of non-state aid to a range of networks and people even in a partly electoral context.

Ostensibly "voluntary" social contributions dwarfed the amount people typically paid in state taxes at the time of the survey in 2016. Research conducted during junta rule suggested that *formal* state tax burden probably comprised a relatively small proportion of average spending, including for emergent business elites (R. Taylor 2009, 456; Turnell 2011, 142). They were replaced with what economist Sean Turnell (2011, 142) terms "implicit" taxes such as financial contributions to GONGOs or village, ward, and township social initiatives. By substituting formal for "implicit" or "informal" taxes in this manner, the junta effectively outsourced a range of social expenditure and governance responsibilities to non-state institutions. Transferring functional and ideological responsibility for social affairs in this way may have ameliorated ideological concerns left over from the BSPP that ideals of equity were being abandoned after the junta's embrace of capitalism, a dynamic seen in a range of post-Soviet republics (Burawoy and Verdery 1999; Collier 2011). Yet, by granting tax reprieves to businesspeople and households in return for social "donations," the fiscal capacity of the Myanmar state was catastrophically hollowed out. Substitution of formal for informal taxation meant that most businesses and households gave more in "donations" to welfare and social institutions than the state itself netted in formal state taxation.[57] These dynamics produced what has been termed elsewhere as "welfare parastate" (Hacker 2016a), funded in this case by informal taxation that in sum may have been more than the state itself collected in formal taxation. The system endured the transition to partial civilian rule, with the 2016 survey finding "donations" averaging 8 percent of household expenditure across wealth quintiles—more than double the amount given in formal taxes and payments to state officials.[58]

Deducting informal contributions from formal tax bills had the structural consequence of reducing the revenues that government agencies could use to fund developmental public goods. As shown in figure 2.4, state tax revenue collapsed to a low of 2 percent of GDP in 2002, a major drop from the already low 6 percent in the early 1990s. This compares starkly with similar regional contexts such as Nepal and Indonesia, where the average tax to GDP ratio during this period was around 8 percent and 10 percent, respectively. The reconfiguration of the welfare

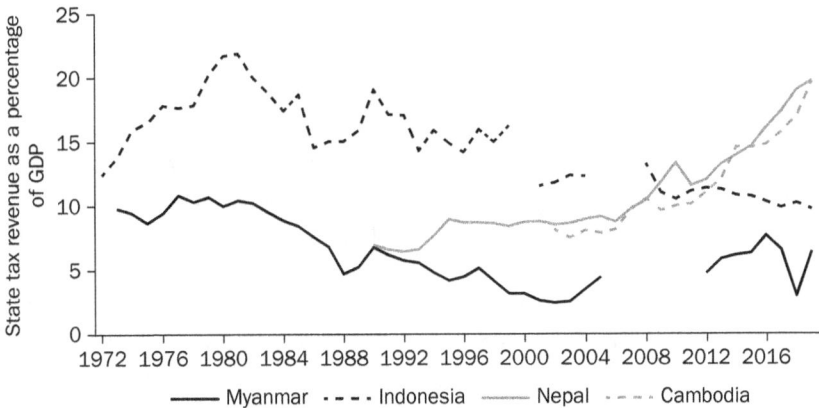

FIGURE 2.4.   Tax revenue as percentage of GDP for Myanmar and counterparts, 1970s–2016. *Source*: World Bank.

regime achieved through formal tax remissions has structurally constrained the fiscal capacity of Myanmar in a way that has proved path-dependent since 2011 as practices of tax remissions—formal and informal—continued to be widely used by state officials during partial civilian rule.

The tax and spending approach of Myanmar's post-socialist regime contrasted with the developmental strategy adopted by regional neighbors during this period. From the 1980s, regimes in South Korea, Taiwan, Thailand, and Singapore converged to form a "productivist world of welfare capitalism" (Holliday 2000, 707). All the countries financed significant direct social expenditures, especially in the education and health sectors, by maintaining formal taxation revenue at over 10 percent of GDP throughout this period. These welfare regimes initially tended to leave unemployment aid, pensions, and aged care to families and the market. However, state social role gradually expanded in each context as political elites sought to garner votes by reducing household out-of-pocket expenditures for health care, education, and aged care while expanding support for the disabled and unemployed (see introduction). In contrast to the productivist model of welfare capitalism, Myanmar's post-socialist junta officials sought to enable its coercive approach to state-building in the periphery by encouraging an informal system of social protection whereby it gave commercial licenses and formal tax remissions to people who made private social expenditures. A doubly "hidden" welfare state emerged from autocratic welfare capitalism. State officials were largely absent from the local administration of non-state welfare at a micro-level (despite financially and ideologically encouraging it), while the costs were ultimately born at a macro-level by the state in the form of diminishing tax revenues and the erosion of bureaucratic capacity to tax the population and economic activity. The coercive penetration of the periphery enabled by social outsourcing thus came at a catastrophic social cost over the short and long term, because it eroded fiscal capacity of the state by entrenching a welfare regime in which non-state actors deliver patchy and suboptimal support to the needy, often in exchange for tax remissions or commercial concessions. Yet the enmeshment of non-state ideals and practices of reciprocity in the welfare mix also paradoxically offered space for grassroots activists to enact ideas of social and political change throughout the otherwise repressive period of the 1990s and 2000s. These normative bonds and practices of localized social obligation formed the basis for a bounded and at times exclusionary democratic politics during the decade of partial civilian rule and later helped to sustain resistance following the return to dictatorship in 2021.

Uncovering the Legacies of Social Outsourcing

After dissolving the socialist dictatorship in 1988, the SLORC/SPDC dramatically reconfigured the social role of the Myanmar state. Rigidly focused on constructing hard infrastructure and wresting control over the borderlands, regional military commanders attempted to address inequities generated by crony capitalism by outsourcing social responsibilities to the emergent business class and community at large. Regime-endorsed interpretations of charity and Buddhist obligation were reinforced by commercial and tax incentives, fostering a moral and political economy from which welfare groups sprang up at the neighborhood, village, and township level across government-controlled areas of the country. These welfare groups and practices helped sustain democratic ideals and resistance efforts amid dictatorship during the SLORC/SPDC junta, a pattern that was repeated following the return to direct military rule in 2021.

A welfare mix reliant on private, charitable, and informal social providers emerged from the post-1988 period of state social retrenchment. As activists and religious authorities framed the provision of materially limited aid to the needy as expressions of Buddhist obligation, potentially mundane social contributions began to accrue metaphysical and civic meaning as acts of meritorious charity (*dana*) that helped sustain a democratic ideal. The notion of "community" popularized during the 1990s and 2000s was thus not limited solely to the ward, village, or even township. Rather, the parameter of social obligation enacted by welfare groups often transcended these local networks and practices of redistribution, most notably in the wake of disasters. In these moments, ideals and networks of localized charity were recurrently extended to some, although certainly not all, distant strangers in need, generating new ideas of moral and political community bounded by the constraints of geographic accessibility, resource availability and common bonds of identity. Focusing on Cyclone Nargis in 2008 and Cyclone Komen in 2015, chapter 3 explores how non-state actors led natural disaster response in the post-socialist period, delivering aid to many while excluding communities mapped ideationally and logistically out of flows of non-state social aid.

DISASTERS AND THE POLITY

In late July 2015, Cyclone Komen and four successive storms made landfall in Myanmar. The deluge and subsequent flooding and landslides were among the worst the country had seen since the devastation of Cyclone Nargis in 2008. Komen affected more than 1.6 million people, directly killed 117, and inundated 800,000 acres of farmland in twelve of Myanmar's fourteen states and regions.[1] It also caused landslides in remote upland areas on the periphery of the country.

In the wake of the initial floods, civilian welfare groups from across the country raised funds in their local community and then traveled to affected areas to disperse relief. In August 2015, following a week of fundraising with a number of these groups, I traveled to flooded townships in the Ayeyarwaddy Delta alongside a team of businesspeople, civil servants, teachers, and university students from central-east Myanmar. For three days I helped load, unload, lug, and distribute rice, oil, clothes, and other supplies to communities devastated by the deluge. We traveled by canoe to remote villages, visited flooded pagodas, and slept alongside one another in crowded monastic compounds.

After the last of our trips to a village engulfed by the rushing backwaters, we returned to the monastery that had been housing and feeding us throughout the week. Before departing on our ten-hour journey home, the abbot invited all forty volunteers into the meditation hall for a ritual to acknowledge our efforts. We all knelt down on the mats set up in front of the abbot, flanked by a few remaining sacks of clothes, food, and other supplies that were stacked up around the hall and loosely covered by a vinyl banner bearing the details of our appeal. The monk reminded volunteers of their bonds and obligations to those experiencing suffering, regardless of geographic or social distance:

> Please help people who are in need as if they were your own father, mother, brother, or sister, without discrimination against their ethnicity, religion, or location. According to Lord Buddha's teachings, everyone is related and they can be your parents or siblings from past lives. So help them as you can with loving kindness (*myitta*). . . . These good deeds you have done will help you to achieve Nirvana where no kind of suffering (*dukkha*) exists. (Field notes, 12 August 2015)

The volunteers, smeared with mud from the day spent dispersing aid, nodded vigorously and bowed to the abbot, affirming the idea of relatedness and mutuality he preached. The abbot concluded by slowly chanting a Buddhist blessing, recognizing the merit shared among all those assembled: "Well done, well done, well done" (*thadu, thadu, thadu*).

Our group was one of thousands that mobilized across Myanmar in the wake of the cyclone to provide aid to people rendered destitute by its torrential downpours. These efforts delivered essential material relief to devastated communities that had yet to receive any support from state authorities and international organizations. The rhetorical framing of distant strangers as potentially reincarnated family demonstrates how ideals of social relatedness and practices of localized reciprocity generated in the wake of market reform in the 1990s have been recurrently stretched to help mobilize support for the needy, near and far.

In this chapter, I argue that natural catastrophes in post-1988 Myanmar have extended the patchy neighborhood- and township-level support generated during the market reform and state social outsourcing of the 1990s and 2000s, stretching ideas of social obligation and mechanisms of welfare capitalism to support distant strangers in need. As charitable groups organized—often at direct encouragement by state officials—to render aid to the needy, they framed some people affected by the floods as belonging to an extended community of reciprocity. Others, especially minority communities in remote upland areas, were implicitly or explicitly excluded from such support. In a context where imaginings of the "nation" (see Anderson 1991) are already fragmented by legally enshrined racial hierarchies along with differential historical experiences of the state (Walton 2018), this chapter examines how non-state mobilization in the wake of disasters has entrenched the role of private and charitable providers in social aid while exacerbating social divides and hierarchies of belonging within the polity. Following a brief overview of the literature on belonging and disasters, the chapter surveys available accounts of the devastation and aftermath of the 2008 Cyclone

Nargis, noting the role of local welfare groups, religious actors, and businesspeople in providing support, often at the behest of junta officials. I then draw on fieldwork conducted with welfare groups from central Myanmar during Cyclone Komen in 2015 to describe how social, geographic, and logistic proximity led Buddhists in flooded lowland regions to receive far more support from these networks than ethno-religious minorities in upland regions affected by landslides. By deliberately and inadvertently cleaving hierarchies of belonging within the polity in this way, non-state aid can undermine shared commitment to state-led collective improvement, which is crucial to justifying taxation and building a more inclusive welfare regime. The chapter concludes that ideals and practices of obligation and redistribution enacted by lowland non-state actors fill important gaps in social aid while also paradoxically fracturing popular commitment to the role of state agencies in achieving social justice.

Disasters and State-Society Relations

The boundaries of social and political community, and the obligations of its members, are often laid bare by catastrophes. Outpourings of aid in the wake of destruction reveal quotidian networks of relief, norms of obligation, and visions of progress that may otherwise be hidden from view. As scholars of catastrophes in the political development of the modern United States have noted,[2] disasters "function as cameras whose snapshots in time allow us to see social transactions in a particular moment" (Remes 2015, 4). The "ties that bind," for which few records may be kept in normal times, are exposed during moments of collective upheaval and enshrined both in media reports and bureaucratic records that record who people turned to at times of trouble. In this way, aid and reconstruction mobilized in the aftermath of disasters can demonstrate the relative protection offered by the state or the centrality of horizontal networks to survival, offering insights into the substantive and symbolic meanings of citizenship or belonging during moments of suffering and devastation.

Yet catastrophes can also transform the way individuals and institutions envision the "social imaginary" (Castoriadis 1997). Disasters create "large groups of apparently 'deserving' needy who could reasonably make claims on the state and their fellow citizens," in some cases resulting in stronger popular expectations of the state, civil institutions, and other individuals (Remes 2015, 5). The governance of disaster relief by the state in some cases lends material substance to *formal* citizenship by creating new categories of entitlement and expectations of the state (Chigudu 2020). Political leaders or entire political regimes may gain legitimacy in the eyes of the public as a consequence of effective disaster response, which governments may then use to expand the role of state agencies in the lives of affected populations.[3] In this sense, disasters have the potential to be "germinal moments" in state-society relations that catalyze movement toward "social citizenship" and greater citizen reliance on state care (Remes 2015, 8) and, in so doing, legitimize (or delegitimize) ruling regimes (Schneider and Hwang 2014).

Inversely, flawed governance of disasters and failure of state officials to support or coordinate relief—including by non-state actors—may also erode trust in the state and reinforce *informal* notions of citizenship beyond the state. Conceptualized by theorists as "social imaginaries," often unwritten idioms, practices, and logics of communal life provide a sense of what political philosopher Charles Taylor (2002, 92) terms "moral order," defined as "the rights and obligations that individuals have in regard to one another, even prior to or outside of the political bond." Central to collective ideals of the polity, political sociologist Rogers Brubaker argues that shared notions of unity and solidarity are administrated "by ordinary people in the course of everyday life, using tacit understandings of who belongs and who does not, of us and them" (Brubaker 2010, 65). These everyday practices and ideas of cultural and political belonging can form "idiom[s] of nationhood" (Brubaker 1992, 162) embraced by a majority or subgroups of the citizenry, and they shape the nature of people's attachment to the national polity. In moments of social rupture such as war or revolution, these idioms, or *informal* dimensions of citizenship and political belonging, are central to contestations over what nationhood means, who it includes, and what is in the interest of the polity.

The inefficacy of state aid during times of natural disaster, along with active attempts to evade responsibility, may deliberately or inadvertently lead to the outsourcing of relief efforts to private and charitable actors. Framed by notions of bounded community and contingent obligation, attempts by non-state social actors to mobilize after disasters can entrench ideas of belonging that run parallel to formal legal notions of political order and legal entitlement.[4] By reinforcing an insecure welfare regime in which the state assumes a minimal role and outsources significant responsibility to non-state responders, disasters can "expose the authorities' incompetence and neglect" while promoting "an intense feeling of national unity and purpose" among the citizenry (Seekins 2009, 731, 718). In so doing, disasters—whether in cyclonic or epidemic form—can mark "the social contours of life and death, belonging and exclusion, privilege and abjection within the body politic" (Chigudu 2020, 4).

These dynamics have played out repeatedly in post-1988 Myanmar in the wake of natural catastrophes, extending and transforming locally oriented practices of charity and idioms of social relatedness. What has been culturally inscribed is a privatized notion of the polity in which commercial elites, welfare groups, and ordinary people must enact moral obligation to the distantly desti-tute. These ideals and practices, generated partly at the direct encouragement of state officials, subsequently informed visions of civic and democratic progress during the decade of partial civilian rule and formed the basis for resistance fol-lowing the return to dictatorship in 2021.

Cyclone Nargis (2008) Extended the Local Welfare Regime

Non-state actors played a crucial role in providing relief in the immediate wake of Cyclone Nargis, one of the worst natural disasters in modern Asian history. In February 2008, a referendum to ratify Myanmar's military-drafted constitu-tion was announced by the ruling junta; the referendum would take place on 10 May 2008. The legal constitution was the fourth stage of the junta's regime-led Seven Step Roadmap to Discipline-Flourishing Democracy, announced in 2003 by General Khin Nyunt (Pedersen 2011, 53). It defines the legal and racial basis of formal citizenship (Cheesman 2017a), reserves 25 percent of seats in Parlia-ment for the military, and enshrines the armed forces' control of three major ministries essential to governance: Home Affairs, Border Affairs, and Defense. It was the basis for Myanmar's constitutional order throughout the decade of partial civilian rule between 2010 and 2021, and at time of writing it remained the military's favored political framework—even though Senior Commander Min Aung Hlaing blatantly violated it by illegally seizing power without the president's permission in February 2021 (Crouch 2021).

Back in 2008, in the days before the fraudulent referendum that ritually rati-fied the constitution, Myanmar was struck by a catastrophic cyclone. The storm made landfall a week before the referendum, on 2 May 2008, ripping through much of the Ayeyarwaddy Delta and coastal areas of Myanmar on the Bay of Bengal and the Andaman Sea. As with disasters throughout history, Cyclone Nargis *demonstrated* and *generated* social ties between citizens and the state that would markedly shape the trajectory of Myanmar's welfare regime in the years that followed.

Reluctant to publish international and domestic meteorological warnings about the impending disaster, government-run media outlets gave almost no cov-erage to the storm (Howe and Bang 2017, 64) and thus no evacuations took place (Lwin and Maung 2011, 240). Uninformed and ill-prepared, an estimated 50,000 people were killed during the storm's initial landfall as houses or struc-tures collapsed around them, buffeted by winds of up to 200 kilometers per hour. Cyclone Nargis and the devastation it wrought, compounded by the subsequent disruption of aid flows by the junta, ultimately took the lives of almost 140,000 people and inflicted catastrophic physical, emotional, and economic trauma on the affected communities.[5]

State officials were slow to respond in the days and weeks following landfall. Junta leaders were reluctant to acknowledge the devastation, and state newspapers thus initially gave limited coverage to the severity of the devastation and its effect on more than 2.4 million people (Seekins 2009, 717). Priority was instead given to the referendum on the 2008 Constitution held in the days that followed (Seekins 2009, 726).[6] Meanwhile, more than US$30 million in aid pledged by twenty-four countries in the week after landfall was initially rejected (Selth 2008, 387). Fearful that foreign powers, including the United States, "might use disaster relief efforts as cover for an invasion" or smuggle in weapons to arm the civilian population, foreign aid was not permitted until 6 May, and even then "only on the basis that [the junta] could control aid distribution" (Selth 2008, 392, 387). For the first two weeks after the storm's landfall, the responsibility for aid dispersal fell to the Ministry of Social Welfare, Relief, and Resettlement (MoSWRR), which had received 0.003 percent of the national budget that year and whose senior leadership were almost entirely on leave or overseas at the time the cyclone hit (Howe and Bang 2017, 67). In contrast, the manpower, resources, and expertise of the military, Myanmar's best resourced institution, were focused on running the referendum. As a result the military was not effectively enlisted in relief efforts until days following landfall, and even then only in a few isolated cases (Selth 2008, 387). It was not until two weeks after Cyclone Nargis made landfall that responsibility was transferred from the MSWRR to the much better funded and staffed Ministry of Finance (Howe and Bang 2017, 72). These factors combined meant that only a trickle of foreign aid arrived in Myanmar in the days following Nargis, with much of this aid remaining at Yangon's airport in Mingaladon for up to a week without being distributed.[7]

Welfare and religious groups around the country recognized that the junta was prioritizing progress on its "roadmap to discipline-flourishing democracy" over the survival of its citizens (Seekins 2009, 726). Thousands of people subsequently mobilized local welfare and religious and business networks—generated with junta encouragement during the 1990s and 2000s—to provide immediate aid to affected areas. What motivated those leading the outpouring of aid? How did they understand their obligations to the many distant people in need of assistance, and how much encouragement, direct or inadvertent, did they receive from state officials? Little ethnographic research was conducted with local aid groups following Cyclone Nargis, making a detailed understanding of their intentions difficult to discern. However, various studies conducted during and after the disaster highlight how idioms and mechanisms of moral duty were mobilized by non-state and market actors as the result of both government inaction and deliberate decisions to outsource the social response.

Notions of Local and Translocal Mutuality

Notions of social obligation that had been enacted locally throughout the 1990s and 2000s played an essential role in mobilizing emergency aid immediately following the landfall of Nargis (South 2012, 184–185). The 2008 report produced by the United Nations, the Association of Southeast Asian Nations (ASEAN), and Myanmar government situated these coping mechanisms as by-products of the state's weak role in delivering formal social protection after 1988:

> Despite, or perhaps because of, the many challenges of delta life, communities are relatively socially cohesive and have strong capacities for collective problem solving and decision-making . . . in the absence of a state or employer safety net, community members support each other in times of need, something particularly evident in their response to Nargis. (Tripartite Core Group 2008, 2–3).

The relative absence of state aid after Nargis only reinforced the need for communities to cultivate what political scientist Donald Seekins (2009, 732) terms as "horizontal solidarity as a survival strategy." Building on networks and activities of local charities that were encouraged to develop after 1988, new community-based groups were formed to distribute relief in devastated areas and coordinate long-term reconstruction efforts. A 2009 study conducted by the Center for Peace and Conflict Studies (CPCS), based on hundreds of interviews with local relief workers, quotes a sixty-year-old leader of a welfare group in the delta:

> I used my own money to buy 10 bags of rice, pack them and start distribution. Being in civil society, many people contacted me to assist with distribution of food and non-food items (blankets, etc.). Slowly other donations started coming in apart from rice including tinned food, canned fish, and cooking oil. We started distributing to the delta area first. . . . We could only start work with INGOs [international nongovernmental organizations] after one and a half months. (Interview in CPCS 2009, 169)

Skepticism of the state's capacity to redistribute fairly played a key role in the formation of many of these local groups. As the leader of a welfare team remarked, "We cannot guarantee that if the government becomes involved in distribution and construction that the donor funds will go to the most needy. The government ones will get priority" (interview in CPCS 2009, 172, 171).

Charity networks outside the delta also mobilized to respond to immediate relief and medium-term reconstruction needs.[8] Although state-controlled media provided little coverage of the devastation and aftermath of the cyclone, groups who had traveled to affected areas returned to Yangon with images and stories of the devastation and dire needs of the victims.[9] Some expressed grievances during the disaster that could not be uttered openly in public. Indeed, a few lay activists and entrepreneurs openly criticized the junta's failure to inform the people of impending catastrophe, a risky move in a context where political dissent was usually harshly suppressed (Brac de la Perriere 2010). The authorities restricted the efforts of activists who did not have transactional or personal relationships with local officials or were viewed by junta officials as politically linked to the leading resistance party, the National League for Democracy (NLD), and in some cases arrested and imprisoned them (Seekins 2009, 731).

The active role monks had been playing in collecting and redistributing wealth since the 1990s continued at a larger scale in the wake of Nargis. Religious authorities acted as nodes of information and material redistribution throughout the country. They also played an interpretive role in framing disaster relief work using Buddhist notions of "work for others" (*parahita*) and meritorious "giving" (*hlu dan*). Prominent monks such as Sitagu Sayadaw (see chapter 2) gave public sermons emphasizing that compassion toward cyclone-ravaged communities was meaningless without meaningful material action:

> Meditating in a room with the doors shut won't help the [cyclone] victims suffering over there. But most Burmese who traditionally believe in Theravada [Buddhism] don't appreciate the need for compassionate action. That is why I am talking about it to people every day. It is essential to make social merit [parahita] stronger.[10]

While acknowledging that the state response was abysmal, Sitagu argued that the disaster exposed the need for Buddhists to extend and strengthen notions of the "common good" achieved through individual moral action. "We can't blame the government alone," he told a journalist a few months after Nargis in 2008:

> People need to think about what others need and what they can do for them. Only then can they work together for the common good. . . . The suffering in Burma, the killing in Iraq and Afghanistan, the killing fields in Cambodia—all of these have come from selfishness. All disasters are driven by that selfishness [*atta seit*].[11]

The appeals to moral obligation made by religious actors, especially monks, helped stretch the idioms and mechanisms of non-state welfare from the neighborhood and township level to translocal people in need. The need for lay selflessness in the absence of other sources of aid was a recurring theme in interviews conducted by Jaquet and Walton (2013); interviewees emphasized that their "primary concern was to alleviate the suffering of people affected by the storm" who had received no state aid. Reflecting discourses evoked by Sitagu Sayadaw and other monks, volunteers framed their assistance as a "Buddhist duty, citing practices of *myitta* (loving-kindness) and *karuna* (compassion)" and "natural" emotional responses to the intense suffering of flood victims (Jaquet and Walton 2013, 7). Notions and mechanisms of social relatedness, often framed with Buddhist idioms that had formed the basis for localized reciprocity since the 1990s, helped bridge the social and physical distance between the public at large and activists, on the one hand, and those experiencing the misfortune of the cyclone, on the other, while also being limited by divides of geography, logistics, and social ties.[12]

Religious authorities and lay activists enlisted Christian and Buddhist concepts of "grace" and "merit" and emphasized the role of "charity" in these faiths. These philosophical alignments eased the path to partnerships between Buddhist organizations and local and international Christian nongovernmental organizations (NGOs) that otherwise would have been strange bedfellows (Jaquet and Walton 2013, 6). Many local appeal and aid groups also included volunteers from a range of religious and ethnic backgrounds residing in lowland areas. As the head of one group commented, "We worked with all groups from diverse religious and ethnic backgrounds. We are human beings and assist on that basis" (CPCS 2009, 170). Others described how faith communities began to collaborate at a grassroots level following the cyclone in ways they had not done before:

> Before Nargis . . . monasteries stuck to themselves, churches, et cetera, did their own thing. They would live in the same village but carry out their own separate activities. The mind says work together but the spirit says stay as a family. . . . For Cyclone Nargis, people went to the monasteries and the churches. As a result of the different religions of those affected, the spiritually formed civil society came to assist. (CPCS 2009, 152)

By imbuing concepts of abstract mutuality and obligation derived from religion into their appeals for aid, welfare activists and religious leaders helped bridge social distance between givers and receivers and secured contributions to relief efforts from people and groups across ethnic, class, and religious divides. These ideals helped extend the geographic boundaries of autocratic welfare capitalism from the local destitute to the distant needy.

Welfare Capitalism Resourced Relief Efforts

Consistent with the local dynamics of welfare outsourcing after 1988, Myanmar's commercial class played a significant role in religious, lay, and state relief efforts in the wake of Nargis. As a result of transactional and social ties developed between provincial businesspeople and junta officials throughout the 1990s and 2000s, many businesspeople engaged directly with the military authorities in ways that many other groups were not (Htet Aung 2009, 18–20). According to a report by the Irish NGO Trocaire, based on interviews with more than sixty businesspeople involved in disaster relief efforts, donors saw their contributions as an extension of the localized patronage they had been providing to funeral associations, orphanages, religious institutions, and other social organizations since the 1990s (Trocaire 2011, 20). Religious authorities encouraged their wealthy donors to enact moral obligations toward distant strangers in disaster areas.[13] Some locals contributed to initiatives led by businesspeople or associations while many others donated to monastic appeals (Jaquet and Walton 2013, 60–63. In addition to these religious networks, ethnic or religious minority businesspeople reported donating directly to identity-based groups to which they had already been donating since the year before, including ethnic associations (Trocaire 2011, 20). Numerous large international companies also supported relief efforts.[14]

Moral obligations to fictive kin were reinforced by the social licensing processes that the junta officials had been using to outsource state social obligations to businesspeople since the 1990s. According to a former director general of MoSWRR, senior members of the State Peace and Development Council (SPDC) eventually acknowledged the limitations of state "financial and technical capacities" in the wake of Nargis and had allocated "duties and responsibilities" to companies and businesspeople "with capability to perform relief operations" (interview with MSWRR DG, cited in Trocaire 2011, 21). Professional associations that had received junta support during the 1990s were also enlisted by senior ministers to assist with state relief and reconstruction efforts (Kyaw Yin Hlaing 2007a, 161–162). A degree of distance between these appeals and junta officials was maintained in order to mitigate perceptions that donations were given under implicit or explicit threat of financial or physical coercion. After initial encouragement by junta ministers, the national and provincial chambers of commerce as well as pharmaceutical and agricultural industry groups, for instance, led appeals themselves by establishing committees and assigning roles to specific companies "based on their respective competences" (Trocaire 2011, 22). They coordinated these distribution efforts, with the vast bulk of translocal aid mobilized in a largely "organic manner due to well established trust, long term relations and social networks" connecting religious, business, and local administrative networks (Trocaire 2011, 6).[15] Despite the minimal formal role of the junta within these appeals, some domestic businesspeople expressed frustration at needing to prop up the junta's ill-preparedness. A businessperson interviewed for the Trocaire study, for instance, argued: "The government should have money ready for disasters, and not ask businessmen for it when a catastrophe happens!" (interview in Trocaire 2011, 22). Yet he still donated to a non-state flood appeal led by a monk (Trocaire 2011, 22). Even entrepreneurs who contributed to junta-initiated appeals argued that their donations were free acts of generosity as they were given "under no influence, just to help" those affected by the disaster (interview in Trocaire 2011, 22).

Alongside the ratification of the formal 2008 Constitution, an *informal* or moral conception of citizenship was envisioned and popularized in response efforts that made it clear that businesspeople, volunteers, and religious authorities had an obligation to care for people and communities beyond their local area. The failure of the junta to adequately respond to Cyclone Nargis thus led non-state welfare, which had been largely centered on neighborhoods and townships until that point, to extend their ideals and practices to include distant people struck by dire misfortune. The absence of in-depth ethnographic accounts of relief work during Nargis, however, means we have a limited sense of how charitable and philanthropic actors who had become central to the welfare regime after 1988 stretched their notions of spiritual and civic obligation to mobilize aid for those left out of largely local efforts. The next section fills this gap by examining the idioms, performances, and rituals whereby obligations to people outside direct family and neighbors were stretched to provide support to flooded communities in lowland areas in the wake of Cyclone Komen in 2015 while excluding upland people mapped out of the lowland social imaginary.

Cyclone Komen (2015) Reinforced the Post-Socialist "Social"

Between 2008 and 2015, Myanmar military leaders initiated major changes to the political regime. After the 2008 Constitution was "ratified" in the week after Nargis, the November 2010 elections—considered rigged by most observers—led to the formation of a civilianized government helmed by former junta officers.[16] Aung San Suu Kyi was freed from house arrest, and restrictions on her NLD party were lifted ahead of by-elections in 2012 in which the party chose to compete. The new government, led by President Thein Sein, commenced a process of liberalization, abolishing prepublication censorship of the media and reducing the military's mediating role in the economy by issuing competitive tenders and auctions for most major commercial licenses and construction projects. Yet despite these changes, ideals and practices of non-state welfare played an essential role in recovery efforts when Cyclone Komen and four subsequent weather events occurred between late July and August 2015, resulting in some of the worst flooding in Myanmar since 2008, months ahead of national elections in November 2015.

The cyclone tore through the delta and Magway Region, dumping heavy rains over upper Myanmar and causing severe flooding and landslides that affected more than 1.6 million people (Howe and Bang 2017, 73). Twelve of fourteen states and regions were affected, and four of them were declared disaster zones by government officials, including Chin State, where severe landslides devastated numerous townships. The United Nations declared more than 117 people dead and over 800,000 acres of farmland unusable.[17]

Unlike what happened during Cyclone Nargis, the government and military quickly recognized the scale of the need created by the devastation. President Thein Sein immediately requested international aid and deployed civilian and military resources to assist in aid distribution. Building on interagency disaster planning and coordination established following Nargis, government agencies and international partners led round-the-clock situational monitoring throughout the flooding that followed the cyclone's landfall to support relief efforts.[18] Officials also delegated greater decision-making powers to local responders, state and non-state, and promptly approved the vast bulk of international visas within one day of application. Despite increased resourcing and coordination, evacuation efforts were undermined by miscommunication, and aid often failed to reach affected communities. In a rare public acknowledgment of fault, the commander of the Myanmar armed forces, Min Aung Hlaing, also issued an apology after soldiers dropped rations intended for affected communities from military helicopters into muddy floodwaters.[19] Yet, even with a more proactive government response, after Cyclone Komen non-state social actors again enlisted ideals and practices of reciprocity and obligation beyond the state to render aid. These groups evoked notions of social duty and intimacy with disaster victims throughout fundraising and aid dispersion efforts, exposing the boundaries of inclusion and exclusion in Myanmar's privatized welfare regime.[20]

Social Obligation Extends to Translocal Needy

Emotive engagement with the suffering inflicted by the cyclone was central to the outpouring of charitable assistance mobilized during the 2015 floods. The precipitous drop in the price of SIM cards to 1,500 kyat (around US$1.2) following the deregulation of the telecommunications sector in 2014 and subsequent expansion of 3G cellular network coverage prompted spontaneous and at times coordinated social action by individuals, communities, businesses, and government agencies. Whereas word of the devastation of Nargis spread slowly by word-of-mouth and religious authorities, by mid-2015, millions of Burmese people had web-enabled smartphones. Images of collapsed houses and rushing stormwaters were shared widely across the country, throughout the region, and around the world by diaspora networks in the hours and days following landfall (G. McCarthy 2018b).

As reports and images of the flooding and devastation circulated on Facebook, thousands of people in Yangon, Mandalay, and provincial towns across the country began local fundraising and relief efforts often connecting with these diaspora networks. Many joined roadside appeals through the traffic of Yangon, in some cases taking leave from work to lead the efforts and travel to flood-affected communities.[21] Minster for Information, Ye Htut, regularly shared photos from disaster zones to his official Facebook account, serving as a central node of information about the floods and relief efforts. Community organizations in affected areas also used Facebook to source donations from Yangon and overseas while keeping family and friends abroad informed about recovery efforts (Pursch et al. 2018, 38).

In Taungoo, exposure to images on Facebook of the devastation and the subsequent fundraising efforts in major cities inspired local groups to start relief campaigns of their own. Within days of Cyclone Komen, interlocutors began changing their profile pictures to images of flooded villages or emblazoned images of themselves with the Burmese or English words "Save Myanmar." Motley crews of students, civil servants, traders, and unemployed young people began traveling to markets, highway rest stops, and small towns around Taungoo to raise funds for flooded communities.

Many volunteers recounted feeling a sense of obligation to support the distant victims of the floods after seeing images on Facebook of the flooding or relief efforts elsewhere in the country. One nineteen-year-old university student who coordinated a fundraising group said he was moved to action when he encountered a photo of a student from Chin State weeping over her soaked schoolbooks on Facebook. "We all live in the same country," he said. "They are suffering from the flood, while we are not. . . . We have to give them help" (interview, 3 August 2015). Moved by these images, university students and welfare groups led sporadic appeals through markets, singing songs emphasizing the suffering wrought by the deluge and their shared kinship with the flood victims. Outside a small teashop, students gathered in front of a vinyl banner bearing an ominous image of a hand rising out of murky waters, clutching for help. A local musician lay a *lungyi* out on the ground for donations and proclaimed, "We all came here because we cannot look at our brothers and sisters and see them hurting. So we wrote these songs for them" (field notes, 3 August 2015). As shopkeepers and passersby began to congregate, they broke into a song titled "Give a Lift Up," which the students had written together the night before, accompanied by guitars and a tambourine:

> Help each other, give a helping hand.
> They are our friends who are living with hope of a helping hand.
> Waiting by gazing for people who will help them with pure intentions
> [*cedana*].
> Brother and sister, give a helping hand by having a sympathetic heart
> from seeing the other human beings.
> Beautify your history!
> Sacred brother with a wonderful heart, help the flood victim as much
> as you can!

Songs, poems, and speeches recited those days interspersed evocative depictions of suffering with claims of thick familial and relational obligation. The Pali-derived term for sufferer, *dukkha-theh*, recurred in speeches and songs, referencing the notion of misery or dissatisfaction, *dukkha*, used widely by both Buddhist monks and ordinary people to describe worldly pain for which the victim cannot be fairly blamed.[22] Echoing the symbolic mechanisms of what anthropologist Erica Bornstein (2012, 148) terms "liberal altruism," the emotional framing of distant sufferers as blameless social kin sought to inspire and obligate passersby to

FIGURE 3.1. A group of artists, students, and musicians gather in a local market to give speeches and sing songs to raise funds for flood victims. *Source*: Photo by author.

support relief efforts. One of the volunteers who helped lead the appeal was a civil servant in a local government department. She explained that these emotive appeals helped remind local people of their ties to others:

> Compared to Yangon, in Taungoo people feel distant and ignorant of the crisis. But only if it is really serious will the government take responsibility. So small charity groups and government departments like mine need to help raise money and provide assistance. (Interview, 3 August 2015)

Symbolic intimacy with victims cultivated through songs, speeches, and images of the devastation helped to extend the boundaries of obligations from neighbors and the local needy to distant others—and by framing these people as social kin, it encouraged others to respond and render aid through private and charitable appeals.

Personal Virtue Transforms Society

Fundraising appeals were underpinned by an emotive impulse to help others in the absence of state aid as much as by the spiritual and civic idea that supporting the destitute would alter the social consciousness (*parahita seit*) of donors and volunteers. A sense of energy, excitement, and even joy permeated discussions and songs as volunteers sat together at the back of crowded light trucks on lengthy rides to fundraising events. Animating these interactions was an assumption, informed by the failure of the state during Cyclone Nargis and flaws in the Thein Sein government's response after landfall of Cyclone Komen, that the government would not provide sufficient support to families whose lives were devastated by the deluge. Some openly discussed the state's role in exacerbating the disaster, sharing diagrams on social media that blamed logging by military-linked companies in Chin State for the landslides there (field notes, 4 August 2015). A local activist, who earlier that year helped lead a march for education reform, delivered a speech in a local market emphasizing that the failure of the state to care for the needy compelled ordinary people to respond to support their civic kin:

> They are our family, living in the highlands in Magway. They are flooded near the ocean in Ayeyarwaddy. . . . They are like our brothers and sisters; they are our relatives. If something is happening in our family, it is happening in our hearts. Our government doesn't give any help, so we are like fatherless children who need to help each other. We need to help them! (Field notes, 4 August 2015)

Many who engaged in social work for the first time during Cyclone Komen felt that organizing fundraising appeals and liaising with authorities transformed their own social and civic consciousness. A sense of energy, excitement, and joy mixed with slightly delirious exhaustion overcame volunteers following those days of fundraising. The companionship of those days extended their ideas of spiritual and civic obligation to others. It also led many to view grassroots charity and social work as a way to achieve social justice, even in the face of state social inaction. This vision of social change through private action was encouraged by NLD candidates at the November 2015 election, an ideological coherence that led many young volunteers to join the party's local campaign events in the months following the cyclone to sing the same songs of solidarity they had performed during the days of fundraising. However, not all activists who supported the NLD at the 2015 election signed up to a vision of privatized obligation in which ordinary people alone should provide for the distant needy.

Welfare Capitalist Critiques of Appeals

Some welfare activists disagreed with seeking small donations from provincial folks for flood appeals, despite the personal and societal transformations they felt such appeals were achieving. A prominent local welfare activist and vocal critic of the Myanmar military, Ko Tin Win, claimed that the town's *parahita* groups were already stretched thin dealing with local problems: "We have enough to do organizing blood donors, free funerals, and helping the sick here" (interview, 1 August 2015). He argued that fundraising efforts should collect from wealthy "cronies" in Yangon rather than "grassroots people":

> What they are doing now is all wrong. It is strange for ten people to drive to Kawlin [in Sagaing Region] or Pathein [in Ayeyarwaddy Region] and deliver only US$6,500 worth of stuff. The area is huge, so you are not going to make much impact.... In Yangon, there are cronies and rich people who donate in one day what we raise in one month here. In Taungoo, people are collecting money for the floods, but I think it is useless because the money we are raising is nothing! We should send people from the village to help [distribute and rebuild], but only raise money from the wealthy people; that is the most effective way. (Interview, 1 August 2015)

Implicit in his critique of inefficient fundraising and disaster response was an expansive vision of the social obligations of the wealthy. His critique did not reject the emotive framing of obligations to flood victims envisioned in these appeals. Nor did he present an alternative framing of the distant stranger in need: for example, as the "bearer of rights" to whom the state had an obligation to render aid, or as the "victims" of landslides caused by excessive commercial logging authorized by the military, as posts that circulated on Facebook had sought to do (field notes, 4 August 2015; 9 September 2015). Rather, the preference for fundraising from the wealthy reflected the enduring appeal of welfare capitalism and social licensing embedded during junta rule. He pointed out that tycoons such as Aung Ko Win, the chairman of Kanbawza Bank, had donated to relief efforts during Cyclone Nargis and were doing so again. Over tea, he pulled up a list from his Facebook feed of donations made to local appeals from prominent business-people and Burmese diaspora networks in Singapore as proof, he claimed, of the power of compassionate capitalism to deliver for the needy.[23]

Ko Tin Win's critique of local welfare groups exposed a widespread perception that relief efforts supported by commercial elites were more effective and efficient than delivering social welfare and public goods through grassroots initiatives. Yet his vision was not that the government should play a greater role in response, or even that grassroots volunteers should play a less important role in responding to need and distributing aid. Instead, experiences of governmental social absence and welfare outsourcing over decades, including during Nargis, led him and many other activists to assume that philanthropic tycoons had a crucial role to play in resourcing non-state relief efforts led by local volunteers in the context of assumed state social inaction. Despite being a vocal supporter of Aung San Suu Kyi and the NLD in the months preceding the 2015 elections (see chapter 5), Ko Tin Win's skepticism of state institutions only compounded his belief in the moral and practical superiority of non-state action.

Moral Recognition Determines Permissible Intermediaries

A perception that state actors were inefficient or corrupt led most welfare groups from central Myanmar to organize travel directly by truck and bus to the affected areas to disburse aid themselves. There were clear practical reasons for this approach, since it ensured that material aid reached the needy amid the logistic challenges of the floods. Numerous volunteers critiqued other groups who simply dropped their assistance in the most accessible town close to flooded areas but made no attempt to distribute it directly to the flood victims. They claimed that this "lazy" approach created more work for already overburdened volunteers, religious institutions, and government administrators in disaster zones. It also led many to doubt whether donations ever reached their intended beneficiaries, leading to a strong preference for delivering aid directly to victims and bypassing intermediaries wherever possible. Yet the concern about directness did not extend to the skepticism of *religious intermediaries*. Indeed, senior religious figures played a prominent role in coordinating and dispersing relief throughout the country. In order to prevent duplication of efforts among groups from Taungoo, for example, the Sayadaw (abbot) of a prominent pagoda complex hosted a meeting for the leaders of over thirty local appeals to discuss the best way to disperse aid around the country, mostly through monastic networks.

Beyond practical concerns about aid leakage or diversion, the reticence of private appeals to partner with state intermediaries was also motivated by a *moral* and *karmic* imperative to ensure that the virtuous actions of donors and volunteers would be appropriately recognized throughout aid dispersal. Throughout the weeks of flood fundraising and aid effort, I repeatedly heard cautionary rumors from volunteers that relief groups in some parts of Myanmar were labeling aid from external networks with their own names, claiming credit and thus good spiritual merit for the relief they had intermediated. "So, we will go to Monywa and give help directly," the leader of one welfare group concluded, emphasizing the importance of all donors being appropriately recognized for their contributions (field notes, 4 August 2015). The most severe moral outrage was reserved for government efforts to claim credit for aid. During the second week of the flood, images of sacks of rice contributed by international donors crudely rebranded with a single piece of A4 paper with the English and Myanmar text "Donated by Myanmar Government" went viral on Facebook. The sacks became the subject of ridicule among local Facebook groups and among welfare activists, who viewed them as further evidence of why any cooperation with the government in aid distribution was neither functionally nor morally beneficial: "They are trying to claim merit from the donations of others!" (field notes, 6 August 2015).[24]

As Erica Bornstein (2012, 65) observes in her ethnography of humanitarianism in New Delhi, stories and images framed as evidence of corruption serve a dual moral function: "They circulate suspicion in attempts to keep corruption at bay, and they express (more indirectly) suspicion of contemporary institutions." In the context of Myanmar's 2015 floods, rumors and stories questioning the capacity of the government to effectively redistribute aid in a materially and morally effective manner reinforced for activists the need for a direct, relational connection between donors, volunteers, and disaster victims. Reflecting these moral and practical imperatives, many groups enlisted techniques or technologies of attribution that had long been used in more localized practices of charitable giving to communicate a direct flow from giver to receiver. Bags of material assistance including clothes and rice were clearly branded with the name of the group, business, family, or individual who had made the donation. In cases where the contribution filled an entire box or bag, labels bore the name of the giver family or business. In other cases, the "parents and families" of a town from which rice or old clothes had been collected for victims were recognized collectively. Terms referring to Buddhist meritorious religious charity (*hlu dan*) were inscribed on these sacks, referencing a far broader social scope of beneficial charitable action than scholars described encountering during the 1950s and 1960s (see chapter 1). Most of these individual and collective gifts retained their attribution throughout the distribution process in the delta, until they were broken down into individual parcels for gifting to heads of households.

Parahita teams similarly were at pains to ensure that their social and moral intentions were exhibited throughout the distribution effort. T-shirts emblazoned with the name of our organization were disbursed to all volunteers before our departure to the delta, and printed vinyl banners bearing the organization and geographic details of our appeal in English and Burmese were affixed at the front of the minibus, trucks, and other vehicles in our convoy. As we drove ten or so hours to Hinthada via Yangon and Pathein (the capital of Ayeyarwaddy Region), we encountered hundreds of similar groups, some with more than ten vehicles in convoys and each with the same style of organizational vinyl banner tied to the front. The regional, organizational, and ideological diversity of these groups—from local ward appeals and NLD Youth Teams to a chapter of the Buddhist chauvinist group 969—was exhibited at the Shwemokhtaw pagoda in Pathein, where dozens of teams from across the country converged to pay homage to an iconic image of the Buddha while en route to or from flooded regions.

Directness Is Essential to Rituals of Verification

The urge for a direct connection between volunteers and the flood victims determined the way private aid was distributed to affected households. In each village where assistance was dispersed, volunteers and beneficiaries engaged in public spectacles recognizing the generosity of donors. On our second day of distribution in the delta, for instance, we canoed to a small monastery elevated on stilts above the floodwaters. The umbrella at the top of a nearby *zeti* (small pagoda) poked out from the water, a visual measure of the extent of the deluge. The simple one-room monastery was constructed on high wooden beams, which allowed us to enter using the top two wooden steps without having to wade through the water. Rather than unloading at the monastery and asking the abbot to coordinate dispersion, which would have allowed us to proceed directly to the next village and speed up distribution, we waited as the abbot broadcast an announcement from the loudspeaker system on the roof: "Donors have come. Donors from Taungoo have arrived. Please come and meet the generous-minded people and receive their help. One person from each household. Well done, well done, well done [to them]" (field notes, 8 August 2015). As the message echoed across the floodwaters, a nurse on our trip delicately checked the blood pressure of the monk, who was sitting on a wooden chair in the center of the room. A few minutes later, I glanced out of a nearby window to see dozens of villagers paddling small wooden canoes through the teeming rain toward the bustling monastery.

As villagers arrived, we opened the sacks of aid—which had been labeled with donors' names until that point—and apportioned handfuls of their contents into individual plastic bags. At the abbot's encouragement, a ritualized gift exchange then followed, with the head of every household posing for photos of them receiving assistance from members of our team (field notes, 8 August 2015). These photographs and exchanges continued for almost an hour and were repeated at another monastery and a school later that afternoon. Deeper, more meaningful interactions occurred between volunteers and recipients in these rituals than I saw in most local welfare initiatives. However, the material demands that recipients could make on donors were delimited both by the brevity of our presence and the potential shame that recipients might feel if they were seen to reject our gifts by requesting cash or other kinds of aid that may have been more helpful for them. Instead, all households received the same bags of aid, and no attempt was made to customize the contents to their specific needs. These interactions and the photo evidence they produced ritually verified for donors back in central Myanmar that funds raised and goods donated had reached their intended beneficiaries—a common practice in non-state humanitarian efforts (Bornstein 2012, 73). Given the widespread doubt about the effectiveness of government aid distribution during Nargis and the scandals regarding government agencies taking credit for the generosity of non-state actors, leaders of the relief efforts quickly loaded images of donation efforts and photos of ritualized giving to floor victims to their personal pages and to local news-oriented Facebook pages. This material aid, however, was neither sufficient relative to the scale of the devastation nor was it customized to the needs of recipients. Despite this, it was the directness of our welfare provision, and the removal of "untrustworthy" state agencies and intermediaries, that reinforced the credibility of non-state charitable welfare efforts relative to the experiences of inept government social response and corruption over decades of autocratic austerity. For participants in circuits of relief, however, sharing images of their service on social media was also aimed at propagating a broader notion of "social consciousness" (*parahita seit*) in which ordinary people and community groups willingly assumed social and redistributive obligations to others in need— near and far—regardless of the role of the state in welfare provision.

Charitable Action as Informal Citizenship

Participating in relief efforts reinforced a moral and civic ideal of non-state social responsibility for many volunteers. The ideological spillover from charity into sociopolitical thinking became evident as volunteers in our group boarded

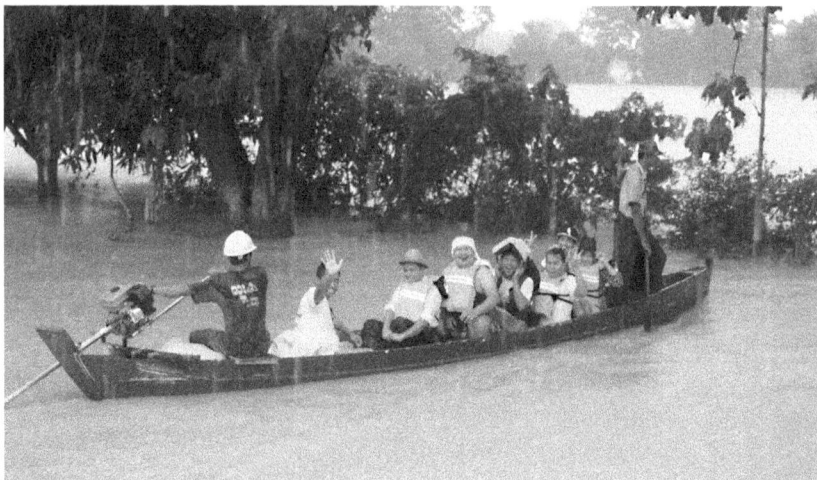

FIGURE 3.2.   A group of volunteers in a wood canoe travel to flooded villages with sacks of food and other aid. *Source*: Photo by author.

a bus bound for Yangon. As we drove out of the archway of the monastery compound in Hinthada, the leader of the team (who was the principal of a private school) passed the bus driver a CD. A few seconds later, a classic Burmese nationalist song blared from the speaker system (field notes, 12 August 2015). The song was about Aung San and the "martyrs" who were assassinated soon after independence, praising their valor in Myanmar's independence struggle against British rule. After the Buddhist ritual of recognition and social kinship (described earlier in this chapter), as we wound our way through the backstreets of Hinthada to commence our journey to central Myanmar via Yangon, everyone on the bus boisterously sang the chorus—symbolically connecting our labor of these past days to a lineage of struggle for the good of the nation.

A few hours later we pulled into the grounds of another monastery, this time a street away from the iconic Shwedagon pagoda in Yangon. We were met in the yard by a monk, an acquaintance of the school principal leading the trip. He directed us to an elevated timber house where mosquito nets and mats were laid out for us in a large shrine room. After bathing from a concrete well outside, I joined a group of university students paying homage at the nearby Shwedagon pagoda. Together, we walked the few hundred meters to the eastern entrance, crossing over Martyr's Road (*Azani Lan*) as we ascended the stairs to the top of the complex, a junction that symbolically echoed the nationalist song we had been singing hours earlier. On the warm mats, still damp from a late-afternoon monsoonal downpour, students joined the crowd giving thanks at the glistening pagoda. As I sat cross-legged and watched the spectacle, a second-year philosophy student with whom I had a chatted on long bus rides grabbed my hand and quietly led me to a small statue of the Buddha in one corner of the compound. A group of students from the trip were pouring water over the statue. He handed me a small silver cup, and I poured a few drops over the icon (field notes, 13 August 2015). Ritually pouring water with others in this manner following meritorious action is seen by many Burmese Buddhists as a means of creating bonds between individuals across lifetimes and increasing chances of reincarnation in social proximity to each other in subsequent lives (Kumada 2015). The pouring of water with other volunteers following days of "work for others" (*parahita*) exposed the complex ideas of relationality and obligation animating non-state relief efforts, including in the wake of disasters. The notions of social and civic duty mobilized those days helped extend localized reciprocity practices to the distant needy imagined as potentially reincarnated family. These leaps of social, ideational, and geographic distance were only possible because of the welfare capitalist ideals and institutions generated after 1988, which had only become further entrenched by 2015. Although notions of kinship certainly had a role in animating individual and collective action, these were not the ideas of biological kinship bound to a notion of "national races" that were used as the basis of indigeneity in Myanmar's 2008 Constitution. Rather, what was critical in determining whether or not the needy received aid from private flood relief appeals was whether they had been fully or contingently mapped into a social imaginary of reciprocity and mutuality heavily reliant on the contingencies of geography, logistics, and identity.

The Limits of the Post-Socialist Welfare Regime

Ideals and practices of civilian relief mobilized during disasters expose a social imaginary that runs parallel to legal definitions of political community embedded in the 2008 Constitution. Myanmar's 2008 Constitution, ratified through a fraudulent referendum, limits formal citizenship to those who can trace and document their lineage to "sons of the soil" (*taingyintha*) or the people who resided in Myanmar before the First Anglo-Burmese War in 1824. Defining belonging in this way links citizenship to the social, moral, and economic trauma wrought by British colonial rule, an approach that contrasts with independence constitution of 1947, in which commitment to a redistributive political community surpassed the idea of "national races." The 2008 Constitution embeds "national races" as the basis for full citizenship within the Republic of the Union of Myanmar, lending pseudo-legal legitimacy to the violent expulsion of minorities, particularly the Rohingya, labeled as "nonindigenous" by the military and civilian leaders alike.[25]

Alongside pernicious *formal* notions of social and political community enshrined in the 2008 Constitution, non-state relief efforts during disasters expose post-socialist notions of "society" and "duty" that are materially and symbolically limited. Consistent with the welfare regime generated during the 1990s, the state plays only a minor role in the post-socialist imaginary of informal citizenship. Instead, religious authorities, commercial elites, and welfare activists assume a central role in extending mechanisms and idioms of welfare capitalism beyond the geographic and social limits of local reciprocity. As ideas of empathy and obligation beyond kin are mobilized by private, charitable actors and even state officials, the moral bonds that determine the boundaries of social belonging or *informal* citizenship are exposed (Brubaker 2010, 65). Imagining the distant other as a member of a shared moral or social community and polity to whom one owes obligations relies on considerable symbolic, affective, and physical labor—the kind mobilized in the wake of recurrent disasters. Yet it also relies on resources raised from donors predisposed or emotively encouraged to see needy and destitute strangers as co-participants in a privatized polity in which citizens, rather than the state, have a leading role to play in achieving social justice. When relief workers or coordinators have few social ties to communities in need, or when the social distance generated by ethnic or religious difference frays these already-tenuous ties, the limits of protection and solidarity offered by non-state welfare is brutally exposed.

Hierarchies of Belonging Exacerbate Inequality

The civilian response to the upland landslides that followed Cyclone Komen in 2015 demonstrated the material and emotive boundaries of a welfare regime that was so reliant on private, non-state actors. The vast majority of flood assistance teams from Taungoo in 2015 provided aid largely to the lowland regions of Ayeyarwaddy, Bago, Magway, and Sagaing that were accessible by the main Yangon–Mandalay highway. In addition to being logistically accessible, communities in these areas that received support were largely ethnic Bamar and Buddhist who were socially and geographically proximate to most volunteers from central-east Myanmar. Indeed, decades of internal migration and trade within lowland areas made it easy to identify friends, family members, or monks who could help distribution efforts in these regions—networks that we called on repeatedly in our distribution efforts. Coupled with the common Buddhist framework of most volunteers, organizations, and recipient communities, these strong ties meant volunteers tended to view and describe people experiencing "misery" (*dukkha*) within a shared moral and even familial community of obligation and aid. However, when severe landslides hit the upland region of Kayah State northeast of Taungoo in the weeks after we returned from the delta, a hierarchy of belonging and obligation emerged that limited the material and metaphorical stretch of localized networks of reciprocity.

The leaders of Taungoo's largely Buddhist welfare groups were already physically, financially, and emotionally fatigued when word of severe landslides in mountainous parts of the Chin, Kayah, and Rakhine States began to trickle through volunteer networks. We already knew these regions had been hard hit before our visit to the delta. Yet none of the groups I followed had discussed traveling to predominantly non-Bamar or non-Buddhist areas at the time. There were certainly logistic constraints to delivering aid to these regions relative to the delta, which is fairly well connected by road to Yangon and the main national highway. Kayah and Chin States are poorly linked to the geographically proximate regions of lowland Myanmar. In addition, telecommunication coverage in these upland areas was spotty at the time of the 2015 floods, hampering coordination of logistics with potential local partners over the phone or on Facebook. Besides volunteer and donor fatigue, ethnic and religious differences served to extend social distance further as the population of both Chin and Kayah States are predominantly ethnic minority Christians. Without the dense social linkages connecting lowland areas to upland people, communities, and institutions, it became difficult to even imagine organizing local relief partnerships in these areas. Different ethnic and religious frameworks also meant that fundraising and relief campaigns based on obligations to potentially reincarnated kin in need would be harder to mobilize.

For all these reasons, once we returned from the delta to find images of devastation from landslides in Kayah State, there was little interest in our social media feeds from activists or volunteers to mobilize again. Logistic barriers, donor and volunteer fatigue, and social distance proved insurmountable for most lowland welfare groups to overcome, and thus none of the local networks in Taungoo raised funds or traveled up to devastated areas of Kayah State, which was just a few hours' drive away. With little non-state aid trickling in from lowland regions, communities in Kayah and Chin States relied on support from ethnic diaspora networks in Thailand and abroad, along with church networks of aid from Yangon and some limited state aid. Without substantive translocal or international aid, similarly remote regions of Rakhine State recovered much slower than other areas in the delta that were comparably affected.[26]

The partiality and contingency of non-state welfare provision can worsen the geographic and social exclusion of minorities, especially where state action to level out inequities is limited. For those mapped into the lowland welfare regime, non-state relief can, in the right circumstances, stretch vast distances to deliver support in the immediate wake of disaster. Yet there is an insecurity built into this reliance on non-state actors; that is because the needy have a limited right to demand specific support from donors but also because logistic, social, and emotive boundaries mean that preexisting social exclusion of ethno-religious minorities can be compounded at times of disaster. By further fragmenting already partial ideas of "nation" and "citizenship," the same social imaginary that leads non-state welfare actors to support (largely lowland) people in need can hollow out expectations that the state can and should play a role in achieving social justice, entrenching a fragmented and partial notion of the polity.

Exclusion from Welfare Regime Entrenches Regressive Politics

By reinforcing the perception that state institutions are unable to deliver social protection or relief, and by exacerbating divides of political belonging through biases (often unintended) in aid distribution, privatized welfare regimes of the kind that emerged in Myanmar after 1988 can undermine common imaginings of the "national" community (see, by way of comparison, Anderson 1991). As political scientist Evan Lieberman (2001, 2003) argues in his study of tax states in South Africa and Brazil, the boundaries and cleavages within the polity shape the capacity of states to justify raising revenue critical to delivering essential public goods for citizens. Lieberman argues that ideas of political community enshrined in the founding legal constitutions shape the long-run capacity of state agencies to tax citizens and deliver redistributive social programs in both states by affecting the willingness of upper classes to quasi-voluntarily cooperate with state social efforts through progressive income and corporate taxes (see also, Levi 1988).

It is easy to see how the formal fusing of national races and citizenship in Myanmar erodes notions of inclusive political community and polity, especially given the widespread domestic support for the military's campaign to expel hundreds of thousands of Rohingya Muslims in 2017. Yet alongside the 2008 Constitution, which cleaves political community according to problematic blood-based theories of racial belonging, also run bounded ideas of mutuality and obligation generated through the welfare work of private, non-state actors since the 1990s. As discussed in chapter 2, the outsourcing of responsibility from state to non-state providers left a legacy of businesspeople negotiating tax remissions with local officials in exchange for contributions made to both state and non-state social initiatives outside formal tax arrangements. These concessions, which continued throughout the decade of partial civilian rule between 2011 and 2021, provided the financing for an immense web of charitable, philanthropic, and non-state social providers to emerge across the country. These groups respond to diverse crises near and far playing a leading role in organizing local response efforts to socioeconomic and public health catastrophes, including during waves of COVID-19 infection in 2020 and 2021.[27] These networks, however, cannot be expected to deliver effective, inclusive, and consistent aid given the contingency of funding and the geographic, logistic, and identity barriers to inclusion. Indeed, the reliance of private welfare providers on donations makes them highly vulnerable to economic downturns as the capacity of businesspeople to donate a slice of their surplus profit is eroded by recurrent cycles of boom and bust caused by dramatic drops in global economic demand (as in the wake of COVID-19 in 2020) or by trade and financial crises caused by the collapse of domestic political order (as following the 2021 coup). These systemic vulnerabilities mean that in addition to eroding the fiscal capacity of the state to fund social initiatives more directly, the central role of non-state welfare actors in the welfare mix entrenches highly variable and often deeply unequal social outcomes that only compound discriminatory legal hierarchies of citizenship.

Civic Consequences of Social Outsourcing

The governance of disasters by successive post-1988 regimes established the social role of non-state actors and popularized a notion of social duty to distant others. As charitable and philanthropic networks stretched local ideals and practices of non-state welfare during catastrophes such as Cyclone Nargis in 2008 and Cyclone Komen in 2015, their physical and ideological labors integrate distant others in need into bounded and privatized visions of social, moral, and political community. Many genuinely do benefit from the material aid and solidarity that these efforts provide to the needy in the wake of disaster. Yet the emotional impulse that underpins the provision of non-state aid is also deeply contingent on the strength of the social and moral ties binding donor and recipient in the absence of state intermediation or action. For remote communities with few family, trade, or ethno-religious connections to lowland areas, the minimal role played by the state in providing timely and materially substantive aid can compound preexisting inequities generated both by discriminatory laws and the often inadvertent exclusion of minorities from flows of predominantly Bamar Buddhist charitable aid. A hierarchy of belonging parallel to the racial distinctions of citizenship enshrined in the 2008 Constitution is thus exposed, which determines who is included and excluded from private flows of aid.

The contingency and inequities inherent in a welfare regime so reliant on non-state relief has the potential to fragment ordinary people's commitment and attachment to notions of the polity in which the state plays an actively redistributive social role. The recurrent process of social outsourcing, especially during moments of disaster, can thereby create a vicious cycle: Cleavages of identity and exclusion within the polity weaken the appeal of paying tax to state institutions, undermining the long-run capacity of the state to raise revenue and thereby constraining the fiscal potential for government now and in the future to deliver more consistent social safety nets that level out social hierarchies. These factors combined result in outsourcing to non-state welfare actors remaining a favored option for diverse actors—elite and grassroots—over time, suppressing the state's capacity to engage in taxation and redistribution. Part 2 explores the path dependency of non-state welfare during Myanmar's decade of partial civilian rule between 2011 and 2020, examining how ideals of private welfare provision and mutuality, generated locally and expanded during disasters, found their way into visions of social progress and distributive justice enacted by parliamentarians, welfare activists, tycoons, and villagers alike.

Part 2
DEMOCRATIC WELFARE CAPITALISM

DEMOCRACY, FREEDOM, AND MORALITY

A few weeks after Myanmar's historic November 2015 national elections, images of the soon-to-be state counselor Aung San Suu Kyi crouching in grass to pick up trash went viral on Facebook. Following high-profile meetings with President Thein Sein, Senior General Min Aung Hlaing, and former dictator Than Shwe, Suu Kyi made one of her first public appearances since the poll collecting rubbish in her electorate in Yangon. After fifteen minutes flanked by jostling photographers—commanding them to "Help pick up the garbage!"—she disappeared back into her car and sped away.[1]

At Suu Kyi's orders, similar clean-ups were occurring across the country, led by local members of the National League for Democracy (NLD) and welfare groups. In Taungoo, volunteers from local welfare groups and private schools collected rubbish from the streets surrounding a government housing project next to the railway tracks that ran through the town. Above an entrance to the housing project, a large green signboard erected before the November 2015 election declared this a "Union Solidarity and Development Party village." That morning, though, an oversized dump truck backed slowly through the gate, driven by a member of a local welfare group wearing a red T-shirt emblazoned with Aung San Suu Kyi's image.

Within the housing project, in a small clearing surrounded by dilapidated wooden houses and filled with decades of accumulated domestic waste, women bathed and washed clothes from a well while chatting about the spectacle surrounding them. As the dump truck reversed into the clearing, incoming NLD parliamentarians fresh from their political clean sweep of the township a few weeks earlier helped a squatter move his makeshift bamboo hut out of the path of the incoming vehicle. A few minutes later, a bulldozer driven by an off-duty police officer began to scoop up piles of old rubbish, *lungyis* (sarongs), and even a writhing snake and dumped everything into the waiting truck.

The businessman who donated the industrial vehicles for the day stood proudly alongside the township development officer, watching as decades of accumulated filth was removed. Both took photos on their phones, loading them to Facebook as local residents looked on, bemused yet pleased. I asked the businessman, "Is this a political campaign [*siyoneyay*]?" He was wearing a "Titleist" golf cap to keep the sun off his face. "Oh no," he responded. "This is 'work for others' [*parahita*] . . . charity!" he responded. "Haven't you seen the photos of Daw Suu collecting rubbish in Yangon? This is the same. This is democracy!" he declared.

The mobilization of political and welfare activists in the name of local improvement and "democracy" that day provided an insight into how ideals and practices of non-state welfare, which became entrenched during junta rule, endured and evolved alongside political liberalization in 2011. As this chapter demonstrates, conceptualizations of reform and democracy enacted by my interlocutors envisioned charitable service and philanthropic donations as necessary given the inefficient and corrupt state bureaucracy. Yet beyond the practical appeal of delivering social outcomes with minimal state involvement, welfare and political activists also viewed their work as generating social and moral bonds necessary for a truly free democracy. In this chapter, I examine how this notion of "freedom" tied "democracy" to ideals and practices of non-state welfare that reinforce rather than undermine the precarity and socioeconomic inequality bequeathed by junta rule.

The chapter proceeds by highlighting how the ideal of "democracy," as enlisted by ethnic Bamar Buddhist political activists and enacted during the decade of partial civilian rule, framed moral conduct as a prerequisite for individual and societal liberation. It then explores the role of non-state welfare in ideas of liberty and democracy enacted by activists in their work and campaigns ahead of the 2015 election. *Practical* preferences for delivering aid and redistributing wealth through non-state practices are typically coupled with an *ideal* of non-state welfare generating and restoring the moral and civic bonds necessary for free, democratic society. By examining attempts to regulate the behavior of youth and businesspeople, especially Muslims, the chapter reveals how ideals and practices of non-state welfare were socially reproduced in ways that also entrenched new hierarchies of belonging. Ideals and practices of non-state social aid thus became a cornerstone of grassroots "democracy" during partial civilian rule, providing a normative justification for an insecure welfare regime and a social basis for minority exclusion.

Moral Democracy in Myanmar

How do ideals and practices of non-state welfare shape the practice and possibilities of electoral politics? A wide literature in political science and anthropology outlines the diverse forms the ideal of "democracy" often takes, depending on linguistic, cultural, and political contexts. Political scientist Frederick Schaffer's research in Senegal, for instance, highlights how prior experiences of self-help and informal social insurance shape the way Wolof-speaking peasants and poor urbanites understand "demokaraasi." These reciprocity mechanisms are often organized around social hierarchy and play essential roles in managing the risks of dire poverty within a community. Drawing on ordinary language interviews with Wolof speakers, Frederic Schaffer (2000, 64–65, 69–76) argues that these preexisting ideals and systems underpin political behavior—such as striking collective agreements to support the same candidate at election time in return for a local public project or simply to avoid discord—that more educated French-speaking Senegalese view as antithetical to "democracy."

Moral practices and ideas rooted in social life similarly shape the practice of democracy in Asia. Studies of Tibetan democracy advocates suggest that the emphasis that Tibetan Buddhism places on leaders possessing an "enlightened mind" generates logics of accountability that diverge from classical political theories, which charge the electorate with overseeing representatives (Frechette 2007, 99). Cambodian political actors and aid organizations similarly emphasize the "personal qualities" and relationship of candidates to various communities rather than the ideas and ideologies they represent (Baaz and Lilja 2014, 8). As a result, many democracy activists in these contexts view corruption as indicative of individual moral failings rather than the inadequacy of institutional frameworks. The focus on the moral virtue of leaders and their capacity to make decisions in the interests of the collective often undermines the scrutiny of representatives and institutions, allowing elites to make policies and laws that are not in the interests of ordinary voters (Rodan and Hughes 2014).

These studies highlight the need to examine the underlying "circumstance-attached logic" from which vernacular connotations of democracy emerge, especially in post-authoritarian contexts like Myanmar, where suppression of political opposition often bequeaths weak party organizations (Stokke, Khine Win, and Soe Myint Aung 2015). In these setting, parties must rely heavily on preexisting social ideals, practices, and organizations that endured or were generated during earlier regimes in order to build an electoral base. Interpretive methods such as ethnographic and interview methods provide the ideal means of studying the complex linkages that can emerge between these social institutions and vernacular concepts of "freedom" and "democracy." Visions of "democracy," as enacted by lowland activists in Myanmar, bear the imprint of the 1988 mass uprising and the junta's subsequent embrace of autocratic welfare capitalism. The major opposition party, the NLD, that formed during the mass movement against Ne Win's socialist junta in 1988 won a majority of votes in the subsequent 1990 election. After disregarding the results, the State Law and Order Restoration Council and (after 1997) the State Peace and Development Council (SLORC/SPDC) eviscerated NLD party structures through the concerted destruction of ties between local branches and the central executive committee. Activists labeled as democracy "agitators" by SLORC/SPDC representatives were regularly jailed, and local party branches were violently disbanded and suppressed. Suu Kyi herself was placed under house arrest for much of the 1990s and 2000s. As a result, many reform-minded people were deterred from formal affiliation both with the NLD and party politics more broadly. Despite authoritarian suppression, abstract and morally imbued notions of democracy circulated widely among elites and ordinary people after 1988 (Houtman 1999).

Moral conduct was central to elite notions of freedom and reform during this period. Aung San Suu Kyi's speeches, writings, and interviews throughout junta rule drew heavily on U Nu's earlier moral discourse of freedom in a democratic society (Wells 2018, 9–10). True "freedom" in Suu Kyi's formulation implied not just the end of oppression by junta officials but also "liberation from the wheel of *samsara* [cycle of rebirth]" for all people (Houtman 1999, 197). Suu Kyi's summarized the moral inflections of Bamar Buddhist conceptions of democracy in her essay *Freedom from Fear*, in which she referred to the Buddhist concept of the four "corruptions": desire, anger, ignorance, and fear. Fear, she argued, was the worst of these as it destroyed a sense of right and wrong, hindered efforts to reform the other three, and, in the case of Myanmar, had led the military to repress citizens and their aspirations for self-transformation and transcendence of this worldly suffering (Aung San Suu Kyi 1991, 181). Suu Kyi called for a "revolution of the spirit," framing liberation from the mundane and the concept of "I" (*atta*) as a prerequisite for "the attainment of democracy in the collective sense" (Walton 2012, 197). As she wrote in *Freedom from Fear*:

> A people who would build a nation in which strong, democratic institutions are firmly established as a guarantee against state-induced power must first learn to liberate their own minds from apathy and fear. . . . Free men are the oppressed who go on trying and who in the process make themselves fit to bear the responsibilities and to uphold the disciplines which will maintain a free society. (Aung San Suu Kyi 1991, 183)

High-profile monks popularized similarly moral concepts of democracy and freedom. Anthropologist Mikael Gravers recounts how monks involved in the

2007 Saffron Revolution argued that empowerment through "study" and "education" were essential prerequisites for democracy. Protesters defined their "knowledge" in opposition to the actions of the generals who "lacked knowledge" as they contravened the precepts of respect for life and were thus "*a-dhamma*, [or] anti-dhamma," meaning they were against the teachings of the Buddha (Gravers 2015, 10). Following the liberalization in 2011, these moral associations of democracy became the subject of public sermons by prominent monks. Political scientist Matthew Walton quotes Yangon monk Ashin Eindaga as conflating democracy with "Buddha's doctrine" at a public sermon in Yangon in 2012: "If you have *taya*, you will have democracy. . . . Democracy means acting in accordance with *taya*, having laws. [2] If society is fully endowed with *thila* (morality), won't it also be fully endowed with democracy?" (Eindaga, quoted in Walton 2016, 179).

The associations between political reform and moral conduct deeply imbued the thinking of Burmese democracy activists. Political scientist Tamas Wells conducted interviews with fifty democracy and civil society campaigners between 2012 and 2014. Many of them framed moral discipline as an essential attribute not just for democratic leaders but for societies more broadly. Echoing the notions of moral democracy endorsed by Suu Kyi, activists repeatedly emphasized that democracy required "the public, community and all parties [to] set aside obsessions and stand together" (Wells 2016, 163). Some activists went so far as to blame the "moral immaturity" of citizens for the longevity of dictatorship. The leader of the political organization 88 Generation Peace and Open Society, Min Ko Naing, argued that military rule endured for so long because "we understood that the government needed to go, but we did not understand society also needed to change" (quoted in Wells 2016, 153). To achieve true liberation, he argued that citizens needed to set aside their "own desires" and cultivate moral "discipline" (*si kan*) (quoted in Wells 2016, 153).[3] As Wells (2018, 4) concludes, for these ethnic Bamar Buddhist democracy activists, "liberty" was interpreted as "freedom for moral conduct, freedom to bear moral responsibilities, rather than freedom for the exercise of individual entitlements" from the state.

The notion that moral conduct can form the basis for genuine democracy allowed a range of activities, including welfare work, to accrue political value. By the transition to partial civilian rule in 2011, Matthew Walton (2016, 129) notes that the scope of political participation for Burmese Buddhists had widened to include not just electoral politics and civil society activities but also moral conduct in everyday life. These moral inflections of democracy provided a basis for a degree of ideological coherence within the democracy movement, unifying diverse networks from Buddhist revivalists to social welfare activists. Moralized, selfless connotations of "democracy" diffused widely in provincial areas of Myanmar, providing the normative basis for re-emergence of the party as an electoral force at the 2012 by-elections despite a weak party organization (Stokke et al. 2015, 25–27). Little noted in existing literature on the ideology and practice of democracy in Myanmar, however, is how visions of freedom, democracy, and reform enacted at a grassroots and elite level have integrated ideals and practices of non-state welfare entrenched during junta rule.

Democracy as "Work for Others"

In the months preceding the November 2015 election, charitable volunteers and their private donors had great difficulty balancing their "apolitical" welfare work with their partisan affiliations. At an organizational level, many township, ward, and village welfare groups in central Myanmar had diverse ties to political parties, often through their well-connected donors. Managers and volunteers of groups formed in the 1990s or early 2000s under the patronage of military-linked businesspeople mostly eschewed any kind of *organizational* affiliation with the NLD. The appearance of impartiality partly reflected the complex political positions of the patrons who remained the primary source of funds for many of these groups. As the 2015 township campaign manager of the Union Solidarity and Development Party (USDP) complained, the businesspeople who financed welfare initiatives during the 1990s and 2000s had shown themselves to be flexible political "animals" after the 2011 liberalization.[4] Most bankrolled the USDP campaign in 2010, before distancing themselves at the 2012 by-election and then openly supporting the NLD and other parties in 2015. Businesspeople such as Khin Maung Aye, the "Taungoo son" and chairman of CB Bank (discussed in chapter 2), had made contributions throughout the 1990s and 2000s to local social initiatives and financed and seconded staff to the township NLD campaign. Meanwhile, other locally oriented "town elders" supported non-USDP candidates, including from the National Development Party, a political vehicle established by one of President Thein Sein's former advisers.

Perhaps wary of the evolving partisan affiliations of their donors, I rarely encountered volunteers from welfare groups established before 2011 discussing politics within the bounds of their organizations. Beyond concerns about donor relations, this reticence may also have been a strategy of conflict avoidance with other volunteers. Otherwise jovial discussions could come to a grinding halt at the mere mention of the upcoming election, as occurred at a Buddhist merit-making event I attended a few months before the poll. One of the older volunteers I was sitting alongside loudly placed his spoon in the bowl and walked away from the table when I commented on the number of people in an NLD campaign parade that was passing by. A few weeks later, I encountered one of the other men from the table at a tea shop. Unprompted, he declared that he "admired Suu Kyi" and was planning to vote for the NLD, though he admitted that some of the other volunteers from his group—including the one who left when I commented on the parade—were supporters of either the USDP or the Buddhist chauvinist group Ma Ba Tha, which had openly criticized Suu Kyi throughout the campaign.[5]

Members of welfare groups formed after liberalization in 2011 more openly supported the NLD. One township-level association formed in 2012 and managed by activists imprisoned by the junta during the 1990s and 2000s was funded by monthly contributions from a diverse range of donors, including traders and civil servants. It also received regular contributions from the local veterans' association that had ties with several volunteers. Despite the group receiving funding from former military personnel, none of the volunteers made a secret of their support for the NLD in their discussions either in the office or at tea shops after shifts. Throughout 2015, Tin Win (pseudonym), a member of the group, ran one of the largest local Facebook groups in the township, sharing photos of welfare activities along with news articles that were often critical of President Thein Sein, the Tatmadaw, and the 2008 Constitution. Once the election campaign started in earnest in late August, I saw many volunteers with the group wearing vintage party T-shirts or covering their motorbikes in stickers with the campaign slogan "Time for Change." One volunteer, a former political prisoner, swapped a funeral hearse for a heavy industrial truck in the weeks before the election, driving an NLD float decked out with LED lights and a troupe of musicians around the town. Others took on roles as ward or village campaign managers and coordinators helping to organize rallies, run village visits, or train polling-station observers. Yet while on duty, they studiously differentiated their welfare work from political "campaigning" (*siyoneyay*). There were no NLD materials posted in the office or disbursed while on shift. Volunteers with whom I worked were particularly conscious not to wear party clothing or symbols while on duty as they explained that "work for others" (*parahita*) should not be conducted for political benefit.

In addition to the partisan affiliations of welfare organizations, political parties themselves offered a range of social services to potential voters. The USDP, for instance, provided low-interest loans to families in wards and villages around Taungoo, creating relationships of financial dependence with poor households in the months prior to the poll. The nexus between welfare and politics in the USDP reflected the long-running role of the party's predecessor organization, the Union Solidarity and Development Association (USDA), in providing social benefits to card-carrying members throughout the 1990s and 2000s. In contrast, the NLD similarly began providing its own charitable social services after the easing of restrictions on the party in 2011. In central Myanmar, the most consistently provided form of support linked to Suu Kyi was a program providing free tutoring to help high school students pass their matriculation exams. The initiative was linked to the Daw Khin Kyi Foundation, a philanthropic organization established and chaired by Aung San Suu Kyi in honor of her mother, which received foreign funds after 2012 to run education programs around the country.[6] The classes I visited in central Myanmar were attended by a dozen or more young people from urban wards of the township and were delivered by a volunteer teacher in a compound across the road from the house of a NLD parliamentarian. Smaller, more informal social services were also coordinated by local NLD networks. These were evident during the funeral processions of local party elders and supporters, for which the township committee coordinated light trucks, "free of charge" on an ad hoc basis, sporting "National League for Democracy" vinyl banners and flags. Donations were also collected for the family of deceased members by party representatives, in order to help allay the costs of funeral rituals, an adaptation of the same rotating funds structure described in chapter 2. Comparative research suggests that political loyalty is rarely "created" or "bought" in the gifts and welfare assistance provided by parties, such as free tutoring or funeral aid. As Javier Auyero (2000) argues in his political ethnography of Peronism in late-twentieth century Argentina, political loyalty instead emerges from the way the language and ideas surrounding these regular interactions and material exchanges help generate and reinforce a political identity of solidarity enacted in everyday life. In a similar manner, volunteers with NLD-affiliated social groups rhetorically framed the help they provided as an expression of a moral ideal of "democracy," which they contrasted with the "selfishness" and "coercion" exhibited by the USDA and junta officials during military rule.

The association of charitable aid as a critique of dictatorship recurred at campaign events in the months leading to the November 2015 poll. At numerous village and ward gatherings that I attended, candidates for office and local NLD sympathizers swapped stories about the egregious abuses they had experienced at the hands of state officials and police during the 1990s and 2000s. As candidates and local elders recounted these narratives, a hushed lull would descend on the shrine rooms or living areas in which we were all crammed. Juxtaposed with the solemnity of these accounts of suffering, however, were narratives of candidates or other well-intentioned people circumventing authorities who had tried to suppress or disrupt small acts of kindness or works of local improvement. One female candidate and former schoolteacher recounted the callousness of being dispatched by her superiors to a rural school without notice, transportation, or accommodation—only to meet local villagers with "goodwill" (*cedana*) who offered her food and lodging. The story elicited knowing cheers from assembled supporters and ended with a comparison between the immorality of the military junta's Union Solidarity and Development Party and the generosity both of "the people" (*pyithu ludu*) and of the NLD more broadly: "Working only for your own interest is not politics. Politics is working for the interests of all, with loving kindness (*myitta*)," she declared at the end of her story. The charitable practices and idioms of obligation through which populations in lowland areas pooled risk during the 1990s and 2000s were here positioned as not just socially virtuous but also reflective of a *democratic* ideal of reciprocity beyond the state. The USDP was not depicted as a generous yet repressive "philanthropic ogre," as political vehicles in one-party regimes sometimes present themselves (Magaloni and Kricheli 2010). Rather, the political identity of democracy activists was defined with reference to the selflessness and "loving kindness" exhibited by Aung San Suu Kyi and the millions of people who engaged in non-state welfare work during the 1990s and 2000s.

Realizing the depth of popular distain for Myanmar's military-linked party, as well as the positive moral connotations of charitable giving, local representatives of the USDP personally financed their own social welfare initiatives. Beyond the special benefits offered and promised to members or supporters of the local USDP, throughout 2015 the upper-house member of Parliament for Taungoo helped finance a clinic that provided free treatment and vitamins for pregnant women every Monday. The clinic was run from an office at the back of a charitable aged-care home (described in chapter 2) and was staffed through a rotation of six doctors, some of whom had direct ties to the USDP through their partners or family. The clinics also received institutional support from administrative staff seconded from the USDP who greeted patients on arrival and disbursed various vitamins after their consultation.

Staff members at the clinic were careful not to be seen to exploit the help provided for electoral benefit. During the weeks that I attended the clinic between June and November 2015, there was no obvious symbolic or discursive attempt to link treatment and vitamins provided to the generosity of either the parliamentarian or the USDP. The iconic USDP lion symbol was nowhere to be seen within the clinic, and most patients interviewed over the weeks I attended had little or no direct contact with party representatives before receiving treatment, most having been referred there by doctors at the general hospital. In the months preceding the 2015 election, I visited the homes of eight of the women I met during visits to the clinic every fortnight to learn about welfare and reciprocity practices within their ward or village. None had been contacted by the administrator of the clinic by the time of the election to convince them to vote for USDP candidates. Few even knew the clinic was patronized by the USDP parliamentarian at all. After the November 2015 election in which the NLD won over 80 percent of seats across Myanmar, I visited the women again—a number of whom had recently given birth. Two had preexisting ties to the USDP through their husbands and reported having voted for USDP candidates; two women said they did not vote because they were traveling and "were not interested" in the election; and the other four voted for the NLD. All recognized the generosity of the "donor" or "master of the gift" (*ah-lushin*) who supported the clinic, even though seven out of eight of the women could not recall his name.

As a vote-buying strategy, the clinic was a dismal failure. In electoral terms, the NLD won a robust majority in practically every urban ward and rural village in the township in 2015. Yet rather than serving solely as a mechanism of clientelism, the clinic must instead be read as an attempt by the patron-parliamentarian to signal his enactment of a notion of moral and political community defined by ostensibly "self-less" and charitable provision of aid to the needy or destitute. Ideals and practices of non-state welfare were here associated with a notion of democracy to which the USDP candidate sought to align himself. Similarly, volunteers who offered their time or resources at charitable welfare initiatives linked to political parties including the USDP and NLD framed their social work as helping to build a political community that restored and rejuvenated individual and societal moral virtues—rather than simply being motivated by electoral self-interest. The need to strike a careful balance between assisting with the care of pregnant women and maintaining a veneer of partisan neutrality denoted the degree to which ideals of non-state welfare came to merge with visions of freedom and democracy during the decade of partial civilian rule.

Practical Preferences for Non-State Welfare

Many interlocutors in welfare groups and parties alike felt that providing welfare and public goods through non-state mechanisms was often more practical than waiting for state action. Having experienced decades of informal taxation and social austerity from the state, few expected that a change in government would dramatically expand social service or public goods provision. Indeed, stories about the ineptitude and inefficiency of bureaucracy were a recurring feature of political discussions at the tea shops I attended nightly throughout 2015. Attendees would share Facebook video clips and news articles and discuss the latest local or national political events with mouths full of betel nut. In making meaning of the various stories they encountered involving government officials, the expression *thabu-oo*—literally, a loofa-like gourd evocatively translated in Burmese dictionaries as "Gordian knot"—was frequently used to describe Myanmar's bureaucracy. Municipal and commercial taxation often came in for particular criticism, both because of the concessionary tax rates that many said were granted to wealthy businesspeople and the opacity of how state officials spent revenues. As a close interlocutor opined after he had paid land tax on his

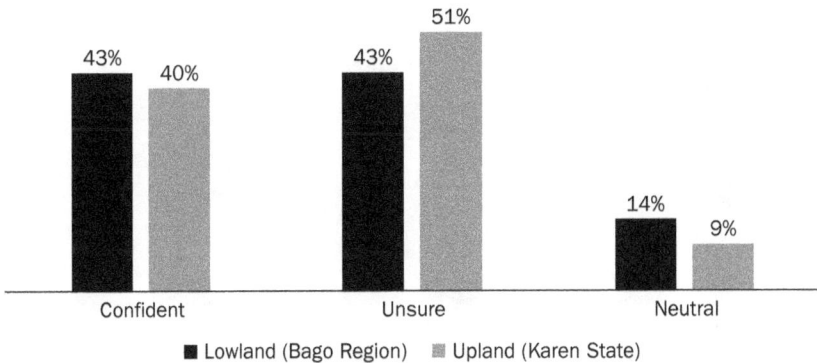

FIGURE 4.1. As many people in lowland areas were unsure of where the taxes they paid went as were confident, with even greater doubt among upland respondents (percentage by township). *Source*: Author survey, March 2016.

plantation: "I have no idea where the tax goes—it probably goes into the pockets of the generals!"

Perceptions of government taxation and bureaucracy as circuitous and ineffective were borne out in the household survey fielded in the weeks before Suu Kyi's NLD took power in 2016. The survey of 1,000 households in central-east Myanmar asked respondents how confident they were that taxes paid reached where they were needed most or if they thought funds were used inefficiently or corruptly.[7] Despite user fees comprising a sizable proportion of overall formal tax burden, in lowland areas the sample was perfectly split: As many people were confident (43 percent) as were unsure (43.4 percent) of how taxes paid were redistributed (see figure 4.1). Upland areas that experienced conflict throughout the 1990s and 2000s until a 2012 ceasefire were even more uncertain (51.3 percent).

These perceptions of tax were in stark contrast to trust in donations, for which almost double the proportion of lowland respondents (81 percent) said they felt confident their contribution to non-state actors reached where they were needed most (see figure 4.2). This pattern was starkest in sample areas of Thandaungyi in Karen State, where 89 percent said they were confident about the way non-state institutions used their donations. These strong levels of trust likely derive from the role religious authorities play in intermediation, along with the persistent focus in non-state circuits of aid on intentionality and directness, both of which strengthen perceptions that contributions are spiritually meritorious.[8] These factors help explain the incredible magnitude of money, goods, and time that both rich and poor households contribute to non-state welfare institutions, a pattern of reliance only further compounded by the expansive role played by charitable networks in the COVID-19 pandemic response and in sustaining local resistance following the 2021 coup.

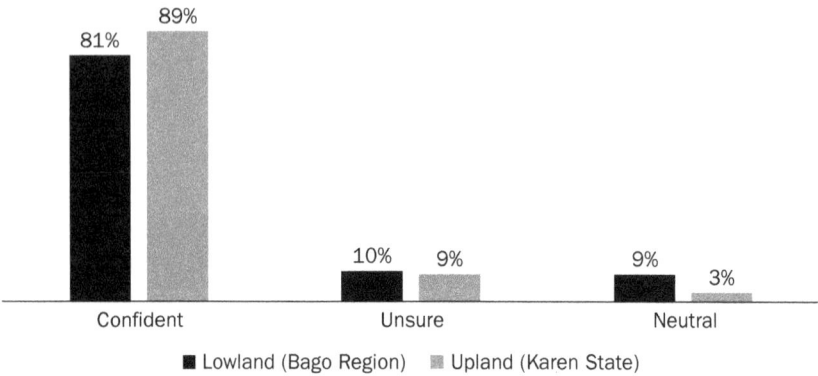

FIGURE 4.2. People expressed high levels of confidence that donations reached where they are needed most (over 80 percent among upland and lowland respondents). *Source*: Author survey, March 2016.

Non-State Welfare Rejuvenates Free, Moral Community

Beyond practical preferences, the visions of reform conjured by both NLD and welfare activists in 2015 and 2016 often framed non-state welfare as morally superior to inefficient state social action. Discussion about the corruption of government social initiatives relative to more direct and accountable non-state welfare often blended with the idea that charitable and philanthropic provision of care and public goods regenerated civic and moral bonds that had been weakened by decades of autocracy and earlier colonial rule. In this sense, many welfare activists saw charitable and philanthropic aid to the needy as practically helpful while also forming the normative basis for a genuinely "democratic" Myanmar. The ideational appeal of non-state welfare was exposed a few months before the 2015 elections, when the blood centrifuge machine at the general hospital broke down, disrupting the literal and metaphorical flow of life-giving aid during the peak of dengue-fever season.

Dengue outbreaks are common during Myanmar's rainy season between May and October and often claim the lives of infants, the elderly, and the infirm whose weak immune systems are unable to fight off the virus. Platelet transfusions, which require large numbers of blood donations processed by centrifuges, have become a common form of treatment for dengue fever.[9] For these reasons, when the only blood centrifuge machine at Taungoo General Hospital broke down in June 2015, the peak of dengue outbreak, news spread quickly. After local activist Tin Win had posted the machine's failure to the 5,000-member Facebook page of a township welfare group, fears about patients dying from a lack of transfusion prompted demands for immediate action. "Can we lease a new one?" one commenter suggested. "How long till they can fix it?" asked another. When group members heard that the South Korean manufacturer had refused to send out a replacement immediately, instead requesting a recall and inspection through the Ministry of Health, a former doctor turned gold merchant intervened in the Facebook thread: "Of course the government machine broke! Let's just buy a new one. Lives can't wait!" The comment was interpreted by other users as imputing corruption in the purchase of the machinery and received supportive likes and comments from other followers of the group. One Facebook user extended the criticism of the government, arguing that the "shit-bag" (*cheetoh*) centrifuge machine was probably purchased by one of the many former military officers who had recently been appointed to senior positions in the Ministry of Health in the final months of the Thein Sein administration, sparking widespread backlash from civilian staff.[10] A fundraising appeal was promptly commenced by the gold merchant and other local welfare activists. Within a week, over US$20,000 had been raised, predominantly from local businesspeople and prominent "town elders," and a new machine was ordered from Yangon within days.

Alongside concern about restoring the flow of blood donations, activists viewed their fundraising effort as enacting a societal ideal crucial to building a more democratic Myanmar. Over tea during the week of fundraising, Tin Win explained the larger societal and political stakes of the centrifuge appeal. Tin Win was a prominent supporter of the Buddhist chauvinist group Ma Ba Tha along with the NLD. Beyond the individual patients—who he claimed would die if they did not receive a platelet transfusion—Tin Win argued that the appeal and the donations of blood it enabled helped to enact an abstract notion of "social consciousness" (*parahita seit*) essential for a truly "free" society. "If Myanmar is to become a true democracy (*tageh demokrasi*)," he said, "we need more people to have goodwill [and] good intentions (*cedana*) and be willing to give their blood for others to reduce suffering (*dukkha*) among our kin (*amyo*)."

The notion of *amyo*, conceived here as beneficiaries of non-state aid including blood donations, is an amorphous term used flexibly in Burmese to refer to family, type, race, or nation. It forms one of the three founding concepts of the Buddhist chauvinist group Ma Ba Tha, which the organization itself interpreted and translated variously as the "Patriotic Association of Myanmar" as well as the "Organization for the Protection of National Race and Religion" until it was banned by state Buddhist authorities in mid-2017 during the term of the NLD government.[11] The associations Tin Win made between blood, kinship, and democracy conjured a racialized conception of polity, potentially rooted in the state ideology of "national races" or "sons of the soil" (*taingyintha*) embedded in the 2008 Constitution (Holliday 2014). Other interlocutors, usually those affiliated with Ma Ba Tha or the

USDP, used the term *amyo* in a similar manner—often in the context of quoting sermons by the Buddhist monk Wirathu that suggested Suu Kyi and the NLD would grant special opportunities and positions of power to Muslims over and above real sons of the soil. Yet, for Tin Win and many other activists, true democracy was not solely defined by racial purity. Rather, his ideal of democracy was also practice-oriented, a notion of the body politic generated by ordinary people giving aid and even blood to those in need through institutions of non-state welfare.

Though grassroots ideals of democracy in this framing rely heavily on compassionate-minded donors and volunteers taking social action, government agencies still had some (minimal) role to play. At the "thank you" ceremony held to recognize the contributions of donors to the centrifuge, for instance, both nurses and doctors praised the ideal of a democratic form of welfare capitalism as practically and morally necessary to improve public welfare. Even though the Ministry of Health had received a larger slice of the overall national budget after 2011, allowing more patients to be treated at subsidized government rather than private hospitals, they argued that charitable and philanthropic groups were needed to supplement meager state funding. In a speech to a crowd of fifty or so local businesspeople, social activists, and civil servants, the hospital's head doctor reminded wealthy donors assembled that they had a special role to play in enabling ordinary people to engage in charity. After handing each of the donors a certificate of appreciation and posing for photos, the doctor then espoused his vision for a new hospital building, to be funded entirely by local philanthropists and a grassroots donations campaign. Contrasting the incompetency of government initiatives with the efficiency and directness of fundraising for the blood centrifuge, he declared: "We can't wait for the government. . . . The people need these facilities now."

A practical critique of the state, rooted in past experience of government austerity, can easily morph into a normative endorsement of non-state public goods provision. As the former doctor turned gold merchant who helped coordinate the blood centrifuge appeal explained as he thanked donors: "No matter how much the government does, it will never be enough. Your contribution is vital!" Their donations were crucial, he explained, not just because they filled a specific need within the hospital and health system. Rather, they were also enacting a social ideal in which compassionate-minded people willfully provided for those in need, generating the bonds necessary for a truly free political community. Rather than charitable and philanthropic aid being a temporary salve for a malfunctioning system, this vision of "democracy" depicted non-state welfare as delivering for the needy while simultaneously reweaving social fabric fragmented by centuries of autocratic and colonial rule.

Non-State Welfare Restores Precolonial Glory

Many lowland welfare and political activists idealize a period before colonial and military rule that, they claim, was a golden age for Burma morally and civically. In this imagining, achieving democracy relies as much on military withdrawal from politics as it does ordinary citizens regenerating moral and political bonds through their daily social practices and moral conduct. Notions of reform as restoration of a glorious past were often evoked at NLD campaign events in the months before the 2015 election, echoing elite ideas of reform (*pyu pyin*) as renovation or rejuvenation to return to the glorious monarchical periods before colonial rule (Candier 2011; Wells 2016, 170). As the NLD candidate for the upper house of Parliament emphasized at an election rally:

> The people have suffered such terrible things since the 1962 coup. Because of the coup people were tortured; this country became so terrible, and the education system was destroyed. People no longer have morals or shame. This is not the mistake of people; it is the fault of the government! If you really want change, we need to leave this system and mind (*seit*) behind.

Embedded in the idea that society was better before autocratic ritualization of morality is the notion that societal and political reform requires the restoration of practices inherent to Burmese culture and people (Wells 2021, chap. 6). In contrast to earlier Buddhist conceptions of monarchical "just rule" and "reform," however, in this version the sovereign ruler no longer bears the primary obligation and duty for care of subjects. Instead, the sovereign's subjects assume them in the monarch's stead, inverting the traditional expectations of the role of kings and imposing them on the citizenry.[12] The notion of democratic rejuvenation enacted by local welfare and political activists thus framed institutions of welfare capitalism generated during junta rule as crucial to civic revival after decades of autocracy, highlighting how ideals of social outsourcing were moralized and normalized in ways that ensured their durability in a more democratic context.

Democratic Welfare Capitalism Outsources Social Obligation

Embedded in the project of restoring precolonial glory is a configuration of freedom, rights, and responsibilities that deviates substantively from liberal notions of the social contract. Rather than democracy implying a system "in which every individual is the bearer of potentially enforceable rights," freedom in this moral configuration relies on relationality with people and groups to whom one both belongs and is obligated.[13] This ethos of social obligation, often framed in familial terms, has found its way into the heart of welfare discourse in diverse countries as governments have sought to redefine and retrench their direct role in the provision of social services. Encouragement provided to non-state groups to fill the breach left by state social absence or retrenchment is often made on the basis of naturalized metaphors of private or charitable aid being expressions of familial or fraternal love and obligation. As anthropologist Andrea Muehlebach (2012, 69) recounts from research on austerity in northern Italy, instead of relying on the state for welfare assistance, these discourses endorse a configuration of social responsibility in which citizens should "attach themselves to each other, through spontaneous, sympathetic acts," rather than to the state. Claims of belonging or entitlement from the state are thus replaced with kinship-imbued welfare and philanthropy framed as "a form of life-blood swirling through the arteries of a human body . . . having a total reach that the state could never have" (Muehlebach 2012, 69). Given these natural obligations, the suffering and need experienced by citizens in precarious welfare regimes compels action not by the state but by generous and compassionate members of the community, especially virtuous capitalists.

Ideals of non-state welfare and formal institutional constraints combined to shape the way activists prioritize and imagine what should be changed in Myanmar's junta-drafted 2008 Constitution during the decade of partial civilian rule. Wells (2016, 220–221) conducted extensive interviews with democracy activists after 2011 and found that while many had clear ideas about what should be altered or added in the constitution, social affairs and economic injustice were largely absent from these priorities. He recounts attending a regional meeting of NLD activists held during the campaign for constitutional reform coordinated in 2013 by party leaders and civil society partners. Attendees at the session were asked to sign in at the door and commit themselves to amendment of the 2008 Constitution. The sections cited for reform in the petition, however, were articles related to the provision of parliamentary seats to the armed forces, the processes of constitutional amendment, and restrictions on eligibility for the Myanmar presidency that precluded Suu Kyi's ascendance to the role. Wells (2016, 220) recounts that in the subsequent "discussion" session, all attendees were encouraged to vocally repeat three times a commitment to *amending* the constitution—a practice that he argues likely masked potential disagreements about the diverse democratic aspirations of loyalists present. This ritual affirming the NLD's amendment priorities was followed by a collective rejection of entirely rewriting the document, a proposition that reflected the formal party position.

Many of the welfare and political activists who coordinated the blood centrifuge appeal shared similar opinions and priorities about reform of the 2008 Constitution. They often emphasized the need for amending specific sections, mostly regarding reducing the number of military seats in the legislature or ensuring ci-vilian control over the bureaucracy. At a betel-nut shop in the weeks following the November 2015 elections, I asked a number of prominent welfare and political activists what else should be changed—specifically, whether they felt the constitu-tion provides adequate redress to those dispossessed or abused during junta rule or whether it sufficiently commits the state to providing for the welfare of citizens. One of the assembled activists, a volunteer with a charitable health clinic run out of a nearby monastery and a vocal critic of the Thein Sein government on Face-book, responded: "There are lots of problems with the 2008 Constitution. But we need to have priorities about what to change and who our real opponent is."

The commitment of NLD activists to amending only very specific sections of the 2008 Constitution could be seen as reflecting a realpolitik approach by the party's leadership. In a context where military dominance is institutionally and economically entrenched, it is unsurprising that activists were reluctant to chal-lenge the impunity established within the 2008 Constitution for past and ongo-ing military atrocities or economic injustices such as land grabs. However, notwithstanding these strategic choices, we also see how the role of non-state actors in the post-1988 welfare regime shapes the imaginable and desirable pos-sibilities of democratic reform. The constitutional reform "discussion" recounted by Wells (2016), along with scenes such as the ceremony for the donors of the blood centrifuge machine organized by avowed democracy and welfare activ-ists, share a common emphasis on the moral value of unity to achieving both reform and restoration of political order. For welfare activists, ideals of unity and obligation enacted through private and charitable redistribution are the very ba-sis of free moral and political community and define how good and virtuous democratic citizenship is enacted and envisioned within the polity. Consequently, rather than seeking to constitutionally enshrine rights to redress for past injus-tices or clarify the redistributive obligations of the state to citizens, democracy activists instead seek to revitalize civic and moral bonds of reciprocity and ob-ligations, using non-state welfare as the path to freedom.

Economic elites play an essential role in this privatized vision of the demo-cratic polity as their donations and patronage are crucial to grassroots social ac-tion. Perhaps as a result, few of my interlocutors envisioned legal reforms that would expand taxation of these same elites or their businesses in order to finance state-mediated social expenditure. In framing the parameters of imaginable re-forms and the role of non-state actors in social mutuality, these welfare capital-ist ideals constrain the possibilities of state social action. Instead, activists who call for reforming aspects of the constitution simultaneously seek to revitalize and entrench ideals and practices of non-state welfare, endorsing them as both practically and normatively preferable to state social action.

Social Discipline as Normative Reproduction

The ideal of a welfare regime in which charitable, philanthropic, and private actors take a leading role in social aid recurred in initiatives and debates that aimed to form the moral behaviors of youth and socially sanction business-people accused of being "stingy" and "immoral"—especially Muslims whose religious identity often saw them treated prejudicially.

Social activists throughout my fieldwork often urged youths to do charitable work as a way of strengthening democracy. Teachers, monks, and volunteers at welfare groups and Dhamma schools frequently disparaged young people for failing to appreciate and enact social virtues by helping others. Anxiety about the moral degradation of young people is hardly a new phenomenon in Myanmar. Indeed, contemporary expressions and discourses of moral regeneration echo anxieties that run back to the independence movements of the colonial period.[14] Many Buddhists, especially monks, now blame what they claim has been the erosion of social morality on the ritualization of Buddhism during military rule. They urge the need to strengthen practices of reciprocity if "democracy" is to endure.

Sunday Dhamma schools, often inspired by the example of Christian Sunday schools, were a key forum where interlocutors sought to morally cultivate youth after the transition to partial civilian rule. After 2011, thousands of Dhamma schools proliferated across the country to teach Buddhist ethics to students (Walton 2014). The lay founders and volunteers that run Dhamma schools sought to revive knowledge and engagement with Buddhist teachings during a period of political reform and transition.[15] At the time of my research in Taungoo, over ten weekly Dhamma schools were run each week, all but one established after 2011. Every Sunday afternoon throughout my fieldwork, close to 2,000 children from around the township would flock to these monasteries. Activities typically included sermons given by monks along with lessons and songs about the life of the Buddha and the virtues he preached. Classes were taught by volunteer teachers, and meals were occasionally provided by local donors. The abbot of the largest Dhamma school in Taungoo argued that these largely layperson-led efforts were essential to rejuvenating moral virtue after decades of autocratic rule: "Until 1962, they had Dhamma education in schools, so people kept their morality and ethics. But military rule shook people's morality. All children know how to do now is pray. They don't know anything about the Buddha's life and what he taught," he argued. So what did these classes, aimed at reviving the normative basis for a free society, actually teach?

Echoing the concerns of prospective parliamentarians, the Dhamma school classes that I sat in and the teaching materials that I reviewed emphasized the need to regenerate bonds of national moral community through acts of social service. The concept of *parahita* was repeatedly mentioned unprompted in interviews with volunteer teachers, senior monks, and school committee members when I asked them about practices that rejuvenated moral community. The concept of giving (*dana*) also recurred in the "objectives" listed at the top of textbooks developed by the national Dhamma School Foundation: (i) to educate youth about the Buddha; (ii) to instill discipline and virtues of charity (*dana*) and "social consciousness" (*parahita seit*); and (iii) to protect "national religion" (*amyo batha thathana*). Ideals and practices of mutuality beyond family (*amyo*) were here directly tied to a conception of the polity.[16] Dhamma schools and youth social education thus served to embed the idea of non-state welfare as a crucial basis for rejuvenating morality and political culture after decades of autocratic turpitude.

Activists closely linked to the local NLD campaign shared many of the same concerns about the moral degeneracy of youth. Many sent their own children to Dhamma schools on a weekly basis, and some were involved as committee members. Throughout 2015 and 2016, I followed a group of NLD-aligned welfare activists, businesspeople, and civil servants who had established a trash-collection initiative aimed at cleaning up the town and cultivating "social consciousness" (*parahita seit*) among local youth. The group met weekly and was run by principals from local private schools, which had proliferated following their legalization in late 2011. Local businesses provided funds for printing T-shirts that bore a Burmese slogan for "Let's take responsibility for trash!" The group proved popular among private school parents. As the initiative grew, the piles of rubbish and organic waste collected each week fast became too much for the light truck/school bus that was initially used for the cleanup. In early 2015, the coordinators of the group approached contacts in the municipal government and asked them to "work together" by providing a truck each week to dispose of collected rubbish. The municipal officers were keen to support the initiative, seeing it as a chance to develop and beautify the town. The collaboration between the garbage-collection initiative led by middle-class NLD activists and the municipal office quickly flourished, eventually leading to the postelection cleanup described in the opening vignette to this chapter.

I joined the group on many Sunday afternoons throughout 2015 and 2016, often at the invitation of activists I had been lunching or drinking with at tea shops or restaurants right before. After finishing our drinks, we would stop off at pharmacy shops to pick up plastic gloves before helping pick up garbage and weeds—usually from an overgrown field in the center of the town that surrounded the local soccer stadium. Under the supervision of teachers and these local activists, students who were ten to sixteen years old would wander around the oval—often in sweltering afternoon heat—muddying their gloves and clothes as they cleared small patches of the oval. The mostly male adults chatted as they helped gather the piles of plastic or organic waste into small bins, occasionally encouraging the students. Yet mostly the group of thirty or so students scampered around on their own, dumping armfuls of gathered waste into the back of a municipal pickup truck. Their sweaty work was an uphill battle: miniscule progress was made in these weekly sessions of an hour or so, and the garbage usually more than replaced itself from week to week as attendees at soccer games or other events held at the adjacent stadium regularly dumped bottles, wrappers, and other waste throughout the clearing.

Despite the initiative barely making a dint in the garbage strewn across the field, the organizers saw their efforts as encouraging youth to "take responsibility" for the ubiquitous litter that plagues Myanmar's urban centers.[17] Other local activists critiqued the effort, saying it absolved the municipal government of their own responsibility and was an ineffective use of young people's time and labor. Apart from confronting the litter problem, however, the coordinators of the initiative also saw themselves as rejuvenating an idealized notion of civic and moral community by cultivating the "social consciousness" of local youth. Offering labor for the benefit of others (*parahita*) through even small acts such as rubbish collection strengthened the bonds of a selfless, compassionate community that they saw as foundational for a genuinely free democracy.

The civic value of these acts became evident in the week proceeding Martyrs' Day in mid-2015. A national holiday that commemorates the assassination of General Aung San and his cabinet on 19 July 1947, local NLD activists organized a public memorial to mark the day at an obelisk located in the center of the oval cleaned weekly by the local youths. The Sunday before, I had joined the group in a collection that was far larger than usual. A cross-section of activists, including local business associates of Khin Maung Aye, the prominent national tycoon, fell to their knees to clear rubbish and weeds from around the obelisk before they swept and prepared the ground for the planned memorial service. Thousands of people attended a somber commemoration there a few days later. Local NLD dignitaries, representatives from the municipal office, as well as dozens of nurses, police, and firefighters all assembled wearing their respective uniforms. Hundreds of students from Taungoo University also joined, many wearing black clothes to mark the solemnity of the event. NLD flags were flown on bamboo poles around the obelisk, symbolizing the lineage between General Aung San and the party. At the exact moment that the assassination occurred, a horn was blown and a minute of silence was observed. Monks then led a procession to the obelisk, followed in train by local party and government dignitaries, along with university students and youths who bowed deeply and placed flowers and other offerings around the obelisk.

The participation of young people in the memorial ceremony highlighted how practical concerns are intimately tied to conceptions of democratic citizenship in ways that help expand the social boundaries of "politics." The same NLD activist who helped organize the cleanup event a few days earlier clearly distinguished the enactment of "democratic" virtues from partisan campaigning. He emphasized that the participation of local youth wasn't aimed at "mak[ing] political advantage" for the NLD but simply at encouraging them "to give respect to martyrs and to remember them." He differentiated the memorial from a Martyrs' Day public feast (*studithar*) hosted by a USDP candidate later that day, which he and other NLD activists considered to be a gratuitous attempt to influence voters ahead of the election. He argued that the students who cleaned the obelisk and oval ahead of the event were "learning from the example of the martyrs" by engaging in parahita—work for others. An abbot at a nearby monastery made a similar connection, arguing that "parahita in the original sense meant working for others and for the benefit of 'sons of the nation/kind' (*amyotha*)." Following this logic, he explained that if small actions such as garbage collection were done selflessly, then anyone could draw merit while strengthening "the nation" (*amyo*). Seen through this symbolic lens, small acts of service are comparable to the sacrifice made by Myanmar's independence "martyrs" and have become, for some, synonymous with ideas of freedom and democracy.

While young people have a clear role in these efforts, so too do comparatively affluent elites. Local democracy activists often praised businesspeople who provided financial or in-kind support such as dump trucks and excavation machines to local improvements efforts. The valorization of philanthropy as crucial to democracy highlights that the moral ideal of freedom enacted by local welfare groups relies as much on ordinary people as it does on generous commercial elites. A culture of civic philanthropy, which cultivates youth and socially praises generous businesspeople, is crucial to sustaining the moral economy on which Myanmar's outsourced welfare regime is predicated. When the affluent do not comply with the generosity expected of them by post-1988 welfare capitalism, activists and communities seek ways to correct their behavior. Yet publicly accusing them of stinginess—either because of immorality or illiquidity—can markedly effect their reputations and possibly damage commercial interests. Uttering such claims against businesspeople from the majority community is thus socially awkward and risky, given that it may sour relations with people who may be crucial sources of funding and material support in the future. In these contexts, already-excluded ethnic and religious minorities can serve as useful scapegoats for asocial and immoral behaviors seen to pose a threat to non-state welfare systems that are understood as crucial to the normative bonds of a democratic polity.

Islamophobia Regulates All Commercial Elites

Throughout my fieldwork, I often encountered accusations about the unwilling-ness of commercial elites to contribute to charitable welfare causes. Local activists frequently labeled local businesspeople, especially those who did not share their political commitments to the NLD, as "stingy" (*gatsayne*) or "self-interested" (*atta seit*). A local hotelier and landowner who supported the Thein Sein–affiliated Na-tional Democratic Party at the 2015 election, for instance, was criticized on social media by NLD-aligned welfare volunteers for refusing to contribute to local road improvement initiatives nearby one of his properties. The same activists also re-peatedly claimed that some businessmen only supported parahita teams so that they could engage in morally or legally questionable activities, such as evading tax bills or avoiding responsibility for commercial accidents that harmed people or the environment. In questioning the moral intentions of the affluent, these stories had the potential to damage the reputation of individual businesspeople. Yet they also served the broader social function of publicly declaring the obligations *all* busi-nesspeople were expected to fulfill in a democratic society. While I often heard stories about self-interested Buddhist commercial elites, the most common and vicious condemnations of selfish profiteering I encountered usually involved Mus-lim entrepreneurs.

Anti-Muslim sentiment, especially the notion of Islam as a threat to both per-sonal and societal security, was ubiquitous across Myanmar in the years follow-ing the 2011 liberalization (Schissler, Walton and Phyu Phyu Thi et al. 2015). In 2012, communal violence broke out in Rakhine State following the rape of a Bud-dhist woman by a group of Muslim men. Stories detailing rape, violence, and forced conversions by Muslim men not just in Rakhine State or in Myanmar but across the globe were frequently retold and disseminated by prominent monks, by ordinary people, and by senior members of President Thein Sein's adminis-tration in old and new media.[18] These narratives commonly depicted Muslims as disproportionately wealthy relative to ordinary Burmese people. Though such stories were often factually inaccurate or entirely fabricated, this genre recurred repeatedly during efforts to incite intercommunal violence throughout the coun-try and were central to fueling riots in Meiktila in 2013 and Mandalay in 2014. Stories of Muslims as stingy and immoral businesspeople also recurred in a pub-lic signature campaign led by the Buddhist chauvinist group Ma Ba Tha, which demanded the government take legislative action to "protect race and religion."[19] The subsequent laws, and the stereotype of the wealthy, violent, and immoral Muslim man associated with them, served to embed moral distinctions, socially and legally, between Buddhists and Muslims. Throughout 2015 and 2016, I conducted dozens of lengthy interviews about the "race and religion" laws with Buddhist revivalists, many of whom were also vociferous NLD supporters.

The character of the sexually aggressive Muslim man who weakens the moral fabric of democracy by forcing his Buddhist wife and children to convert to Islam was a recurring motif in these stories.[20] Embedded in this depiction of imbalanced domestic relations were also thinly veiled grievances regarding the perceived economic dominance of Muslims and their apparent "stinginess" to people outside their community during the 1990s and 2000s (G. McCarthy 2016b: 323). In retelling stories, activists often elevated the religious identity of key figures. Muslims in particular were depicted as having experienced the suffering of the SLORC/SPDC period differently from Buddhists. By virtue of their commercial success, these stories claimed, Muslims were able to avoid the worst excesses of authoritarian rule by bribing government officials for special deals and citizenship papers. Alternatively, it was claimed that Muslims would use "terrorism" (*agyanbyet-hmu*) to force others into submission using practices of high-interest lending or brute force (G. McCarthy and Menager 2017b).[21] Post-socialist Buddhist notions of merit and virtue recurred in stories of violence, coercion, or cow-slaughter recounted by welfare volunteers. These narratives often concluded with the moralistic claim, expressed by local activist Tin Win, that "the major problem with Muslims is that they believe killing gives merit (*kutho*). That's the meaning of jihad" (fieldnotes, 10 July 2015). Such stories and their interpretation helped to reframe memories of past and present interactions of local collaboration across religious lines, rendering Muslims the scapegoats for decades of junta-era suffering in place of the central role played by military leaders and their tycoon allies in the economic and social suffering experienced by many during junta rule (G. McCarthy 2016b, 323–324; G. McCarthy and Menager 2017a, b).

In addition to projecting blame and creating hierarchies of suffering, however, narratives about Muslims also served to clarify and reinforce the obligations of businesspeople in a more democratic Myanmar. The gossip, stories, or cautionary tales repeated in interviews or at betel-nut shops often depicted Muslims as commercially successful yet morally bankrupt. In contrast to Buddhists, who my interlocutors claimed would demonstrate their compassionate intentions (*cedana*) through donations and "work for others," Muslims were described as "stingy" (*gatsayne*), greedy, and aggressive businesspeople who offered help "only to their own kind (*lumyo*)" (G. McCarthy 2018a). "Look at my Facebook—there are so many images of Buddhists helping each other," a Buddhist Ma Ba Tha member exclaimed while showing me images of a local ward road project that had appeared in his feed. "I never see Muslims making donations or volunteering for these kinds of projects," he claimed.[22] Such claims were not empirically true: Muslim respondents to the household survey conducted in March 2016 contributed to public goods and to people of other religions at a disproportionately higher rate, on average, than Buddhist and Christian respondents.[23] As often occurs with the extension of new liberties, however, social outgroups—in this case Muslims—became a socially acceptable mechanism through which the obligations of new social, political, and economic liberties were thought through and clarified (McGovern 2015).

Thinly veiled behind these religious and racial prejudices is a welfare capitalist ideal of democracy. Provision of welfare and redistribution of wealth through charity and philanthropy is depicted as practically and morally superior to state-led social development initiatives. Narratives featuring allegedly wealthy Muslims refusing to share their wealth, though factually inaccurate and deeply prejudicial, thus serve multiple functions. First, they bolster hierarchies of moral virtue in which religious identity defines the extent of generosity an individual feels toward those in need; second, they project blame for past abuses and ongoing economic vulnerability onto Muslims rather than the junta and military-linked businesspeople who built fortunes through land expropriation and monopolies during post-socialist dictatorship (G. McCarthy and Menager 2017a, b); and third, they define the terms of morally respectable capitalism and thereby regulate the social behavior of economic elites more broadly. State institutions are not the primary bearers of social responsibility to the needy. Rather, in this imaginary, moral bonds generated through practices of service and charitable giving are the basis for material aid and the civic fabric of the polity. Ethnic and religious minorities become the social mechanism through which the limits of these obligations can be openly discussed, further exacerbating cleavages and eroding notions of "national" political community on which more progressive state-led redistribution might otherwise be based (E. Lieberman 2001). Beyond "rigged" formal political institutions, ideals and practices of nonstate welfare that exacerbate insecurity and inequality may thus endure from one regime to another because they fulfill needs both of beneficiaries and seemingly well-intentioned people who contribute to and help to manage these private systems of risk-pooling and reciprocity.

Social Outsourcing as Political Ideal

Ideals and practices of non-state welfare found their way into the heart of grassroots democratic aspirations during Myanmar's decade of partial civilian rule. Past experiences of state inefficiency and corruption underpinned a preference, on behalf of many reform-minded activists, to deliver social aid and local improvement through charity and philanthropy rather than state institutions. Practical concerns were reinforced by a normative ideal of freedom in which bonds of reciprocity generated through charity and philanthropy helped to revive the kind of "free" political community that was imagined as existing before autocratic rule and colonization. For activists who subscribed to this worldview, taxing the wealth of economic elites and expanding the state's role in the welfare mix were low political priorities. Instead, beyond removing the military's direct role in politics, their agenda largely focused on ensuring that ordinary citizens and wealthy people alike assumed the moral obligations necessary for a free society—tensions often born out in scapegoating of ethnic and religious minorities as "stingy" for being insufficiently philanthropic.

Non-state actors, especially commercial elites, thus have a crucial role to play in generating the social bonds of the welfare capitalist polity. The affluent are obliged to give away a portion of their wealth to support non-state initiatives that sustain Myanmar's outsourced welfare regime. Yet the centrality of the already-affluent to private mechanisms of public goods provision leaves plenty of scope for questionable military-linked tycoons to defend their wealth from taxation or regulation. Focusing on the gifting practices of a prominent tycoon, chapter 5 explores how philanthropy can make economic elites so central to public goods and civic culture that state social action to resolve economic injustices and inequities becomes undesirable, even for elected representatives.

PHILANTHROPY AND WEALTH DEFENSE

In August 2017, Myanmar's elected government led by Aung San Suu Kyi faced one of the biggest challenges of its tenure in office. With resentment intensifying among the Rohingya people about the restrictions placed on their lives and movement in Myanmar's western Rakhine State, an armed group calling itself the Arakan Rohingya Salvation Army (ARSA) staged a series of fatal raids on Myanmar police and military outposts. The attacks claimed the lives of twelve state security personnel. The Myanmar military and cooperative vigilantes responded with "clearance operations" in which hundreds of villages were burned and civilians were executed across northern Rakhine State. Within weeks, the onslaught prompted more than 750,000 people, almost all Rohingya, to flee to Bangladesh.

The actions of army personnel, and the civilian government's defense of them as "counterterrorism," drew widespread condemnation of both the Tatmadaw and Suu Kyi herself from the international community. By November 2017, the Rohingya crisis was the subject of a United Nations Security Council resolution calling on the government "to end the use of excessive military force." While some global leaders claimed Suu Kyi was hamstrung by the military's autonomy of civilians enshrined in the 2008 Constitution, others called for her to be stripped of her Nobel Peace Prize for inaction in the face of war crimes.

In Myanmar, the perception among many following the Tatmadaw atrocities in Rakhine State was that their country was under siege from the global community. An image of Suu Kyi and a dove with the caption "I stand with Aung San Suu Kyi" went viral on Myanmar Facebook as international outcry intensified. Many Burmese interlocutors I spoke with felt that the State Counsellor and

Myanmar's democratic leaders more broadly were being unfairly held responsible for what they regardless viewed as the legitimate actions of the Tatmadaw in response to "terrorist" attacks by ARSA.

In the weeks that followed the military offensive in Rakhine State, Myanmar's civilian leaders scrambled to contain the diplomatic, geopolitical, and reputational damage of the crisis. By mid-October 2017, an economics and peace adviser to Suu Kyi, Professor Aung Tun Thet, conceived a public-private partnership to show the Myanmar government's commitment to the return of Rohingya refugees from Bangladesh. The entity, called the Union Enterprise for Humanitarian Assistance, Resettlement, and Development (UEHRD) and chaired by State Counsellor Suu Kyi herself, promised to deliver employment opportunities, infrastructure, and housing in villages destroyed by Tatmadaw "clearance operations" through partnerships between corporate interests and agencies of the Myanmar government.

Charitable donations immediately began to pour into UEHRD from local organizations, state and regional government authorities, companies, and some international actors. In November 2017, Suu Kyi herself hosted a "giving ceremony" in Naypyitaw where she posed for photos surrounded by tycoons from the old regime who had pledged close to US$13.5 million to UEHRD activities.[1]

The initiative exposed the critical role tycoons and economic elites played in addressing social challenges during Myanmar's decade of partial civilian rule. Yet the reliance even of state agencies on donations from and partnerships with commercial elites also raises a broader question increasingly central to comparative research on the politics of inequality: What do business interests gain by assuming social obligations through philanthropy, including contributions to the state? Are they able to exert influence over policymaking through public giving, and if so, how?

These questions are particularly pertinent as Myanmar's tycoons engaged in increasingly public-facing philanthropy throughout the decade of partial civilian rule (Ford, Gillan, and Thein 2016; Menager 2017; Prasse-Freeman and Phyo Win Latt 2018). In contrast to the obligatory giving that helped tycoons accumulate business empires during the 1990s and 2000s, the personalized and civic orientation of elite giving between 2011 and 2021 resembled philanthropy in more established democracies like the United States and Europe.[2] Scholars and activists who debate the merits and pitfalls of foundations, endowments, and private donations in these contexts have begun to identify mechanisms whereby such contributions distort public debate and political decision making in ways that perpetuate inequality (Roy 2014; Reich 2016; Skocpol 2016; Nickel 2018; Reich 2018; Giridharadas 2019). Yet beyond the confines of industrialized democracies, where discourses and logics of corporate social responsibility are increasingly ubiquitous, dynamics of public giving by economic elites have received comparatively little attention. Examining these patterns during the period of partial civilian governance in Myanmar thus exposes how the appeal of social outsourcing to diverse interests can allow tycoons to use donations to projects of public and civic value to justify and defend their wealth from redistributive action by the state.

This chapter examines the evolution of philanthropic networks and practices of one of Myanmar's most prominent tycoons throughout the decade of partial civilian rule. Dynamics of patronage and philanthropy at the local, provincial, and national level show that in resource-poor contexts, tycoons who renounce a small percentage of their wealth to support social, political, and cultural causes and projects generate bonds of imbalanced mutual dependence with political elites and the public at large. By rendering themselves crucial to social aid and public goods provision, established elites can cultivate a publicly rooted form of social license that erodes the commitment and capacity of state officials, including elected representatives, to redress economic injustice and structurally address the social needs of citizens through governmental action. The structural dominance granted to tycoons by public philanthropy, and the impediments their influence presents to state-led social action, help to explain why outsourcing social functions to private and non-state actors continues across successive regimes.

The chapter starts by focusing on the chairman of one of Myanmar's largest banks, tracing his rise as a military-linked businessman and subsequent metamorphosis into a patron of Myanmar's leading democratic party. It examines broadly the role played by tycoons as creditors, employers, and philanthropists in the post-socialist period and specifically how one tycoon adapted these levers of influence during partial civilian rule to defend his wealth from demands of redistribution and to expand his commercial empire. Focusing on the contingent legitimacy generated by elite provision of public goods, the chapter concludes that when tycoons become crucial to the public goods and collective identities, the welfare regimes that emerge tend to ensure that wealth trickles up to the already affluent, while the working poor are ensnared in debt and precarity.

Philanthropy and Patronage in Contemporary Myanmar

Public philanthropy by Myanmar's tycoons relies on networks of patronage and practices of gifting generated during the post-socialist period in the 1990s and 2000s. Theories of clientelism suggest that patronage relationships can have coercive, instrumental, and emotive dimensions, with the balance of each shaped both by underlying commercial logics and the role of the state in economic regulation.[3]

Reciprocity between patrons and their clients relies on moral bonds built through frequent face-to-face interactions. As anthropologist James C. Scott (1972b, 95) notes in his study of clientelism, the need for a degree of social intimacy between patron and client, coupled with the constraints of a patron's financial resource base, generally "limits the number of direct active ties a single patron can have" to between twenty or thirty people.[4] The significant opportunities and other assistance that commercial patrons are able to offer, however, can extend their influence as their direct clients develop transactional and affective patronage bonds with associates of their own. Clients in these second-tier clusters often have no face-to-face contact with the pinnacle patron, yet they can usefully be conceived within what Scott terms a patron-client pyramid (figure 5.1). Through this larger social structure, pinnacle patrons may be able to command loyalty from, or at least influence, hundreds if not thousands of people across industrial sectors, regions, and tiers of government through relations of (often contingent) loyalty that comprise a patronage pyramid. Many of those lower in the pyramid never meet the pinnacle patron yet might still perform functions that serve their interests.

Throughout the period of the State Law and Order Restoration Council and State Peace and Development Council (SLORC/SPDC) in the 1990s and 2000s, the military-mediated nature of market reform (discussed in chapter 2) meant that junta officials became the pinnacle patrons in provincial and national patronage pyramids.[5] Dyadic relations with their direct clients allowed military commanders to shift social obligations over to businesspeople, and under this arrangement, both could grow rich. The result was some of the worst social outcomes in the region. During the period of partial civilian rule between 2010 and 2021, however, government agencies began to run competitive tenders for state-issued licenses, projects, and contracts. Military officials during this period thus became only one of a number of actors alongside political party representatives and civil servants with the capacity to influence commercial and regulatory decisions. For the dozen or so tycoons who accumulated immense capital and built diversified conglomerates throughout the 1990s and 2000s, these shifts meant that civilian politicians

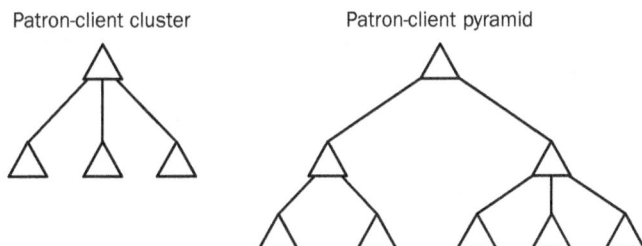

Patron-client cluster   Patron-client pyramid

FIGURE 5.1.   Patronage clusters versus pyramids. *Source:* Scott 1972b, 96.

and "the public" replaced junta officials at the pinnacle of patronage pyramids. The introduction of electoral processes in this way shifted relations of social licensing as formerly military-dependent "cronies" were forced to enlist a range of strategies to institutionalize their economic dominance and defend their wealth from potential redistribution in a more democratic context (Jones 2014; Ford, Gillan, and Thein 2016). In addition to "incubating" personal connections and patronage "at or near the center of the regime," as wily business interests across Southeast Asia are renowned for doing (Winters 2011, 159), strategies of "wealth defense" during the post-2011 period relied heavily on philanthropic giving, which showed the donor's commitment to a vision of a capitalist democratic polity in which private contributions are crucial to public welfare. The evolution of elite philanthropy in Myanmar during partial civilian rule reflects a global trend over decades toward "the lasting interpenetration of gifts and personal identities" (Silber 2001, 394). Instead of "detachment" being the distinguishing feature of elite wealth renunciation as earlier "scientific" forms differentiated themselves, sociologist Illana Silber (2001, 395) argues that a defining feature of current philanthropy is precisely the "contempt for anonymous, impersonal giving." Rather than maintaining a degree of social and institutional distance from beneficiaries, as encouraged by early-twentieth-century advocates of scientific philanthropy, studies of elite giving in the United States and India highlight donors' attempts at "forging, consolidating, or changing" their identity through personal gifts or institutional donations mediated by corporate or family foundations (Silber 2001, 396).[6] The embeddedness of donor identity and intentions within the "gift" means that philanthropy can simultaneously shape the social reputation of donors while also contributing to the "constitution of a highly dispersed and localized sphere of 'public'" that reflects and protects their interests (Silber 2001, 397). These personal and public dimensions of philanthropy are essential to understanding the historical evolution and contemporary forms of gifting in Myanmar, along with the enduring appeal of social outsourcing across successive regimes.

Practices of public gifting have been a source of social hierarchy and elite prestige since at least the precolonial period in Burma. Echoing ethnographies conducted in postindependence Burma, research on gifting in early 1990s Myanmar emphasized the social and moral stratification generated by ritualized wealth renunciation. Drawing on anthropological theories of "the gift" (Bourdieu 1977; Mauss 2002), Naoko Kumada (2004, 10) argued that the "eternal value" of money and material objects in 1990s upper Myanmar was revealed in their "consumption" on pagoda construction, feasts for others and provision of public goods such as wells. Viewing these practices through the prism of "symbolic capital"—an asset that Pierre Bourdieu (1977, 179) considered "perhaps the most valuable form of accumulation"—Kumada (2004, 13) argued that social and religious philanthropy in 1990s Myanmar constituted both a "form of renunciation and a form of manifestation of power . . . [that] maintain or enhance . . . [a donor's] position in society." These donations, in addition to accruing good merit to the renouncer as they were conceived as *dana* or religious charity, also served mundane functions for the donor by "totalizing . . . his biography, his labor and his social milieu" for those who witnessed his generosity (Kumada 2004, 11). Giving away profits, either to government-organized nongovernmental organizations (GONGOs) or local social initiatives, was not only a path to commercial expansion during the SLORC/SPDC period, but it simultaneously helped embody, generate, and legitimize social hierarchies by allowing donors to depict themselves as crucial to the public good.[7]

The period of partial civilian rule between 2011 and early 2021 shifted dynamics of commercial licensing considerably. Myanmar's tycoons were forced to compete to proactively generate a social license congruent with a more democratic welfare capitalist ethic by expending their capital in a way that crafted their public image as willingly "generous." In so doing, tycoons propagated the notion that taxing or regulating their businesses was unnecessary as they already delivered public goods on behalf of or in lieu of state agencies.

Public Philanthropy Generates a Democratic Social License

Elite public philanthropy after 2011 took a variety of forms. Gifts from tycoons to support education, social welfare, and infrastructure provision became much more common and public-facing, with funds and in-kind contributions to organizations often disbursed through corporate or family foundations (Menager 2017, 116). Alongside the increased magnitude of philanthropic giving, however, perhaps the most significant qualitative shift following the transition to partial civilian rule was the growing emphasis on gifts that expressed or augmented the public identity of donors.

Tycoons as Creditors, Employers, and Philanthropists

By crafting identities as patrons of both public goods and collective identity, tycoons accrue symbolic capital that morally legitimizes their past and present accumulation of capital and assets. In the years after 2011, lower-tier clients had two essential roles to play in enabling the identity-shaping public philanthropy of tycoons: first, by executing the commercial and social initiatives of their patrons and, second, by identifying opportunities for both business expansion and impactful public philanthropy. In the context of central-east Myanmar, the most prominent businessperson engaged in elite gifting after 2011 was Khin Maung Aye, the founder and chairman of KMA Group of Companies (see chapter 2). Born in Taungoo in 1964, his proactive philanthropy throughout the 1990s and 2000s enabled his "incubation" of senior members of the junta and subsequent emergence by the late 2000s as a nationally prominent businessman. After political liberalization in 2011, his business interests formalized and expanded amid efforts to meet foreign compliance and investment standards. Hundreds of bank branches opened throughout provincial areas during the decade of partial civilian rule after 2011. Coupled with the company's rapid uptake of digital banking, by 2019 CB Bank—which he chairs—was considered the second-largest private financial institution in Myanmar. After the transition to partial civilian rule, Khin Maung Aye's philanthropy was increasingly mediated through his companies and related foundations with some gifts framed in global discourses of "corporate social responsibility."[8] His hometown in central Myanmar remained a focal point for his philanthropic efforts even as his business and political interests led him to spend most of his time in Yangon and Naypyitaw.

Networks of clients generated during the 1990s and 2000s were essential to facilitating his local patronage of sports teams, welfare groups, and cultural festivals, along with communal projects like road construction and pagoda renovation after 2011. Cash and in-kind gifts often arrived at pivotal moments in the development of the social initiatives or projects that I followed, and they were usually coupled with rituals of recognition, vinyl banners, and signboards bearing the Khin Maung Aye name or that of his companies CB Bank and "Good Myanmar Victory" (Kaung Myanmar Aung or KMA). Identifying people, groups, or initiatives for which patronage would be of strategic value and then ensuring symbolic attribution of philanthropy to his generosity are processes that require significant time, an understanding of local context, and resources. Given that Khin Maung Aye mostly resided in Yangon or Naypyitaw after 2011, a network of business associates developed since the mid-1990s helped him to identify causes worthy of his personal support. Part of this network comprised direct employees, as central-east Myanmar remains a major hub for a number of his commercial ventures, including those in hospitality, mining, and construction. Employees with these businesses fulfilled various administrative tasks but were also integrated into a pyramidal structure of corporate hierarchy, the higher tiers of which are based largely in Yangon. Few of these local employees had any direct contact with Khin Maung Aye himself. However, they occasionally played minor roles in the execution of philanthropic initiatives at the request of their managers, and they were only rarely involved in these activities outside of work hours.

Beyond his employees, the core of Khin Maung Aye's local patronage network was a small group of direct clients who received personal or commercial loans at his intercession during the 1990s and 2000s or after 2011. The role of these clients provides insight both into how credit scarcity—historical and contemporary—shapes structures of patronage and mechanisms of influence. During the post-socialist period of the 1990s and 2000s, most private banks—including the three institutions that merged in 2004 to form Cooperative Bank, of which Khin Maung Aye became chair—"conducted very little formal banking business" (Turnell 2009, 266). A major barrier to formal lending was that prospective borrowers unconnected either to the banks, their owners, or junta officials were commonly required to give collateral equivalent to around 200 percent of the value of a loan up front, in addition to paying hefty "establishment fees" on loans (Turnell 2009, 272). Without formal lines of credit, the owners of most small and medium-sized enterprises in the 1990s and 2000s thus relied on self-financing through funds from friends and family that were backed by intimate social obligations and the security of personal property (Mieno 2006, 158; Turnell 2009, 273).

Some aspiring entrepreneurs, however, were able to secure lines of credit by cultivating personal ties with regime-linked businessmen like Khin Maung Aye. These credit ties between wealthy businesspeople and their personal clients at lower tiers of the commercial world relied on relationships of patronage lubri-cated through regular face-to-face contact and the (often unequal) exchange of favors. At the personal intercession of the pinnacle patron, who would vouch for these clients to junta officials if required, banks would then relax conditions of formal institutional loans such as collateral requirements, interest rates, loan lengths, and so on. This informal form of institutional credit combined the so-cial and familial obligations typical of "self-financing" with the heft and credi-bility of private or semiprivate banks and their junta-linked executives. A large proportion of Myanmar's provincial commercial class seemingly sourced ini-tial capital for business expansion by entering into these kinds of patron-client arrangements during the 1990s and 2000s. These arrangements offered a way for junior businesspeople to cultivate junta officials by being vouched-for by pa-trons who had shown their commitment to the social outsourcing logics of au-tocratic welfare capitalism (see chapter 2).

Regulatory reform and banking sector development after 2011 saw the relax-ation of collateral and other requirements for commercial loans (Foerch, Thein, and Waldschmidt 2013). Yet most wealthy tycoons maintained their credit rela-tions with direct clients in provincial areas throughout the decade of partial ci-vilian rule. During my fieldwork, for instance, interlocutors who managed or funded local welfare and social activities often complained about the difficulty they faced securing loans for business expansion. In cases where their commercial aspirations outstretched the lending limits or collateral requirements of formal bank loans, they would often seek a concessional loan through a social tie to wealthy financiers. While these loans were usually institutionally mediated by banks, they were not negotiated by bank branch managers as with typical lines of credit. Instead, recipients secured loans by engaging directly with Khin Maung Aye's office in Yangon. Though receiving lines of credit from the tycoons helped secure cheap financing, it also brought with it complex obligations to maintain the reputation of the patron at a subnational level.

Borrowers Become Clients Who Facilitate Public Philanthropy

Pyramids of patronage formed through credit relations were essential to the provincial philanthropic footprint of tycoons after 2011. The case of Khin Maung Aye's direct client, the speaker at the town-hall meeting vignette that opened this book, provides a prism into these dynamics. Dr. Kyaw Tu is a Taungoo native who studied medicine in the 1990s before returning to open a small private clinic. Following the liberalization of private health care in 2007, he secured a license to open one of Taungoo's first private hospitals, a business that proved highly profitable in the context of minimal state health spending and a poor standard of treatment at government facilities.[9] It is difficult to determine how credit to fund the hospital and other enterprises during this period was acquired since publicly available documentation is sparse. Attempts to probe these details in interviews with business associates of Khin Maung Aye solicited vague and sometimes evasive answers.[10] However, it is clear that a relationship of close commercial and social loyalty existed between Dr. Kyaw Thu and Khin Maung Aye. The two frequently appeared alongside each other in donations records of various religious and social initiatives in the late 2000s and especially after 2011 (field notes, 4 September and 7 September 2015). As will be discussed, Dr. Kyaw Tu was instrumental in the execution of large-scale public philanthropy projects financed by Khin Maung Aye from late 2010. Along with twenty or so other businesspeople and prominent former civil servants, he also fulfilled the role of "town parent" or elder (*myo mi myo pah*) on the township development committee, in many cases representing the interests of Khin Maung Aye (interview, 23 February 2016). By the commencement of my fieldwork in early 2015, Dr. Kyaw Tu's business had expanded from medical services into hospitality. He then formed a construction company partially underwritten by Khin Maung Aye, which he hoped would be granted permission to construct a shopping center and condominium complex on the former site of the Taungoo market (interview, 27 October 2015).

Clients such as Dr. Kyaw Tu played significant roles in identifying social and welfare initiatives worthy of Khin Maung Aye's support. One highly strategic form of gifting was the use of philanthropy to responsively or preemptively co-opt and silence Khin Maung Aye's most vocal critics, such as local welfare volunteer Tin Win. As discussed in earlier chapters, throughout 2015, Tin Win ran the largest locally oriented Facebook page in Taungoo that had more than 5,000 followers. The page featured up to a dozen posts daily depicting various *parahita* or welfare activities by volunteers as well as Burmese-language articles about local, national, or global news. Alongside posts suggestively linking Myanmar Muslims and Islam more broadly to violence and terrorism in the period before the expulsion of more than 750,000 Rohingya Muslims from Myanmar (G. McCarthy 2018a), many posts criticized the military and the allegedly corrupt dealings of "cronies." Khin Maung Aye was a common focus of Tin Win's posts, some of which detailed his alleged involvement in land grabs and questioned his plans to construct a "green" industrial zone on the fringe of the town. They also detailed his attempts to secure an extension of a highly concessional lease from the municipal authority for his luxury hotel in the center of town. In late 2015 and early 2016, however, Facebook posts critical of Khin Maung Aye became markedly less frequent. Over tea in early 2016, Tin Win explained to me that the chairman of his welfare group had asked him to hold back from publicly criticizing Khin Maung Aye as his business associates were planning to donate an ambulance to the organization in lieu of earlier promised funds (interview, 11 February 2016). For politically conscious activists passionate about charitable work, being forced to choose between either addressing local social problems or critiquing tycoons for their land grabs and commercial self-dealings can quiet public scrutiny of questionable business dealings and undermine incentives for ameliorative action by elected officials.

Seeding the formation of new volunteer and welfare organizations can similarly offer tycoons ways to shape public debate and protect their personal and commercial interests. For instance, at the same time that business associates of Khin Maung Aye were promising Tin Win's welfare group a sizable donation, another group of his clients in the local Sino-Burmese community were establishing a new relief team with his direct support. Founded in the wake of Cyclone Komen and flooding that was occurring around the country in mid-2015, the group tried to mobilize to respond to local and national disasters. Official-looking uniforms that bore the logo of the group were produced and disbursed to members, who also received mobile phones, ostensibly for use when they deployed but that they were able to keep full-time. In early 2016, the team began irregularly posting images to a newly created Facebook page of their efforts responding to local accidents such as fallen trees or fires. Their social media presence was led by a Sino-Burmese business associate of Khin Maung Aye who had been prominent in disaster relief activities in 2015 and also led a Chinese dance troupe. Though posts on the Facebook page exclusively focused on their relief activities, the leaders of the relief group regularly posted videos both to their personal Facebook pages and to township noticeboard pages profiling Khin Maung Aye's philanthropic activities (field notes, 16 December 2015). One of the Sino-Burmese activists was particularly vocal in support of the shopping center and condominium proposal led by Dr. Kyaw Tu and financed by Khin Maung Aye. In the months before and after a major town-hall meeting about the future of the market, he posted architectural animations of the proposed shopping center to Facebook and accused the municipal authority of "failing the people of Taungoo" as they had not yet approved the redevelopment of the market that had burned down in 2014 (field notes, 12 January and 7 February 2016). The use of patronage ties and targeted public philanthropy by associates of tycoons such as Khin Maung Aye can silence vocal critics while helping to disseminate corporate and personal propaganda that frames them in a positive light. Much like the dynamics of political party social provision, as discussed in chapter 4, public philanthropy should not be interpreted solely as a means of co-opting critics into quiescence. Instead, public philanthropy also serves to express the donors' commitment to the logics of social outsourcing in which the generosity of private interests generates bonds of mutuality crucial to democratic rejuvenation.

Philanthropy Demonstrates the Donor's Commitment to Democracy

Tycoons used philanthropy during the decade of partial civilian rule to publicly demonstrate their commitment to democracy and political reform. Many local and nationally prominent tycoons quietly funded the Union Solidarity and Development Party (USDP) at the 2010 election. However, a majority shifted their political affiliations to the National League for Democracy (NLD) in 2012 or 2015. How these political gifts from tycoons to parties and their campaigns were discursively framed is crucial to understanding the way economic elites incubated influence among state officials after 2011 while cultivating a public reputation as reformist-minded democrats working in the public interest.

In addition to providing direct funding to the NLD party at the 2015 parliamentary election, as many tycoons did, Khin Maung Aye recast himself as a lifelong democrat by directly supporting the campaign of NLD candidates in his hometown. He provided funds to the township NLD office and also gave in-kind support to the campaign, including by temporarily assigning one of his business associates to manage rallies and voter outreach. I encountered the NLD's brash campaign manager, a wiry man in his forties, early in my fieldwork at a hotel restaurant owned by one of Khin Maung Aye's direct clients. At the time he was working as a fixer for Khin Maung Aye's latest commercial project, attempting to negotiate a deal with farmers for the acquisition of land for the construction of a proposed industrial zone on the fringe of the township. A few months later, we traveled together to the delta to engage in relief efforts with a group that received funds from Khin Maung Aye. During this trip, he exclusively wore tattered old T-shirts bearing the image of Aung San Suu Kyi (field notes, 1 August 2015). Soon after our return from the delta, he took up the position of NLD township campaign manager and began organizing candidate visits to rural villages training party loyalists in campaign tactics, coordinating large urban rallies and liaising with electoral observation teams.

While he appeared confident, competent, and commanding at these gatherings, his interactions with local activists, many of whom had spent lengthy periods imprisoned for their political activities during the 1990s and 2000s, were often tense. In a number of village visits, for instance, grassroots NLD members—especially female activists—jokingly called him a pervert or "hot nose" (*nahboo*) during casual banter after the formal proceedings had finished. It was a crude insult often hurled between men at betel-nut shops, and I had never heard it uttered so openly in public by women. The public nature of the jibe by party loyalists went beyond expressing grievances with the campaign manager himself; it may also have reflected discontent with the moral compromise which his role in the NLD campaign represented. Indeed, in the weeks before the 2015 elections, a number of grassroots activists complained about the muddying of commercial and altruistic motivations within the campaign. They contrasted the campaign manager with grassroots village or ward activists like themselves. Whereas the manager was being paid by a tycoon who they said was "close to President Thein Sein" from the rival USDP, they were lending their time to support the NLD for free with "goodwill" (*cedana*)—invoking a Buddhist term referring to actions taken with pure and selfless intentions (interview, 13 August 2015).

At the same time as these moral misgivings circulated a narrative depicting Khin Maung Aye as a long-term democrat began to recur in my interactions with campaign staff and candidates linked to him. At a village campaign event, an NLD candidate—who party activists also described as a business associate of Khin Maung Aye—recalled working closely with him during the 1988 uprising. As the campaign manager commented at the same event, though Khin Maung Aye "did business" during the 1990s and 2000s, he "always loved democracy" (field notes, 23 October 2015). His role in the 1988 protests was highlighted in Facebook posts by the campaign manager and other local welfare activists that circulated in the later months of 2015. By the time of the poll, the majority of my interlocutors—welfare volunteers, shopkeepers, restaurateurs, students, monks—acknowledged

Khin Maung Aye's commercial exploits during junta rule yet also promptly mentioned his long support of democracy. One prominent local monk explained that "he has good sides and bad sides," an assessment shared by several interlocutors in the run up to the elections (field notes, 25 October and 4 November 2015).

It is difficult to determine why the story of Khin Maung Aye's involvement in the 1988 uprising circulated so widely in 2015. Yet it was clear that Khin Maung Aye's clients in the NLD campaign worked hard to frame his philanthropic support of the NLD in 2015 as an expression not of a *newly found* commitment to democracy but of a *long-held* belief that preceded the period he spent as a prominent crony. Indeed, by the time of the election, this framing of Khin Maung Aye as a closet democrat became "established fact" among local activist networks and parliamentarians who subsequently took seats for the NLD in Myanmar's national parliament in early 2016. The power generated by elite gifting in electoral contexts is not just derived from the influence it has on political elites, however. Rather, elite patronage of projects and initiatives of collective identity and improvement can also generate a degree of public consent for, and state inaction toward, their disproportionate economic and political influence.

Public Philanthropy (Re)invents Collective Identity

Public patronage of religious and cultural initiatives can offer economic elites a way to reinforce their centrality to collective identity and community, raising the cost of disloyalty. Khin Maung Aye's spectacular support for the historic revival of the Taungoo dynasty following the November 2010 elections illustrates how philanthropy can generate and revive civic and historic imaginaries that bind the voting public to economic elites. Between the fourteenth and sixteenth centuries, a Burmese kingdom based nearby the contemporary city of Taungoo conquered parts of Myanmar and much of Southeast Asia (Aung-Thwin and Aung-Thwin 2012, chap. 6). According to the curator of a local museum, in the 1990s Khin Maung Aye grew disappointed that many local people knew little about the local lineage of the dynasty, which was taught in schools during this period and was pivotal to the nationalist propaganda endorsed by the SLORC/SPDC junta. Starting from the mid-1990s, he began to memorialize the period in symbolic ways such as by funding gates and statues commemorating the monarchical leaders of the dynasty, King Tabinshwehti and his successor King Bayinnaung, at the entrance to the town. He also collected artifacts from various periods of monarchical history in Myanmar, including teak racing boats, ceramics, and weapons, and exhibited them around the grounds of the luxury hotel, Royal Kaytumadi, located on the largest lake in Taungoo.

His commitment to historic revival and public memorialization of the Taungoo dynasty became much more public-facing after the end of direct SLORC/SPDC military rule. A few weeks after the November 2010 election in which Khin Maung Aye supported the USDP, he held a cultural festival celebrating the 500th anniversary of the Taungoo dynasty. Financed through his companies CB Bank, Golden Myanmar Airways, and KMA Group, the festival was held annually in November every year between 2010 and 2020.[11] In November 2015, barely ten days after the NLD convincingly won national elections, the festival was held once again. The five days of the festival resembled what anthropologist Clifford Geertz (1980) conceptualized as political "theater": complex rituals and performances symbolically tied together to conjure into existence a shared notion of historically and regionally situated political community. Stages were set up at the entrance to the town, where reenactments of the sack of Ayuthaya (in present-day Thailand) were performed by costumed actors and acrobats riding horses and elephants (see figure 5.2). A parade was then held through the town to the ballroom of Khin Maung Aye's Royal Kaytumadi hotel, referencing the dynastic name for the historic capital of the Taungoo dynasty. Famous actors from Yangon played the parts of princes and princesses, waving to thousands of people who crowded the streets as they were carried aloft by elephants and actors dressed as courtesans.

The (re)invention of the Taungoo provincial imaginary artfully interwove dynastic and Buddhist symbolism. In addition to unveiling a pagoda renovated in the style of Bagan-era temples, Khin Maung Aye integrated a long-running

FIGURE 5.2. Parade of horses, elephants, and performers enter Taungoo following the reenactment of the sacking of Ayuthaya. *Source:* Photo by author.

Buddhist festival into the celebration, hosted a Dhamma recitation competition for young Buddhists, and held a merit-making ceremony for 505 monks from around Taungoo, a number chosen to commemorate the 505th anniversary of the dynasty. The Dhamma recitation event was conducted at the Bayinnaung ballroom of the Royal Kaytumadi hotel, named after the king of the Taungoo dynasty who invaded Ayuthaya. At Khin Maung Aye's invitation, hundreds of children, monks, and teachers from every Dhamma school in Taungoo assembled to compete in recitation of Buddhist *suttas*. The competition served to demonstrate his commitment to the rejuvenation of morality among young Buddhists while also channeling funds from Khin Maung Aye to Dhamma schools and local monasteries. Cash prizes totaling US$15,000 were awarded to three winners of the Dhamma recitation competition, many of whom gave their prize money to local abbots to support the tuition and moral cultivation of youth (field notes, 25 November 2015).

Khin Maung Aye's clients enabled the pagoda parade to be held on the second night of the festival. Twenty-eight floats depicted scenes from the life of the Buddha (*Jatika*) and stories about *nat* spirits central to Burmese Buddhist cosmology. A team from every urban ward in the township competed in the parade, with Taungoo's Hindu community also participating with an effigy of a sacred cow. The origin of the parade runs back to the independence movements of the 1930s, with smaller-scale iterations receiving the support of local businesspeople for decades. In 2010, however, the pagoda festival was integrated into the memorialization of the Taungoo dynasty at the direct request of Khin Maung Aye. Though the merger met with some initial resistance from monks and local people, Khin Maung Aye negotiated the integration of the two festivals by committing to providing a grant to each ward to cover the costs of float materials. In 2015, these funds were disbursed to ward-based committees by Khin Maung Aye's business associates in the weeks prior to the festival, extending pyramids of financial and symbolic patronage down to a neighborhood level. These teams were led in some wards by the local administrator who coordinated the workmanship, vehicles, and volunteers for each float and raised additional funds from local businesspeople for special decorations. As with the Dhamma recitation competition, the top three floats as judged by a committee of artists received cash prizes of up to US$15,000 provided by Khin Maung Aye.[12] The bulk of winners again donated funds to pagodas and monasteries within their ward, further deepening Khin Maung Aye's financial and moral ties of patronage down to a neighborhood level (field notes, 25 November 2015).

By funding and coordinating the dynasty and pagoda festivals in such a spectacular manner after 2011, Khin Maung Aye made himself the linchpin in a circuit of morally and culturally significant wealth redistribution symbolically linked to provincial collective identity. Alongside paid actors and employees, patron-client relationships formed through concessionary business and personal loans were essential to Khin Maung Aye's execution of the Kaytumadi festival. His direct clients, most of whom had earlier received concessionary lines of credit, helped to recruit volunteers for the parade, pagoda procession, and various other events held to mark the anniversary. Though competition between, and tensions among, second-tier clients were exposed by these requests, their ties of dependence to Khin Maung Aye helped ensure the festival was executed with the resources it needed to succeed. Using civilizational philanthropy of this kind, enabled by pyramids of clients, tycoons place themselves at the center of a privatized ideal of moral and civic community in which their outsized dominance comes to be viewed as not just defensible but even desirable.

Patronage of Collective Identity Generates Democratic Social License

By patronizing collective identities, elites raise the cost of challenging their political and economic dominance. The pride individuals garner from perceived membership and participation in collective political imaginaries of unity and progress such as the Taungoo dynasty can shape beliefs, attitudes, and behavior in ways that complicate political accountability. Yoshihiro Nishizaki's political ethnography of provincial Thailand documents the role of identity in the resilient popularity of Barnharn Silpa-archa, a politician reelected repeatedly to represent Suphanburi Region between 1976 and 2008, despite a reputation for blatant corruption. Nishizaki documents how Barnharn systematically cultivated pride in provincial identity and made himself the primary patron of the region's material and cultural advancement. Through well-publicized personal donations to local cultural schemes along with large-scale public ceremonies to mark the opening of new buildings and highways within the province, Barnharn effectively raised the cognitive and social costs of voters abandoning him electorally (Nishizaki 2004, 2011). In Indonesia, the reinvention of dynastic lineages has been a feature of the country's post-Suharto period, with political entrepreneurs resurrecting long-lost monarchies throughout the archipelago to lend communitarian heft to electoral appeals or elite demands for advanced district-level autonomy (Van Klinken 2007, 151–153).

Khin Maung Aye's spectacular revitalization of the Taungoo dynasty, which became markedly more public during the decade of partial civilian rule, similarly sought to cultivate a collective identity that justified his political and economic domination. After decades of what many local activists and moral authorities framed as economic, social, and moral degeneracy, the revival of the

Taungoo dynasty historical memory encouraged pride and identification with a provincial imaginary half a millennia old. By encapsulating diverse local social and religious institutions into circuits of public philanthropy of which he is the primary donor, Khin Maung Aye sought to render himself indispensable to the reform and restoration of a provincial moral community based on mutuality beyond the state. The co-optation of these groups also lent credibility to his business activities, which he framed as essential to the revival of provincially rooted moral community. In a speech to the business and cultural leaders of the historic town of Mogok in Mandalay Region in 2018—shared publicly by one of his local clients to Facebook—Khin Maung Aye made the commercial benefits of civilizational philanthropy explicit, explaining:

> In promoting Taungoo, I started with the 500 anniversary festival. I had a plan to develop the industrial zone (*setmoozone*). By organizing the festival, local people became really motivated to develop the city and supported my project. City development in this way also contributes to national restoration and development (*naingan pwun pyo doh teh*). (Field notes, 19 March 2018)

In this sense, the intensification of civilizational philanthropy by tycoons such as Khin Maung Aye during the decade of partial civilian rule can be read as an attempt to generate a more publicly rooted form of the authoritarian-era social license that had been crucial to their commercial success during junta rule (see chapter 3).

Though local and diffuse in its focus, the "public" hailed by the (re)invention of the Taungoo dynasty was not just provincial in its scope. Rather, it also targeted a national audience including high-profile military and civilian patrons. Reflecting the national commercial footprint of CB Bank and KMA Group, an array of prominent national politicians and military officers were integrated into the 2015 celebrations alongside local politicians and dignitaries. President Thein Sein was invited to place the golden umbrella (*tee*) atop a pagoda specially renovated to resemble a prominent Bagan temple (field notes, 27 November 2015).[13] NLD parliamentarians from Bago Region and beyond, freshly elected in the weeks earlier, also attended the festival wearing the party's iconic orange outfits. Myanmar's largest pay-TV provider SkyNet was invited to broadcast the festivities while journalists at various newspapers, including the government-run *Global New Light of Myanmar*, were granted special access to ensure the celebrations were witnessed across the country.[14] By ensuring that national elites and the public at large could see the scale of his public gifting, Khin Maung Aye was able to use subnational patronage to generate a broader contingent social consent for his continued wealth accumulation throughout the decade of partial civilian rule.

Civilizational Philanthropy Binds Donors into Continued Patronage

Funding spectacular expressions of culture and collective identity is a powerful though paradoxical way to acquire public or political loyalty. The dominance of a single donor in efforts of cultural revival can render them indispensable to collective identity, generating a form of symbolic reliance that can bind and commit them in perpetuity. This bind was exposed in 2016 when rumors circulated among Taungoo's welfare and political activists that Khin Maung Aye was not planning to fund the festival again. In the weeks before the town-hall meeting described in the opening vignette to this book, various unrelated contacts repeated rumors that Khin Maung Aye had grown impatient with municipal officers: Despite spending what he claimed was more than US$1 million on the festival in 2015, he was apparently angry that local officials had still not approved the shopping center redevelopment proposed by his protégé. As another local businessman explained, he might not have wanted to fund the festival again out of spite to the municipal officers. Yet failing to do so would signal a financial liquidity problem that could unsettle his social license: "[Khin Maung Aye] must continue to fund the festival. . . . If he didn't," the businessman said, "it would be a disaster for his reputation as people would think he has run out of money and is no longer a reliable supporter of the people" (interview, 3 September 2016).

If tycoons such as Khin Maung Aye fail to publicly and prominently fund expressions of provincial identity that they had supported previously, their reluctance may be viewed by voters or politicians as an inability—or worse, a lack of commitment—to fulfilling the social obligations of welfare capitalism that allowed them to evade state redistributive action after 2011. Here we see how the need to sustain public consent to domination via philanthropy (loosely) ties the hands of proto-oligarchs in a way that ensures the endurance of precarity and inequality for the working poor.[15] Satisfying the expectations of democratic welfare capitalism through quasi-public performances of philanthropy and renunciation generates a symbolically meaningful reputation for the donor. As Bourdieu (1977, 179) theorized, this symbolic capital is then "convertible back into economic capital" as it allows disproportionate commercial and political influence at both a local and national level. The failure to be perceived as a "reliable supporter of the people," however, can unleash scrutiny of the sources of wealth or prompt demands to redistribute assets among the broader national "public." In the same manner that moral bonds with junta officials needed to be cultivated by emergent businesspeople during the 1990s and 2000s, the effort and resources tycoons put into public philanthropy expose how the looming threat of regulatory action by elected officials and public scrutiny shift dynamics of social licensing. Whereas during the

1990s and 2000s businesspeople competed to be recognized as reliable clients by military officers, the introduction of electoral politics and greater scrutiny of economic elites forced tycoons to compete by donating their wealth in ways that accrued them the esteem of politicians and the public alike.

Tycoons were not trying to legitimize *all* businesspeople through their generosity, however. Rather, donors used their public gifting as a way to morally compare themselves with other commercial elites. During a May 2016 town-hall meeting on reconstruction of the burnt-down local market, for instance, both the Chief Minister of Bago Region and the business protégé of Khin Maung Aye threatened the possibility of less enlightened and "generous" businesspeople intervening to exploit the town if the shopping center they proposed was not approved. In other words, failure to accept the commercial demands of "generous" tycoons and business elites could lead to the dominance of *even more* exploitative capitalists who could not care less about contributing to the public good. Increasingly proactive performances of generosity by tycoons after 2011 in this sense reflects the shifting configurations of power and accountability during the period of partial civilian rule. Yet the competition between tycoons to engage in philanthropy after 2011 also served to further entrench the appeal of social outsourcing, hollowing out expectations that state agencies could play a more active role in addressing inequality and shackling state officials from doing more to address social disparities.

Philanthropy Constrains Democratic Redistribution

Elite philanthropy reinforces an ideal of social outsourcing in which a greater state role in the welfare mix can be framed as unnecessary, undesirable, and infeasible. By helping deliver suboptimal though critical public goods through private means, commercial elites undermine the capacity of state officials to resist their demand for regulatory concessions, fairly resolve land-grab disputes, and tax them to fund a greater government role in the welfare mix.

Elite Provision of Public Goods Generates Contingent Legitimacy

Patronizing the public functions that state agencies fail to adequately deliver makes commercial elites crucial to the provision of "public" goods. The reputational benefit gained from supplementing inadequate state service delivery was evident in the months before Myanmar's November 2015 elections, when large green dumpsters emblazoned with the name "Khin Maung Aye, Chairman of CB Bank" began to appear on street corners around the urban core of Taungoo. According to state legislation passed in 2012 that devolved revenue and expenditure powers to subnational agencies, municipal offices are legally responsible for collecting taxes for waste and providing rubbish-collection services. Up until mid-2015, however, the cash-strapped municipal authority in Taungoo had provided no local dumpsters and only one small rubbish truck to cater to the waste management needs of more than 100,000 people living in urban wards. Consequentially, many people dumped nonorganic household waste on roadsides or burned it in bonfires in family compounds, creating a thick gray haze that often loomed over the town in the late afternoon hours. Associates of Khin Maung Aye who led voluntary efforts at small-scale rubbish collection throughout 2015 and 2016 (described in chapter 4) recognized that the absence of government dumpsters left a major gap in waste management, which a philanthropic contribution could help fill. Khin Maung Aye was informed, and a month or so later his associates helped the municipal authority order dozens of new dumpsters. Each was branded with his name and title ("CB Bank Chairman U Khin Maung Aye gave this . . .") and then placed on street corners around the town. Within days they were overflowing with waste, and a welfare group began providing occasional volunteers to the under-resourced municipal waste team to help empty the bins into dump trucks.[16]

Municipal officials were at pains to frame the contribution as a gift to the public rather than a bribe to state employees. A municipal officer explained that they marked the dumpsters with Khin Maung Aye's name and position on the bin in order "to honor him as the master of the gift (*alu shin*)." However, he insisted that they felt no pressure to approve any projects related to him since "his donation is to develop his native town or city, not to help the government" (interview, 2 February 2016). Yet the gifting of dumpsters did coincide with efforts by Khin Maung Aye's local clients to elicit concessions from local officials. Within weeks of the donation, Khin Maung Aye's business associates requested municipal officers extend the peppercorn lease for his hotel located on the lake. They also urged approval of the shopping mall project on the site of an old local market, in which his local client had a commercial interest. Both of these requests were posted to Facebook by local welfare activists, where they received considerable criticism by social media users. When I asked two local volunteers who posted these articles whether they thought public gifts such as the dumpsters would benefit Khin Maung Aye personally, they were surprisingly ambivalent. Regardless of his plans or intentions, they saw the bin as filling an important gap in public service delivery and hygiene. A municipal official avoided commenting on whether the donation might have had "selfish" intentions. Musing on the gifting from a Buddhist viewpoint, he emphasized that regardless of whether his aim was "clean and pure" enough to be spiritually beneficial, the donation was still critically needed because of how cash-strapped the local authority was:

> The merit of his donation depends on the *cedana* (goodwill) of his donation. I'm not sure if he gets merit every time people use the dumpsters, as merit depends on the intention, not on what you donate. But even if he doesn't get good merit for his donation, it is good for the town, and he will still have a good image and reputation. (Interview, 2 February 2016)

Welfare activists similarly interpreted the contributions as a sign that Khin Maung Aye grasped local problems (reported to him by his clients) and was committed to improving the town. Shwe Linn (pseudonym) a former political prisoner and prominent local critic of Khin Maung Aye, strongly supported the dumpster donation. In the months before he had vocally called out on his popular public Facebook page what he considered Khin Maung Aye's "greedy" activities. In a viral post shared more than a thousand time, he had claimed the spectacle of the 505th Taungoo dynasty and pagoda festivals were as worthwhile as "burning money" (field notes 26 November 2015). In the week after the November 2015 election, however, Shwe Linn posted an image to his followers of an overflowing dumpster on the road outside his home (figure 5.3). The post acknowledged the

FIGURE 5.3.   One of dozens of dumpsters sponsored by a prominent tycoon placed on street corners around Taungoo ahead of the November 2015 election. *Source*: Photo by author.

public hygiene problem posed by poor waste management and urged readers to "say 'thadu' [good work] for the donor, and put your rubbish in the bins."

I asked Shwe Linn privately whether it was inconsistent to praise Khin Maung Aye for his dumpster donation given the otherwise critical views he expressed toward him. He responded that "we should acknowledge good deeds when we see them" and that it was not his place to judge the motivations of the donation (interview, 15 November 2015). The criterion of intentionality within Buddhist understandings of merit (discussed in chapter 2) allows plenty of scope to critique public philanthropy on the basis of potentially selfish motivations, such as securing sweetheart deals from the municipal authority. However, even for critically minded activists, the reality that state agencies are resource-poor—a legacy of decades of tax remissions in exchange for indirect social expenditures—means that former "cronies" contributing to public goods and welfare coheres with practical and normative expectations of the wealthy entrenched during junta rule.

There are limits to the praise some activists believed tycoons should receive for their philanthropic contributions. These boundaries were exposed in late 2017 when Khin Maung Aye contributed to the renovation of a degraded road behind his hotel that ran out to the town cemetery and crematorium. A Facebook post by one of Khin Maung Aye's business associates detailing his donation, accompanied by photos of him from the Taungoo dynasty festival and images of the road project, circulated widely among my interlocutors. It received over 1,100 likes and elicited more than 200 effusively supportive comments including "Respect!" and "Good work!" Shwe Linn interjected with an obscene comment that stuck out from the others, receiving dozens of likes: "We can acknowledge his gift, but don't lift his testicles for him!" I initially read the explicit interjection as an attempt to resist the impunity of apolitical tycoons who had shifted their political allegiances in 2012 to the NLD after years of collaborating with junta officials. Yet another way to interpret it is that even activists such as Shwe Linn who criticize the outsized influence of emergent oligarchs embrace the idea that businesspeople have a significant role to play in delivering public goods in the social absence of the state (author notes, 3 October 2017). Rather than criticizing the logic of social outsourcing, which let the state off the hook for public goods provision, Shwe Linn instead accepted the centrality of tycoons to road construction as so commonsensical that he felt the community should not feel obliged to him for performing his "natural" social role as a tycoon.

In assuming that economic elites *should* substitute for the state in public goods provision, activists and the public implicitly accept that an insecure welfare regime in which state institutions play a minimal role is the best they can and should expect. Rather than demanding officials collect more taxes to fund public services that the state is often legally mandated but insufficiently resourced to provide, self-professed democracy activists instead praise Myanmar's tycoons for helping to deliver those same public goods. In this way, forms of public philanthropy that supplement the failure of the state reinforce an ideal of social outsourcing that undermines incentives for government officials to expand state fiscal and redistributive capacities. Using the levers of state power to directly address social needs is seen as *ineffective* but also as *counterproductive*. Doing so may undermine the moral and social bonds from which political and social actors imagine the bonds of a "free" and "moral" polity emerge. Seen through this lens, taxing tycoons or redistributing questionably acquired assets becomes an attack not just on economic elites but on the fabric of the polity—provincial and national.

Redistributive Role of Tycoons Complicates Resolution of Past Injustices

The influence and symbolic capital accrued by tycoons through public philanthropy complicated efforts by elected officials to resolve some of the most difficult distributive challenges facing the country during Myanmar's decade of partial civilian rule. This was especially the case in relation to land grabs, one the most pernicious and complicated issues in the country. Millions of hectares of agricultural land changed hands throughout the 1990s and 2000s, often through patronage-based relationships and commercial arrangements between junta officials and emergent businesspeople. Military state officials who initiated these transactions often declared land used or occupied by villagers for decades as "vacant" or "fallow" land over which the state had public domain. As businesspeople sought to capitalize on land received or purchased in this manner, especially after the liberalization of 2011, hundreds of thousands of families were evicted and lost usage rights over land that many had cultivated and improved for decades. Many were forcibly evicted from land to make way for commercial redevelopment such as mining, agribusiness, forestry, and industrial or tourism purposes. The extent of land expropriated in this manner is difficult to quantify, though by 2016 almost a fifth of Myanmar's agricultural land (17 percent) had been transferred for agribusiness purposes (see chapter 2). Since 2012, the issue of rural dispossession gained increasing political attention, with a growing movement of farmers across the country demanding compensation for (or the return of) land from which they were alienated. The NLD recognized the need for a policy on the issue and committed to resolving land-grab disputes during the 2015 election campaign.

Land-grab disputes were especially rife in central-east Myanmar. Junta and state officials leased significant allotments of land in the area to companies in the 2000s under frequently opaque contractual arrangements. Throughout my fieldwork, a number of ostensibly farmer-focused political parties, some supported by civil-society activists, attempted to mobilize villagers who had lost access to land and had not been properly compensated. The largest of these local protests involved land over which Khin Maung Aye claimed ownership. In mid-2015, farmers in an area nearby the new Yangon–Mandalay highway claimed they had received inadequate compensation for land on which KMA Group was planning to develop an industrial zone. In an interview with English-language newspaper *The Myanmar Times* in November 2015, Khin Maung Aye admitted that the land initially acquired for the zone was purchased "very cheaply." However, he argued that the quality of the land was poor, and he emphasized that if garment factories were to open in the area as planned, they could create 100,000 new jobs "and the township will prosper."[17] Business associates of Khin Maung Aye closely linked with the NLD's campaign team repeated these claims while also working to appease local farmers. Their efforts saw KMA Group acquire the final allotments necessary for the industrial zone at more than 300 times the amount paid per acre to smaller landholders earlier in the process, creating divisions within the protesting villagers.[18] Protests gradually dissipated as larger landholders were paid more, better mobilized farmers received some compensation, and families began to leave the area.

On 12 January 2016, however, claims of land grabs reemerged. A group of around 200 villagers and activists marched through Taungoo alleging they had been dispossessed *without* compensation by Khin Maung Aye's KMA Group during the final years of junta rule. The origins of the case ran back to transactions that occurred in 2009, when the company claims it signed a thirty-year lease with the Ministry of Agriculture, Livestock, and Irrigation to create a commercial teak nursery on 2,400 acres of land in northeast Bago Region bordering Karen State.[19] In December 2015, the company publicly committed to reducing the amount of land apportioned for the teak nursery to 511 acres and returning the remaining 1,189 acres of land at a "renunciation ceremony" to be held at Khin Maung Aye's hotel on 11 January 2016. SkyNet's MNTV channel broadcast the ceremony the day before the protest, edited segments of which were shared to Facebook by Khin Maung Aye's local clients (field notes, 14 January 2016). Videos and images from the event depicted him ceremoniously renouncing the majority of the land by personally giving deeds to villagers and providing cash payments to people his associates had negotiated with directly. Only a portion of the affected villagers attended the ceremony, however. A larger group of villagers claimed that the company had seized more than double the amount of land—over 5,000 acres total, which was 3,600 acres more than what it had legally leased from the Ministry of Agriculture in 2009.[20] Their protest the following day, and another similar demonstration in

February 2016, thus challenged the depiction of Khin Maung Aye as generously returning land, as had been broadcast on MNTV and circulated online. Instead, the protesters claimed that the extent of his company's land expropriation, and thus the magnitude of injustice, was far larger than he had admitted.

Local NLD activists were quick to respond, and within a few days Khin Maung Aye's local clients within the NLD mobilized counterprotests. The march coordinated by party loyalists did not mention the grievances of the villagers or the amount of land they claimed had been seized. Instead, the counter-rally featured farmers, some of whom had received compensation in the earlier renunciation ceremony, carrying signs explicitly criticizing the Eleven Media journalist who was reporting on the alleged land grabs.[21] One Facebook post by a local activist that received 1,100 likes and over 180 shares in the days following the January 2016 protest, including from prominent local NLD loyalists, made the dispute a collective conflict by accusing the reporter of "attacking the chairperson of CB Bank who provided a lot of support to Taungoo" (field notes 13 January 2016). The post listed "good things" that Khin Maung Aye had done for development of the township, including "working hand in hand with the NLD and USDP." It also criticized the journalist for linking the protests to land disputes regarding the industrial zone. Citing limits to "freedom of expression," the post concluded with an indictment of the journalistic ethics of both the reporter and the outlet itself: "A few years ago, prior to the entry of so-called journalists from Eleven Media, we did not have this kind of problem" (field notes, 13 January 2016). Instead of acknowledging and addressing the grievances of the farmers, activists linked to welfare and political groups patronized by Khin Maung Aye mobilized against the reporter who was scrutinizing land deals made by KMA Group during junta rule.

A provocative meme that circulated on Facebook among local NLD activists in the days that followed superimposed the question "Is your goal to create a riot in Taungoo?" over an image of the gates to the city, which Khin Maung Aye had donated during the SLORC/SPDC period. The image evoked Khin Maung Aye's patronage of the town, but it also had a potent subtext, referencing the bloody intercommunal riots in 2001 in which more than twenty Muslims died. By framing allegations made by the farmers and journalist against Khin Maung Aye as an attack on the city as a whole, the meme could be read as inviting or threatening violent backlash against the journalist. Despite these threatening connotations, the image was shared by various local NLD activists, with some even making it their Facebook cover photo for more than a week following the counterprotest targeting the Eleven Media journalist (field notes, 14 January 2016).

The virulent defense of tycoons by self-professed democracy activists shows how the ideal of welfare capitalism in which private interests are crucial to public goods and collective civic identity can complicate the resolution of economic injustices. While some of the most vocal defenders of Khin Maung Aye were clients obliged to defend their patron's reputation, many people with no financial ties to him at all shared the meme, too. The centrality of commercial elites to public goods and collective identity can in this way create constituencies who support the continued dominance of tycoons, weakening the incentives for state officials to resolve economic injustices at either the micro or systemic level through state action. Indeed, taxing or seizing assets of economic elites becomes undesirable and unimaginable when those same businesspeople are crucial not just to provision of welfare but also to a broader notion of the polity generated through acts of seemingly selfless reciprocity by market and non-state actors.[22]

The virtue of these donations being given willingly means that even when tycoons appear to violate the ethics of welfare capitalism to which they are meant to adhere, activists and elected officials are reluctant to use the levers of the state to address injustice. Instead, they prefer to encourage economic elites to return their misappropriated wealth voluntarily and on their own terms, often through performative expressions of morality and generosity unregulated by law. A welfare mix in which private non-state actors play a major role in public goods and redistribution can in this way entrench precarious outcomes for the poor, posing a constraint separate from the formal constraints on redistributive state action that were embedded in the "rigged" 2008 Constitution.

Philanthropy Is Cheap for Tycoons but Expensive for the State

Rather than waning when Aung San Suu Kyi's NLD took power in March 2016, her government embraced the ideal of philanthropy as a way to address Myanmar's most intractable problems. She personally pressured tycoons to renounce their wealth in the name of democratic moral community, asking economic elites assembled in Naypyitaw in October 2016: "Can't those who have previously worked for their own self-interest work for others in the future? Don't they have the necessary attributes to work for others? I believe it is possible."[23] Suu Kyi herself hosted a number of "giving ceremonies" in Naypyitaw to solicit funds, including one in December 2016 to fund her reboot of Myanmar's peace process and in October 2017 (figure 5.4) to kick-start a "public-private partnership" to repatriate Rohingya from Bangladesh and reconstruct Rakhine State after the campaign of war crimes by security forces. In both cases, requests from Suu Kyi and her advisers for "donations" from Myanmar's most prominent former cronies were responded to with enthusiasm by economic elites.[24] Along with prominent SLORC/SPDC-era tycoons such as Kanbawza Bank Chairman Aung Ko Win and Asia World Chairman Steven Law, Khin Maung Aye featured as one

FIGURE 5.4. State Counselor Aung San Suu Kyi posing in October 2017 in Naypyitaw with Myanmar's most prominent tycoons after they donated to a public-private partnership to "reconstruct" Rakhine State following the expulsion of more than 750,000 Rohingya to Bangladesh by security personnel. *Source*: State Counsellor's official Facebook page.

of the top donors at these appeals. He also contributed to similar efforts by state and regional chief ministers to raise funds to supplement subnational state social initiatives.[25]

Myanmar has a persistently low formal tax revenue, partly a consequence of state officials since the 1990s granting tax exemptions to outsource the government's social functions. In this context of weak state fiscal capacity, it is unsurprising that Suu Kyi and the NLD solicited contributions from tycoons to help achieve social objectives. Yet the emphasis in these initiatives on the moral obligations of businesspeople highlights the enduring appeal of social outsourcing, including to ostensibly "reformist" elected representatives. The normative value placed by the NLD government on wealthy elites donating voluntarily to support state initiatives was highlighted by public posts on the Facebook page of the State Counsellor recognizing these contributions. The subtext of posting these images was that those who failed to make contributions could be scrutinized and their social license legitimately questioned by elected officials and the public. In this sense, the solicitation of donations from tycoons after 2011 can usefully be compared to the dynamics of social outsourcing during SLORC/SPDC rule in the 1990s and 2000s. State social responsibilities and functions were largely outsourced through decen-

tralized dynamics of patronage between businesspeople and provincial junta officials who mediated commercial licensing. In contrast, Suu Kyi and the NLD
sought to symbolically centralize the flow of donations through herself, her office,
and her party—bypassing the role of military patrons, including at a provincial
level. Public philanthropy by tycoons in response to state requests for donations
after 2016 were thus increasingly directed through Suu Kyi, who replaced senior
military officials as the charismatic "patron in chief." Notorious tycoons with long
histories of partnering with the military donated to these appeals and directly to
Suu Kyi and explicitly depicted themselves as "defenders" of democracy who were
"on the same page as the government."[26]

In the 1970s and 1980s, Indonesia's President Suharto similarly solicited donations directly from tycoons, staging public "shakedowns" of tycoons to help
finance schools, mosques, and other initiatives run by tax-free philanthropic
foundations he personally chaired (Vatikiotis 1998, 50–52). Suharto often specifically targeted ethnic Chinese businessmen since economic liberalization had
created public outcry about their perceived privileged status as commercial partners of the Indonesian military since the 1940s (Vatikiotis 1998, 50). Suharto's
approach netted him slush funds he later redistributed for political benefit. It
also showed the public his willingness to extralegally regulate and extract funds
from specific businesspeople under the guise of benefiting ordinary Indonesians
(Vatikiotis 1998, 51). Though Suu Kyi acted similarly as the intermediary of elite
donations, her vision of welfare capitalism did not appear to vary significantly
by the ethnic background of tycoons. In contrast to Suharto's shakedowns, which
aimed to assuage public discontent about racial economic inequity, elected officials in Myanmar held all commercial elites to the same standard by encouraging (or implicitly requiring) them to substitute or supplement state social
initiatives, regardless of their ethnicity.

Proactively fulfilling the obligations of democratic welfare capitalism in this
way came relatively cheap for Myanmar's tycoons during the decade of partial
civilian rule. The amounts they gave through public philanthropy and state-
sponsored "giving ceremonies" after 2011 were a fraction of what business empires
often accrued through legally and ethically dubious means during the 1990s and
2000s. Myanmar's major conglomerates expanded rapidly after 2011, especially
following the lifting of major international economic sanctions on even the most
infamous "cronies" in 2016 at Suu Kyi's personal urging.[27] Donations by tycoons to
foundations or national initiatives such as the peace process or Rohingya repatriation thus constituted a small proportion of their opaque but growing annual company profits—a small price to pay to legitimize questionably expropriated and
accrued land and assets. Meanwhile, government attempts to boost tax revenue
are complicated by a tax code that permits up to 25 percent of assessable income to

be deducted through donations to private charities and causes—an approach that creates both a legal basis and a financial incentive for the perpetuation of social outsourcing.[28] In early 2018, Myanmar's largest private financial institution Kanbawza Bank, for instance, claimed to have donated more to charity than it paid in overall tax since 2011—citing US$103 million given to philanthropic activities of the KBZ Brighter Future Foundation since 2009 compared with US$80 million paid in taxes since 2011.[29] Such imbalances are perfectly consistent with current tax regulations and the logics of welfare capitalism. Yet they also rob the state of revenue crucial to delivering a more consistent social safety net and entrench the role of often self-interested commercial actors in the achievement of social justice.

The dominance of economic elites in non-state social aid provision distorted the reform of tax policy after 2011. Rather than boosting state revenue by more consistently taxing the corporate profits and income of the affluent, both the Thein Sein and Suu Kyi administrations sought to fund public goods by instead expanding consumption taxes that disproportionately burden the poor.[30] The human and social consequences of ideological and practical preferences for private redistribution were born out during the COVID-19 pandemic. Concerned about accruing public debt given Myanmar's low tax revenue, the elected government spent little relative to its neighbors to keep poor households afloat amid the worst economic downturn in decades. Instead, Aung San Suu Kyi encouraged Myanmar people, including businesspeople, to support local efforts to contain the virus and encouraged donations to finance the government's purchase of vaccines.[31] None of these outcomes were formally established by the "rigged" 2008 Constitution, which set the parameters of partial civilian rule between 2011 and the military coup of 1 February 2021. Instead, outsourcing social functions to non-state actors continued as it aligned at least partly with the material and ideational interests of diverse political and economic actors—from ordinary voters to democracy activists and tycoons. For economic elites, their centrality to non-state social aid and projects of collective identity allowed them to protect their fortunes from potential democratic claims to state-led redistribution while ingratiating themselves with elected officials throughout the decade of partial civilian rule.

Social Outsourcing Erodes Faith in State Social Action

Elite philanthropy shifted markedly in its logics and scope during Myanmar's decade of partial civilian rule. During the period of autocratic welfare capitalism in the 1990s and 2000s, emergent businesspeople used charitable giving to generate transactional and moral bonds with military patrons who would then grant them licenses and contracts on which they built commercial empires. The political economy of philanthropy evolved with the introduction of electoral politics in 2011 as licensing and contracting became more competitive and civilian scrutiny of business activities intensified. In this context, public philanthropy became a tool for economic elites to justify and defend their wealth, since it allowed them to artfully demonstrate their moral and civic commitments while contrasting themselves with disreputable and stingy "cronies." These ideals and practices of philanthropy rendered private interests crucial to welfare provision and governance, despite the transition to partial civilian rule, enabling the emergence of oligarchs who could defend and expand their commercial empires regardless of which political party held power (Hutchcroft 1991).

The entrenchment of private donors and practices of gifting between 2010 and 2020 thus followed a process of social outsourcing similar to that seen in more established capitalist democracies. Many elected officials and voters were practically and normatively satisfied when tycoons gave away a sliver of their mammoth wealth for ostensibly civic causes, even though they were paying minimal tax to the state (Reich 2018). The enduring appeal of social outsourcing in this sense relies on a cruelly optimistic ideal: that it is possible for commercially minded actors to *voluntarily* deliver fair, efficient, and just social outcomes with minimal state involvement or formal regulation (Berlant 2011). Though this rarely happens in reality, since the promise of social outsourcing aligns with the interests and ideals of diverse actors, state officials come to frame government social action as redundant and undesirable. Indeed, especially in a context of weak state capacity, taxing elites to fund potentially ineffective state social aid could be risky and might even weaken the incentive for philanthropy from which the normative bonds of freedom—individual and civic—are imagined as emerging from in the first place.

Even in sectors where the state was expanding its social footprint, the preference for non-state social action led state officials to award communities deemed "self-reliant" far more government social aid than their equally needy counterparts. Chapter 6 explores these dynamics, examining how post-2011 local development assistance was disbursed in ways that required local populations to earn their social "rights" through projects of communal improvement, inscribing conditionality and exclusion at the heart of democratic social governance.

6

SELF-RELIANCE AND ENTITLEMENT

How do logics of state social outsourcing distort the way communities access government aid? Does the expansion of state social spending over time erode expectations that private actors must contribute to public welfare? Following the austerity of the 1990s and 2000s, government social outlays in Myanmar increased markedly, though inconsistently, during the decade of partial civilian rule.[1] Comparative literature suggests that the expansion of state agencies into new areas of social service provision, as occurred in Myanmar after 2011, can generate new expectations among citizens that bind successive regimes and shape the trajectory of welfare state formation over time (L. MacLean 2011b). This chapter, however, highlights a contrary and puzzling dynamic. Villages and neighborhoods that received aid from the state during partial civilian rule were far more likely to have engaged in "do it yourself" local improvement projects before receiving state aid than communities excluded from these schemes. Many of these local initiatives received some form of support from government officials and schemes outside the community. Yet even as state agencies spent more on social development than they had in decades during the period of partial civilian rule (2011–2021), the idiom of "self-reliance" remained a central way that communities and people lobbied for social aid from the Myanmar state.

This chapter unpacks the politics of self-reliance in post-2011 Myanmar: how it shaped who was considered worthy or deserving of state aid and what this suggests about the persistence of social outsourcing across regimes. Informed by case studies of local improvement initiatives and data from the 2016 household survey, I argue that state officials burdened poor communities with an obligation and moral responsibility to prove themselves good "partners" for develop-ment.[2] By encouraging community contributions to social improvement in this way, state officials institutionalized a zero-sum conception of entitlement in which access to "rights" was determined not by citizenship but by personal and collective contributions to non-state efforts of social improvement.

The chapter opens by probing the historical roots of so-called self-reliant de-velopment in Myanmar, arguing that the rise of do-it-yourself projects correlates temporally with the decline in "forced labor" from the early 2000s. Case studies and interviews are used to explore how local hierarchies of wealth, along with state support for these initiatives, were artfully hidden by community leaders so that they could depict themselves as self-reliant and appeal to more senior state officials for more substantive government aid. The chapter concludes by examin-ing how the persistence of social outsourcing as a primary logic of citizen-state relations throughout the decade of partial civilian rule exacerbated the vulnera-bility of poor and excluded populations—especially minorities—despite state so-cial expansion.

Self-Reliance and Collective Improvement

Myanmar has a long history of forced contributions to infrastructure and state initiatives. The use of corvée labor to construct pagodas, bridges, roads, and ir-rigation canals was common during precolonial monarchies (R. Taylor 2009, 43–44). Reports of forced labor during the Burma Socialist Programme Party (BSPP) period were not uncommon; however, following the 1988 uprising, the State Law and Order Restoration Council (SLORC)—later renamed the State Peace and Development Council (SPDC) and subsequently referred to as the SLORC/SPDC junta—became globally notorious for using involuntary labor to construct national and local infrastructure. Although Myanmar was a signatory to the International Labour Organization (ILO) Forced Labour Convention, re-ports throughout the 1990s detailed the use of forced portering in conflict zones and involuntary labor to construct infrastructure, especially irrigation aimed at improving national rice output.[3] Military officers or headmen of villages over-saw these projects and would often claim a portion of subsequent crop yield at a fraction of market rates, both to meet junta quotas and for personal benefit (Thawnghmung 2001, 247). If these requests were refused, or if laborers grew tired, beatings, imprisonment, or fines were common (Horsey 2011, 4–5). Rural development projects such as these increased significantly after 1988, apparently resulting in an increase in the total irrigated area of Myanmar from 2.5 million to 4.1 million acres between 1991 and 1995.[4] Data released in 1997 by the Ministry

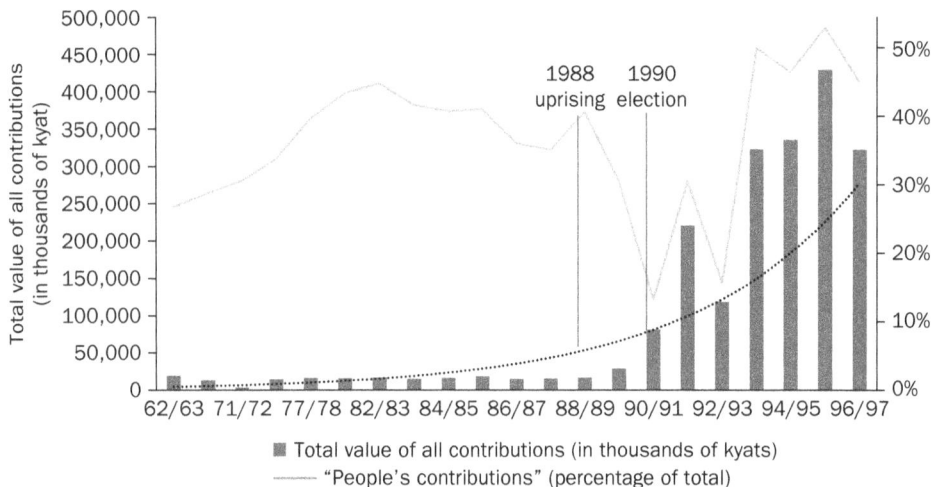

Total value of all contributions (in thousands of kyat) — y-axis left

500,000 / 450,000 / 400,000 / 350,000 / 300,000 / 250,000 / 200,000 / 150,000 / 100,000 / 50,000 / 0

Right axis: 50% / 40% / 30% / 20% / 10% / 0%

1988 uprising   1990 election

x-axis: 62/63 71/72 77/78 82/83 84/85 86/87 88/89 90/91 92/93 94/95 96/97

■ Total value of all contributions (in thousands of kyats)
------- "People's contributions" (percentage of total)

FIGURE 6.1. Increasing value of community contributions to local improvement, 1962–1997. *Source:* Adapted from Thawnghmung 2001, 247 based on 1997 data from the Ministry of National Planning and Economic Development.

of National Planning and Economic Development, depicted in figure 6.1, highlights the marked increase in the value of rural development initiatives after 1988. In addition to reporting the overall monetary value of these projects running back to Ne Win's 1962 coup, the data also cited "the people's contribution" to these projects of rural development through "in-kind services." With massive increases in the overall value of rural works after 1988, "the people's share" as a percentage of overall projects—including "donations" in cash as well as in-kind and labor contributions—was acknowledged by the state as regularly exceeding half the total value of projects.[5] Despite international outcry into the early 2000s that much of this "contribution" was in the form of forced labor, senior junta officials argued that "people's contributions" were coherent with Buddhist ethics along with British colonial-era laws (Horsey 2011, 11, 35).

In the early 2000s, the junta began to rely less on forced labor. Facing pressure from the ILO and the Federation of Trade Unions of Burma based abroad, top officials from the regime started to allow egregious cases of forced labor to be heard in Burmese courts, resulting in the sentencing of local government officials on charges of forced labor from 2004 onward (Kyaw Yin Hlaing 2007b, 246; Horsey 2011 1, 137–140). During the decade of partial civilian rule after 2011, the practice declined but certainly was not eliminated, as local officials began to be elected and state agencies increased spending on local infrastructure.[6]

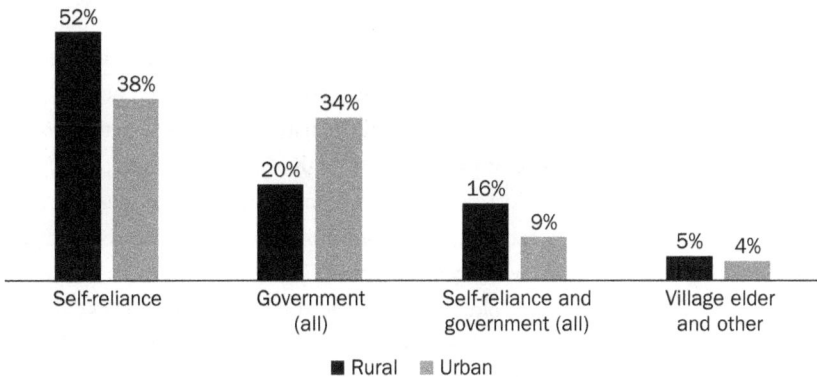

FIGURE 6.2. Perception of who built local roads in urban and rural areas (multiple options permitted). *Source*: Author survey, March 2016.

A range of local development funds were established, many run by the Ministry of Agriculture, Livestock, and Irrigation, providing new opportunities for interaction between state officials and local communities and delivering improved infrastructure and rural livelihoods outcomes, especially in remote areas of the country (see Griffiths 2016 for an evaluation).[7]

Though rural development projects involving corvée labor declined as government spending on local infrastructure increased after 2011, community contributions to public goods provision did not cease. Indeed, the 2016 household survey conducted in central-east Myanmar (Bago Region and Karen State) found that 70 percent of respondents in rural areas and 47 percent in urban areas attributed local roads to "self-reliance" or a "partnership" between "the community" and the state (see figure 6.2).[8] Though state-led corvée projects declined from the mid-2000s, local improvement initiatives framed by participants as "self-reliance" thus appear to have markedly increased during the decade of partial civilian rule. So, what distinguishes self-reliance initiatives from forced labor?

Self-Reliance as Idiom and Ideal

Self-reliance is a descriptive idiom and normative ideal that denotes the need for individuals and households to take control of their own affairs. Achieving political and economic self-reliance from foreign capital and markets was a primary objective for independence-era leaders who legitimized state-driven import-substitution industrialization with reference to ideologies of collective labor and sacrifice (Tharaphi Than 2013, 651; Maung Maung 1953, 117–118). Following the dissolution of the BSPP, the post-1988 junta subsequently abandoned Ne Win's socialism and embraced autocratic welfare capitalism. Self-reliance faded as a primary plank of state ideology and foreign relations during the 1990s. Yet interlocutors in central-east Myanmar frequently characterized a "self-help" outlook as "practically" necessary to survive economic liberalization and the withdrawal of the patchy social support previously ideologically promised, though sparingly delivered, by the BSPP (see chapter 1). The subject or agent in idiomatic accounts of these periods almost always reference oneself (*ko*), as in common idioms "stand on one's own" (*kothu kotha*), "rely on one's own strength" (*ko ah koko*), and "eat one's own rice" (*kothamin kosa*). As a former soldier and village tract administrator explained, "After 1988, people started to develop a self-reliance/do-it-yourself (*kothu kotha*) attitude as the government totally collapsed. So, people developed the mindset that if they don't work for themselves, they won't have food to eat."

Interviewees used the idiom of "self-reliance" to describe the creative livelihood strategies necessary for survival as sources of contingent social aid, such as rations from BSPP food stores, ceased or were radically reconfigured. Yet, in a major interpretive shift from U Nu's 1950s vision of self-reliance as the path to a modern welfare state, many interlocutors used the term to denote a normative commitment to looking "beyond the state" for aid. Though the "self" evoked in these idioms refers to the individual or the family unit, it also became increasingly common for civil society activists, religious authorities, and administrators to enlist earlier connotations of collective self-reliance to encourage people to cooperate with village, ward and neighborhood projects of improvement.[9] Accounts of local initiatives undertaken during the late 1990s and early 2000s emphasized that these contributions were "voluntary." Indeed, leaders of self-reliance projects often made careful distinctions between the labor provided by villagers, commonly in partnership with local religious authorities such as monks and pastors, and the coercive and "unfair" deployment of forced labor by military officials after 1988.[10]

In the absence of in-depth accounts of local development projects in the 1990s and 2000s, it is difficult to assess the extent of organizational and interpretive overlap between what the state labeled as "people's contributions," what activists considered "forced labor," and what ordinary people and local administrators now describe as "self-reliance." By 2015 and 2016, interlocutors in provincial Myanmar commonly described self-reliance projects during junta rule as overwhelmingly small scale and locally oriented, often focusing on repaving high-use village roads with dirt and stone or digging drainage ditches to prevent flooding. The local focus of these initiatives seems to have cultivated a strong sense of ownership and benefit for many participants in these initiatives.[11] State officials were not always absent from these projects, however. Interlocutors recounted local administrators, military-linked businesspeople, and even military commanders leading or contributing to many of these improvement initiatives.

Businesspeople also recalled being encouraged by military officials to proactively contribute to local public goods provision, organize fundraising campaigns, and coordinate "volunteer" labor in order to secure annual renewal of their commercial licenses, as discussed in chapter 2.

Despite the role that authorities and commercial elites often played in these initiatives, use of the term "self-reliance" allowed local improvements to be attributed to the collective efforts of all residents, rich and poor alike, regardless of their formal or informal associations with the junta. The contemporary discourse of self-reliance rhetorically embeds local administrators, junta-linked businesspeople, and even military officers into notions of the "self" or community, an encapsulation of market actors into the collective common in post-socialist contexts of state social retrenchment (Lal 2012). The fact that most projects are led by residents means that coordinators are able to solicit labor or cash from local residents far more willingly than forced labor projects. The 2016 survey found that participants at least retrospectively viewed their contributions to these initiatives as freely given. Of respondents who said they had made contributions to local road construction in the 2016 survey, 97 percent said that their actions or donations drew good karmic merit or grace as the projects contributed to the welfare of others.[12] Given that merit is widely seen to accrue only to actions taken or possessions renounced willingly, these perceptions suggest a stronger sense of local ownership relative to the more coercive local improvement projects of the 1990s and 2000s.[13]

The sense of ownership that accompanies self-reliance improvement projects cultivates a perception that coproducing development is fair or normatively appropriate. Almost a quarter (24 percent) of respondents in the 2016 survey agreed with the statement that the local community *should* bear some or all responsibility for construction of village or ward roads. Previous involvement in self-reliance projects, and exposure to ideologies skeptical of state attempts to minimize its social responsibility, were strong predictors of support for this ideal of coproduced public goods; those who said road construction should be the sole responsibility of government were far less likely to have participated in these kinds of projects previously.[14] Beyond being a descriptive term used to collapse social hierarchies and promote collective responsibility for communal development, the framing of local improvement initiatives as "self-reliance" may thus instill a preference for social affairs being managed and resolved at the lowest level possible.[15] Contrary to theoretical expectations that the state will seek to take credit for local development executed wholly or partly from government resources (Sacks 2011), these ideals did not fade with the expansion of state local development expenditure after 2011. Rather, self-reliance became a basis on which communities competed against each other for finite government aid.

Self-Reliance Endures Expansion
of State Social Spending

As the state spent more money on poverty alleviation and infrastructure development during the decade of partial civilian rule, idioms of communal self-reliance continued to be widely used by leaders of village and ward improvement initiatives—including government officials. Many of the projects I followed between 2015 and 2018 were led by commercial elites with assistance in funding, organization, and engineering from government officials. Despite the significant role often played by both state staff and resources, the coordinators of these projects often described the initiatives as "self-reliance," regardless of the extent of state involvement.

Local administrators involved in improvement projects explained this veneer by saying it was "not good" to talk about the support they received from government officials. Doing so could evoke memories of forced labor and undermine the notion that residents were giving their time freely and earning merit in the process, they said. As a result, it was important to refer to government support as part of or supporting the collective "self" or "community." They referred to projects using Buddhist idioms of giving (*dana*) and "work for others" (*parahita*) and supplemented this spiritual content with an adapted socialist discourse that emphasized the collective problem solving and "unity" (*sii lone hmu*) exhibited in the initiative.

The framing of collective self-reliance allowed authorities to solicit disproportionate financial and labor contributions from poorer households. The amounts donated to projects by more affluent households often appear to be highly progressive; in some urban contexts surveyed, these contributions comprised between two and five times the amount donated by poorer households.[16] When the foregone wage value of labor contributions to self-reliant initiatives are considered, however, there is reason to doubt the fairness and progressivity implied by the discourse of collective unity enlisted in projects of local improvement. Poorer households in the survey, for instance, were 8 percent more likely to contribute labor for road initiatives than richer households and 12 percent more likely than middle-income respondents, while more affluent households were 6 percent more likely to give cash alone than poorer respondents (see figure 6.3).[17] Moreover, when overall household donations to social and religious causes are calculated as a proportion of household expenditure, the amounts donated are almost equal between poor households (7 percent) and more affluent households (10 percent). The poor thus carry a larger burden for non-state provision of public goods relative to their wealth, their use and role in their degradation, or their benefit from the improvement—a dynamic common in other contexts where informal taxa-

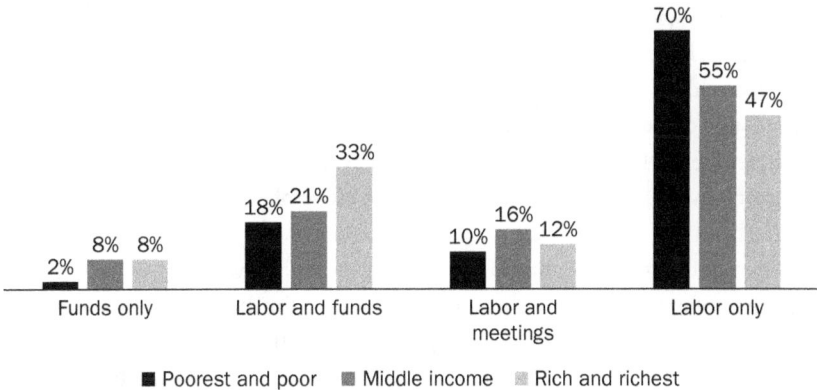

FIGURE 6.3. Types of contributions made to road projects. *Source*: Author survey, March 2016.

tion is widespread (Jibao Prichard and van den Boogaard 2017). The idiom of self-reliance deployed in local initiatives thus morally legitimizes an unfair allocation of burden for public goods provision and entrenches an insecure welfare regime in which non-state actors, especially the poor, carry a disproportionate burden to improve the communities in which they live.

The endurance of these dynamics and inequities during partial civilian rule, when state officials were electorally accountable for the first time in generations, is puzzling. Why would both community leaders and ordinary people work so hard to maintain the veneer of local improvement initiatives as "self-reliance"? And even more puzzling, why would state officials, including members of Parliament (MPs), permit the leaders of projects to hide the support given by state agencies? A case study of a village road-improvement initiative helps to tease out the practical, symbolic, and strategic stakes of "self-reliant" local development projects in a context of deeply ingrained logics of social outsourcing.

Seeking State Aid by Demonstrating "Self-Reliance"

Many local administrators and ordinary people framed self-reliance as a central basis on which resource claims could be made to authorities and decision makers after 2011. A road project led by a local leader in a village on the fringe of a provincial town provides an insight into the perceived relationship between self-reliance projects and eligibility to receive aid from state officials, including parliamentarians.

Kyaw Naing lives with his family in a small rural hamlet with around twenty or so other households about 200 meters from a bitumen inter-town road connecting

Bago Region with northern Karen State. A former Tatmadaw soldier now in his mid-sixties, he retired from active duty in the 1990s to this quiet agricultural area where he and his family could enjoy rural life as well as the benefits of proximity to schools and clinics less than a twenty-minute ride away by motorbike. We first met in September 2015 at a small Union Solidarity and Development Party (USDP) campaign event held in the village before the November election, to which I was invited by one of the candidates.

After meeting a chatty group of locals, including Kyaw Naing, at the biriyani feast that followed the event, I was invited to return for the upcoming wedding of the local village administrator's daughter. In the months that followed, I became a regular visitor to the village before and after the November 2015 elections to chat about the national election campaign or swap local gossip. As I rode into the village on one of these visits in late January 2016, Kyaw Naing was sweeping the front yard of his small compound and invited me into his home. A few minutes after our first sips of tea, he passionately declared his admiration for Aung San Suu Kyi and informed me of his recent election as ten-house administrator—the lowest tier in the administrative structure of the Myanmar government bureaucracy.[18] Repeatedly using the term "democracy," he explained his plans to repave the hamlet laneway. I immediately grasped the value of the project as I had been embarrassingly bogged on the same road a few months earlier.

The road slated for repair led at one end through an adjacent hamlet to a bitumen inter-town road and trailed off into paddy fields at the other. Kyaw Naing had initially sought help for the project from the village tract and township administrators, but they claimed to have spent all available funds until the next financial year. Convinced that "doing it yourself" was the only option in the short term, Kyaw Naing subsequently collected around US$20 per household for gravel and soil to cover the road. He insisted that all financial contributions were entirely voluntary, though every household in the hamlet had contributed by the end of the project. When I returned the day of the road construction in late February 2016, ten or so local men—their *lungyis* (sarongs) hitched up around their thighs—were shoveling stone from the back of a reversing truck onto the road where a group of jovial women with large pans were then disbursing the stones onto the muddy tracks of the road. Two household leaders who lent their labor expressed pride at the road improvements when I interviewed them later, emphasizing that their labor and financial contributions drew good grace.

Though violence was not threatened to compel contributions, the small road-improvement project was in some ways similar to rural development initiatives that relied on forced labor during the 1990s and 2000s. The project was technically led by a local state official who "encouraged" households—rhetorically and socially—to contribute both funds and labor. As with some forced labor initiatives after

1988, the project also delivered a clear benefit to local residents—though the road came to an abrupt stop at the end of the hamlet and did not continue the extra fifty meters or so through the rest of the village and on to the main bitumen road to Taungoo. "That road is another administrator's responsibility," he explained to me when I asked why the improved road ended prematurely—an infrastructure gap that highlighted the patchy salve that self-reliance initiatives often provide in rural contexts. Despite the limited efficacy of the project, however, Kyaw Naing saw the project as achieving strategic as much as practical ends. He framed the project as a deeply political act that generated collective pride and set the standards for receipt of assistance from the National League for Democracy (NLD) government elected in November 2015. For him, the road repaving was an expression of "self-reliance" that resonated with ideas of people power evoked by Aung San Suu Kyi and NLD parliamentarians throughout the election campaign:

> Really, this project is about pride that we don't have to rely on the government. If I talk with the government I can be confident and have pride, without feeling small. Now the government is elected by the people, so by doing this work and sharing responsibility, we are showing we have power, too.

The emphasis on "sharing responsibilities," "collective pride," and "showing power" resonated with discourses of morality and democracy that circulated throughout the 1990s and 2000s and recurred during the November 2015 election. Embedded within this demonstration of self-reliance, however, was also an expectation that representatives of the state would view them as collectively worthy of government poverty alleviation and development aid. Kyaw Naing explained:

> We are trying to influence the government by showing them we are working hard. Once we lay the foundation for the road, then the government could come later and do a better road. . . . When we do self-reliance projects, we can ask for more help from the government because it shows we are organized and want to share responsibility.

From Kyaw Naing's perspective, the small road repaving initiative demonstrated to state officials the willingness of the village to "share responsibility" for development, obliging authorities to extend poverty alleviation assistance to the village in the future. Kyaw Naing's promise that the "generosity" of residents would be more than reciprocated by state officials was not simply rural moralizing designed to eke out free labor and cash contributions from local residents. Rather, he had good reason to believe that demonstrating self-reliance could lure state aid to the village. Indeed, sharing responsibility for development became a primary basis for determining eligibility for expanding state aid during the decade of partial civilian rule, forming part of a strategy that political theorist Nikolas Rose (1999) has termed "government by community." [19] Viewed through this lens, "community" became, after 2011, a useful tool "whose vectors and forces [were] mobilized, enrolled, deployed" by policymakers to outsource social functions to non-state actors even in a more democratic context (Rose 1999, 176).

Deservingness and Exclusion

The notion that ordinary people carry considerable obligation and burden to advance the interests of the collective was a recurring feature of Burmese political thought throughout the twentieth century. Drawing on the monarchical logics of precolonial Burmese kings, officials under Ne Win's socialist dictatorship often linked the contributions that individuals made to collective projects of national or local improvement to their worthiness to be the bearers of legal or social rights. Nick Cheesman (2015a), a scholar of Burmese legal and political thought, highlights that during BSPP rule, the concept of "rights" closely followed socialist legal logic (see Markovits 1978). That is, they accrued to individuals or groups by virtue of their role in satisfying Ne Win's policy goals and ultimately derived unilaterally from his goodwill (*cedana*) as sovereign. Individuals who sought redress—sometimes successfully—from BSPP officials would thus often make appeals based on the contributions they had made to Ne Win's project of socialism (Cheesman 2015a, 107–109). Rather than entitlements, rights during BSPP rule were thus "conditional privileges paternalistically bestowed . . . [on] certain people who deserve them because they conform with the sovereign's vision for the community" (Cheesman 2015a, 109).

Despite the dissolution of the BSPP in 1988, the logic of contingent entitlement endured. As discussed in chapter 2, SLORC/SPDC officials outsourced obligations for social governance and redistribution previously ideologically promised (though inconsistently delivered) by the BSPP by encouraging people to be "self-reliant" both in propaganda and by disbursing commercial licenses to clients who accepted obligations to the communities in which they operated. Following this logic, people who had engaged in forced labor, for instance, used participation in local improvement initiatives as proof of their worthiness to receive opportunities or chances from the state—or, in the case of Muslims, as proof of their right to "have" rights (Cheesman 2012, 205–206; Cheesman 2015b). Though the post-1988 junta dispensed with the pretense that it fulfilled parental functions for citizens, the vernacular notion of a "social contract" remained "contextual and contested . . . subject to one's ability to marshal other resources (symbolic, material, social), subject to luck or contingency . . . state agent whim or risk profile, the extant political conditions in the country. . . ." (Prasse-Freeman 2015, 98).[20] As anthropologist Elliot Prasse-Freeman notes from research with contemporary activists, the word "right" (*khwint*) as used in everyday language reflects this slippery subtext—more commonly associated with contingent notions of "permission," "approval," or "opportunity" than an entitlement or "demand for a restoration of what one already 'has'" (Prasse-Freeman 2015, 96).

With the transition to partial civilian rule and the development of alternate, more direct mechanisms of claim-making by political parties, parliamentary committees, and advocacy groups, more assertive forms of claim-making began to emerge. Thousands of ordinary people took up opportunities to make formal appeals to the state in the immediate years after liberalization in 2011.[21] Cheesman (2015a, 227–237) has analyzed letters written to authorities by "citizen-complainants" between 2004 and 2013 in which they asserted their entitlement to rights and redress—often shifting from supplication to stridency when successive attempts to secure redress failed. Prasse-Freeman and Phyo Win Latt (2018, 412) similarly describe assertive claim-making among land-rights activists seeking restoration of land from which farmers had been dispossessed. Despite new opportunities for claim-making through various "representative" institutions, the logic that rights accrue to people or communities who practice and possess virtues coherent with the sovereign's vision of political community was puzzlingly reinforced rather than challenged during the decade of partial civilian rule. Why? Did demonstrating commitment and contribution to the collective really help communities or people solicit aid from state officials? As close study of the politics of entitlement after 2011 highlights, state authorities used the expansion of governmental social aid between 2011 and 2021 to entrench an ideology of coproduced development, granting poverty alleviation support to communities that appeared to be self-reliant while excluding deprived neighborhoods and villages from much-needed state aid.

Self-Reliance, When Rendered Legible, Enables Eligibility

Local improvement projects played a key role in determining eligibility to state aid during the decade of partial civilian rule. Self-reliance initiatives enabled a powerful claim to worthiness from the state as they presented the image of a community unified and bonded across wealth and social hierarchies to which the state could outsource social obligations.

Data on the distribution of state-mediated local development initiatives demonstrated that Kyaw Naing had good reason to be optimistic that renovating the hamlet road could render his village more eligible for state aid. The 2016 household survey of twenty-eight rural villages in Taungoo, Bago Region, and the adjacent township of Thandaungyi, Karen State, found a statistically significant skew in a major government loan scheme, the Green Emerald Fund, favoring communities much like Kyaw Naing's. Administered by the Department of Rural Development (DRD) in the Ministry of Agriculture, Livestock, and Irrigation from 2014 until its suspension following the 2021 coup, the scheme aimed to create revolving funds at the village level to support entrepreneurial activities; although township DRD officers recommended which villages would receive the project, the chief minister and director of the DRD in the state or region gave final approval (Robertson, Joelene, and Dunn 2015, 24).

The 2016 survey found that respondents in villages that had been selected for inclusion in the Green Emerald loans scheme were 17 percent more likely to have contributed labor or funds to road construction in the past than households in otherwise similar villages nearby that had not been selected.[22] Communities that had demonstrated their self-reliance through local improvement projects were thus disproportionately likely to receive the scheme than communities where fewer households had engaged in these initiatives. This difference was not a treatment effect, as the scheme provided household-level loans to support enterprise development across the village and was not intended to fund construction of local infrastructure. Rather, headmen in villages that received the Green Emerald scheme recounted how their communities had been selected for inclusion because they demonstrated their ability to fundraise and contribute to local improvement through earlier road construction projects and other initiatives of local improvement. Local monks or welfare activists often helped coordinate these initiatives, which interviewees repeatedly described using idioms of self-reliance.

Achieving eligibility for government funding during the decade of partial civilian rule was not as simple as engaging in self-reliance projects, however. Village headmen described how local administrators, monks, and businesspeople or state officials connected in various ways to the villages had to lobby relevant government officials to ensure their eligibility for the scheme. State aid was not secured unless the community proved both neediness and self-reliance to decision makers. Bonds to wealthy commercial elites were particularly important in this process, given that businesspeople tend to have strong ties to state officials at the village tract, township, and in some cases, state or national level, as a legacy of decades of autocratic welfare capitalism in which they willingly assumed the social responsibilities of the post-socialist junta. Poverty and engagement in "self-reliance" projects in the past could in this sense be considered necessary but not sufficient conditions for communities to be considered deserving of state assistance. Self-reliance is instead crucial, providing as it does a veneer to convince authorities and patrons at various levels that a community is sufficiently virtuous and unified across hierarchies of power and wealth to be deemed worthy of state social aid.

A zero-sum logic is exposed when communities compete against each other to receive local development schemes on the basis of their self-reliance. For instance, the US$480 million National Community Driven Development Project (NCDDP), funded by the World Bank and the governments of Myanmar, Italy, and Japan, included a "multi-stakeholder consultation" after the majority of villages in a participating township received and used the grant.[23] These competitions were judged by local and regional authorities such as parliamentarians both on the basis of the impact of the projects as well as community participation and contribution to the success of the project. After speeches, presentations, and in some cases performances such as dances by representatives of each community, a first-place prize for "Best Village" as well as second- and third-place prizes were awarded. Villages expended significant time and resources on projects of local improvement, as well as rehearsals and so on, to ensure they were highly competitive for the prizes on offer. Why were these awards so valuable? Because villages recognized in these competitions were then able to lobby for inclusion in other development schemes as they proved their willingness to coproduce public goods alongside the state.[24]

There is a clear link between performances of self-reliance and the eligibility of a community to receive state developmental intervention. The key mechanism linking self-reliance and eligibility is whether and how a community makes itself legible to authorities as collectively deserving of state aid. James C. Scott's (1998, 2) notion of state technologies such as cadastral maps and censuses that simplify complex social phenomena into readable, comprehensible, or "legible" domains for state intervention is relevant here. As extensive ethnographic research across South and Southeast Asia demonstrates, "legibility" to authority can be a bottom-up achievement of the governed population as much as it is inscribed unilaterally by state officials and their practices of governance. Partha Chatterjee's (2004, 33) work on "political society" in India, for instance, explores how community-based welfare groups use various strategies to help squatters in Calcutta "get themselves identified as a distinct population group that would receive the benefits of governmental programs." Andrew Walker (2012, 33) has similarly recounted how ritual performances of "community" and "local development" in northern Thailand "add potency in the form of visibility and moral authority" to claims of eligibility for state aid or subsidy (see also Vandergeest 1991, 433). Legibility may thus best be understood as a key element in what Tania Li (2007, chap. 1) terms the "politics of entitlement" in which the state controls who receives state support and what they must do to be deemed worthy of support. Focusing on local community development projects funded by the World Bank in provincial areas of Indonesia, Li analyzed how various technologies of measuring "community cohesion" were used to make villages the subject of intervention by state and development actors. When state officials and communities are searching for a legitimate basis on which to selectively disburse state aid, "the sacred context of collective endeavor" or "community" provides a useful mechanism for "the mutual construction of both legibility and eligibility" (Walker 2012, 33).[25] Self-reliance initiatives played a similar role during Myanmar's decade of partial civilian rule and expanding state social footprint. Yet, even if legibility of a community to authorities made them eligible to state intervention, proving worthiness did not mean that government agencies would take full responsibility for the provision of public goods.

Eligibility to State Aid Requires Coproducing "Development"

Even when eligibility to receive state aid is established, the logic of social outsourcing means that state-supported initiatives often require households and communities to coproduce development. Willingness to co-contribute to projects in the form of funds or labor was a key selection criterion cited by a representative in the Karen State parliament who had helped coordinate more than sixty state-funded development initiatives between 2010 and 2015. He explained that many government grants and rural development schemes explicitly stated in project guidelines and consultation workshops with prospective communities that villages willing to contribute funds or labor "voluntarily" would be favored over communities unwilling to make these contributions.[26] He argued that this criterion allowed government funds to "go further" and have a wider impact than would be possible if workers were paid. According to a consultant on the World Bank's NCDDP initiative, villages that were "more emphatic in their display of volunteer spirit" during the "multi-stakeholder consultation" were similarly favored in that scheme. Communities that demonstrate a track record of self-reliance initiatives and a willingness to co-contribute to local improvement initiatives are seen as more worthy of these schemes than villages that do not show themselves to be virtuous in the same manner.

There are less dismissive ways to view the absence of self-reliance initiatives. In her examination of local development initiatives in the Philippines, anthropologist Hannah Bulloch (2017, chap. 7) notes that the failure of villages to contribute to improvement projects could also signal the need for a community to receive *more* rather than less assistance from the state. Making the appearance of self-reliance the basis of eligibility to receive state aid thus institutionalizes a logic of deservingness to development aid; poor communities must then compete with each other to share responsibility with the state for development in ways that minimize expectations of the role that government agencies play in social justice and poverty alleviation.

The process whereby a local improvement initiative translates into eligibility to receive development support thus outsources government responsibility for the welfare of citizens to the locus of "community," entrenching a zero-sum logic in which communities must compete with each other in order to be deemed worthy of state aid.

Democracy Justifies Exclusion of the Undeserving Poor

Distinguishing between eligible and ineligible communities relies on creating hierarchies of deserving and undeserving poor. Communities that have not engaged in self-reliance initiatives or have not demonstrated a willingness to co-contribute to state-supported improvement projects are placed at a distinct disadvantage as authorities see them as justifiably ineligible or unentitled compared with communities that accept their shared responsibility for development alongside government agencies.[27]

The ascendency of the NLD to Myanmar's civilian government in 2016 strengthened rather than weakened distinctions between the deserving and undeserving poor. National and local members of the NLD encouraged the coproduction of public goods using the moral discourse of democratic duty (described in chapter 4). At public events between 2015 and 2021, for instance, Aung San Suu Kyi repeatedly urged citizens: "Think of what you can contribute for the development of your country, not what benefits you can have from your country. . . . Only demanding rights without assuming responsibility and accountability, which are wholly left to the government, does not comply with democracy standards" (Suu Kyi, cited in Callahan 2017, 2). The constellation of democracy and "self-reliance" recurred in election campaign events in the months before Myanmar's historic November 2015 elections. At a village meet-and-greet that I attended in provincial Myanmar, one of the NLD candidates explained to villagers how "development" would work if the NLD was elected:

> [After the election], you will be able to ask for your rights (*akhwint ayay*) and try to develop your village. . . . We can cooperate and work together. The NLD needs to know the needs of the village. But the village also needs to discuss and cooperate with us to lead improvements here.

The notion of communities securing rights by "cooperating" with the state and leading improvements was notably absent of promises—such as funding for specific projects or initiatives in exchange for votes, a hallmark of clientelistic politics elsewhere in the region (Aspinall and Sukmajati 2016). Instead, candidates echoed the emphasis Suu Kyi herself placed on democratic "responsibility," further entrenching a category of deserving citizens who willingly assumed social responsibility to the communities in which they lived while expecting little from the state. The continued reliance on these distinctions during the decade of partial civilian rule was *not* the consequence of military control over bureaucracy: indeed, all ministries relevant to rural and local development were led by officials appointed by Myanmar's civilian government.[28]

The perceived practical and civic superiority of non-state social action provided philosophical grounds for excluding some communities and people from government aid. Those that did not fulfill the duties envisaged by a welfare capitalist ideal of the polity were considered legitimately less worthy of state aid. State and region NLD parliamentarians, interviewed in September 2016 about communities being excluded from government social schemes if they had not contributed to local development, strongly support the logic behind this outcome. They repeated the same discourse of reciprocal duties as a requirement of liberty, as discussed in chapter 4, explaining that communities that had not engaged in local improvement initiatives did not deserve state funding because "democracy needs people who take responsibility" for themselves and society.

The role of self-reliance in claim-making and entitlement in this way reveals a politics of entitlement determined by whether potential recipients of state aid or concessions fulfill the obligations of reciprocity generated by decades of social outsourcing and welfare capitalism after 1988 (see chapters 2 and 3). The nature of entitlement in this vision of the polity resembles socialist-era legal reasoning. Eligibility to possess rights could previously be claimed by virtue of sacrifices made willingly or unwillingly for the socialist vision of Ne Win and later in support of the welfare capitalist state-building strategy of the SLORC/SPDC. Post-2011 rights to state aid then began to accrue to those who demonstrated their commitment to a welfare capitalist notion of moral and political community in which businesspeople and communities were expected to assume significant responsibility for social redistribution. The claims of entitlement possible on the basis of forced labor during the junta-era and self-reliance during the decade of partial civilian rule are thus categorically similar: both enabled claims to "a delimited right tied to reciprocal duties" rather than any form of entitlement derived from legal citizenship (Cheesman 2015a, 109; Wells 2018).

The distributive imaginary reinforced through this welfare capitalist politics of entitlement is cruelly optimistic (Berlant 2011). Development and progress are framed as achievable through the unity and generosity of community members alone, with minimal support from institutions of the state. Instead, citizens were expected to engage in practices of private redistribution by cultivating bonds across wealth and social hierarchies. Even state officials were encapsulated into the collective of "community" evoked during these projects, with their contributions to self-reliance initiatives depicted as personal *gifts* dispersed through their goodwill in response to the demonstrated worthiness of subjects.[29] Possession of formal citizenship or payment of taxes lend no inherent weight to claims on the state in this framework. Instead, officials are empowered to withhold state aid from communities they judge are not sufficiently committed to the virtues of self-reliance and the vision of private welfare provision it valorizes.

Putting aside the fact that failure to participate or co-contribute to public goods provision could also logically signal the need for *more* and not less assistance from the state (Bulloch 2017, chap. 7), the moral criteria used to distinguish worthy from unworthy recipients of state aid reinforce pernicious cleavages of deservingness and belonging within the polity.

Zero-Sum Rights and Societal Cleavages

It is not only the poor or those who lack connections to patrons and commercial elites who can find themselves excluded from state aid in a welfare capitalist politics of entitlement. The competition to have rights, which pits the "self-reliant" against the "undeserving poor," exacerbates societal divides by justifying exclusion and even expulsion of minority communities. An imaginary of rights as zero-sum and competitive recurred throughout my fieldwork in violent demands to exclude minorities such as the Rohingya and Muslims more broadly from the slippery and conditional rights and opportunities afforded to legal citizens of Myanmar. Narratives that have framed Muslims and South Asians more broadly as disproportionately wealthy and better resourced than average Burmese people (see chapter 4) circulated alongside state propaganda that excludes Rohingya and other minorities from ideologies of "national races" (*taingyintha*) (Cheesman 2017a, 195–196). The contingency of citizenship and rights as a result can create pernicious incentives to violently excise minorities from territory and political community when they are labeled as "unworthy" to compete with "legitimate" citizens for finite state resources or opportunities (Davies 2018, 145–158). The outpouring of popular support from many Burmese people for the Myanmar military and for the NLD government following the Tatmadaw's 2017 campaign to expel Rohingya—and Suu Kyi's defense of the Tatmadaw in international forums—highlights the tragic and pernicious nature of this competitive logic of rights.

Even minorities included in official ethnic-based notions of citizenship must also work to earn the recognition of state officials, despite long histories of conflict that have often eroded their trust in the state. Decades of violence and insurgency throughout Myanmar's borderlands have entrenched discourses critical of state social failure distinct from the social outsourcing ideology dominant in lowland areas after 1988. In northern Karen State, for instance, ideals and practices of non-state welfare common in lowland areas did not develop in the same way after 1988 due to ongoing conflict.[30] In these areas since the early independence period, the Karen National Union along with its broader societal partners in churches and community-based groups often based in Thailand attempted to deliver essential services such as schools and mobile health treatment to regions where it claims control (Decobert 2015; Brenner 2017a). Rather than mitigating the expectations of the state, the symbolic language enlisted by these non-state institutions in their everyday interactions with populations emphasized the failure of the Myanmar government to deliver development and respect the aspirations of Karen people for cultural and political autonomy (Brenner 2017a; McCarthy and Farrelly 2020). Consequentially, the expansion of state-mediated local development funds in northern Karen State after a bilateral 2012 ceasefire created tensions over the demands these schemes made for local contributions to public goods.

Karen communities in Thandaungyi were far more skeptical of attempts to render them responsible for coproduction of public goods than their counterparts in adjacent lowland areas. At the heart of this reluctance are strong variances in perceptions of state responsibility for public goods. When asked in the 2016 survey who *should* be responsible for building and maintaining roads, 15 percent more respondents in northern Karen State named government agents such as the municipal or state authorities than respondents in lowland areas. Their strength of entitlement from the state contrasts directly with lowland respondents, 15 percent more of whom expected roads be built through "self-reliance" or in partnership with local elders or commercial elites than their counterparts in upland areas. Decades of insurgency thus deeply shaped individual expectations of the appropriate social role of the state. Limited experience with self-reliant projects is a key factor here, with respondents in upland ceasefire areas 10 percent less likely to have contributed to local improvement initiatives and 40 percent less likely to have given money to local road construction than those in lowland areas.[31]

Attitudinal differences between upland and lowland communities, rooted in different lived experiences during the 1990s and 2000s, created tensions over whether communities that refuse to embrace the competitive logics of welfare capitalist rights are worthy of government social aid. After 2011, many ethnic minority politicians and armed groups advocated for a federal system that would devolve considerable budgetary and expenditure powers to the subnational level, enabling intermediation of development through previously insurgent social orders (Brenner 2017a; McCarthy and Farrelly 2020). Since the military returned to power in February 2021, demands for federal political reform have only intensified, especially among ethnically and religiously diverse coalitions of pro-democracy activists (Dunford 2021; Thawnghmung and Noah 2021). If and when a new political settlement is reached, idioms of self-reliance are unlikely to disappear as a feature of citizen-state relations because of their practical and normative appeal. Karen elites who reside in lowland Taungoo, for instance, expressed anxiety before the 2021 coup that if communities in ceasefire areas did not willingly contribute to local improvements, they would achieve minimal developmental progress. As a Karen pastor involved in social development in northern Karen State explained to me in 2018:

> We can say that in terms of their Christian faith, the mountain Karen villagers are very strong. But there is a problem with their mindset as they expect others to support them and will not take responsibility for themselves. They refuse to accept that they must stand on their own in a unified way in order to develop fully.

The unwillingness of poor minorities to co-contribute to development, a legacy of decades of conflict, is here reframed as a problem that will hold some of Myanmar's most deprived people back from state aid that may improve their lives. If and when negotiations toward a more democratic and federalized political structure eventually progress, the question of which governmental entities will intermediate development—national-level ministries, subnational governments, or state-like apparatuses of armed groups—will be a stumbling block to the emergence of a stable political settlement across the country (South 2017; McCarthy and Farrelly 2020). Given these dynamics, the ideal of coproduced development will need to be consistently challenged by Myanmar's diverse anti-dictatorship coalition, and a more just and redistributive ideal of the polity institutionalized, if postcoup demands for federal political change are to prevent social outsourcing from simply taking on new or mutated forms.

Austerity and Slippery Entitlement

Following the transition to partial civilian rule in 2011, ideals and practices of social outsourcing found their way into the heart of claim-making from the elected government. Hierarchies of worthiness were institutionalized as communities competed to render themselves worthy to coproduce development and welfare alongside state agencies. The insecure welfare regime that emerged was legitimized by a cruelly optimistic vision in which development and social justice more broadly were seen as achievable through the unity and generosity of community members, non-state actors, and virtuous tycoons, with minimal support from state agencies (see Berlant 2011). Residents concerned about their remoteness from emergency medical care or the spread of disease from open sewers were encouraged by this cruel optimism to turn to each other and not to expect the state to respond—even though state agencies after 2011 were better resourced than they had been in generations to help address these problems.

Inequality permeated every element of this precarious welfare regime. Less affluent households shouldered an unfair share of the burden for "self-reliant" projects relative to richer neighbors whose proportionally far smaller donations received widespread praise. Yet the poor tended to benefit far less from the provision of collectively provided public goods than commercial elites, who were often disproportionately responsible for degrading local infrastructure in the first place. More broadly, by encouraging competition over who has a "right" to receive government social aid, this ideal justified the exclusion of people and communities unable or unwilling to "stand on their own" because of poverty or historical grievances against state oppression.

The role of non-state welfare initiatives in determining which communities receive government aid bears striking resemblance to the distributive politics of neighboring countries such as India, Indonesia, and Thailand and also more established democracies such as the United States and austerity Europe. Across these contexts, ideologies legitimizing state retrenchment or absence have sought to uproot notions that a state-mediated social safety net is "a matter of entitlement" and reframe such aid as a generous "gift" from authorities, patrons, or companies for which recipients should be "grateful" (Nickel 2018, 63).[32] Reflecting the intensification of populism and xenophobia globally in recent years, what emerged in Myanmar during the decade of partial civilian rule was a precarious and sometimes vicious politics of entitlement in which notions of social "rights" were replaced by slippery claims of worthiness mediated through ideals and mechanisms of self-reliance. The already-affluent were able to expand their economic dominance by evading taxation while the poor and working class were mired in a precarious web of debt, conditional state aid, and for some, outright social exclusion on the basis of their identity.

In Myanmar, the drive to encourage ordinary people to assume responsibility for development may shift in the wake of the widespread civil disobedience movement which emerged following the 2021 return to dictatorship. As ordinary people have withheld their cooperation from projects of the military state, labor and social activists have directly challenged the expectation that the poor must "stand on their own," instead demanding a new political order in which social justice and inclusion are core priorities of the state (Jordt, Tharphi Than, and Sue Ye Lin 2021). The reliance of the postcoup resistance movement on local mechanisms of non-state reciprocity and collective endeavor created during the 1990s and 2000s highlights the paradoxical legacy of social outsourcing: it can both exacerbate the vulnerability of the poor while also creating ideals and practices of mutuality beyond the state that can enable grassroots struggles against egregious state repression. The concluding chapter of the book draws these insights together, examining what the long and complex legacies of social outsourcing in Myanmar suggest about the origins of precarious welfare regimes, their persistence over time, and the role of non-state welfare in sustaining alternative visions of the polity during periods of political upheaval.

PATH-DEPENDENCE AND WELFARE REGIME CHANGE

This book has examined why outsourcing social responsibility from state to non-state actors continues over time despite changes in political regimes. Through close study of Myanmar's modern political history, where ideals and practices of non-state welfare have formed a critical tool of governance for decades, the book raises critical questions about why precarious and unequal welfare systems endure in autocratic and democratic regimes alike and the conditions in which they can be changed.

Existing comparative research on inequality and state social action largely focuses on the constraints imposed on governmental welfare provision by limited state capacity and the enduring influence of authoritarian-era constitutions and laws (Albertus and Menaldo 2013; Soifer 2013; Ansell and Samuels 2014). The previous chapters have sought to shed light on a related though less examined impediment to governmental action for the poor: how the earlier outsourcing of welfare to non-state actors shapes both the ideals and material interests of ordinary people, state officials, and commercial elites regarding how social aid and development should be delivered and achieved. In doing so, we see the value of an interpretive approach that takes seriously the way political and moral ideals can markedly shape policy and social outcomes over time.

Informed by extensive mixed-methods fieldwork, the book has further shown that non-state welfare can exacerbate inequality and fracture the polity in ways that undermine state redistributive action. Yet outsourcing state social responsibility to private, charitable, and philanthropic providers will continue because outsourcing often partly aligns with the interests and ideals of diverse actors. Poor voters, for instance, contribute to and receive often patchy social support and public goods from non-state sources—viewing their contributions and those of others to charity and philanthropy as enacting a moral ethic of civic duty. Meanwhile, commercial elites who donate a fraction of their wealth to charity and public goods can accrue public reputations and cultivate political support, allowing them to evade direct taxation and influence government regulation. Elected representatives may also avoid taxing commercial elites or their constituents to fund state social spending, instead encouraging non-state welfare provision through tax remissions and a moral discourse of citizen duty to "co-produce" development. The combination of these material and ideational factors has an effect that ensures social outsourcing continues, even in electoral regimes in which representatives should theoretically use the state to respond to the needs of vulnerable voters. Yet even when created by official strategies of state social outsourcing, non-state welfare can sustain social and political visions opposed to officially sanctioned ideologies, enabling survival and resistance amid dictatorship and disorder.

The book makes theoretical, empirical, and methodological contributions that aid in understanding both Myanmar's insecure welfare regime and the legacies of social outsourcing in a comparative perspective. In these concluding comments, I examine implications of the research in three areas: first, the origins of non-state welfare ideals and institutions; second, why social outsourcing can endure even with regime change; and third, how non-state welfare can paradoxically perpetuate systems that ensnare the poor in precarity and debt while sustaining efforts to contest the autocratic state and reimagine social and political order.

The Origins of Non-State Welfare

The experiences of Myanmar clarify how non-state welfare can come to occupy a central place in welfare regimes. Focusing on postcolonial institutional inheritances from British rule, chapter 1 showed how decades of grievances with the extractive colonial economy, especially unfair practices of taxation, sparked rebellion when the Great Depression dispossessed scores of indebted farmers. By the time of independence, elite and popular animosity toward the colonial economy had enshrined a vision of a welfare-oriented, economically interventionist state in the 1947 Constitution. However, lingering anti-tax sentiment along with a weak postcolonial apparatus of administration, especially in upland periphery areas, narrowed the options for financing a more just, state-led welfare regime. For the first fifteen years of independence, the elected government pursued a welfare capitalist vision of postcolonial modernization, the Pyidawtha Plan, which encouraged foreign investment while regulating private enterprise to co-contribute alongside employees to a formal social protection scheme for workers. Rather than develop an apparatus of direct taxation, however, the state instead funded its role in welfare provision by indirectly taxing the rural population through price controls set by a government trading monopoly. As the military rapidly expanded and institutionalized itself, and as declining rice export revenues through the 1950s led modernization plans to falter, General Ne Win justified the 1962 coup on the grounds that civilians had continued colonialism by enabling private enterprise and embracing foreign investors. Between 1962 and 1988, Ne Win's Burma Socialist Programme Party (BSPP) attempted to build a wholly state-controlled economy and welfare regime. As untaxed borderland trade proliferated to fill booming demand for scarce goods in lowland Burma, the contradictions in the BSPP's autarkic economic strategy and expansive state commitment to welfare prompted demonetization in 1987 and outright political crisis in 1988.

The consensus against unregulated capitalism and direct taxation that shaped the welfare regime after independence mutated over time to reinforce the expansive role of non-state welfare actors in social justice and welfare provision. Part 1 of this book, informed by extensive fieldwork in lowland provincial areas, revealed a form of rule that I term *autocratic welfare capitalism*. Unable to sustain the BSPP's autarkic state-mediated welfare model, post-socialist military officials after 1988 instead mediated market reform and retrenched the social state by transferring state welfare obligations to commercial elites and non-state actors. Chapter 2 examined the proliferation of local practices and ideals of charity and philanthropy during the 1990s and 2000s, often enabled by the patronage of businesspeople who received commercial licenses and tax remissions from junta officials in return for these contributions and cooperation with the military state. Probing the ideals underpinning these practices, we saw how religious authorities, commercial elites, ordinary people, and activists enlisted Buddhist notions of "charity" (*dana*) and "work for others" (*parahita*) to ideologically justify extensive social obligations to the needy at the same time as the state retrenched itself from the welfare mix. A postcolonial commitment to an economically interventionist and socially oriented state thereby mutated into a welfare regime in which non-state actors, including regime-aligned economic elites, played a more central social role than ever before.

Though non-state welfare practices were initially locally oriented in their scope after 1988, chapter 3 examined how these mechanisms extended to strangers during moments of disaster in ways that shaped durably popular conceptions of citizenship and the polity. Non-state relief efforts during Cyclone Nargis in 2008 and Cyclone Komen in 2015 were crucial to the governance of both natural catastrophes, despite the evolution of the political regime in the intervening periods. In both cases, volunteers who raised funds from rich and poor alike and then disbursed relief, often at state encouragement, mobilized emotive ideas of empathy and obligation beyond kin. These ideals made it possible to deliver tangible support to the distant needy. Yet most aid went to communities that shared the ethnoreligious identity of volunteers and were geographically accessible to lowland areas where relief efforts were largely being coordinated. The exclusion of some regions and communities badly affected by disasters from non-state aid for reasons of logistics or identity demonstrates the informal boundaries of citizenship that emerge when the state outsources social aid and plays a minimal direct role in relief efforts. In the absence of government action to address inequities between communities and regions, the exclusion of populations from non-state welfare reinforces preexisting social cleavages—of race, ethnicity, religion, and region. The fracturing of social solidarity exacerbated by these efforts of non-state welfare can erode the collective consensus necessary to finance and build a more just and developmental welfare regime.

From postcolonial socialism to autocratic welfare capitalism, the tensions between ideals and institutions that embedded non-state welfare after 1988 in Myanmar have markedly shaped social development in a range of other contexts from West Africa to the Middle East to Latin America (L. MacLean 2004, 2010, 2011a; Cammett and MacLean 2014; McGovern 2017, chap. 7). Indeed, welfare regimes that rely on private provision of social welfare often have their roots in the ideals and anxieties of decision makers during key moments in time, as the experience of welfare state development in the United States of America has demonstrated (Orloff 1988; Béland and Hacker 2004). However, comparative research on overall social spending by both public and private actors, and the origins of welfare regimes that deliberately reinforce the expansive role of charitable and non-state institutions in the welfare mix, has largely focused on affluent countries in the Organization for Economic Cooperation and Development (OECD). Given the significant role played by private and non-state institutions in welfare provision in both developed (Adema 1999) and developing contexts alike (Wood and Gough 2006), further mixed-methods research on evolutions in the welfare mix is needed to identify the pathways and historical processes whereby social outsourcing can create and perpetuate insecure welfare regimes.

Non-State Welfare and Political Transitions

Part 2 of the book shed light on why social outsourcing can remain a go-to governance strategy across regimes even during and after political transition. A growing body of literature on private welfare demonstrates that once ideals and practices of non-state social provision become established, they often shape the modalities of social policy in ways that exacerbate inequities over time (Hacker 2002; Béland 2005; Hacker 2016a). Chapter 4 took the case of grassroots democracy activists and wealthy donors to examine how non-state welfare can be both *practically* and *normatively* appealing to elites and ordinary voters alike. Activists and wealthy donors who became the core of the local campaign apparatus of the National League for Democracy (NLD) during the decade of civilian rule between 2011 and early 2021, for instance, frequently compared the functional efficiency of non-state welfare and public goods provision with the bureaucratic opacity and corruption of the Myanmar government. Beyond these practical benefits, though, they also praised non-state welfare as normatively superior to state-led provision of social support—believing it helped restore moral and civic bonds of "democracy" and citizenship that were degraded over decades of colonial rule and dictatorship. Even activists who sought to reform the rigged 2008 Constitution between 2011 and 2021 worked to socially embed ideals and practices of non-state welfare, including by circulating prejudicial stories about "stingy" Muslims in order to encourage philanthropy by all business elites. The centrality of non-state welfare to notions of "democracy" can ideationally justify an insecure welfare regime since it absolves elected officials of obligations to alleviate the precarity of the working poor through state action. Yet even when political expression by non-state welfare providers is tightly bounded due to fear of state repression and financial reliance on the patronage of economic elites loyal to an autocratic regime, mechanisms of local reciprocity can still maintain a degree of autonomy from direct government control. These factors can ensure social outsourcing remains appealing to diverse actors seeking to take meaningful micro-level social action independent of the state. The net result is that charity and philanthropy can retain crucial roles both in the welfare mix and in resisting autocratic repression over time.

By giving a slice of their wealth away to support public goods and collective identities, tycoons can perpetuate ideals and practices of social outsourcing while enabling the expansion and defense of their commercial empires. Chapter 5 showed that the practices of philanthropy required for capital accumulation during post-socialist junta rule in Myanmar shifted and intensified with the transition to partial civilian rule. During the decade between 2011 and 2021, it was not enough to simply satisfy provincial and national military patrons that the obligations of wealth and commercial success were being fulfilled through social philanthropy, as was the case during the 1990s and 2000s. Rather, throughout partial civilian rule, elites in Myanmar became far more public-facing, and they increasingly sought to patronize social welfare groups, local infrastructure, political parties, and collective projects of religious and regional identity (re)invention in ways that would generate symbolic and financial bonds with ordinary people. Using the case of prominent tycoon Khin Maung Aye, chapter 5 showed that philanthropy by economic elites between 2011 and 2021 aimed to generate a degree of social consent to their economic and political dominance, a dynamic that helped them defend their wealth from scrutiny and potential democratic demands for market regulation or asset redistribution.

In exposing the normative and practical appeal of non-state redistribution to partisan, bureaucratic, and economic elites, the book contributes to literature on why precarious welfare regimes endure even in electoral contexts. The bulk of existing research on path dependency of private and market sources of welfare primarily focuses on periods of policy contingency in industrialized democracies such as the United States and Canada (Béland and Hacker 2004). Meanwhile, existing literature on the perpetuation of regressive distribution in new democracies and during political transition either focuses solely on "rigged" or "gamed" formal institutions such as constitutions (Albertus and Menaldo 2013) or on vote-buying and clientelism as explaining suboptimal social policy (Keefer 2007). This book couples formal institutional analysis with an interpretive "thick-descriptive" approach to the study of politics, especially vernacular understandings of democracy and the social and institutional milieu from which they emerge (Schaffer 2014, 329). By taking seriously how moral ideals can entrench systemic inequality, the book shows how precarity and conditionality can come to define social linkages between citizens and the state. Chapter 6 considered the seeming paradox that contemporary state poverty alleviation and development initiatives in Myanmar were disproportionately awarded after 2011 to communities that demonstrated their independence *from* the state. Case studies and household survey data showed that communities that performed their collective "self-reliance" by proactively contributing cash or labor to local public goods initiatives were markedly more likely to receive state social aid. Here again we see how the normative and practical appeal of social outsourcing to ostensibly reformist politicians and officials can entrench welfare regimes that saddle the poor with significant responsibility to bootstrap themselves out of poverty before they are considered worthy of government support.

From the perspective of bureaucrats and politicians seeking to avoid taxing their wealthy patrons, it might make sense to reward "self-reliant" communities with additional state support because it allows finite government funds to be stretched further than if support was extended to all communities in need. Yet, beyond being practically appealing, achieving development without the state was also framed as *normatively* superior by many state officials and party activists who viewed volitional acts of giving and service as generating the bonds—especially between the affluent and the poor—required to achieve their vision of civic renewal through voluntary private action. In contrast, communities that did not proactively contribute to social initiatives because of poverty or histories of con-flict were viewed as less eligible to receive state aid, even though they are arguably the most in need of support. Demanding people contribute to local development at implicit threat of exclusion from state aid resembles a mutated liberal form of the forced labor practices for which Myanmar became globally notorious during the 1990s and 2000s junta. Yet the *practical* and *normative* appeal of social outsourc-ing to state officials and party representatives, and the incentives for villages to compete against each other in order to receive finite state aid, can entrench auster-ity and conditionality even when government social spending is expanding.

Welfare Outsourcing Privatizes the Polity

The book showed how ideals and practices of social outsourcing stymie progress toward a more secure and just socioeconomic system by eroding expectations of state social leadership. The role of economic elites in non-state welfare provision can distort incentives to redress socioeconomic injustices and inequities through state action. As demonstrated in the attempt to suppress activism against land grabs described in chapter 5, tycoons are able to cultivate civic and moral bonds with political elites, activists, and even their harshest critics by filling the vacuum left by the state in key areas of public goods provision. Similar patterns have been observed in established democracies such as the United States, where scholars and policy activists are increasingly debating whether the influence that foundations, endowments, and private donations grant to tycoons over public debate and politi-cal decision-making is "repugnant to the whole idea of democracy" (Reich 2016; Skocpol 2016; Nickel 2018; Reich 2018; Giridharadas 2019). The experience of Myanmar shows how the symbolic capital and contingent loyalty accrued through public gifts of these kinds can complicate the commitment of state officials to re-dress economic injustice and precarity through governmental intervention. State-led redistribution during Myanmar's decade of partial civilian rule was certainly constrained by the legal terms of Myanmar's 2008 Constitution and the realpolitik of civil-military relations. However, the social license that economic elites were able to accrue by fulfilling their roles in a welfare capitalist ideal also shielded their past and ongoing economic exploitation from scrutiny, allowing them to evade state social action.

The critical role of private, non-state actors in the welfare mix can also erode the development of state social capacity by absolving elected officials of addressing social injustices directly. In many contexts, philanthropic donations by tycoons and companies can be used to reduce taxable income. During Myanmar's decade of partial civilian rule, domestic and international companies were permitted by tax code to deduct up to 25 percent of their income through donations, a right that was used extensively after 2011 for businesses and tycoons to make regular and public contributions to personal or corporate foundations. These contributions can help achieve positive social outcomes, including supporting specific communities in need especially in the wake of disaster. Still, the net effect of tax-deductible donations, especially in contexts of weak state capacity, is to deprive government institutions of the revenue essential for them to take robust state social action to support the poor and drive inclusive development. Here we see how the normative appeal of social outsourcing as more effective and virtuous relative to tax-funded government spending can undermine the development of state social capacity over time, reinforcing the constraints to state redistributive action, including toward Tatmadaw businesses, that were enshrined by Myanmar's military-drafted 2008 Constitution. Indeed, following constitutional procedure laws on taxation could in theory be amended between 2011 and 2021 by civilian governments with a simple majority of the Union parliament even if military representatives opposed such moves. Yet, throughout Myanmar's decade of partial civilian rule, many democratically elected legislators and activists, including State Counselor Aung San Suu Kyi, framed philanthropic provision of public goods as not just functionally necessary but also *normatively admirable*—a perception shared by lawmakers across the political spectrum in established democracies such as the United States. When preference for low taxes and outsourcing of social redistribution to private and non-state actors are framed in civic cultural terms, elected political elites have little incentive to reform the business concessions of the past, pass laws to tax natural resource extraction, or even ensure the enforcement of existing tax codes. Instead, the Myanmar government's revenue-raising efforts after 2011 predominantly focused on boosting regressive consumption taxes, a strategy that tends to compound preexisting inequalities by disproportionately burdening the poor far more than the affluent.[1] The enduring legacies of social outsourcing thus impose constraints on state social capacity, separate from those of rigged legal institutions, feeding back in ways that exacerbate inequality despite electoral incentives.

State social schemes that reward informal contributions to social welfare or public goods initiatives can similarly exacerbate pernicious social and economic inequities. As discussed in chapter 6, self-reliance as a criterion on which state officials and parliamentarians dispersed poverty alleviation and development programs rendered "rights" contingent on competing with other poor communities and people for who was more "deserving" of government aid. Hierarchies of wealth and power are encouraged to be hidden behind a veneer of collective unity and self-reliance in the hope that demonstrating such bonds may convince state officials that their community is worthier than others to receive social support.

What emerges is a zero-sum game in which the poor must bond themselves to local elites and proactively regulate who is considered deserving of state aid—a sentiment that legitimizes the expulsion of minorities such as the Rohingya, who have been demonized for decades in state propaganda and by political elites as free-riding noncitizens seeking to "steal" the opportunities of native populations. Making participation in private improvement a key criterion for receiving state aid thus serves to hide economic hierarchies and entrench coproduction of public goods while encouraging individuals to viciously regulate the boundaries of political community and entitlement.

Insecure welfare regimes that rely on non-state actors can thus place inequity and precarity at the heart of the polity—even in electoral regimes. Access to social support provided by welfare groups, religious authorities, and economic elites is often shaped both by intermediaries who broker aid and collective or individual moral performances of 'worthiness' by potential beneficiaries. As a result, contractarian notions of social aid as a "right" to which one is entitled by virtue of citizenship or payment of taxes are replaced by a more slippery, bounded, and contingent conception of eligibility which must be constantly reproved. Precarity is inherent in this type of welfare regime since providers of aid can withhold assistance in the context of scarcity or if the correlative duties of *reciprocal* relationships with authorities are viewed as unfulfilled (Wood 2003). Moreover, the expansive idea of "duty" that is required to resource non-state provision of welfare may exacerbate social cleavages of race, religion, and region while further entrenching perceptions of the state as inefficient, stingy, and aloof from citizens. By giving oxygen to the idea that social justice can be achieved without state involvement, and further fracturing notions of national political community, support for non-state welfare can also constrain the ability of elected officials to win over economic elites and ordinary voters, both of whom are crucial if progressive tax reforms necessary for developmental nation-building are to be progressed (E. Lieberman 2001, Lieberman 2003). By eroding the expansion of state revenue capacity and undermining the practical and normative commitment of elected officials to state-led support to the poor, non-state welfare can entrench suboptimal social outcomes and permit wealth to be further concentrated in the hands of the wealthy few.

Toward a Redistributive Polity?

Despite limiting the possibility of more inclusive and socially progressive governance in ordinary times, the vibrancy of non-state action enabled by social outsourcing can also lay the groundwork for revolutionary new possibilities during periods of political upheaval. Throughout the decade of partial civilian rule,

Myanmar's elected leaders, including Aung San Suu Kyi and her senior advisers, continued to rely on social outsourcing as a core tool to deliver public welfare and pursue civic renewal. Rather than use the levers of the state to achieve more progressive or redistributive social policy Suu Kyi's NLD, in alliance with economic elites, sought to intensify market capitalism and foreign investment while further entrenching ideals and practices of non-state welfare, even going as far as making them pathways to accessing state aid (as discussed in chapter 6). The cruelly optimistic ideal of achieving social justice through private redistribution and low direct taxation resulted in unequal social and economic outcomes and foreclosed more sustainable solutions to the dire vulnerabilities and injustices bequeathed by decades of dictatorship.[2]

Yet localized mechanisms and ideals of non-state welfare can also sustain societal resistance to autocracy and dictatorship. Within days of the February 2021 coup in Myanmar, for instance, neighborhood groups comprised of local activists, elders, ousted parliamentarians, and civil servants were formed around the country, building on preexisting non-state social ideals and practices to erect an apparatus of local administration parallel to the military state (Jordt, Tharaphi Than, and Sue Ye Lin 2021, 26–29). Networks of solidarity began to pool resources to feed striking civil servants, conduct nighttime patrols to ensure public safety, and mobilize residents to defy orders and laws issued by the junta. These ideals and practices of reciprocity, often rooted in the 1990s and 2000s, animated the work of local welfare teams who, even when facing harassment, helped coordinate and deliver treatment during the brutal COVID-19 wave that the struck the country in mid-2021. With ordinary people boycotting government health facilities in protest at the occupation of public clinics and hospitals by security personnel, private and philanthropic clinics linked to foundations of tycoons stepped in with junta encouragement to administer hundreds of thousands of COVID-19 vaccinations. As conflict intensified between the Myanmar military and various resistance organizations opposed to the coup, schools run by ethnic social service providers also began offering basic education to children forced to flee violence. All these dynamics deepened the social role of non-state actors, ensuring that private, charitable, and ethnic armed groups will retain major roles in Myanmar's welfare regime over the near term.

The civil disobedience and resistance movements formed on the back of non-state aid networks in 2021 highlight how the legacies of past social outsourcing can paradoxically enable a challenge to political regimes during moments of institutional contingency. For the first time in decades, the unequal political economy bequeathed by autocratic welfare capitalism has been vocally challenged after the February 2021 coup by diverse constituencies previously largely ignored by state officials. Labor activists, youth, women, ethnic and religious minorities, and diverse subaltern communities spearheaded a popular movement to abolish the military-drafted 2008 Constitution and establish a "federal democratic union" in the months after the coup. A more just and inclusive democratic economic and social system is at the heart of their political demands. As female garment workers chanted in the early weeks following the coup: "We must resist! We have nothing to lose but our chains!" (Jordt et al 2021, 8). The opposition National Unity Government, formed by parliamentarians ousted in February 2021, have followed their lead—committing itself to drafting a new charter in partnership with diverse resistance forces fighting for social justice.

Whether the terms of a future political order can lay to rest logics of state social absence entrenched over decades remains to be seen—depending as it does on the resistance movement successfully setting the terms of negotiations toward a reimagined status quo. What is clear is that ideals and practices of non-state welfare, generated during the autocratic rule of the 1990s and 2000s, have after the February 2021 coup helped sustain a revolutionary struggle that could dramatically challenge the vicious cycles of inequality, austerity, and repression that have governed Myanmar for almost two centuries.

Notes

INTRODUCTION

1. The section that follows draws from field notes, 20 May 2016.

2. Throughout the book, all interlocutors and organizations with whom I had direct contact have been given pseudonyms to protect their identity. Publicly prominent people with whom I had no direct contact, such as Khin Maung Aye, along with nationally significant institutions have retained their real names.

3. Throughout the book, I refer to Myanmar's regime type between early 2011 and the February 2021 coup as "partial civilian rule." I use this term to signal the more representative form of governance that was created after the discredited November 2010 election. Although not contested by the NLD, Myanmar's main opposition party, the election was not considered free and fair because it resulted in the formation of a government largely led by civilianized former military officers who initiated a process of political, economic, and social liberalization before holding an openly contested election in November 2015. Because Myanmar's military retained 25 percent of seats in the legislature, plus formal control over the Ministries of Defense, Home Affairs, and Border Affairs and a veto on constitutional reform by virtue of the 2008 Constitution, I continue to refer to governance after the November 2015 election as partial civilian rule, albeit a more democratic form. The critical juncture or transition that I refer to throughout this book denotes the categorical shift from direct military rule to partial civilian governance between 2011 and the military coup in early 2021, as well as the more specific transition from an unfairly elected government comprised largely of civilianized military officers (2011–2015) to a democratically elected civilian government led by Aung San Suu Kyi (between March 2016 and February 2021).

4. Allocations to social sectors—health, education, and welfare—jumped as a share of Myanmar's national budget from 5.8 percent in 2011 to 12.5 percent in 2019 and 2020, which was an increase from 1 percent of gross domestic product (GDP) to around 3 percent total (UNICEF 2020, 2). According to the ASEAN Secretariat, government budget allocations to education *alone* (excluding health and welfare) averaged 3.45 percent of GDP across the Association of Southeast Asian Nations (ASEAN) in 2017—a disjuncture that highlights Myanmar's status as a laggard on state social spending, specifically on welfare, relative to its neighbors (ASEAN Secretariat 2018, 13, average by author).

5. The Ministry of Defence budget was maintained at between 13 and 15 percent between 2012 and 2013 and 2018 to 2019, although it dropped to 11 percent in the 2019–2020 period, following a 29 percent year-on-year increase of the overall size of the Union budget (UNICEF 2020, 3, fn2). For context on military budget allocations, see Nyein Nyein, "Parliament Approves Reduced Budget for 2017–2018," *The Irrawaddy*, March 17, 2017. On attempts to cut the military budget amid COVID-19, see Nyein Nyein, "Myanmar Parliament Slashes Military's Budget Request for First Time," *The Irrawaddy*, May 28, 2020.

6. The overall percentage of the national budget dedicated to social welfare was 0.38 percent of Union budget in 2019–2020, a proportionally significant increase from the miniscule base of 0.05 percent from 2011 to 2012. Despite budget expansion, total actual expenditures by the Ministry of Social Welfare, Relief, and Resettlement (MoSWRR)

comprised only US$36.5 million in 2017–2018. For detailed analysis of MoSWRR budget allocations between 2011 and 2019, see MOPFI 2020 and UNICEF 2020. For simplicity's sake, "welfare" is defined as the primary responsibility of MoSWRR, which takes the lead on state social initiatives aimed at reducing vulnerability of core population groups across the life course—from support for mothers of nutritionally deprived newborns and care for people with disabilities to financial aid and care for displaced populations and the elderly. Other government ministries also run programs with a social focus; for example, there are Ministry of Health and Sport schemes aimed at reducing extremely high levels of out-of-pocket health expenses and Ministry of Agriculture, Livestock, and Irrigation programs to promote rural development. However, these initiatives comprised comparatively small slices of overall ministry budgets and, like MoSWRR, often rely on non-state social actors to help implement or achieve program objectives, as discussed in chapter 6.

7. On economic impacts and governance responses to COVID-19 before the 2021 coup, see Brancati et al. 2020 and Kyu Khin Gar 2020. On local community impacts and responses to COVID-19, see Rhoads et al. 2020. On government solicitation of donations, see Zaw Zaw Htwe, "Donations Pour in as People of Myanmar Dig Deep to Help Cover Cost of Vaccine," *The Irrawaddy*, January 12, 2021.

8. In April 2020, the NLD government announced its US$2 billion COVID-19 Economic Relief Plan, which provided a range of supports including emergency loans to businesses and trade financing and around US$210 million in cash and food to support the most vulnerable. The initial package accounted for 2.5 to 3 percent of GDP, below the average ASEAN commitment of 3.7 percent of GDP and significantly less than Thailand, which had committed close to 9 percent of GDP by mid-2020. For analysis of Myanmar's pre-coup COVID-19 stimulus, see Bello et al. 2020 and Wai 2020; on ASEAN-wide stimulus, see Martinus and Seah 2020.

9. See Wittekind 2021 on the post-coup collapse of the government COVID response and the role of reciprocity networks in the subsequent mobilization against dictatorship.

10. As economists Olken and Singhal (2011) note, it is common for redistributive systems such as taxation to be regressive but still deliver valuable public goods. Regressive in this sense refers to a system of public goods provision in which the poor contribute a larger proportion of household income or labor than the wealthy but receive less proportional benefit from those goods relative to the more affluent.

11. Here I draw on the work of political theorist John Dryzek in framing the "normative integration of the polity" around a "range of acceptable [policy] options" as crucial to the democratic health of a political system or community (Dryzek 2017, 626). He also offers an analysis (625–627) of how the worsening of inequality and intensification of austerity across the globe in recent decades has been accompanied by the fraying of polity-level normative bonds and the narrowing of state redistributive action—at least prior to the COVID-19 pandemic.

12. Thelen (1999, 394) has a useful overview of literature on path dependency in relation to the welfare state.

13. Ansell and Samuels (2010, 2014), Perotti (1996), Ross (2006) and Scheve and Stasavage (2012) offer critical empirical assessments of redistribution under democratic rule.

14. Acemoglu and Robinson (2006, 222) provide this assessment. Slater, Smith, and Nair (2014) also offer a useful critique of the theory and empirics on which these economic explanations for democratic breakdown largely rest.

15. Where the state has little ability to implement redistributive initiatives, scholars argue that economic elites have "little to fear" from taxation while the voting public has little to gain from democratization, making the relationship between inequality and democracy "conditional on the strength of the state" (Soifer 2013, 2).

16. Herrold (2020, 1–49), Teets (2014), and Brass (2016) present in-depth case studies of non-state social actors in autocratic contexts.

17. As Haggard and Kaufman (2008, 259) explain: "In Korea and Taiwan, for example, politicians were attracted first and foremost to broad middle-class entitlements—pensions and particularly healthcare—and in Thailand a number of initiatives were less redistributive in design than they might have been. When government either initiated unemployment insurance or expanded it . . . they did so in conjunction with initiatives designed to increase labor-market flexibility."

18. Esping-Andersen (1990) explains how the ideal of single-breadwinner families entrenched in Germany's state social policies discouraged female labor market involvement. Skocpol (1992) notes that the emergence of an American working class capable of advocating expansion of the welfare state was undermined by a patronage-based party system and the competing interests of national and state executives (Thelen 1999, 394). Studies from the Middle East and North Africa similarly highlight how state social schemes entrench notions of government welfare responsibility in ways that narrow the options of later governments, authoritarian and democratic alike, to retrench those social functions (Kawamura 2016; Eibl 2020).

19. Perversely, these enduring logics have produced lower life expectancy in the United States than in other industrialized democracies, despite households, employers, and the American state together spending far more on health care as a percentage of GDP than their counterparts in the OECD (Prasad 2012, 8).

20. Since the 1970s, American policymakers and legislators have cut or instituted strict conditions on access to progressive state social programs such as Medicare, Medicaid, "welfare" (Temporary Assistance for Needy Families or TANF), food stamps, public housing, and other social initiatives (Howard 2009, 90). In contrast to direct state social programs that disproportionately benefit the poor and destitute, especially the elderly poor who receive over half of all direct government welfare spending, tax expenditures such as credits and exemptions overwhelmingly benefit the middle class and the affluent, adding further to preexisting economic and social inequalities (Howard 2009, 89; Hacker 2016b).

21. In the United States, for example, Democratic lawmakers have embraced indirect social expenditure through tax concessions both as a way of granting aid to needy populations and as a countercyclical measure aimed at stimulating the economy through increased spending (Howard 2009; Martin, Mehrotra, and Prasad 2009, 17; Hacker 2016a).

22. See also Chatterjee 2004, Kohl-Arenas 2015, Skocpol 2016, and Walker 2012.

23. In addition to "gamed" laws and constitutions, Michael Albertus and Victor Menaldo (2013, 581) identify a number of "informal mechanisms" of elite leverage whereby elites shape formal institutional outcomes including clientelism, vote-buying, and bribery. A wide literature on political patronage examines how political parties and elites use their mediating influence over state schemes and programs to shape popular political norms or identities or raise the social cost of vote defection, especially in developing democracies. See, for example, studies of patronage, clientelism, and brokerage of state social programs in Argentina (Auyero 2000; Levitsky 2001), Brazil (Ansell 2014), Indonesia (Hadiz 2004; Berenschot, Hanani, and Sambodho 2018; Berenschot and van Klinken 2018), the Philippines (Hutchcroft 1991; Aspinall and Hicken 2020), and Thailand (Nishizaki 2011).

24. Two rare exceptions were crucial in development of this study: research by Lauren MacLean (2004, 2010, 2011a) on welfare, mutuality, and citizenship in West Africa; and the work of Melani Cammett (2014) on Hezbollah's mediation of state health care to fund party provision of welfare in Lebanon. Cammett and MacLean (2011, 2014) also give a useful introduction to the political consequences of non-state welfare.

25. See Béland and Hacker 2004 for a useful discussion of these dynamics in relation to health care reform in the United States.

26. As discussed in chapter 2, Taungoo was also known as Toungoo during the colonial period. As the town is referred to as Taungoo by my interlocutors, I use this term throughout the book unless referring to the precolonial period.

27. The World Bank, "Urban Population (% of Total Population)—Myanmar," United Nations Population Division, World Urbanization Prospects, accessed 23 July 2017, https://data.worldbank.org/indicator/SP.URB.TOTL.IN.ZS?locations=MM.

28. Official government data on ethnicity and religion recorded at the 2014 census had not been released at township level at the time of this research or writing. According to discussions with township officials familiar with the demographic data of the 2014 census, as well as extensive qualitative fieldwork and survey data collected by the author, Taungoo's Karen Christian population comprises around 20 percent of the township while other minorities—including Muslims, Hindus, Shan and Chinese Buddhists, and others—comprise around 10 to 15 percent or so. The remaining 65 to 70 percent of the township was considered by most local interlocutors to be Bamar Buddhist.

29. I am using definitive ethnic labels for simplicity's sake, although in practice, many people identify as numerous ethnicities without any sense of exclusivity. National-level data on ethnicity collected at the 2014 census had not been released at the time of this writing because of political sensitivities. However, it is widely reported that 68 percent of the 53 million population, or around 36 million people, identify as at least partly Bamar, as enumerated at the 2014 census. Data on religion used here is drawn from the 2014 Myanmar Population and Housing Census ("The Union Report: Religion Census Report Volume 2-C," Department of Population and Ministry of Labor, Immigration, and Population, July 2016, 12–15).

30. The 2001 riots in Taungoo resulted in the deaths of at least ten Muslims and the destruction of a historic mosque that dated back to the precolonial period.

31. The KNU signed the Nationwide Ceasefire Agreement (NCA) in October 2015, just before the November election. Between 2016 and the February 2021 coup, however, the peace process and negotiations over institutional reform and transition to a federal system stalled as Myanmar's military authority, known in Burmese as the Tatmadaw, insisted that all of Myanmar's armed groups must commit to the NCA before constitutional changes could proceed (Lwin Cho Latt and Hillman et al. 2018). The lack of progress frayed the patience of local communities and regional brigade commanders of the KNU's armed wing, the Karen National Liberation Army (KNLA), which increasingly resisted Tatmadaw efforts to expand territorial control into ceasefire areas (McCarthy and Farrelly 2020). In the wake of the 2021 military coup, these KNU brigades subsequently provided shelter and military training to anti-coup protesters and resistance fighters—resulting in the upland regions of southeast and central-east Myanmar being termed "liberated" areas and prompting debates within Karen elites about whether to declare the 2015 NCA "void." See "Myanmar Ceasefire Agreement Is Void: KNU Concerned Group," *The Irrawaddy*, 3 September 2021.

32. As a result, parts 1 and 2 of the book focus predominantly on distributive politics in government-controlled areas. However, some comparisons with the ceasefire area of Thandaungyi are noted in chapter six and the book's conclusion, drawing especially on the March 2016 household survey.

33. Kuhonta, Slater, and Vu (2008, chap. 1) present a longer discussion of this method.

34. These contexts varied both by their demographic profiles (rural/urban, ethnicity, religion) along with the role of state development initiatives and by the proportion of residents employed by the government in each context.

35. To roughly reflect the proportionality of urbanization across the two townships and Myanmar as a whole, 300 rural respondents and 200 urban respondents were recruited in each context.

36. In contrast, I treat *publicly* accessible Facebook posts made by groups, media outlets, or prominent local and national individuals as citable without informed consent, although in most cases I have given pseudonyms to the pages or people who made these posts. There are complex issues of informed consent involved in using social media for research purposes. Yet there are also clear benefits to studying social media commentary because opinions expressed are less subject to social desirability bias (Townsend and Wallace 2016).

1. DISTRIBUTIVE POLITICS SINCE COLONIZATION

1. For a discussion of the banknote in the context of Myanmar's socialist history, see Campbell (2019).

2. Creditors were unconstrained by legal restrictions on the alienation of agricultural land to foreign or nonagricultural interests, the likes of which British administrators had instituted in Malaysia following major uprisings (Brown 2013, 42).

3. See Adnan Naseemullah and Paul Staniland (2016) for a discussion of varieties of indirect rule in South Asia.

4. Saha (2013, 3–5) examines the extension of colonial order into the delta. These systems were later imposed in Upper Burma following the Third Anglo-Burmese War in 1885, which led to the British dissolution of the monarchy seated in Mandalay and formal abolition of rural hereditary rule (Thant Myint-U 2001, chap. 8).

5. In 1923, the post of lieutenant-governor was granted additional autonomy and administration of these noncritical areas and transferred to Burmese ministers (Nash 1965, 4).

6. While the justice system was used by some elites embroiled in disputes often involving land (Thant Myint-U 2001, 231–233), in the booming delta region, courts were avoided by most small-scale cultivators (Taylor 2009, 103–107; Saha 2012; Saha 2013, 44–45).

7. Areas with particularly high rates of armed robbery and murder, especially in the socially fragmented delta, were forced to pay additional taxes on top of the normal land rates to cover the cost of additional Karen and Indian police (Taylor 2009, 102–103).

8. Land tax comprised 31 percent of total revenue before the Great Depression, while customs duties, business tax, and forestry levies combined delivered only 42 percent of revenue (Brown 1999b, 385–386; Taylor 2009, 258).

9. Exemptions granted were proportional to the loss incurred (Brown 1999b, 386 citing Furnivall 1931, 204–225. This fairly flexible approach was in contrast to land tax in colonial India, which was calculated on the total acreage of the holding and rarely reassessed (Adas 1979, 201).

10. As Brown (1999, 387) notes, there were exemptions for "government officials, schoolteachers and monks" and scope was also provided for exemptions on grounds of poverty. A less stringent form of the head tax, inherited and subsequently adopted by colonial rulers after the dissolution of the monarchy in 1885, was applied in Upper Burma (Scott 1976, 99; Thant Myint-U 2001, 228–229).

11. There was significant regional variation in British policies regarding existing local elites. Thant Myint-U (2001, 235–40) includes a discussion of variation in policies toward aristocrats in lowland Upper Burma.

12. Turnell (2009, chap. 2) includes a history of the *chettiar* class, and Egreteau (2011, 36) has a discussion of Indians as the first target of xenophobia before the more affluent Anglo-Burmese, European, and Chinese communities.

13. Popular kinds of rice lost almost half their value between July 1930 and January 1931 (Brown 1999b, 388).

14. Both Adas (1979) and Scott (1976) analyze the context surrounding the Saya San Rebellion while Aung-Thwin (2010) analyses the historiography surrounding this period. Scott (1976, 151–155) argues that the capitation tax "provided the detonator" for the uprising, since it was "a unifying issue par excellence. . . . [Whether] smallholders, tenants or labourers, [it] was the single material claim weighed on all of them at a given, regular time."

15. Colonial authorities reduced head taxes by 25 percent for the period 1931–1932 and then 20 percent through to June 1935. However, with the collapse in the price of paddy, the head tax tripled in its real burden despite these reductions (Brown 1999b, 384). Although the perceived unfairness of the head tax fed anti-colonial sentiment, the low cost of its administration relative to its revenue yield meant it was not abolished until 1941, after the outbreak of the Second World War (Brown 1999b, 391).

16. The Dobama movement was heavily involved in the student strikes of 1936 and oil field strikes of 1938, both of which devolved into violence targeting Indians and Muslims and led to lethal clashes with mostly British, Indian, and Karen police in Rangoon and Mandalay (Callahan 2003, 36; Walton 2016, 25). Dobama activists criticized the role Karen troops played in suppressing these uprisings, as well as the earlier 1930 Saya San Rebellion, accusing them of failing to "love their own country, cherish their own literature, or respect their own language" (Nemoto 2000; Callahan 2003, 36). See Than Tun 1938 for a Burmese socialist critique of the British colonial response to the 1938 riots.

17. Fearing potential rebellion, the British had explicitly avoided recruiting or training men from the plains and delta after the creation of the British Burma Army in 1937, instead focusing prewar recruit efforts on ethnic minorities from upland areas (Callahan 2003, 31–42; R. Taylor 2009, 100–101). Following an intensive recruitment drive between 1939 and 1941, the British Burma Army around the time of the Japanese invasion reported more than double the number of soldiers from upland ethnic minority groups (a force of 4,907 made up of 2,797 Karens, 1,258 Chins, and 852 Kachins) than Burman troops (1,893), in addition to 2,578 Indians and small numbers of Chinese recruits (R. Taylor 2009, 101).

18. Political scientist Dorothy Guyot (1966, 209, 212–214) calculates government revenues at 5 percent of the prewar level in the period from 1943 to 1944, and 3 percent in 1944 to 1945. The Japanese claimed revenues from customs, business income tax, and forests for themselves, while the land taxes, which had provided the largest source of revenue until the Depression, collapsed further in the absence of export opportunities for rice.

19. Aung San was appointed the chairman of the Supreme Council along with independence leaders Let Ya and Ne Win. The leader of the moderate White Flag faction of the Communist Party was made secretary general, and members were appointed to the fifteen-member working committee (Maung Maung 1989, 180–183).

20. The White Flag faction of the Communist Party joined Aung San's AFPFL alliance after the more radical Red Flag faction moved into underground rebellion against the state (Badgley 1974, 244).

21. SAMB became critical to state revenue with land revenue comprising only 4 percent of tax revenue and 2 percent of state income by 1956 to 1957 while income from ministries, state trading corporations, Japanese war reparations, and customs together comprised 60 percent of total revenue (R. Taylor 2009, 222, 258). A smaller proportion of revenue (22 percent) was also derived from an income tax, although this was almost exclusively paid by state employees as the government was reluctant to force traders and shopkeepers in the private sector to shoulder increased tax burden (Khin Maung Kyi 1966, 101; R. Taylor 2009, 258).

22. Wartime exodus, combined with attempts to nationalize the economy after independence, saw the numbers of Indians in Burma drop from 1.1 million in 1942 to 700–800k by the 1950s (Egreteau 2011, 36, 40, Brown 2013).

23. As Secretary of Commerce, Hoover spent much of the 1920s responding to down-turns and social crises by formulating plans with "enlightened" corporate capitalists to "meet the needs of industrial democracy without the interference of government bureau-crats" (Wilson 1975, 89).

24. Between 1906 and 1935, the Burma Corporation held one of the largest mining concessions in upland Burma, in Namtu, Shan State. As an early investor, Hoover per-sonally managed mining operations and developed a corporate apparatus of welfare ser-vices, including both education and health care for mine workers (Baillargeon 2020).

25. Tharaphi Than (2013, 649, 643 fn19) provides context to the legally mandated wel-fare capitalist schemes created in the postindependence period, noting the considerable discord among Burmese political elites about the role of foreign investment and aid in the Pyidawtha Plan.

26. Many Progressives, including Roosevelt, feared that state-led social schemes that did not require co-contribution of beneficiaries could prove fiscally "irresponsible" and promote a sense of entitlement, which could discourage beneficiaries from working (Orloff 1988, 67–70). Roosevelt's New Deal subsequently required employers and employees to co-contribute to social insurance schemes, enshrining a worker-based system of social protec-tion that continues to shape the welfare regime in the United States (Orloff 1988, 37–81).

27. U Nu's campaign was not regionally unique; it reflected similar attempts by Gan-dhi in India to enlist Hindu vernacular notions of giving (*dan*) and service (*seva*) to en-courage contributions to development, including "education, sanitation, protection and promotion of . . . village industries to help local handicrafts and artisans, and the fight against untouchability" (Bornstein 2012, 35).

28. Government data on industrial production notes a significant increase in its contri-bution to gross national product, from 6.5 percent in the 1950–1951 period to 15.1 percent in 1960–1961. However, the data is not disaggregated between state and private production, hiding the growth in the private sector, which likely occurred during this period (Tin Maung Maung Than 2007, 82). Total employment in private manufacturing in 1957 was 154,000, compared with 250,000 civil servants employed across all departments, boards, and corporations (R. Taylor 2009, 284–285). The average private manufacturing establish-ment employed thirty-nine people, suggesting that the scale of the private industrial sector in Burma during this period was small relative to other Southeast Asian contexts (Brown 2013, 114–15). See Tin Maung Maung Than (2007, 89–90) for a longer discussion.

29. Many of these local militias allegedly engaged in widespread robbery and illegal activities into the early 1950s, prompting attempts by U Nu and army leaders to integrate more "respectable" members into the Tatmadaw and disband less "reliable" ones (Callahan 2003, 143).

30. Most innovations during this period, including professional training, foreign study trips, military ceremonies, discipline, and incentives, were adopted by Ne Win and his senior planning staff without any civilian oversight (Callahan 2003, 159–169).

31. Burmese civilian and armed elites imposed martial law in the Shan States in 1950, fearing an invasion by the People's Liberation Army and seeking to increase control over a restive region increasingly occupied by anti-Chinese and anti-Rangoon forces, some which were receiving regular supply drops from the US Central Intelligence Agency (CIA) (Callahan 2003, 155–156). Already stretched by civilian administration duties, the military engaged in a number of failed operations against the KMT between 1950 and 1953, the last of which saw them roundly defeated by superior KMT firepower and re-doubled the drive for Tatmadaw modernization and expansion (Callahan 2003, 159).

32. The military also actively encouraged military officers to start small businesses by issuing loans to purchase vehicles and equipment, a welfare capitalist approach that would later inform the SLORC's and, subsequently, the State Peace and Development

Council's (SPDC) embrace of authoritarian welfare capitalism to fund retirement of some veterans after 1988 (Callahan 2003, 169; G. McCarthy 2019).

33. Civilian participation in the BSPP was tightly restricted until the party became a mass organization following the 1974 national constitution, albeit only at the sub-township village, ward, workplace, and cell level.

34. A commitment from the government "to redeem the notes of those who had saved the money honestly" apparently allowed a sizable proportion of domestic entrepreneurs to avoid confiscation (Mya Maung 1970, 542).

35. From 1973 onward, efforts were made to narrow the beneficiaries to exclude workers who were not classed as active members, while schemes to address the welfare needs of workers, such as emergency loans and direct purchasing through factories, were introduced (Tin Maung Maung Than 2007, 141, 282, fn59, 273).

36. The distribution of goods through the private market during the civilian period involved perhaps 2 million people, whereas "the entire system of [BSPP] public stores employed just 50,000" throughout the 1960s (Brown 2013, 146).

37. These loans were estimated to cover around 11 percent of average cultivation costs by the late 1960s (Brown 2013, 140; Mya Maung 1970, 546).

38. Agricultural yield was also constrained by laws that banned cooperative cultivators from selling or mortgaging their holding or purchasing other holdings. These constraints undermined the potential for cultivators to legally invest in expanding their agricultural capacity (Brown 2013, 142).

39. The legislation created three categories of citizens—full, associate, and naturalized—which essentially relegated ethnic minorities to associate status at best. Attaining citizenship also required presentation of government identification cards that had often not been issued in rebel-held areas or in government-held territory where local populations could not speak Burmese. As Josef Silverstein (1997) argued, many minorities subsequently "lost their equal standing with other indigenous peoples of Burma and were treated as stateless." Some were issued foreigners' registration cards that subsequently barred them from key occupations and disqualified their children from university (Silverstein 1997, 182).

40. Conservative estimates were that 40 percent of all trade activity occurred outside of state control during this period (Smith 2007, 19), while others placed illegal trade in the early 1980s at 75 percent of total official trade (Mya Than 1992, 58).

41. Rice exports collapsed from 1.7 million tons in 1960 to just 0.6 million in 1980, down from 3 million tons in 1940 (Brown 2013, 163).

42. However, as Kyaw Yin Hlaing notes, the black market was mostly tolerated at a local level throughout the 1960s and 1970s, given it was central to party functions and for keeping order by supplying and distributing goods unable to be sourced in required amounts through state monopolies.

43. Kyaw Yin Hlaing (2003, 51) discusses the donation practices of illegal traders during BSPP rule.

44. BSPP propaganda barely enlisted Buddhism or religious concepts at all, instead simply claiming Ne Win and its leaders were "men of excellent morals" (Tin Maung Maung Than 1993; Campbell 2014).

45. Enterprises employing between ten and a hundred workers almost halved from 4,792 in 1974 to 2,531 in 1988, with particularly steep declines in the private sector (Tin Maung Maung Than 2007, 260–261).

46. Social Security Board membership peaked in 1973, despite sizable state investment in the manufacturing sector. With the inclusion of health care benefits in 1978, however, disbursals as a percentage of contribution increased from around 20 percent in 1978 to 45 percent by the mid-1980s (Tin Maung Maung Than 2007, 273).

47. These figures do not include the sizable untaxed trade in the informal or black-market economy already mentioned, probably overinflating tax revenue as a proportion of overall trade (licit and illicit) and thus as a percentage of GDP.

48. For useful descriptive and analytical accounts of these events, including chronologies and estimated death counts, see accounts by Kyaw Yin Hlaing (2003, 53–57) and Federico Ferrara (2003, 323).

2. POST-SOCIALIST WELFARE OUTSOURCING

1. The BSPP successor party, the National Unity Party, which also contested the election, failed dismally. Apparently, lacking trust in the ability of civilians to manage either the apparatus of the state or the demands from ethnic minority elites for greater autonomy, the SLORC disregarded the results of the 1990 elections. SLORC generals viewed the potential for an alliance across the colonial-era divides of lowland Ministerial and upland Excluded areas as the "single greatest threat to the military's power and to Burma's continued existence as a unitary state" (Callahan 2004, 103).

2. Two key laws—the Foreign Investment Law (November 1988) and the State-Owned Economic Enterprises Law (March 1989)—were made by the new junta during this period, allowing private foreign capital after twenty-five years and authorized private enterprises to be engaged in all but twelve stipulated industries (Kudo 2005, 12). Tin Maung Maung Than (2007, 356–357), Fujita and Okamoto (2009, 191–197, 219–221, 237), and Woods (2015, 8) provide sector-specific analyses of these processes.

3. Myat Thein (2004, 147), Selth (2002, 253), and Turnell (2011, 141) examine military and budget allocations during this period. G. McCarthy (2019, 14–19) discusses the significant off-budget revenues netted by military-owned enterprises reestablished after 1988.

4. Anthropologist Julianne Schober (1997, 221, fn9) interprets the junta's emphasis on physical religious infrastructures as a strategic attempt to move away from relying on monks to legitimize their rule through participation in merit-making rituals, as many monks openly opposed junta rule. Schober describes the SLORC as a "modern theatre state" that claimed hegemony through "self-consciously constructed legitimation" grounded in the public performance of Buddhist cosmology materialized most commonly in physical religious structures. Prasse-Freeman (2020, 129–130) critiques this interpretation, arguing instead, à la Geertz (1980, 126), that the junta may have been more concerned with making the state "the numinous center of the world . . . round which the public life of society revolved" rather than being concerned with the perception of its subjects and thus legitimation per se.

5. Signatories to ceasefires were permitted to attend the national convention convened to provide "input" to what later became the 2008 Constitution.

6. In the years following these ceasefires, many armed elites entered into joint ventures with Myanmar military and commercial elites in extractive industries such as logging, mining, agribusiness, as well as illicit production, distribution, and money-laundering for drug kingpins (K. MacLean 2008; Meehan 2011, 398; Jones 2016, 102).

7. As Callahan notes, indigenous leaders, religious authorities, language and cultural associations, refugee and diaspora communities, political parties, and social assistance groups initially received some funds from ceasefire signatories during the SLORC/SPDC period (Callahan 2007, 3–4). In the years following these agreements, however, the extent of local elite benefit often narrowed as the Myanmar military-state took control of valuable mines and ensured that circuits of extraction in timber, jadeite, gemstones and other commodities were sold or left port in Yangon or Naypyitaw. This had the effect of cutting businesses linked to armed groups out of trade flows and thus eroding lucrative border checkpoint rents (Jones 2016, 105). Trade in illicit goods such as methamphetamines,

which flourished in borderland areas during this period, also provided an essential means of financing the regime with state-controlled banks levying a "whitening tax" in return for accepting "deposits of dubious origin without question," providing an opportunity for laundering while improving the junta's budget bottom line, and lining the personal pockets of senior generals (Meehan 2011, 391).

8. Brenner (2015), Callahan (2007), K. MacLean (2010), G. McCarthy and Farrelly (2020), Sadan (2016), and Smith (2007) all discuss the paradoxes at the heart of junta-era and post-2011 ceasefires.

9. For instance, while government hospitals continued to function after 1988, the costs for most supplies were shifted onto patients, resulting in considerable increase in out-of-pocket expenses for families of the sick or elderly (Kyaw Yin Hlaing 2007a, 163).

10. Mekong Regional Land Governance (U San Thein et al. 2018, 37) cites agricultural concessions by 2016 at 2,086,894 hectares (ha). This is 17 percent of total land sown in 2014 (11,990,000 ha), according to data from Open Development Myanmar, accessed 12 June 2018, https://opendevelopmentmyanmar.net/topics/land/. These figures do not include land allocated for extractive investments or special economic zones, so the proportion of land declared vacant, fallow, or virgin and transferred is likely to be even higher. Although not all land allocated for these purposes or regions is disputed, the scale of the problem of landlessness and land grabs is evidently immense.

11. See Myat Thein (2004, 146) for a more skeptical discussion of government economic and tax data in the context of the rampant inflation of the early to mid-1990s.

12. United Nations Development Programme (UNDP) creates an index for every year of available data based on four key variables: life expectancy at birth, expected years of schooling, mean years of schooling, and gross national income (GNI) per capita. For each variable, a range of international data sources are used, some of which rely on declared data from national governments, which, especially during junta rule in 1990s and 2000s Myanmar, was of questionable quality and must thus be taken skeptically. For technical notes on human development index (HDI) calculation and data, see UNDP, "Technical Notes: Calculating the HDI," *Human Development Report 2016*, https://hdr.undp.org/sites/default/files/hdr2016_technical_notes.pdf. Data for health expenditure across the region is only available from 1995 onward. An increase in health spending was observed in 2000–2001, but it was largely spent on infrastructure and human resource development rather than for hiring new staff (James 2005, 57).

13. Other mixed-method studies (James 2005; Fujita, Mieno, and Okamoto 2009), along with less reliable human development indicators based partly on government-declared data, demonstrate improvements in social outcomes by the late 2000s. These moderate HDI advances have held since more reliable surveys were conducted by international agencies after 2011, suggesting mild improvements in absolute terms, despite questionable data for earlier years. For technical notes on HDI calculation and data, see UNDP, "Technical Notes: Calculating the HDI," *Human Development Report 2016*.

14. Junta social expenditures largely took the form of hospitals and school buildings built by Ministry of Defense construction battalions (Myat Thein and Khin Maung Nyo 1999; James 2005, 57). Direct expenditures on formalized social welfare were mostly disbursed to charitable providers such as Buddhist centers for the elderly or to regime loyalists through the welfare association that the junta endorsed, the Union Solidarity and Development Association (Schober 1997, 238).

15. A widely referenced 2006 study found an estimated 214,000 community-based organizations (CBOs), including neighborhood organizations, native-place and ethnic organizations, and welfare groups operating throughout the country (Heidel 2006, 60). These groups and networks of risk-sharing and non-state welfare provision are described

by a range of scholars who conducted research in Myanmar in the late 1990s and early 2000s including Helen James (2005), Ashley South (2004), Jasmin Lorch (2006, 2007, 2008a), Khin Zaw Win (2006), Kyaw Yin Hlaing (2001, 2007a), and Petrie and South (2014).

16. Accounts of charitable and non-state welfare groups during the SLORC/SPDC period from Lorch (2008b, 28–29), S. McCarthy (2012, 4), and Dove (2017), for instance, give little attention to how political economy dynamics were linked to the proliferation of communal risk-sharing during the post-socialist period.

17. Initially, this autonomy derived from the fact that some regional commanders held more senior ranks than a number of military officers who led the 1988 coup, a major contradiction to the highly hierarchical logic that governed the military during the socialist period. While junta members were summarily promoted soon after deposing Ne Win, Mary Callahan argues that the discrepancy in earned rank between the junta and regional commanders resulted in "extraordinary authority [being granted] to the more senior regional commanders" to ensure the stability of the new regime (Callahan 2001, 38). The commanders of Myanmar's twelve military regional commands thus possessed considerable autonomy over administration, economic management, and "law and order" in their territories after 1988, driving the "unambiguous rise in power and status" (Callahan 2001, 38) of regional commanders, especially in resource-rich border areas such as Kachin, Shan, and Rakhine States.

18. As Schober (1997) recounts, Myanmar's military commanders and officers engaged in widespread merit-making at pagodas and monasteries around the country throughout the 1990s, a practice she argued was aimed both at building a form of Buddhist-based legitimacy in the absence of popular sovereignty and lubricating military social life.

19. This was despite the covert reliance of the military and civilians on the black-market trade to supplement the haphazard system of government food stores and quotas, discussed in chapter 1.

20. Isolated accounts from this period suggest that anxieties regarding inequities generated by unregulated market trade continued to shape the behavior of junta officials. Economic liberalization, for instance, was partly constrained by the fact that some SLORC members feared that privatization of state assets could generate politically risky economic inequities (Jones 2014, 149). As a result, the agency responsible for privatization initially required private purchases to totally avoid retrenchment of staff (Brown 2013, 191) while senior members of the junta also engaged in vigorous campaigns against emergent agricultural trading tycoons by accusing them of "forgetting their social responsibilities and fuelling inflation through excessive profiteering" (Cook 1994, 133) and setting up committees at the subnational level, which required private traders to sell to government distribution and "welfare" centers at prices fixed by the government-appointed Rice Traders Association (Mya Maung 1991, 288–289).Compulsory rice acquisition from farmers and rice rationing also endured until 2003 and 2004, respectively, although the beneficiaries were narrowed to military and state employees (Brown 2013, 191).

21. For in-depth accounts of ideological adaptation and path dependence following the collapse of the Soviet Union in Bulgaria, Hungary, Poland, and Russia, see Burawoy and Verdery 1999 and Collier 2011.

22. Similar dynamics of transactional patronage were also observed by other scholars conducting research during this period, albeit predominantly in borderland areas that were sporadically under ceasefire during the early 1990s (Callahan 2007; K. MacLean 2010; Woods 2015; Jones 2014; Ford et al 2016).

23. BSPP notions of state ownership of all rural land continued to be reflected in the junta's ongoing land confiscation as well as continued collection of rural agricultural quotas during the 1990s and 2000s. A battalion commander interviewed in the 1990s by Kyaw Yin

Hlaing (2007b, 253), for instance, claimed that he "had the right to do what he wanted with the land since it belonged to the state." The resilience of this ideational understanding of land reinforces the contrast with the approach taken to the social regulation of commerce.

24. Political scientist Matthew Walton (2012, 63) notes that the Mangala Sutta "probably enjoys the widest circulation of any of the Buddha's teachings in Myanmar," often being the subject of monastic and lay books, sermons, speeches, and comics.

25. See the "Exchange Rates" section for discussion of official relative to black-market exchange rates during the 1990s and 2000s.

26. In a repeat of the 1990s and 2000s, since the military coup of 1 February 2021, there have been almost daily reports in the state media of renovations to Buddhist religious sites attended by Senior General Min Aung Hlaing and his entourage. See, for example, Myanmar News Agency, "It Is Necessary to Divide Tasks into Sectors for Carrying Out Full Renovation of Maha Pasana Cave: Senior General," *Global New Light of Myanmar*, 1 November 2021.

27. Julianne Schober (1997, 238) notes the "enormous expenditures" donated by private individuals and junta-linked groups to support "social welfare programs—such as hospitals and homes for the elderly" during the 1990s.

28. Civil servants were also involved in the management of religious and welfare groups. According to records seen by the author, the founding committee of a charitable funeral and welfare association in Taungoo included a senior civil servant from the Department of Railroads along with the local Rice Traders Association and the owners of numerous local restaurants, hotels, and other small businesses.

29. Similar dynamics of abbots serving as patrons of organizations that were largely run by lay persons were noted in a study of thirty-five welfare groups in Sagaing Region (Griffiths 2017, 8).

30. Though Buddhist groups claim to service all religious communities, most Karen churches as well as Muslim mosques that I encountered ran their own welfare groups also. Many churches, especially the Paku Baptist, Catholic, and Anglican dominations, provided assistance to parishioners with medical bills, education costs, and loans and also played a role in preserving sub-ethnic Karen languages such as Paku, Bweh, Gehko, and Gehpa through special classes. Many members of these Karen church networks had kin with links to northern Karen State and areas that were administered by the Karen National Union (KNU), with some having family members serving in the armed wing of the KNU, the Karen National Liberation Army. Karen Christian churches are thus linked in complex and sometimes contradictory ways to Karen ethno-nationalism, a common dynamic of non-state welfare provision in other contexts; see Cammett and L. MacLean 2011.

31. These expenses were usually waved entirely for families who are unable to afford them.

32. A civil servant with intimate knowledge of military battalion administration in the 1990s suggested that these "donations" would usually derive from contributions made by local military families as well as goods sourced from military food stores, which until 2003 derived from compulsory procurement from nearby farmers (interview, 6 September 2016). See also Fujita and Okamoto 2009.

33. Here I appropriate the concept of the "social license to operate," coined by researchers of extractive industries, to refer to the degree to which business operations granted a *legal* commercial license by governmental authorities also received the endorsement of the public or community from which resources were extracted. Business ethics scholars Geert Demuijnck and Björn Fasterling (2016, 675–676) define a "social license" as a "contractarian basis for the legitimacy of a company's specific activity or project . . . [which justifies] an institution or a moral or political rule by referring to the consent of all persons concerned with it." My use of the concept to describe state-business relations

in post-socialist Myanmar is not meant to suggest that the public at large endorsed the businesses operated by the emergent commercial elites.

34. Information in this paragraph was sourced from interviews with various unconnected contacts involved in the local events of the 1988 protests (field notes, June 2015, November 2015, April 2016) and triangulated with Khin Maung Aye's official CB Bank profile at "Our Leadership Team," CB Bank website, accessed 12 February 2020.

35. The company name translates as "Good Myanmar Victory," although the acronym of the company also mirrors his English initials (KMA).

36. For an official biography of Khin Maung Aye, see "New Chairman of Myanmar Banks Association: 2016–2017 (MBA)," ASEAN Bankers Association, accessed 29 January 2017, http://www.aseanbankers.org/ABAWeb/index.php/regional-updates/myanmar /61-president-2022.

37. Yeni, "Burmese Bank Rumored on Verge of Bankruptcy," *The Irrawaddy*, 14 January 2011.

38. The result of this dispute was the formation of Myanmar's second international airline, Golden Myanmar Airlines. Khin Maung Aye is its chairman.

39. For excerpts of a rare interview with Kyaw Thu, see Hilary Whiteman, "Myanmar Movie Star Buries the Dead," *CNN*, 8 October 2013.

40. The September 2007 uprising, labeled the "Saffron Revolution" by some observers because of the involvement of thousands of monks in dark maroon robes, was the largest demonstration against the junta since 1988. Stephen McCarthy (2008) has a useful overview of the context to the uprising and the political implications of the junta's violent response.

41. Interview with Kyaw Thu, 16 May 2016, Yangon.

42. Anthropologists who conducted fieldwork during this period recounted contentious debates about merit. The attitude of the donor to the gift, the attitude of the recipient to receiving it, the type of gift, its value, and the appropriateness of the gift to the recipient were recurring elements in discussions about the meritorious nature of a gift (Jordt 2007, 101–102; Kumada 2004, 5). Contributions made to monks or monasteries with an expectation of material return were seen as morally inferior to acts or gifts renounced with detachment from its material value or hope of future benefit from its renunciation (Jordt 2007, 100; Kumada 2004, 5). Participants in state-endorsed meditation networks regularly questioned whether funds pledged by military officials or their civilian business clients to GONGOs and other regime-aligned welfare groups were gifted with the requisite "sincerity" to be considered meritorious (Jordt 2007, 137).

43. The necessity and feasibility of private networks of aid and redistribution became evident with Sitagu's significant role in coordinating assistance following the devastation of Cyclone Nargis in 2008, as discussed further in chapter 3.

44. Para or "others" is the inverse concept of atta or self, and it is here conjoined with the concept of benefit (*hita*). Thus, *parahita* refers to "for the benefit of others" or "work for others."

45. See Turner (2014) for a comprehensive examination of independence-era Buddhist revivalism. As Walton (2016, 152) notes, in the decades following independence the prominent abbot Mingun Sayadaw enlisted Buddhist notions of charitable giving and selflessness to support construction of a university and a range of social service organizations. Yet the conceptual confines of *parahita* appear to have remained fairly limited during the BSPP period due to the tight constraints on civil society and absence of a sizable private commercial class capable of bankrolling non-state social initiatives.

46. Suu Kyi framed the concept of *myitta* as the central criteria for evaluating the junta after 1988. She argues that during the precolonial monarchical periods, myitta was considered an attribute of "good" power, becoming a key part of King Mindon's coronation

ceremony: "O King . . . love compassionately everyone . . . treasure their lives as though your own. . . . Look after everyone as though after yourself. Guard their welfare as though your own. . . . Deign to watch over the country's inhabitants' welfare. . . ." (quoted in Houtman 1999, 325). Suu Kyi also repeatedly referred to her father Aung San's approach of governing "on the basis of loving kindness and truth," placing herself and the NLD within a regal lineage of just rule (quoted in Houtman 1999, 325).

47. For more background on the growth of the initiative see Zon Pann Pwint, "Kyat Thu: From Actor to Funeral Director," *Myanmar Times*, 2 December 2013.

48. Thanks to Mee Mee Zaw for helping to clarify this terminology. See Mee Mee Zaw (2018) for a useful discussion of similar parahita practices and ideals among Yangon Buddhist youth networks prior to liberalization.

49. The 1990s and 2000s saw significant internal migration, both within Bamarmajority areas of central Myanmar as well as from lowland areas to ethnic minority regions in a process labeled by some scholars as "Burmanization" (Boutry 2016). Migrants' experience of exclusion from kin-based mechanisms of reciprocity in their host communities may have been one of the driving forces behind the proliferation of welfare groups in government-controlled areas of the country during the post-socialist period. The social isolation often experienced on migration elsewhere in the country, as well as the exposure to new ideas and practices in their host communities, might help explain why migrants are, according to survey research, disproportionately likely to "remit funds for religious and social activities" to their home communities (LIFT/QSEM 2016). Indeed, a survey exploring "social remittances" in Myanmar similarly found that villages with high levels of out-migration were over 20 percent more likely to have local social organizations than those with lower levels of migration (Ito and Griffiths 2016).

50. The aged are considered one of the "Five Jewels" worthy of veneration in Buddhism (Buddha, Dharma, Sangha, parents, and teachers). Ceremonies to pay homage to elders (*bu zaw kadaw bwe*) older than seventy years of age highlight how respect for the elderly in post-socialist Myanmar is often understood as gifting cash, soap, toothbrushes, clothing, slippers, blankets, and food. Contributions to honoring ceremonies comprised nearly one-third of all reported expenditure by thirty-six parahita organizations surveyed in the Sagaing Region (Griffiths 2016; Griffiths 2017). A HelpAge International report similarly includes elder care groups in Magwe Region that hosted honoring ceremonies twice a year where all local elderly received 10,000 kyat, in cash, alongside a range of essential household items (Leehey 2016).

51. For instance, many welfare groups organize female chanting troupes (*dhamma seh gya*) on behalf of the families of the deceased in addition to subsidizing the financial costs of funerals and cremation. These troupes accompany funeral processions and recite blessings for the deceased as per Burmese funeral customs. The secretary of a township-level group formed in the early 2000s emphasized that satisfying both the material *and* ritual needs of the deceased was essential to "helping the spirit to reach a better place" (interview, 3 August 2015).

52. Similar amounts were raised by groups that collected funds for medical emergencies such as motorbike accidents.

53. Funeral rituals followed by the author regularly totaled more than three months of average household income. These costs were often in addition to the catastrophic debt families assume to extend the life of a sick, injured, or elderly relative. Average individual income in provincial Myanmar at the time of this writing ranged between US$100 and $250 per month for a day laborer and around US$200 to $300 for a schoolteacher or civil servant. Income was more seasonal for agricultural households, with many relying on urban remittances from children as well as windfalls from harvests that varied considerably depending on the size of seasonally cultivated land. Total costs for funeral rituals and ceremonies at-

tended by the author, including the amount spent on food, gifts for guests, donations to monks, costs of coffin, cremation, ritual adherence, and so on ranged between US$300 to $500 for rural and poor households and upwards of US$1,000 for wealthier trading households.

54. To financially support administrative costs or enable provision of other social support for local residents, some village or neighborhood welfare groups issue loans to villagers from funds withheld from appeals or donated by businesspeople. These loans are often at the same or lower interest rate as that of commercial money lenders. As credit from welfare groups satisfies immediate financial needs of loan recipients and contributes to the social insurance of the "community," anthropologist Jennifer Leehey (2016, 34–35) notes that many people who take loans from welfare groups see themselves as "drawing good merit," an intriguing way to use the Buddhist concept of karma to frame receipt of a loan.

55. Social researcher Mike Griffiths (2017, 9) recounts how managers of groups justify inclusion of recent arrivals or non-Buddhists with reference to the "Bamar ethnicity's compassionate attitude (cedana)," which they suggest is, or at least should be, shared by all residents.

56. These contributions are in addition to in-kind contributions such as labor, which, if valued as foregone wages, would constitute a significant and regressive burden on poor households (see chapter 6). Respondents were asked to allocate ten stones to various household expenditures made in the past three months, including donations, formal state taxes, and other categories of spending. Each stone reflected 10 percent of expenditure, and thus the total allocation of stones reflected the entirety of the household budget for the preceding three-month period. "Donations" were defined as the aggregation of all contributions to social and religious groups, as the parameters between these spheres is difficult to distinguish organizationally and financially. Poverty quintiles were constructed based on a multivariable household-level poverty indicator adapted from Schreiner (2012).

57. In order to make a direct comparison with financial "donations," here I am excluding nonmonetary and informal forms of taxation from formal tax burden. Informal forms of taxes during this period included the rural rice quota, which continued to be enforced until 2003, along with forced labor on state infrastructure projects, which was ubiquitous until the early 2000s and still continues in some areas of Myanmar. See chapter 6 for a detailed discussion of patterns of involuntary labor and the disproportionate contribution of poor households to ostensibly "voluntary" contemporary local improvement projects. On arbitrary, corrupt, and in some cases financially catastrophic extraction framed as "taxation" during junta rule, see Vicary 2010.

58. Across poverty quintiles, taxes comprised 4 percent while donations and community contributions comprised 8 percent of household spending. Along with business, income, and land taxes, "taxes" here include various user fees and charges, since these are referred to by the same term in Burmese (akun) and are by far the most ubiquitous form of payment made to state officials by people across poverty quintiles.

3. DISASTERS AND THE POLITY

1. Four administrative divisions were declared disaster zones: Rakhine State, Chin State, Sagaing Region, and Magway Region.

2. Scholars of welfare state development in the United States, for instance, trace the New Deal passed in the aftermath of the social disaster of the Great Depression to the language, ideology, and legal powers of disaster intervention accrued and used by the federal government during city fires in the 1910s and 1920s (Brandes 1976; Dauber 2012).

3. Disasters can also place a spotlight on systematic corruption, social inequality, and discrimination (Schneider and Hwang 2014), eroding the authority and legitimacy of a regime or government and mitigating the value of formal citizenship (Shindo 2015).

4. Adams (2013) examines how Hurricane Katrina and subsequent relief efforts shaped popular notions of fictive kinship.

5. The initial report of the Tripartite Core Group, comprised of representatives from the United Nations, the Association of Southeast Asian Nations (ASEAN), and the Myanmar government, cited the official death toll on 24 June 2008 as 84,537 with 53,836 missing and 19,359 injured. The bulk of the missing were later considered deceased, bringing the total number of dead to over 138,000.

6. Officials claimed that 92.4 percent of voters approved of the constitution, with 26 million out of 27 million eligible voters casting ballots.

7. Some of this aid was confiscated and placed in storage by the authorities but later released. Aid workers were subjected to long visa application processes at the Myanmar embassy in Bangkok and elsewhere, planes waited at airports in neighboring countries for permission to deliver their supplies, and relief personnel already in the country were given little or no assistance by the government in getting to the worst hit areas. See Seekins 2009.

8. Anthropologist Benedicte Brac de la Perriere (2010) recounts that Yangon middle-class networks were some of the first private groups to respond, collecting in-kind donations from street and neighborhood groups as well as companies and then forming convoys of cars to disburse the aid to survivors in the delta.

9. Videos from some of these trips were even being sold at traffic lights in Yangon in the weeks following landfall (Brac de la Perriere 2010).

10. Quoted in Kyaw Zwa Moe, "Putting Compassion into Action," *The Irrawaddy*, 9 May 2014.

11. Kyaw Zwa Moe, "Putting Compassion into Action."

12. Brac de la Perriere (2010) mentions some groups using the terms "meritorious donation" (Burmese: *hlu*) and "misfortune" (Pali: *dukkha*) while others used more neutral discourse, possibly to avoid conflict with junta officials.

13. Numerous businesspeople stated that they had "decided to donate after hearing appeals to do so by one of several Sayadaw," or abbots, including Sitagu Sayadaw and his Sitagu Association, who were encouraging a stronger emphasis on the "common good" (Trocaire 2011, 19–20).

14. A number of large international companies operating in Myanmar during this period also provided donations of fuel along with the transportation and distribution of aid to affected communities, framing this aid as a form of "corporate social responsibility" (Trocaire 2011, 25–26).

15. For detailed accounts of the spontaneous nature of some of these appeals, see CPCS 2009 and Brac de la Perriere 2010.

16. These successive reforms were consistent with the military's "Seven Step Roadmap to Discipline-Flourishing Democracy." Pedersen (2011, 53) discusses the roadmap and the 2010 elections.

17. Rochanakorn, K. "More than one month after Cyclone Komen, some impacted people remain homeless," United Nations High Commissioner for Refugees, 21 September 2015.

18. Emergency response teams comprised of technical specialists were deployed by the ASEAN as well as twelve UN agencies and the US, Australian, and Japanese governments (Howe and Bang 2017, 73).

19. T. McLaughlin and Hnin Yadana Zaw, "Myanmar government, Military Win Pre-Vote Plaudits for Flood Response," *Reuters*, 10 August 2015.

20. The following sections on Cyclone Komen response efforts draw on interview transcripts and notes from fieldwork conducted between 1 August and 19 September 2015.

21. For an analysis of the civilian flood response, see Justine Chambers and Gerard McCarthy, "Amid the Deluge, Solidarity and Leadership Emerge," *The Myanmar Times*, 18 August 2015.

22. The concept is commonly deployed in everyday life to describe grave suffering over which an individual has little or no agency, reflecting a notion of misery intimately tied to Buddhist notions of lack of control (Pali: *anatta*) as well as the impermanence and finitude of this world (*aneitsa*) (Walton 2016, 40–42). The term *dukkhatheh* is also used in Burmese discourse to refer to people displaced internally or to border areas of Thailand or China as a result of Myanmar's ongoing civil conflicts; the term carries a connotation of suffering as a result of misfortune devoid of agency—victims who cannot be blamed for their situation but who must rely on themselves and others for aid and assistance. The mobilization of aid in largely lowland areas and its encouragement by authorities stands in contrast to the limited assistance mobilized from central Myanmar to conflict areas where state violence and propaganda often imply or explicitly impute blame for conflict on rebel groups and the communities that sustain them.

23. Aung Ko Win was sanctioned by the United States until October 2016 for links to the State Law and Order Restoration Council and State Peace and Development Council (SLORC/SPDC) junta. Media reports named him as the "top donor" during the 2015 floods, claiming he had contributed more than US$3.6 million to relief efforts in the form of flight services and donations from his charity group, the Brighter Future Myanmar Foundation. See "Aung Ko Win's KBZ Charity Tops $3.6M in Flood Aid," *The Irrawaddy*, 7 August 2015.

24. This suggests a notion of merit earned only through social recognition and also a lack of trust in institutions of redistribution—especially the state, which was already perceived as having disrupted or diverted aid in its own interests during the devastation of Cyclone Nargis in 2008 (Jaquet and Walton 2013).

25. The official schedule of "sons of the soil' or "national races" is comprised of groups that the state recognizes as having resided in Myanmar before 1823, when British forces first invaded Burma. The list has fluctuated over decades from over 140 groups down to the present 135. Cheesman (2017a, 470) conceives of the national races concept as a "trope for Myanmar's many linguistic and cultural groups pulled together in a state-building enterprise." In the absence of inclusive institutions capable of bridging social distance and generating shared social imaginaries, the notion of national races contentiously frames Myanmar's diversity in "a mythic unity that has never emerged" (Holliday 2014, 410). The discourse that the Rohingya are not a "national race" and thus do not "belong" in Myanmar has been repeatedly enlisted by the Tatmadaw to justify withholding legal citizenship from the Rohingya and has also featured, since August 2017, in justification for the purge of more than 700,000 Rohingya people to Bangladesh. For an example of the Tatmadaw leaders legitimizing anti-Rohingya sentiment with reference to the "national races" discourse, see Richard C. Paddock, "Myanmar General's Purge of Rohingya Lifts His Popular Support," *New York Times*, 26 November 2017.

26. Some welfare groups from Yangon traveled to Kayah State in the weeks following the initial landfall of Cyclone Komen. However, none of these groups came from Taungoo, despite the immediate geographic proximity to the flooded areas.

27. Rhoads et al. (2020) describes the local community impacts and responses to COVID-19.

4. DEMOCRACY, FREEDOM, AND MORALITY

1. T. Fuller, "After Victory in Myanmar, Aung San Suu Kyi Quietly Shapes a Transition," *New York Times*, 22 December 2015.

2. While Eindaga also mentions the need to have laws, the "taya" referred to here was the Buddhist truth of dhamma, which carries with it a particular understanding of cause and effect.

3. In one of his first public comments following his release from prison, Min Ko Naing, the 88 Generation Peace leader and democracy activist, emphasized that "it is very

important to have discipline and unity, we have to show that we deserve democracy" (quoted in Wells 2016, 168). The discourse of "discipline" runs back to the colonial period (Walton 2015), and recurred on NLD signboards and campaign materials and in speeches of political leaders after 2011.

4. He described these businesspeople using an obscene Burmese idiom about "goat testicles" (*seh gweh sii*) while making a hand gesture to evoke them moving from left to right with each step (field notes, 9 November 2015).

5. Some leaders of Ma Ba Tha, especially firebrand monk Wirathu, claimed that Suu Kyi would empower Muslims, so her party could not be trusted to protect "national religion." Not all Ma Ba Tha–affiliated interlocutors supported the USDP, however. Indeed, the endorsement of the USDP appeared to carry little weight for many of my welfare-group interlocutors, most whom either proudly voted for the NLD or avoided voting entirely.

6. The foundation also ran a project developing public libraries across the country and delivered relief assistance during the 2015 floods. For background on the Daw Khin Kyi Foundation education project, see Zaw Win Than, "NLD Targets Overhaul for 'Ruined' Education System," *The Myanmar Times*, 15 October 2012.

7. The Burmese word for tax or payment to an authority (*akun*) was used in order to elicit a general perception of all state-levied payments referred to with this term, including user fees for roads and electricity usage typically referred to in Burmese as "tax."

8. The same level of confidence was also expressed in relation to translocal redistribution during the 2015 floods, with over 80 percent of those who donated saying they were confident that their contributions reached "where it was needed most."

9. As the number of patients treated at the local Taungoo General Hospital increased during the decade of civilian rule with additional government funding, flows of charitable blood to support patients also intensified. According to the hospital's blood bank, there was a 40 percent increase in the number of 500 milliliter (ml) bottles of blood donated for patients in the hospital—from less than 3,900 donated in 2013 to over 5,500 bottles by 2016—and they were mostly uncompensated, voluntary donations.

10. The criticism of the militarization of civilian-led ministries proved prescient after the larger social mobilization that occurred in the months that followed. In August 2015, nurses in Mandalay Bone Hospital and Taungoo General Hospital placed a black ribbon on their uniforms in protest of appointment of former military doctors into senior positions in the Ministry of Health. The resulting "Black Ribbon" campaign spread across Myanmar, with other sectors including the Ministry of Education, Ministry of Electrical Power, and Ministry of Energy starting their own ribbon campaigns as well—a form of small-scale disobedience that was scaled up following the February 2021 coup as the basis for the civil disobedience movement that saw hundreds of thousands of government staff go on strike. G. McCarthy (2018b, 98–99) further discusses the 2015 Black Ribbon campaign, while Dunford (2021) examines the civil disobedience movement formed after the 2021 coup.

11. As Brac de la Perriere (2015, 5) observes, Ma Ba Tha connects three forms of belonging: *amyo* as "nation," *batha* as individual belief or faith in religion, and *thathana* as institutions of religion. For a discussion of *amyo* since the colonial period, see Phyo Win Latt 2016.

12. Political scientist Matthew Walton (2016, 68) gives the example of Asoka, a third-century ruler in present-day India commonly praised as the exemplar of Buddhist kingship after he committed himself to governing and expanding his empire "through the strength of *dhamma* (the Buddha's teachings)." Candier (2007) examines how successive nineteenth-century Burmese monarchs and their courts interpreted these royal duties, including the compulsion to care for the welfare of subjects. However, the locus of responsibility shifted considerably during the social outsourcing of the 1990s and 2000s. Walton (2016, 159), for instance, recounts a prominent Burmese monk who viewed the rules of

conduct for kings, such as providing for the welfare of the needy and patronizing Buddhism, as "rules of ideal conduct" for all people—arguing that whether the public fulfilled these duties was "a way to evaluate citizen participation in politics" in a democratic society.

13. Anthropologist Erica Bornstein (2012, 172–173) analyzes this ethos in the context of Indian humanitarianism.

14. Historian Alicia Turner highlights widespread anxieties about the decline in Buddhism, especially among young people, during the independence movement. However, earlier revivalists primarily sought to address their anxieties by rejuvenating monastic schools and cultivating moral discipline through meditation training (Turner 2009, 2011, 2014).

15. Most schools teach using the textbook provided by the national Dhamma School Foundation, which as of late 2015 only had materials for third- and sixth-grade classes intended for children ages 5 to 11. Some, however, taught their own curriculum for students in the seventh and eighth grades. Two senior monks interviewed in Taungoo mentioned plans for release of a new Dhamma School Foundation curriculum for seventh grade in 2016 and eighth grade in 2017 that would focus more explicitly on "citizenship" and the role of Buddhism in politics.

16. The association between Buddhist chauvinism and notions of service or social work (*parahita*) was strengthened further in 2017 after the main state body regulating Buddhist affairs, the Sangha Maha Nayaka, formally banned Ma Ba Tha as an organization. Within a week, a new group called the "Buddha Dhamma Parahita Foundation" was established that explicitly referenced the concept of service for others or "social work." See Aung Kyaw Min, "Ma Ba Tha to Continue under New Name," *The Myanmar Times*, 29 May 2017.

17. For a discussion of the chronic problem of urban waste management and questions about "responsibility," see Swe Zaw Oo, "Who Is to Blame? No Trash Talk Please," *Tea Circle Oxford*, 15 March 2018.

18. Alongside stories about Myanmar Muslims, articles and images of violence committed by the so-called Islamic State (IS), rumors of Al Qaeda cells within Myanmar, or posts detailing allegedly "terrorized" conversion of Buddhist women circulated widely on the Facebook pages of welfare groups during 2015 and 2016. The narrative-making framed around these images of global or local violence and coercion regularly involved universal claims about Muslims being intrinsically violent or morally deviant. Beyond serving to reframe memories of past suffering and to project blame on Muslims (Schissler, Walton and Phyu Phyu Thi 2017), grievances about economic inequality melded with allegedly differential notions of the "value of life" to morally legitimize attempts to exclude Muslim from formal and informal belonging.

19. The campaign resulted in the passage of a package of four pieces of legislation, signed into law by President Thein Sein in the month before the 2015 election, restricting inter-religious marriage and conversion, enforcing monogamy, and limiting the reproductive rights of families. See G. McCarthy and Menager 2017b for a longer discussion.

20. A similar cosmological discourse of moral decline recurs in contemporary Sri Lanka. For useful comparisons see Gravers 2015 and Schonthal and Walton 2016.

21. Similar characterizations recurred in stories that circulated before the intercommunal riots in Meiktila in 2013 and Mandalay in 2014, with Muslims traders or shop owners depicted as behaving in an aggressive or exploitative manner toward their employees or customers. For a useful and anonymous eyewitness account, see "Rumour, Religion and Riots in Mandalay," *New Mandala*, 3 July 2014.

22. Ironically, the reverse theme recurred in the Facebook feeds of Muslim contacts about Buddhists during this period, with one post shared repeatedly by Muslim contacts that included six images—five of which depicted alleged assaults and attacks on Muslims in

Myanmar, including burning mosques, and the final image being a photo of Muslim men in religious headwear handing sacks of rice to what appeared to be Buddhists affected by the floods. Above the images was the caption: "They do this to us. . . . And we do this for their benefit."

23. Muslims scored an average of 9.4 points out of 20, compared with 7.7 for Buddhists and 7.4 for Christians (Baptists) in a social capital index constructed from the March 2016 survey results. The 20-point index combined a series of variables focused on interaction and contribution to public goods along with donations to other ethnic or religious communities.

5. PHILANTHROPY AND WEALTH DEFENSE

1. For discussion of donations to UEHRD and controversy around the public-private partnership for Rakhine State, see "Suu Kyi-led Rakhine Development Agency Says UN Report 'Intended to Harm' Myanmar," *The Irrawaddy*, 8 August 2019.

2. For instance, Jacqueline Menager (2017, 116–118) documents the marked intensification of philanthropic donations to schools, hospitals, and pagodas by the prominent tycoon Tay Za after 2011. Prasse-Freeman and Phyo Win Latt (2018, 405) argue that vertical bonds of patronage could degrade with Myanmar's integration into global marketplaces, along with the spread of an ethos of individual accomplishment.

3. Some patron-client relationships are purely transactional and short term; others are based on longer-term interactions and claims of obligation, affection, and fictive kinship. While the balance of "calculation" to affection may vary from dyad to dyad, the maintenance of direct patron-client ties relies on a "continuing pattern of reciprocity . . . creat[ing] trust and affection between the partners" (Scott 1972b, 94). The balance of protection and exploitation involved in these patronage relationships has evolved over time along with shifts in underlying commercial logics and the regulation of assets that form the economic basis of patronage networks. Stability of patronage ties between commercial elites and their clients in rural areas of Myanmar's delta, for instance, have historically derived and continue to emerge from the willingness of patrons to render social protection or defer debt repayment at times of disaster or family crisis (Scott 1972a; Adas 1974; Boutry 2013).

4. Scott (1972b, 95) contrasts commercial networks with politicians who, he argues, tend to have small, dense, and largely familial networks of support.

5. These networks ultimately linked to senior members of the SLORC/SPDC junta. The instability within and competition between patronage pyramids was exposed when Khin Nyunt and all networks perceived as linked to him across business and military networks were dramatically arrested amid his purge in 2004 (R. Taylor 2009, 394).

6. Reich (2016, 2018b) discusses foundations and endowments in the United States; Roy (2014) and Crabtree (2018) provide an analysis of tycoons, capitalism, and philanthropy in India.

7. In the context of tensions associated with capitalist activity and the inequalities it creates, businesspeople thus sought to answer questions about how they "take the otherworldly into their life" (Kumada 2004, 10) through renunciation in the form of often-localized philanthropy. Large-scale public ceremonies, especially those "performed without the help of others," become the "object of public admiration," while "failure to meet people's expectations, on the other hand, can result in a lowering of the donor's dignity and reputation" (Kumada 2004, 11).

8. See, for example, the bank's statement about its platform for "Corporate Social Responsibility," CB Bank, accessed 2 April 2022, https://www.cbbank.com.mm/en/about -cb-bank/corporate-social-responsibility.

9. At the time of my fieldwork in 2015 and 2016, there were three private hospitals providing both inpatient and outpatient services. In the absence of quality public health

services, treatment at private clinics and hospitals comprised a significant proportion of middle-class household expenditure in the area. See G. McCarthy 2016 for a fuller discussion.

10. Details about the life of Khin Maung Aye and his business interests and philanthropic practices in provincial Myanmar are based on the author's interview transcripts and field notes between 15 July 2015 and 20 March 2016. This original research is supplemented with digital ethnography with interlocutors and official biographies available online accessed prior to the February 2022 coup.

11. The festival ran from 2016 to 2019, though on a smaller scale than the spectacular 2015 celebration. It was not held in 2020 because of the pandemic. Following the return to dictatorship in February 2021, the dynasty festival was canceled and only a scaled-back version of the original pagoda festival was held, though with very few participants.

12. A spectacular float supported by one Khin Maung Aye's protégés, Dr. Kyaw Thu, was disqualified from receiving a prize as it was clearly better funded than any other in the parade. His float had won the top prize in previous years, which sparked frustration and speculation about favoritism, given his close relationship with the primary patron of the festival.

13. As the president was unable to attend because of a meeting of the Association of Southeast Asian Nations (ASEAN), military-appointed Home Affairs Minister General Ko Ko took the honor of cutting the ribbon and placing the *tee* (golden umbrella) atop the pagoda in his absence.

14. See coverage of the festival in *Global New Light of Myanmar*, 27 November 2015, http://www.burmalibrary.org/docs21/GNLM2015-11-27-red.pdf.

15. A similar dynamic was observed in early 1990s upper Myanmar. Large-scale public ceremonies, especially those "performed without the help of others" became the the "object of public admiration." Conversely, "failure to meet people's expectations . . . can result in a lowering of the donor's dignity and reputation" (Kumada 2004, 11).

16. Similar donations from businesspeople to support municipal waste management, including the provision of trucks for rubbish collection, have been witnessed by the author and other researchers elsewhere in provincial Myanmar, including Shan State.

17. Tin Yadanar Htun, "CB Bank Chair to Open Industrial Zone," *The Myanmar Times*, 30 November 2015.

18. Tin Yadanar Htun, "CB Bank Chair to Open Industrial Zone"; field notes, August 2015.

19. Tin Yadanar Htun, "Farmers Protest KMA Group Project in Taungoo," *The Myanmar Times*, 9 December 2015.

20. Moe Myint, "Taungoo Farmers Restate Claims of Land Grabbing against Well-Known Businessman," *The Irrawaddy*, 12 February 2016.

21. A volunteer at a local welfare group, however, filmed a Facebook Live interview with one of the protesting farmers who claimed he did not know the name of the journalist and "just wanted his land back" (field notes, 15 January 2016).

22. This is not to say that such redistribution is impossible in contemporary Myanmar. In September 2017, for example, the NLD's agricultural minister of Magwe Region committed to redistributing nearly 13,0000 acres of "unused" land it had seized from two companies as part of a national scheme led by the Ministry for Agriculture, Livestock, and Irrigation and funded by international donors. See Htet Naing Zaw, "Myanmar Govt to Redistribute Vacant Land," *The Irrawaddy*, 26 September 2017.

23. See Htet Naing Zaw, "Aung San Suu Kyi Woos Tycoons in Naypyidaw Meet-Up," *The Irrawaddy*, 24 October 2016.

24. Over US$8 million was donated to Suu Kyi in early 2017 to support the peace-related initiatives projects she favored, including US$2.2 million from Kanbawza Bank,

Myanmar's largest private financial institution. Following the Tatmadaw's campaign of ethnic cleansing in Rakhine State in August 2017, a similar appeal was made and tycoons pledged close to US$13.5 million to UEHRD. While many of the donors were the same, their initial contributions were far less—though a number have provided in-kind services of various forms as well. See Nyein Nyein, "Burmese Tycoons Contribute $8 Million to Govt Peace Fund," *The Irrawaddy*, 24 January 2017, and B. Dunant, "Tycoons on the Frontline of Rakhine Reconstruction," *Voice of America*, 23 January 2018.

25. Over US$13 million was donated for Rohingya repatriation by Myanmar's top tycoons. According to a list of donations released by the state counselor's office, Khin Maung Aye was the twelfth largest contributor to the UEHRD in Rakhine. He was recognized as contributing the equivalent of around US$380,000 while Kanbawza Bank's Aung Ko Win was the top donor, contributing over US$1.5 million. See also "Bago Region Chief Minister Pledges to Assist Development in Rakhine," Republic of Union of Myanmar Information Committee, accessed 24 September 2019, removed following the February 2022 coup.

26. Consider, for example, the inclusion of comments from Khin Swe, a former USDP member of Parliament and notorious tycoon, in a public statement from the State Counsellor's office explaining his donation of one billion kyats to UEHRD on the basis of "defending" the Rakhine State and democracy more broadly.

27. See Khet Mar and Roseanne Gerin, "In Myanmar, Mixed Reactions to the Lifting of U.S. Sanctions," *Radio Free Asia*, 15 September 2016.

28. See "Myanmar Corporate—Deductions," PricewaterhouseCoopers, 17 January 2002, http://taxsummaries.pwc.com/ID/Myanmar-Corporate-Deductions, and "Myanmar Individual—Deductions," PricewaterhouseCoopers, 17 January 2002, http://taxsummaries.pwc.com/ID/Myanmar-Individual-Deductions.

29. See "KBZ Bank Largest Taxpayer for Six Consecutive Years," *The Myanmar Times*, 23 January 2018.

30. See Aung Thein, "Tax Reforms in Myanmar," Internal Revenue Department, Union of Myanmar Ministry of Planning and Finance (paper presented at the Seventh IMF-Japan High-Level Tax Conference for Asian Countries, Tokyo, 5–7 April 2016), https://www.imf.org/external/np/seminars/eng/2016/asiatax/pdf/at33.pdf. See also "Tax Reforms in Myanmar," Oxford Business Group, accessed 23 February 2018, https://oxfordbusinessgroup.com/overview/taxation-detail-long-road-towards-tax-reforms.

31. On local community impacts and responses to COVID-19, see Rhoads et al. 2020. On government solicitation of donations, see Zaw Zaw Htwe, "Donations Pour in as People of Myanmar Dig Deep to Help Cover Cost of Vaccine," *The Irrawaddy*, 12 January 2021.

6. SELF-RELIANCE AND ENTITLEMENT

1. Social welfare spending grew far slower than education and health, for instance. The overall percentage of the national budget dedicated to social welfare was 0.38 percent of the national budget in the 2019–2020 period—a proportionally significant increase from 0.05 percent in 2011–2012 yet building on a miniscule base. Despite the budget expansion, total actual expenditures by the Ministry of Social Welfare, Relief, and Resettlement (MoSWRR) were only US$36.5 million in 2017–2018 for a population of more than 53 million people. For a detailed analysis of MoSWRR budget allocations between 2011 and 2019, see MOPFI 2020 and UNICEF 2020.

2. This chapter cites data, interviews, and field notes collected from 5 August 2015 until 4 July 2017.

3. For in-depth analysis of these reports, see Horsey 2011, 10–11. The expansion of irrigation was part of the SLORC/SPDC junta's campaign to boost agricultural productivity by shifting from two to three harvests a year (Vatikiotis 1996).

4. Data from the Ministry of National Planning and Economic Development and the Ministry of Agriculture and Irrigation claimed that seventy-four irrigation projects were completed between 1990 and 1996. US Embassy reports placed the value of new irrigation works between 1993 and 1995 alone at around 100 million kyat, compared to 126.7 million kyats for the entire thirty-year period prior (1962–1992) (cited by Thawnghmung 2001, 246–248).

5. These numbers are likely to vastly underestimate the proportion of involuntary labor solicited by junta officials during this period, as many military officers also enlisted "unofficial" forced labor to help tend their gardens, till their lands, or assist with other activities; see, for example, Thawnghmung 2001, 252.

6. While the magnitude of forced labor appears to have dropped, especially in lowland areas, the practice continues to be documented in conflict zones including Rakhine, Shan, and Kachin States; see Fortify Rights, "Myanmar: Investigate Forced Labour of Rakhine Buddhists in Western Myanmar," news release, 15 March 2016, http://www.fortifyrights.org/publication-20160315.html.

7. The most prominent schemes at the time this research was conducted in 2015 and 2016 were the Poverty Reduction Fund, Rural Development Fund, and the Green Emerald Fund, along with the Constituency Development Fund and the Ministry of Cooperative's Agricultural Loan Program (Robertson, Joelene, and Dunn 2015, ii). The Ministry of Agriculture, Livestock, and Irrigation administered the first three of these schemes along with internationally supported initiatives such as the World Bank–funded National Community Driven Development Project (NCDDP). Funding for constituency development, established in 2013, was managed by a Union of Myanmar central committee and a township-level committee comprised of parliamentarians and public servants, with 100 million kyats (US$75,000) provided to each township for basic infrastructure such as roads, bridges, clinics, and schools. Robertson, Joelene, and Dunn (2015, 10–11) give a detailed analysis of local development funds; Egreteau (2017) discusses constituency development funds.

8. Over 60 percent of respondents in the sample townships reported personally contributing to the construction of local roads—92 percent giving labor and 27.5 percent donating funds. Middle-income and rich households were much more likely to have contributed financially. Researchers in other regions of Myanmar have also noted significant community participation and contribution to local public goods provision in recent years (Okamoto 2017; Griffiths 2019).

9. For a discussion of self-reliance and self-help as a practice of everyday resistance "between passivity and open, collective defiance" (Scott and Kerkvliet 1986, 1) against the state during junta rule in Myanmar, see Mullen 2016, chap. 4.

10. Prasse-Freeman (2012, 385–386) includes a discussion of how Burmese people categorized "fair" and "unfair" forced labor in the late 2000s.

11. Research from this period suggests that the extent of benefit to participants was a key determinant of how contributions to improvement projects were perceived. Thawnghmung (2001, 251) argued that perceptions of labor contributions to irrigation projects varied among farmers according to "how it affected their lives, whether they are paid or not, and the season in which they were drafted and called upon." She cites an interview with a farmer who was initially "very angry when he was ordered by the authorities to construct small scale irrigation networks adjacent to his village. In retrospect, however, he was very grateful for the leadership of the military regime and the local political and civilian officials made summer paddies possible" (cited in Thawnghmung 2001, 251). She concludes that those who received a clear benefit from irrigation owing to higher yields on their land had a more positive perception of involuntary labor and financial contributions than those who accrued little or no benefit.

12. This association of work on public goods projects with good merit or grace was consistent at over 95 percent across upland and lowland areas and across all major religious communities for which a sizable sample was gathered (Buddhist, Christian, and Muslim). These associations suggest that the social and cosmological interpretation of "work for others" has been embraced by both non-Buddhist and Buddhist communities alike in the survey areas.

13. The notion that working on village roads could draw merit contrasts sharply with research conducted during the 1950s which suggested that labeling contributions to public goods provision as "meritorious" was highly contentious. Anthropologist Melford Spiro, for instance, recounted a village elder in the 1960s who "*contrary to most of the villagers,* insisted that public works for the common good—for example, the repair of roads—was also dana, which would confer merit on the volunteer worker" (Spiro [1970] 1982, 464, emphasis added).

14. Greater community involvement is a strong predictor of normative support for self-reliance: Respondents who viewed self-reliance as the preferred form of road provision in both contexts had a markedly higher social capital score (8.4/20 in Bago Region, 7.5/20 in Karen State) compared with a mean for all respondents (8.1/20 in Bago Region, 7.19/20 in Karen State). The twenty-point index combined a series of variables focused on contribution to public goods and interaction with other ethnic or religious communities. A complementary explanation for this data is that people unwilling to assume responsibility for local public goods tend to withhold their support for self-reliance initiatives in the first place. Rates of participation in initiatives were 10 percent higher in the lowland context of Bago Region (70 percent) than in upland northern Karen State (60 percent) where the Karen National Union (KNU) has criticized military infrastructure projects and encouraged villages to withhold support from such initiatives for decades. Variations in participation rates thus correlate with exposure to ideologies critical of state attempts to outsource social responsibility along with experience of civil conflict.

15. There were good reasons for residents and local administrators to embrace the ideal of self-reliance during junta rule, as it allowed communities to avoid interaction with higher authorities. For instance, Thawnghmung (2003; 2004, chap. 4 and 5) highlights that headmen who villagers viewed as the most effective were those who strategically managed junta officials in ways that kept state officials at bay while maximizing benefit for locals from state initiatives.

16. In one urban ward road improvement project, the municipal government itself was privately contracted by a ward committee to renovate and repave ward roads and drainage ditches. Commercial elites donated the equivalent of US$200 compared to US$40 for poorer households.

17. Respondents were asked, "Have you ever contributed to local road construction?" If so, they were then asked, "What form of contribution? (Labor; Meetings; Funds; Other)." Eighty-eight percent of poor households reported contributing labor and/or funds to local road improvements, compared with 80 percent for richer households and 76 percent for middle-income households.

18. For discussion of local administration, see Kyed, Harrisson, and G. McCarthy 2016.

19. Rose (1999, 135–136) argues that as the market reforms of the 1970s and 1980s prompted attempts to retrench state welfare schemes in many developed democracies, policymakers increasingly framed "social" problems such as unemployment "in terms of features of communities and their strengths, cultures, pathologies." The social task of government shifted, reframing issues such as joblessness or migrant integration from issues requiring the state to provide material aid or support to individuals or regions affected by economic and social change to enabling, animating, and facilitating "community" as "a self-generating formation capable of governing itself" (Li 2011, 101–102). Solutions to prob-

lems imagined as rooted in community were seen to require interventions that "encourage and harness active practices of self-management and identity construction, of personal ethics and collective allegiances" (Rose 1999, 176).

20. The military state passed orders and laws that, as anthropologist Elliott Prasse-Freeman (2015, 98) notes, "delineated actions that were forbidden without creating any reciprocal 'rights' allowing subjects to make claims against the state." The one-way flow of "rights" reflected precolonial monarchical understandings of power as "self-justifying," in which kings governed their subjects on the basis of performances of divine authority and a system of natural law derived from Buddhist cosmology (Myint Zan 1997).

21. Aung San Suu Kyi's Rule of Law and Tranquility Committee, for instance, received 11,259 submissions in 2012 and 2013 alone. Of these, 3,600 concerned the executive and 3,466 land confiscation cases. Cheesman (2015a, 227–237) notes that many of the claims made in these and other letters referenced notions of a "just" rule of law, claiming an entitlement to fair and impartial treatment and redress for past wrongs.

22. Three hundred respondents were surveyed in fourteen villages of each township, of which seven villages (150 respondents) had received the Green Emerald scheme and another seven villages (150 respondents) in the same village group had not received the scheme. A total of 600 rural respondents across twenty-eight villages were surveyed across both townships. There was a statistically significant difference in road construction assistance rendered by respondents in Green Emerald and non–Green Emerald villages (p-value of 0 percent). Of respondents in villages selected to receive the Green Emerald initiative in 2015 or 2016, 81 percent had contributed previously to local road construction, compared with 64 percent of respondents in non–Green Emerald villages—a robust 17 percent difference. On other relevant indicators such as poverty rates, however, there was no statistically significant variation between the villages as the treatment and non-treatment villages were otherwise in the same village group.

23. The initiative expanded rapidly between 2013 and 2020 with the aim of funding local development initiatives identified by a committee of local residents in at least one village in every village group of the participating township. Poverty rates were the "primary criterion for selecting the participating townships," and below that, level projects were selected from within village groups through a "planning and consultation process." The World Bank's Q&A about the scheme cites the aim of including "at least 63 townships across the country" by the end of the rollout period. International financing for the scheme and all World Bank initiatives in Myanmar were suspended after the military coup in February 2021.

24. Thanks to an anonymous adviser to the scheme for this description of the competition process within NCDDP.

25. Walker links this legibility to the broader dynamic of rural agricultural subsidies, noting the importance of symbolically constructing an entity legible as "community" that can be "an eligible participant in the new fiscal relationship that has emerged between the subsidizing state and the rural economy" (Walker 2012, 185).

26. Conversely, the author also encountered a number of cases where communities spent more than the allocated government budget for a project and then raised additional funds through donations from the local community.

27. Tania Li (2011, 117) recounts similar dynamics in her study of community "cohesion" and development initiatives in Indonesia, where hierarchies of collective virtue justify the exclusion of poor communities "whose failure to perform made them ineligible for assistance."

28. Until late 2018, the General Administration Department (GAD), whose local officers are responsible for grassroots administration and governance across Myanmar, was part of the military-controlled Ministry of Home Affairs. In late 2018, the GAD was transferred to

the Ministry of the Union Government Office headed by a civilian. Kyi Pyar Chit Saw and Arnold (2014) provide more detail; see also "Govt Reveals Plan to Bring GAD under Civilian Control," *Frontier Myanmar*, 22 December 2018.

29. Ethnographers have recorded similar dynamics of rural development assistance provided as a "gift" rather than an entitlement in northern Thailand since the 1980s (Vandergeest 1991, 433), though peasants have seemingly grown increasingly strategic in their interactions with state authorities in recent decades (Walker 2012, 185).

30. Northern Karen State has seen conflict between the Myanmar military and the Karen National Union (KNU) armed group since 1949. Severe clashes initially reduced following a preliminary bilateral ceasefire signed in 2012 and the KNUs subsequent 2015 commitment to the Nationwide Ceasefire Agreement. Following several years of Myanmar military attempts to expand its access through unilateral road construction in ceasefire areas between 2015 and 2020 that led to repeated skirmishes between the Tatmadaw and the KNU (see McCarthy and Farrelly 2020), after the February 2021 coup several KNU brigades provided shelter and military training to anti-coup protesters and resistance fighters. Prominent leaders within the KNU also declared the 2015 NCA "void."

31. Of 301 respondents in northern Karen State who reported contributing their labor to local road construction, only 11 (3.75 percent of contributors) stated they had donated funds. This contrasts with 41 percent of respondents in lowland Bago Region who contributed either funds or funds and labor.

32. See also Chatterjee 2004, Kohl-Arenas 2015, Skocpol 2016, and Walker 2012.

CONCLUSION

1. The Internal Revenue Department at the Union of Myanmar Ministry of Planning and Finance provides this perspective. See Aung Thein, "Tax Reforms in Myanmar" (paper presented at IMF-Japan High-Level Tax Conference for Asian Countries, 5–7 April 2016), https://www.imf.org/external/np/seminars/eng/2016/asiatax/pdf/at33.pdf.

2. For instance, the NLD government placed economic concessions at the heart of its Business for Peace scheme, encouraging armed groups to establish public companies that would then tender for infrastructure projects and attract foreign investment to ceasefire areas, despite extensive experience that shows this will only compound dire social and economic inequalities (G. McCarthy 2019). See also Moe Myint, "Analysis: Trading Armed Struggle for Battle in the Market Place," *The Irrawaddy*, 25 July 2018, https://www.irrawaddy.com/news/trading-armed-struggle-battle-market-place.html.

References

Acemoglu, D., and J. A. Robinson. 2006. *Economic Origins of Dictatorship and Democracy*. New York: Cambridge University Press.

Adams, V. 2013. *Markets of Sorrow, Labors of Faith: New Orleans in the Wake of Katrina*. Durham, NC: Duke University Press.

Adas, M. 1974. *The Burma Delta: Economic Development and Social Change on an Asian Rice Frontier, 1852–1941*. Madison: University of Wisconsin Press.

Adas, M. 1979. *Prophets of Rebellion: Millenarian Protest Movements against the European Colonial Order*. Chapel Hill: University of North Carolina Press.

Adema, W. 1999. "Net Social Expenditure." *OECD Labour Market and Social Policy Occasional Papers*. Paris: OECD.

Albertus, M., and V. Menaldo. 2013. "Gaming Democracy: Elite Dominance during Transition and the Prospects for Redistribution." *British Journal of Political Science* 44 (3): 575–603.

Anderson, B. 1991. *Imagined Communities: Reflections on the Origin and the Spread of Nationalism*. London: Verso.

Ansell, A. 2014. *Zero Hunger: Political Culture and Antipoverty Policy in Northeast Brazil*. Chapel Hill: University of North Carolina Press.

Ansell, B. W., and D. J. Samuels. 2010. "Inequality and Democratization: A Contractarian Approach." Comparative Political Studies 43(12): 1543–1574.

Ansell, B. W., and D. J. Samuels. 2014. *Inequality and Democratization*. Cambridge: Cambridge University Press.

ANU. 2014. *Myanmar Military Presence Index*. Compiled by N. Farrelly. Canberra: Australian National University.

ASEAN Secretariat. 2018. *ASEAN Key Figures 2018*. Jakarta: ASEAN Secretariat Statistics Division.

Aspinall, E., and M. Sukmajati. 2016. *Electoral Dynamics in Indonesia: Money Politics, Patronage and Clientelism at the Grassroots*. Singapore: National University of Singapore.

Aspinall, E., and A. Hicken. 2020. "Guns for Hire and Enduring Machines: Clientelism beyond Parties in Indonesia and the Philippines." *Democratization* 27 (1): 137–156.

Aung, G. 2019. "Reworking Bandung Internationalism: Decolonization and Postcolonial Futurism in Burma/Myanmar." *Critical Asian Studies* 51 (2): 198–209.

Aung San Suu Kyi. 1991. *Freedom from Fear*. London: Penguin Books.

Aung-Thwin, M. 2010. *The Return of the Galon King: History, Law, and Rebellion in Colonial Burma*. Athens: Ohio University Press.

Aung-Thwin, M., and M. Aung-Thwin 2012. *A History of Myanmar since Ancient Times: Traditions and Transformations*. London: Reaktion Books.

Aung Tun Thet. 1989. *Burmese Entrepreneurship: Creative Response in the Colonial Economy*. Stuttgart: Steiner Verlag Wiesbaden.

Auyero, J. 2000. *Poor People's Politics: Peronist Survival Networks and the Legacy of Evita*. Durham, NC: Duke University Press.

Baaz, M., and M. Lilja. 2014. "Understanding Hybrid Democracy in Cambodia: The Nexus between Liberal Democracy, the State, Civil Society, and a 'Politics of Presence.'" *Asian Politics & Policy* 6 (1): 5–24.

Badgley, J. 1974. "Burmese Communist Schisms." In *Peasant Rebellion and Communist Revolution in Asia*, edited by J. Badgley and J. Lewis, 151–168. Stanford, CA: Stanford University Press.

Baillargeon, D. 2020. "'Imperium in Imperio': The Corporation, Mining, and Governance in British Southeast Asia, 1900–1930." *Enterprise & Society* (October): 1–32.

Béland, D. 2005. "Ideas and Social Policy: An Institutionalist Perspective." *Social Policy & Administration* 39 (1): 1–18.

Béland, D. 2010. "Reconsidering Policy Feedback: How Policies Affect Politics." *Administration & Society* 42 (5): 568–590.

Béland, D., and J. S. Hacker. 2004. "Ideas, Private Institutions and American Welfare State 'Exceptionalism': The Case of Health and Old-Age Insurance, 1915–1965." *International Journal of Social Welfare* 13 (1): 42–54.

Bello, W., J. Franco, P. Vervest, and T. Kramer 2020. "How to Improve Myanmar's Covid-19 Emergency Relief Program." Transnational Institute, 9 June. https://www.tni .org/en/article/how-to-improve-myanmars-covid-19-emergency-relief-program.

Berenschot, W., R. Hanani, and P. Sambodho. 2018. "Brokers and Citizenship: Access to Health Care in Indonesia." *Citizenship Studies* 22 (2): 129–144.

Berenschot, W., and G. van Klinken. 2018. "Informality and Citizenship: The Everyday State in Indonesia." *Citizenship Studies* 22 (2): 95–111.

Berlant, L. 2011. *Cruel Optimism*. Durham, NC: Duke University Press.

Block, F. 2009. "Read Their Lips: Taxation and the Ring-Wing Agenda." In *The New Fiscal Sociology: Taxation in Comparative and Historical Perspective*, edited by. I. W. Martin, A. K. Mehrotra, and M. Prasad, 68–85. New York: Cambridge University Press.

Bogais, J. 2015. "Beyond the Critical Juncture: Myanmar's 2015 Elections in Focus." CSIS Asia Program.

Boix, C. 2003. *Democracy and Redistribution*. New York: Cambridge University Press.

Bornstein, E. 2012. *Disquieting Gifts: Humanitarianism in New Delhi*. Stanford, CA: Stanford University Press.

Bourdieu, P. 1977. *Outline of a Theory of Practice*. Cambridge: Cambridge University Press.

Boutry, M. 2013. "From British to Humanitarian Colonization: The 'Early Recovery' Response in Myanmar after Nargis." *South East Asia Research* 21 (3): 381–401.

Boutry, M. 2016. "Burman Territories and Borders in the Making of a Myanmar Nation State." In *Myanmar's Mountain and Maritime Borderscapes: Local Practices, Boundary-Making and Figured Worlds*, edited by. S.-A. Oh, 99–120. Singapore: ISEAS-Yusof Ishak Institute.

Brac de la Perriere, B. 2010. "Le scrutin de Nargis: Le cyclone de 2008 en Birmanie [The Nargis Poll: The 2008 Cyclone in Burma]." *Terrain* 54:66–79. https://journals .openedition.org/terrain/13968.

Brac de la Perriere, B. 2014. "A Woman of Mediation." In *Burmese Lives: Ordinary Life Stories under the Burmese Regime*, edited by E. Tagliacozzo and W. C. Chang, 71–82. New York: Oxford University Press.

Brac de la Perriere, B. 2015. "A Generation of Monks in the Democratic Transition." In *Metamorphosis: Studies in Social and Political Change in Myanmar*, edited by R. Egreteau and F. Robinne, 320–345. Singapore: National University of Singapore Press.

Brancati, E., P. Minoletti, Nilar Win, Aung Hein, and G. Riambau 2020. "Coping with COVID-19: Protecting Lives, Employment, and Incomes in Myanmar." Policy Brief MMR-20100, International Growth Centre, London, October.

Brandes, S. D. 1976. *American Welfare Capitalism, 1880–1940*. Chicago: University of Chicago Press.

Brass, J. N. 2016. *Allies or Adversaries*. New York: Cambridge University Press.

Brenner, D. 2015. "Ashes of Co-Optation: From Armed Group Fragmentation to the Rebuilding of Popular Insurgency in Myanmar." *Conflict, Security & Development* 15 (4): 337–358.

Brenner, D. 2017. "Authority in Rebel Groups: Identity, Recognition and the Struggle over Legitimacy." *Contemporary Politics* 23 (4): 408–426.

Brenner, D. 2018. "Inside the Karen Insurgency: Explaining Conflict and Conciliation in Myanmar's Changing Borderlands." *Asian Security* 14 (2): 83–99.

Brenner, D. 2019. *Rebel Politics: A Political Sociology of Armed Struggle in Myanmar's Borderlands.* Ithaca, NY: Cornell University Press.

Brody, D. 1980. *Workers in Industrial America: Essays on the Twentieth Century Struggle.* New York: Oxford University Press.

Brown, I. 1999a. "The Economic Crisis and Rebellion in Rural Burma in the Early 1930s." In *Growth, Distribution and Political Change: Asia and the Wider World*, edited by R. Minami, K. S. Kim, and M. Falkus, 143–157. London: Palgrave Macmillan UK.

Brown, I. 1999b. "Tax Remission and Tax Burden in Rural Lower Burma during the Economic Crisis of the Early 1930s." *Modern Asian Studies* 33 (2): 383–403.

Brown, I. 2013. *Burma's Economy in the Twentieth Century.* Cambridge: Cambridge University Press.

Brubaker, R. 1992. *Citizenship and Nationhood in France and Germany.* Cambridge, MA: Harvard University Press.

Brubaker, R. 2010. "Migration, Membership, and the Modern Nation-State: Internal and External Dimensions of the Politics of Belonging." *Journal of Interdisciplinary History* 41 (1): 61–78.

Bulloch, H. C. M. 2017. *In Pursuit of Progress: Narratives of Development on a Philippine Island.* Honolulu: University of Hawai'i Press.

Bünte, M. 2016. "Myanmar's Protracted Transition: Arenas, Actors, and Outcomes." *Asian Survey* 56 (2): 369–391.

Burawoy, M., and K. Verdery, eds. 1999. *Uncertain Transition: Ethnographies of Change in the Postsocialist World.* Lanham, MD: Rowman & Littlefield.

Cady, J. F. 1958. *A History of Modern Burma.* Ithaca, NY: Cornell University Press.

Callahan, M. 2001. "Cracks in the Edifice? Military-Society Relations in Burma since 1988." In *Strong Regime, Weak State*, edited by M. Pedersen, 22–51. Adelaide: Crawford House Publishing.

Callahan, M. 2003. *Making Enemies: War and State Building in Burma.* Ithaca, NY: Cornell University Press.

Callahan, M. 2004. "Making Myanmars: Language, Territory, and Belonging in Post-Socialist Burma." In *Boundaries and Belonging: States and Societies in the Struggle to Shape Identities and Local Practices*, edited by J. S. Migdal, 99–121. New York: Cambridge University Press.

Callahan, M. 2007. *Political Authority in Burma's Ethnic Minority States: Devolution, Occupation and Coexistence.* Washington, DC: East-West Center.

Callahan, M. 2017. "Aung San Suu Kyi's Quiet, Puritanical Vision for Myanmar." *Nikkei Asian Review*, 29 March.

Cammett, M. 2014. *Compassionate Communalism: Welfare and Sectarianism in Lebanon.* Ithaca, NY: Cornell University Press.

Cammett, M., and L. M. MacLean. 2011. "Introduction: The Political Consequences of Non-State Social Welfare in the Global South." *Studies in Comparative International Development* 46:11–21.

Cammett, M., and L. M. MacLean. 2014. *The Politics of Non-State Social Welfare.* Ithaca, NY: Cornell University Press.

Campbell, S. 2014. "Rethinking Myanmar's Left Intellectual History: The Subaltern Politics of Banmaw Tin Aung and Thakin Po Hla Gyi." Paper presented at Burma/Myanmar Research Forum, Cornell University, Ithaca, NY, 24–26 October.

Campbell, S. 2019. "Touring Myanmar's Leftist History." *Focaal Blog*, 14 May. https://www.focaalblog.com/2019/05/14/stephen-campbell-touring-myanmars-leftist-history/.

Candier, A. 2007. "A Norm of Burmese Kingship? The Concept of Raza-Dhamma through Five Konbaung Period Texts." *Journal of Burma Studies* 11:5–48.

Candier, A. 2011. "'Conjuncture and Reform in the Late Konbaun Period: How Prophecies, Omens and Rumors Motivated Political Action from 1866 to 1869." *Journal of Burma Studies* 15 (2): 231–262.

Castoriadis, C. 1997. *The Imaginary Institution of Society*. Cambridge, MA: MIT Press.

Chatterjee, P. 2004. *The Politics of the Governed: Reflections on Popular Politics in Most of the World*. New York: Columbia University Press.

Cheesman, N. 2012. "The Politics of Law and Order in Myanmar." PhD diss., Department of Political and Social Change, Australian National University.

Cheesman, N. 2015a. *Opposing the Rule of Law*. New York: Cambridge University Press.

Cheesman, N. 2015b. "The Right to Have Rights." In *Communal Violence in Myanmar*, edited by N. Cheesman and Htoo Kyaw Win, 139–152. Yangon: Myanmar Knowledge Society.

Cheesman, N. 2017a. "How in Myanmar 'National Races' Came to Surpass Citizenship and Exclude Rohingya." *Journal of Contemporary Asia* 47 (3): 461–483.

Cheesman, N. 2017b. "Introduction: Interpreting Communal Violence in Myanmar." *Journal of Contemporary Asia* 47 (3): 335–352.

Chigudu, S. 2020. *The Political Life of an Epidemic: Cholera, Crisis and Citizenship in Zimbabwe*. New York: Cambridge University Press.

Collier, S. J. 2011. *Post-Soviet Social: Neoliberalism, Social Modernity, Biopolitics*. Princeton, NJ: Princeton University Press.

Cook, P. 1994. "Policy Reform, Privatization, and Private Sector Development in Myanmar." *South East Asia Research* 2 (2): 117–140.

Cook, S., and J. Pincus. 2014. "Poverty, Inequality and Social Protection in Southeast Asia: An Introduction." *Journal of Southeast Asian Economies* 31 (1): 1–17.

CPCS. 2009. *Listening to Voices from Inside: Myanmar Civil Society's Response to Cyclone Nargis*. Phnom Pehn: Center for Peace and Conflict Studies.

Crabtree, J. 2018. *Billionaire Raj: A Journey through India's New Gilded Age*. New York: Crown Publishing.

Crouch, M. 2021. "Myanmar Coup Has No Constitutional Basis." *East Asia Forum*, 3 February.

Dauber, M. L. 2012. *The Sympathetic State: Disaster Relief and the Origins of the American Welfare State*. Chicago: University of Chicago Press.

Davies, J. 2018. "Making Myanmar: Democratic Transition and Communal Violence 2012–2014." PhD diss., School of Humanities and Social Sciences, University of New South Wales.

Decobert, A. 2015. *The Politics of Aid to Burma: A Humanitarian Struggle on the Thai-Burmese Border*. New York: Taylor & Francis.

Demuijnck, G., and B. Fasterling. 2016. "The Social License to Operate." *Journal of Business Ethics* 136 (4): 675–685.

Dove, C. 2017. "Giving Trends in Myanmar: More than Merit Making." *Austrian Journal of South-East Asian Studies* 10 (2): 205–222.

Dryzek, J. S. 2017. "The Forum, the System, and the Polity: Three Varieties of Democratic Theory." *Political Theory* 45 (5): 610–636.

Dunford, M. 2021. "Centering Heterogeneity in the Civil Disobedience Movement." Presentation, Myanmar Update Conference 2021, Australian National University, Canberra, 22 July.

Egreteau, R. 2011. "Burmese Indians in Contemporary Burma: Heritage, Influence, and Perceptions since 1988." *Asian Ethnicity* 12 (1): 33–54.

Egreteau, R. 2017. "The Emergence of Pork-Barrel Politics in Parliamentary Myanmar." Singapore: ISEAS-Yusof Ishak Institute.

Eibl, F. 2020. *Social Dictatorships: The Political Economy of the Welfare State in the Middle East and North Africa.* New York: Oxford University Press.

Englund, H. 2008. "Extreme Poverty and Existential Obligations: Beyond Morality in the Anthropology of Africa?" 52 (3): 33–50.

Esping-Andersen, G. 1990. *The Three Worlds of Welfare Capitalism.* Princeton, NJ: Princeton University Press.

Fairfield, T., and C. Garay. 2017. "Redistribution under the Right in Latin America: Electoral Competition and Organized Actors in Policymaking." *Comparative Political Studies* 50 (14): 1871–1906.

Farrelly, N. 2008. "Patronage and Power in Northern Burma." *New Mandala*, 10 August.

Farrelly, N. 2013. "Discipline without Democracy: Military Dominance in Post-Colonial Burma." *Australian Journal of International Affairs* 67 (3): 312–326.

Ferguson, J. 2015. *Give a Man a Fish: Reflections on the New Politics of Distribution.* Durham, NC: Duke University Press.

Ferrara, F. 2003. "Why Regimes Create Disorder: Hobbes's Dilemma during a Rangoon Summer." *Journal of Conflict Resolution* 47 (3): 302–325.

Foerch, T., S. Thein, and S. Waldschmidt. 2013. *Myanmar's Financial Sector: A Challenging Environment for Banks.* Yangon: Deutsche Gesellschaft für Internationale Zusammenarbeit (GIZ).

Ford, M., M. Gillan, and H. H. Thein. 2016. "From Cronyism to Oligarchy? Privatisation and Business Elites in Myanmar." *Journal of Contemporary Asia* 46 (1): 18–41.

Frechette, A. 2007. "Democracy and Democratization among Tibetans in Exile." *Journal of Asian Studies* 66 (1): 97–127.

Fujita, K., F. Mieno, and I. Okamoto. 2009. *The Economic Transition in Myanmar after 1988: Market Economy versus State Control.* Singapore: National University of Singapore Press.

Fujita, K., and I. Okamoto. 2009. "Overview of Agricultural Policies and the Development in Myanmar." In *The Economic Transition in Myanmar after 1988: Market Economy versus State Control*, edited by K. Fujita, F. Mieno, and I. Okamoto, 169–215. Singapore: National University of Singapore Press.

Furnivall, J. S. 1931. *An Introduction to the Political Economy of Burma.* Rangoon: Burma Book Club.

Geertz, C. 1980. *Negara: The Theatre State in Nineteenth-Century Bali.* Princeton, NJ: Princeton University Press.

Giridharadas, A. 2019. *Winners Take All: The Elite Charade of Changing the World.* London: Penguin.

Goldfarb, K. E., and C. E. Schuster. 2016. "Introduction: (De)materializing Kinship— Holding Together Mutuality and Difference." *Social Analysis* 60 (2): 1–12.

Gravers, M. 2015. "Anti-Muslim Buddhist Nationalism in Burma and Sri Lanka: Religious Violence and Globalized Imaginaries of Endangered Identities." *Contemporary Buddhism* 16 (1): 1–27.

Griffiths, M. 2016. *Poverty Reduction through Rural Development: The Evergreen Village Project.* Nay Pyi Taw: SPPRG/DRD.

Griffiths, M. 2017. *Parahita Organizations in Rural Myanmar: The Politics of Emergent Forms of Redistribution*. Singapore: Asia Research Institute, National University of Singapore.

Griffiths, M. 2019. *Community Welfare Organisations in Rural Myanmar: Precarity and Parahita*. New York: Routledge.

Guyot, D. H. 1966. *The Political Impact of the Japanese Occupation of Burma*. DPhil diss., Department of Political Science, Yale University.

Hacker, J. S. 2002. *The Divided Welfare State: The Battle over Public and Private Social Benefits in the United States*. Cambridge: Cambridge University Press.

Hacker, J. S. 2016a. "America's Welfare Parastate." *Perspectives on Politics* 14 (3): 777–783.

Hacker, J. S. 2016b. "Insecurity, Austerity and the American Social Contract." In *Progressivism in America: Past, Present and Future*, edited by D. B. Woolner and J. M. Thompson, 109–127. New York: Oxford University Press.

Hadiz, V. R. 2004. "Decentralization and Democracy in Indonesia: A Critique of Neo-Institutionalist Perspectives." *Development and Change* 35 (4): 697–718.

Haggard, S., and R. R. Kaufman. 2008. *Development, Democracy, and Welfare States: Latin America, East Asia, and Eastern Europe*. Princeton, NJ: Princeton University Press.

Hawley, E. W. 1974. "Herbert Hoover, the Commerce Secretariat, and the Vision of an 'Associative State,' 1921–1928." *Journal of American History* 61 (1): 116–140.

Heidel, B. 2006. *The Growth of Civil Society in Myanmar*. Bangalore: Books for Change.

Helmke, G., and S. Levitsky. 2004. "Informal Institutions and Comparative Politics: A Research Agenda." *Perspectives on Politics* 2 (4): 725–740.

Herrold, C. E. 2020. *Delta Democracy: Pathways to Incremental Civic Revolution in Egypt and Beyond*. New York: Oxford University Press.

Himmelberg, R. F. 2001. *The Great Depression and the New Deal*. Westport, CT: Greenwood Press.

Holliday, I. 2000. "Productivist Welfare Capitalism: Social Policy in East Asia." *Political Studies* 48:706–723.

Holliday, I. 2014. "Addressing Myanmar's Citizenship Crisis" *Journal of Contemporary Asia* 44(3): 404–421.

Horsey, R. 2011. *Ending Forced Labour in Myanmar: Engaging a Pariah Regime*. New York: Routledge.

Houtman, G. 1999. *Mental Culture in Burmese Crisis Politics: Aung San Suu Kyi and the National League for Democracy*. Tokyo: Institute for the Study of Languages and Cultures of Asia and Africa, Tokyo University of Foreign Studies.

Howard, C. 1999. *The Hidden Welfare State: Tax Expenditures and Social Policy in the United States*. Princeton, NJ: Princeton University Press.

Howard, C. 2009. "Making Taxes the Life of the Party." In *The New Fiscal Sociology: Taxation in Comparative and Historical Perspective*, edited by I. W. Martin, A. K. Mehrotra, and M. Prasad, 86–100. New York: Cambridge University Press.

Howe, B., and G. Bang. 2017. "Nargis and Haiyan: The Politics of Natural Disaster Management in Myanmar and the Philippines." *Asian Studies Review* 41 (1): 58–78.

HRW. 2002. "Crackdown on Burmese Muslims." Human Rights Watch.

Hsu, M.-L. 2019. "Making Merit, Making Civil Society: Free Funeral Service Societies and Merit-Making in Contemporary Myanmar." *Journal of Burma Studies* 23(1): 1–36.

Htet Aung. 2009. "Distrust and Division in the Delta." *The Irrawaddy* 17 (3): 18–20.

Hutchcroft, P. D. 1991. "Oligarchs and Cronies in the Philippine State: The Politics of Patrimonial Plunder." *World Politics* 43 (3): 414–450.

Ito, M., and M. Griffiths 2016. *Migration in Myanmar: Perspectives from Current Research*. Yangon: SPPRG/IOM.

Jacobs, L. R., and T. Skocpol. 2007. *Inequality and American Democracy: What We Know and What We Need to Learn.* New York: Russell Sage Foundation.

James, H. 2005. *Governance and Civil Society in Myanmar: Education, Health and Environment.* London: Routledge Curzon.

Jaquet, C., and M. J. Walton. 2013. "Buddhism and Relief in Myanmar: Reflections on Relief as a Practice of Dāna." In *Buddhism, International Relief Work, and Civil Society,* edited by H. Kawanami and G. Samuel, 51–73. New York: Springer.

Jibao, S., W. Prichard, and V. van den Boogaard 2017. *Informal Taxation in Post-Conflict Sierra Leone: Taxpayers' Experiences and Perceptions.* Brighton: Institute of Development Studies.

Jones, L. 2014. "The Political Economy of Myanmar's Transition." *Journal of Contemporary Asia* 44 (1): 144–170.

Jones, L. 2016. "Understanding Myanmar's Ceasefires: Geopolitics, Political Economy and State-Building." In *War and Peace in the Borderlands of Myanmar: The Kachin Ceasefire, 1994–2011,* edited by M. Sadan, 95–113. Copenhagen: Nordic Institute of Asian Studies.

Jordt, I. 2007. *Burma's Mass Lay Meditation Movement: Buddhism and the Cultural Construction of Power.* Athens: Ohio University Press.

Jordt, I., Tharaphi Than, and Sue Ye Lin. 2021. *How Generation Z Galvanized a Revolutionary Movement against Myanmar's 2021 Military Coup.* Singapore: ISEAS–Yusof Ishak Institute.

Kawamura, Y. 2016. "Social Welfare under Authoritarian Rule: Change and Path Dependence in the Social Welfare System in Mubarak's Egypt." PhD diss., School of Government and International Affairs, Durham University.

Keefer, P. 2007. "Clientelism, Credibility, and the Policy Choices of Young Democracies." *American Journal of Political Science* 51 (4): 804–821.

Khin Maung Kyi. 1966. "Patterns of Accommodation to Bureaucratic Authority in a Transitional Culture." PhD diss., Cornell University.

Khin Yi. 1988. *The Dobama Movement in Burma (1930–1938).* Ithaca, NY: Cornell University Southeast Asia Program.

Khin Zaw Win. 2006. "Transition in a Time of Siege: The Pluralism of Societal and Political Practices at Ward/Village Level in Myanmar/Burma." In *Active Citizens under Political Wraps: Experiences from Myanmar/Burma and Vietnam,* 74–92. Chiang Mai: Heinrich Boell Foundation.

Kohl-Arenas, E. 2015. *The Self-Help Myth: How Philanthropy Fails to Alleviate Poverty.* Oakland: University of California Press.

Korpi, W. 1983. *The Democratic Class Struggle.* London: Routledge & Kegan Paul.

Kubo, K. 2007. "Determinants of Parallel Exchange Rate in Myanmar." *ASEAN Economic Bulletin* 24 (3): 289–304.

Kudo, T. 2001. *Industrial Development in Myanmar: Prospects and Challenges.* Chiba: Institute of Developing Economies.

Kudo, T. 2005. *Stunted and Distorted Industrialization in Myanmar.* Chiba: Institute of Developing Economies.

Kuhonta, E. M., D. Slater, and T. Vu. 2008. *Southeast Asia in Political Science: Theory, Region, and Qualitative Analysis.* Stanford, CA: Stanford University Press.

Kumada, N. 2004. "Rethinking Daná in Burma: The Art of Giving, Buddhism and the Spirit Cult Revisited." Paper presented at the Interdisciplinary Conference on Religion in Contemporary Myanmar, Stanford University, 22–23 May.

Kumada, N. 2015. "Burmese Kinship Revisited: Substance and 'Biology' in the World of Rebirth." *Contemporary Buddhism* 16 (1): 75–108.

Kyaw Htut. 1994. *A Guide to the Mangala Sutta.* Translated by Daw Mya Tin. Yangon: Department for the Promotion and Propagation of the Sasana, Union of Myanmar.

Kyaw San Wai. 2020. "Myanmar's COVID-19 Response Banks on Aung San Suu Kyi." *East Asia Forum*, 31 July.

Kyaw Yin Hlaing. 2001. "The Politics of State-Business Relations in Post-Colonial Burma." PhD diss., Cornell University.

Kyaw Yin Hlaing. 2003. "Reconsidering the Failure of the Burma Socialist Programme Party Government to Eradicate Internal Economic Impediments." *South East Asia Research* 11 (1): 5–58.

Kyaw Yin Hlaing. 2007a. "Associational Life in Myanmar: Past and Present." In *Myanmar: State, Society, and Ethnicity,* edited by N. Ganesan and K. Y. Hlaing, 143–171. Singapore: Institute of Southeast Asian Studies.

Kyaw Yin Hlaing. 2007b. "The Politics of State-Society Relations in Burma." *South East Asia Research* 15 (2): 213–254.

Kyed, H. M., A. P. Harrisson, and G. McCarthy. 2016. *Local Democracy in Myanmar: Reflections on Ward and Village Tract Elections in 2016.* Copenhagen: Danish Institute for International Studies.

Kyi May Kaung. 1995. "Theories, Paradigms, or Models in Burma Studies." *Asian Survey* 35 (11): 1030–1041.

Kyi Pyar Chit Saw, and M. Arnold. 2014. *Administering the State in Myanmar: An Overview of the General Administration Department.* Yangon: The Asia Foundation.

Kyu Khin Gar, G. McCarthy, A. Smurra and R. Toth. 2020. "Myanmar COVID-19 Impact & Recovery Monitor (MCIRM) Survey." Round 1 (Sept/Oct) Briefing, Innovations for Poverty Action, The Asia Foundation, and WaterAid Myanmar.

Lal, P. 2012. "Self-Reliance and the State: The Multiple Meanings of Development in Early Post-Colonial Tanzania." *Africa: The Journal of the International African Institute* 82, (2): 212–234.

Leehey, J. 2016. *Community-Based Social Protection in the Dry Zone.* Myanmar: HelpAge International.

Li, T. M. 2007. *The Will to Improve: Governmentality, Development, and the Practice of Politics.* Durham, NC: Duke University Press.

Li, T. M. 2011. "Rendering Society Technical: Government Through Community and the Ethnographic Turn at the World Bank in Indonesia." In *Adventures in Aidland: The Anthropology of Professionals in International Development,* edited by D. Mosse, 57–80. Oxford: Berghahn.

Lehman, F. K. 1967. "Ethnic Categories in Burma and the Theory of Social Systems." In *Southeast Asian Tribes, Minorities and Nations,* edited by P. Kunstadter, 93–124. Princeton, NJ: Princeton University Press.

Levi, M. 1988. *Of Rule and Revenue.* Berkeley: University of California Press.

Levitsky, S. 2001. "An 'Organised Disorganisation': Informal Organisation and the Persistence of Local Party Structures in Argentine Peronism." *Journal of Latin American Studies* 33:29–65.

Lieberman, E. 2001. "National Political Community and the Politics of Income Taxation in Brazil and South Africa in the Twentieth Century." *Politics & Society* 29 (4): 515–555.

Lieberman, E. 2003. *Race and Regionalism in the Politics of Taxation in Brazil and South Africa.* Cambridge: Cambridge University Press.

Lieberman, R. C. 2002. "Ideas, Institutions, and Political Order: Explaining Political Change." *American Political Science Review* 96 (4): 697–712.

Lieberman, V. 2003. *Strange Parallels: Southeast Asia in Global Context, c. 800–1830. Volume 1: Integration on the Mainland.* Cambridge: Cambridge University Press.

LIFT/QSEM. 2016. *A Country on the Move: A Qualitative Social and Economic Monitoring (QSEM) Thematic Study Domestic Migration in Two Regions of Myanmar.* Yangon: Livelihoods and Food Security Trust Fund.

London, J. D. 2018. *Welfare and Inequality in Marketizing East Asia.* London: Palgrave Macmillan UK.

Lorch, J. 2006. "Civil Society under Authoritarian Rule: The Case of Myanmar." *Südostasien aktuell* 25:3–37.

Lorch, J. 2007. "Myanmar's Civil Society—A Patch for the National Education System? The Emergence of Civil Society in Areas of State Weakness." *Südostasien aktuell* 26 (3): 54–88.

Lorch, J. 2008a. "The (Re)-Emergence of Civil Society in Areas of State Weakness: The Case of Education in Burma/Myanmar." In *Dictatorship, Disorder and Decline in Myanmar,* edited by M. Skidmore and T. Wilson, 151–176. Canberra: ANU E Press.

Lorch, J. 2008b. "Stopgap or Change Agent? The Role of Burma's Civil Society after the Crackdown." *Internationales Asienforum* 39 (1–2): 21–54.

Lwin Cho Latt, B. Hillman, Marlar Aung, and Khin Sanda Myint. 2018. "From Ceasefire to Dialogue: The Problem of 'All-Inclusiveness' in Myanmar's Stalled Peace Process." In *Myanmar Transformed? People, Places, Politics,* edited by J. Chambers, G. McCarthy, N. Farrelly, and Chit Win, 231–250. Singapore: Institute for Southeast Asian Studies.

Lwin, H. H., and K. K. Maung. 2011. "A Study of Public Awareness Education Training on Natural Disaster Risk Reduction in Myanmar." *Universities Research Journal Myanmar* 4 (5): 223–241.

MacLean, K. 2008. "Sovereignty in Burma after the Entrepreneurial Turn: Mosaics of Control, Commodified Spaces, and Regulated Violence in Contemporary Burma." In *Taking Southeast Asia to Market: Commodities, Nature, and People in the Neoliberal Age,* edited by J. Nevins and N. L. Peluso, 140–157. Ithaca, NY: Cornell University Press.

MacLean, K. 2010. "The Rise of Private Indirect Government in Burma." In *Finding Dollars, Sense and Legitimacy in Burma,* edited by S. L. Levenstein, 40–53. Washington, DC: Woodrow Wilson International Center for Scholars.

MacLean, L. M. 2004. "Empire of the Young: The Legacies of State Agricultural Policy on Local Capitalism and Social Support Networks in Ghana and Cote d'Ivoire." *Comparative Studies in Society and History* 46 (3): 469–496.

MacLean, L. M. 2010. *Informal Institutions and Citizenship in Rural Africa: Risk and Reciprocity in Ghana and Côte d'Ivoire.* Cambridge: Cambridge University Press.

MacLean, L. M. 2011a. "Exhaustion and Exclusion in the African Village: State Legacies and Non-State Social Welfare in Ghana and Cote d'Ivoire." *Studies in Comparative and International Development* 46 (1): 118–136.

MacLean, L. M. 2011b. "State Retrenchment and the Exercise of Citizenship in Africa." *Comparative Political Studies* 44 (9): 1238–1266.

Magaloni, B., and R. Kricheli. 2010. "Political Order and One-Party Rule." *Annual Review of Political Science* 13:123–143.

Marcus, G. E. 1998. *Ethnography through Thick and Thin.* Princeton, NJ: Princeton University Press.

Mares, I., and M. Carnes. 2009. "Social Policy in Developing Countries." *Annual Review of Political Science* 12:93–113.

Markovits, I. 1978. "Socialist vs. Bourgeois Rights: An East-West German Comparison." *University of Chicago Law Review* 45 (3): 612–636.

Martin, I. W., A. K. Mehrotra, and M. Prasad. 2009. "The Thunder of History: The Origins and Development of the New Fiscal Sociology." In *The New Fiscal Sociology:*

Taxation in Comparative and Historical Perspective, edited by I. W. Martin, A. K. Mehrotra, and M. Prasad, 1–28. New York: Cambridge University Press.

Martin, I. W., and M. Prasad. 2014. "Taxes and Fiscal Sociology." *Annual Review of Sociology* 40 (1): 331–345.

Martinus, M., and S. Seah. 2020. "Are ASEAN Stimulus Dollars Going towards Sustainability?" *ISEAS-Yusof Ishak Institute Perspective*, 19 August.

Maung Aung Myoe. 2009. *Building the Tatmadaw: Myanmar Armed Forces since 1948*. Singapore: Institute of Southeast Asian Studies.

Maung Htin Aung. 1967. *A History of Burma*. New York: Columbia University Press.

Maung. 1989. *Burmese Nationalist Movements, 1940–1948*. Edinburgh: Kiscadale Publications.

Mauss, M. 2002. *The Gift: The Form and Reason for Exchange in Archaic Societies*. New York: Taylor & Francis.

McCarthy, G. 2016a. *Building on What's There: Insights on Social Protection, Taxation and Public Goods in Taungoo, Bago Region and Thandaungyi, Kayin State*. London: International Growth Centre Myanmar.

McCarthy, G. 2016b. "Buddhist Welfare and the Limits of Big 'P' Politics in Provincial Myanmar.". In *Conflict in Myanmar: War, Politics, Religion*, edited by N. Cheesman and N. Farrelly, 313–332. Singapore; ISEAS-Yusof Ishak Institute.

McCarthy, G. 2018a. "The Value of Life: Citizenship, Entitlement and Moral Legibility in Provincial Myanmar." In *Citizenship in Myanmar: Ways of Being in and from Burma*, edited by A. South and M. Lall, 167–187. Singapore: ISEAS-Yusof Ishak Institute and Chiang Mai University Press.

McCarthy, G. 2018b. "Cyber-Spaces." In *Routledge Handbook of Contemporary Myanmar*, edited by A. Simpson, N. Farrelly, and I. Holliday, 92–105. Abingdon, Oxon: Taylor & Francis.

McCarthy, G. 2019. *Military Capitalism in Myanmar: Examining the Origins, Continuities and Evolution of "Khaki Capital."* Singapore: Institute of Southeast Asian Studies.

McCarthy, G., and N. Farrelly. 2020. "Peri-Conflict Peace: Brokerage, Development and Illiberal Ceasefires in Myanmar's Borderlands." *Conflict, Security & Development* 20 (1): 141–163.

McCarthy, G., and J. Menager. 2017a. "Buddhist Suffering and the Muslim Scapegoat." *Frontier Myanmar*, 10 July.

McCarthy, G., and J. Menager. 2017b. "Gendered Rumours and the Muslim Scapegoat in Myanmar's Transition." *Journal of Contemporary Asia* 47 (3): 396–412.

McCarthy, S. 2008. "Overturning the Alms Bowl: The Price of Survival and the Consequences for Political Legitimacy in Burma." *Australian Journal of International Affairs* 62 (3): 298–314.

McCarthy, S. 2012. *Civil Society in Burma: From Military Rule to "Disciplined Democracy."* Brisbane: Griffith Asia Institute.

McGovern, M. 2012. "Life during Wartime: Aspirational Kinship and the Management of Insecurity." *Journal of the Royal Anthropological Institute* 18 (4): 735–752.

McGovern, M. 2015. "Liberty and Moral Ambivalence: Postsocialist Transitions, Refugee Hosting, and Bodily Comportment in the Republic of Guinea." *American Ethnologist* 42 (2): 247–261.

McGovern, M. 2017. *A Socialist Peace? Explaining the Absence of War in an African Country*. Chicago: University of Chicago Press.

Mee Mee Zaw. 2018. "The Rise of Social Consciousness among Young Buddhists in Burma 2009–2011." Paper presented as Asian Studies Association of Australia Conference, Sydney, 3–5 July.

Meehan, P. 2011. "Drugs, Insurgency and State-Building in Burma: Why the Drugs Trade Is Central to Burma's Changing Political Order." *Journal of Southeast Asian Studies* 42 (3): 376–404.

Meltzer, A. H., and S. F. Richard. 1981. "A Rational Theory of the Size of Government." *Journal of Political Economy* 89 (5): 914–927.

Menager, J. 2017. "Myanmar's New Generation: A Study of Elite Young People in Yangon, 2010 to 2016." PhD diss., Australian National University.

Mendelson, M. 1975. *Sangha and State in Burma: A Study of Monastic Sectarianism and Leadership.* Ithaca, NY: Cornell University Press.

Mieno, F. 2006. "Determinants of Debt, Bank Loan and Trade Credit of Private Firms in the Transitional Period: The Case of Myanmar." In *Recovering Financial Systems: China and Asian Transition Economies,* edited by M. Watanabe and A. K. Kenkyūjo, 146–175. Hampshire: Palgrave Macmillan.

MOPFI. 2020. *Myanmar 2019/20 Social Welfare Budget Brief.* Naypyitaw: Myanmar Ministry of Planning, Finance, and Industry.

Muehlebach, A. 2012. *The Moral Neoliberal: Welfare and Citizenship in Italy.* Chicago: University of Chicago Press.

Mullen, M. 2016. *Pathways That Changed Myanmar.* London: Zed Books.

Mya Maung. 1970. "The Burmese Way to Socialism beyond the Welfare State." *Asian Survey* 10 (6): 533–551.

Mya Maung. 1991. *The Burma Road to Poverty.* New York: Praeger Publishers.

Mya Than. 1992. *Myanmar's External Trade: An Overview in the Southeast Asian Context.* ISEAS Current Economic Affairs Series. Singapore: Institute of Southeast Asian Studies.

Mya Than, and Myat Thein. 2000. "Mobilization of Financial Resources for Development in Myanmar: An Introductory Overview." In *Financial Resources for Development in Myanmar: Lessons from Asia,* edited by Mya Than and Myat Thein, 1–24. Singapore: Institute of Southeast Asian Studies.

Myat Thein. 2004. *Economic Development of Myanmar.* Singapore: Institute of Southeast Asian Studies.

Myat Thein, and Khin Maung Nyo. 1999. "Social Sector Development in Myanmar: The Role of the State." *ASEAN Economic Bulletin* 16 (3): 394–404.

Myint Zan. 1997. "Position of Power and Notions of Empowerment: Comparing the Views of Lee Kuan Yew and Aung San Suu Kyi on Human Rights and Democratic Governance." *Newcastle Law Review* 2 (1): 49–69.

Nakanishi, Y. 2013. *Strong Soldiers, Failed Revolution: The State and Military in Burma, 1962–1988.* Singapore: NUS Press.

Nam, I. 2014. *Democratizing Health Care: Welfare State Building in Korea and Thailand.* New York: Palgrave Macmillan US.

Naseemullah, A., and P. Staniland. 2016. "Indirect Rule and Varieties of Governance." *Governance* 29 (1): 13–30.

Nash, M. 1965. *The Golden Road to Modernity: Village Life in Contemporary Burma.* New York: John Wiley & Sons.

Nemoto, K. 2000. "The Concepts of Dobama ('Our Burma') and Thudo-Bama ('Their Burma') in Burmese Nationalism, 1930–1948." *Journal of Burma Studies* 5:1–16.

Newman, K. S., and R. O'Brien 2011. *Taxing the Poor: Doing Damage to the Truly Disadvantaged.* Berkeley: University of California Press.

Nickel, P. M. 2018. "Philanthropy and the Politics of Well-Being." *PS: Political Science & Politics* 51 (1): 61–66.

Nishizaki, Y. 2004. *The Weapon on the Strong: Identity, Community and Domination in Provincial Thailand.* PhD diss., University of Washington.

Nishizaki, Y. 2011. *Political Authority and Provincial Identity in Thailand: The Making of Banharn-buri*. Ithaca, NY: Cornell Southeast Asia Program.

Oh, S.-A. 2013. *Competing Forms of Sovereignty in the Karen State of Myanmar*. Singapore: Institute of Southeast Asian Studies.

Okamoto, I. 2017. "Village Organizational Capability and Collective Actions in Myanmar." ANU Myanmar Update Forum, University of Yangon, 15–16 March.

Olken, B. A., and M. Singhal. 2011. "Informal Taxation." *American Economic Journal: Applied Economics* 3 (4): 1–28.

Orloff, A. S. 1988. "The Political Origins of America's Belated Welfare State." In *The Politics of Social Policy in the United States*, edited by M. Weir, A. S. Orloff, and T. Skocpol, 37–80. Princeton, NJ: Princeton University Press.

Pedersen, M. B. 2011. "The Politics of Burma's 'Democratic' Transition." *Critical Asian Studies* 43 (1): 49–68.

Perotti, R. 1996. "Growth, Income Distribution, and Democracy: What the Data Say." *Journal of Economic Growth* 1 (2): 149–187.

Petrie, C., and A. South. 2014. "Development of Civil Society in Myanmar." In *Burma/Myanmar: Where Now?*, 87–94. Copenhagen: Nordic Institute of Asian Studies Press.

Phyo Win Latt. 2016. "Protecting Amyo: Constructing Identity and Belonging in Colonial Burma, 1900–1941." Presentation, Department of History, National University of Singapore.

Prasad, M. 2012. *The Land of Too Much: American Abundance and the Paradox of Poverty*. Cambridge, MA: Harvard University Press.

Prasad, M. 2018. *Starving the Beast: Ronald Reagan and the Tax Cut Revolution*. New York: Russell Sage Foundation.

Prasse-Freeman, E. 2012. "Power, Civil Society, and an Inchoate Politics of the Daily in Burma/Myanmar". *The Journal of Asian Studies*. 71 (2): 371–397.

Prasse-Freeman, E. 2015. "Conception of Justice and the Rule of Law." In *Myanmar: The Dynamics of an Evolving Polity*, edited by D. Steinberg, 89–114. London: Lynne Rienner.

Prasse-Freeman, E. 2020. "Of Punishment, Protest, and Press Conferences: Contentious Politics amidst Despotic Decision in Contemporary Burmese Courtrooms." In *Criminal Legalities in the Global South*, edited by G. Radics and P. Ciocchini, 124–142. New York: Routledge.

Prasse-Freeman, E., and P. W. Latt. 2018. "Class and Inequality in Contemporary Myanmar." In *Routledge Handbook of Contemporary Myanmar*, edited by A. Simpson, N. Farrelly, and I. Holliday, 404–416. New York: Routledge.

Pursch, S., A. Woodhouse, M. Woolcock, and M. Zurstrassen. 2018. "Documenting Social and Economic Transformation in Myanmar's Rural Communities." In *Myanmar Transformed? People, Places, Politics*, edited by J. Chambers, G. McCarthy, N. Farrelly, and Chit Win, 23–52. Singapore: ISEAS.

Quadagno, J. S. 1984. "Welfare Capitalism and the Social Security Act of 1935." *American Sociological Review* 49 (5): 632–647.

Reich, R. 2016. "Repugnant to the Whole Idea of Democracy? On the Role of Foundations in Democratic Societies." *PS: Political Science & Politics* 49 (3): 466–472.

Reich, R. 2018. *Just Giving: Why Philanthropy Is Failing Democracy and How It Can Do Better*. Princeton, NJ: Princeton University Press

Remes, J. A. C. 2015. *Disaster Citizenship: Survivors, Solidarity, and Power in the Progressive Era*. Urbana: University of Illinois Press.

Rhoads, E., Thang Sorn Poine, Cho Cho Win, and H. M. Kyed. 2020. *Myanmar Urban Housing Diagnostic & COVID-19 Rapid Assessment*. Yangon: Enlightened Myanmar Research Foundation/World Bank.

Robertson, B., C. Joelene, and L. Dunn. 2015. *Local Development Funds in Myanmar: An Initial Review*. Yangon: The Asia Foundation.

Rodan, G., and C. Hughes 2014. *The Politics of Accountability in Southeast Asia: The Dominance of Moral Ideologies*. New York: Oxford University Press.

Rose, N. 1999. *Powers of Freedom: Reframing Political Thought*. Cambridge: Cambridge University Press.

Ross, M. 2006. "Is Democracy Good for the Poor?" *American Journal of Political Science* 50 (4): 860–874.

Roy, A. 2014. *Capitalism: A Ghost Story*. Chicago: Haymarket Books.

Rozenberg, G. 2010. *Renunciation and Power: The Quest for Sainthood in Contemporary Burma*. New Haven, CT: Yale University Southeast Asia Studies.

Sacks, A. 2011. "Credit or Blame: Non-State Provision of Services and Political Support in Africa." DPhil diss., Department of Sociology, University of Washington.

Sadan, M. 2016. *War and Peace in the Borderlands of Myanmar: The Kachin Ceasefire, 1994–2011*. Copenhagen: Nordic Institute of Asian Studies.

Saha, J. 2012. "A Mockery of Justice? Colonial Law, the Everyday State and Village Politics in the Burma Delta, c.1890–1910." *Past & Present* 217 (1): 187–212.

Saha, J. 2013. *Law, Disorder and the Colonial State: Corruption in Burma c.1900*. London: Palgrave Macmillan UK.

San San Oo. 2018. "How Shall We Die Now? The Rise of Co-Operative of Funeral Service Societies in Yangon." Paper presented at the Thirteenth International Burma Studies Conference, Bangkok, 3–5 August.

Schaffer, F. C. 2000. *Democracy in Translation: Understanding Politics in an Unfamiliar Culture*. Ithaca, NY: Cornell University Press.

Schaffer, F. C. 2014. "Thin Descriptions: The Limits of Survey Research on the Meaning of Democracy." *Polity* 46 (3): 303–330.

Scheve, K., and D. Stasavage. 2012. "Democracy, War, and Wealth: Lessons from Two Centuries of Inheritance Taxation." *American Political Science Review* 106 (1): 81–102.

Schissler, M., M. J. Walton, and Phyu Phyu Thi. 2015. "Threat and Virtuous Defence: Listening to Narratives of Religious Conflict in Six Myanmar Cities." Myanmar Media and Society Working Paper.

Schissler, M., M. J. Walton, and Phyu Phyu Thi. 2017. "Reconciling Contradictions: Buddhist-Muslim Violence, Narrative Making and Memory in Myanmar." *Journal of Contemporary Asia* 47 (3): 376–395.

Schneider, F., and Y.-J. Hwang. 2014. "The Sichuan Earthquake and the Heavenly Mandate: Legitimizing Chinese Rule through Disaster Discourse." *Journal of Contemporary China* 23 (88): 636–656.

Schober, J. 1989. "Paths to Enlightenment: Theravada Buddhism in Upper Burma." PhD diss., Department of Anthropology, University of Illinois at Urbana-Champaign.

Schober, J. 1996. "Religious Merit and Social Status among Burmese Buddhist Lay Associations." In *Merit and Blessing in Mainland Southeast Asia in Comparative Perspective*, edited by C. A. Kammerer and N. B. Tannenbaum, 197–211. New Haven, CT: Yale University Southeast Asia Studies.

Schober, J. 1997. "Buddhist Just Rule and Burmese National Culture: State Patronage of the Chinese Tooth Relic in Myanmar." *History of Religions* 36 (3): 218–243.

Schonthal, B., and M. Walton. 2016. "The (New) Buddhist Nationalisms? Symmetries and Specificities in Sri Lanka and Myanmar." *Contemporary Buddhism* 17 (1): 81–115.

Schreiner, M. 2012. "A Simple Poverty Scorecard for Myanmar." London: United Kingdom Department for International Development and Microfinance Risk Management.

Scott, J. C. 1972a. "The Erosion of Patron-Client Bonds and Social Change in Rural Southeast Asia." *Journal of Asian Studies* 32 (1): 5–37.

Scott, J. C. 1972b. "Patron-Client Politics and Political Change in Southeast Asia." *American Political Science Review* 66 (1): 91–113.

Scott, J. C. 1976. *The Moral Economy of the Peasant: Rebellion and Subsistence in Southeast Asia*. New Haven, CT: Yale University Press.

Scott, J. C. 1998. *Seeing Like a State: How Certain Schemes to Improve the Human Condition Have Failed*. New Haven, CT: Yale University Press.

Scott, J. C., and B. J. Kerkvliet. 1986. *Everyday Forms of Peasant Resistance in South-East Asia*. London: Frank Cass.

Seekins, D. M. 2009. "State, Society and Natural Disaster: Cyclone Nargis in Myanmar (Burma)." *Asian Journal of Social Science* 37:717–737.

Segura-Ubiergo, A. 2007. *The Political Economy of the Welfare State in Latin America: Globalization, Democracy, and Development*. New York: Cambridge University Press.

Selth, A. 2002. *Burma's Armed Forces: Power without Glory*. Norwalk, CT: EastBridge.

Selth, A. 2008. "Even Paranoids Have Enemies: Cyclone Nargis and Myanmar's Fears of Invasion." *Contemporary Southeast Asia* 30 (3): 379–402.

Shindo, R. 2015. "Enacting Citizenship in a Post-Disaster Situation: The Response to the 2011 Great East Japan Earthquake." *Citizenship Studies* 19 (1): 16–34.

Silber, I. 2001. "The Gift-Relationship in an Era of 'Loose' Solidarities." In *Identity, Culture and Globalization*, edited by E. Ben-Rafael and Y. Sternberg, 385–400. Leiden: Brill.

Silverstein, J. 1997. "Fifty Years of Failure in Burma." In *Government Policies and Ethnic Relations in Asia and the Pacific*, edited by M. E. Brown and S. Ganguly, 167–196. Cambridge, MA: MIT Press.

Skidmore, M. 2004. *Karaoke Fascism: Burma and the Politics of Fear*. Philadelphia: University of Pennsylvania Press.

Skocpol, T. 1992. *Protecting Soldiers and Mothers: The Political Origins of Social Policy in the United States*. Cambridge, MA: Harvard University Press.

Skocpol, T. 2016. "Why Political Scientists Should Study Organized Philanthropy." *PS: Political Science & Politics* 49 (3): 433–436.

Slater, D. 2010. *Ordering Power: Contentious Politics and Authoritarian Leviathans in Southeast Asia*. Cambridge: Cambridge University Press.

Slater, D., B. Smith, and G. Nair. 2014. "Economic Origins of Democratic Breakdown? The Redistributive Model and the Postcolonial State." *Perspectives on Politics* 12 (2): 353–374.

Slater, D., and H. D. Soifer 2020. "The Indigenous Inheritance: Critical Antecedents and State Building in Latin America and Southeast Asia." *Social Science History* 44 (2): 251–274.

Smith, M. 1999. *Burma: Insurgency and the Politics of Ethnicity*. London: Zed Books.

Smith, M. 2007. *State of Strife: The Dynamics of Ethnic Conflict in Burma*. Washington, DC: East-West Center and Institute of Southeast Asian Studies.

Snyder, R. 2006. "Does Lootable Wealth Breed Disorder? A Political Economy of Extraction Framework." *Comparative Political Studies* 39 (8): 943–968.

Soifer, H. D. 2013. "State Power and the Economic Origins of Democracy." *Studies in Comparative International Development* 48 (1): 1–22.

South, A. 2004. "Political Transition in Myanmar: A New Model for Democratisation." *Contemporary Southeast Asia: A Journal of International and Strategic Affairs* 26 (2): 233–255.

South, A. 2012. "The Politics of Protection in Burma." *Critical Asian Studies* 44 (2): 175–204.

South, A. 2017. "'Hybrid Governance' and the Politics of Legitimacy in the Myanmar Peace Process." *Journal of Contemporary Asia* 48 (1): 1–17.

Spiro, M. E. (1970) 1982. *Buddhism and Society: A Great Tradition and Its Burmese Vicissitudes*. Berkeley: University of California Press.

Stasch, R. 2009. *Society of Others: Kinship and Mourning in a West Papuan Place*. Berkeley, CA: University of California Press.

Steinberg, D. 1997. "The Union Solidarity and Development Association: Mobilization and Orthodoxy in Myanmar." Burma Debate, Open Society Institute, Washington, DC, 4–11 January/February.

Steinberg, D. 2005. "Myanmar: The Roots of Economic Malaise." In *Myanmar: Beyond Politics to Societal Imperatives*, edited by Kyaw Yin Hlaing, R. H. Taylor, and Tin Maung Maung Than, 86–116. Singapore: Institute of Southeast Asian Studies.

Steinberg, D. I. 1999. "A Void in Myanmar: Civil Society in Burma." In *Strengthening Civil Society in Burma: Possibilities and Dilemmas for International NGOs*, edited by T. Kramer and P. Vervest. Chiang Mai: Silkworm Books.

Steinberg, D. I. 2001. *Burma: The State of Myanmar*. Washington, DC: Georgetown University Press.

Steinberg, D. I. 2006. *Turmoil in Burma: Contested Legitimacies in Myanmar*. Norwalk, CT: East Bridge.

Stephens, J. D. 1979. *The Transition from Capitalism to Socialism*. London: Palgrave Macmillan UK.

Stifel, L. 1971. "Economics of the Burmese Way to Socialism." *Asian Survey* 11 (8): 803–817.

Stokke, K., Khine Win, and Soe Myint Aung. 2015. "Political Parties and Popular Representation in Myanmar's Democratisation Process." *Journal of Current Southeast Asian Affairs* 34 (3): 3–35.

Taylor, C. 2002. "Modern Social Imaginaries." *Public Culture* 14 (1): 91–124.

Taylor, R. 1985. "Burma." In *Military-Civilian Relations in South-East Asia*, edited by Z. H. Ahmad and H. A. Crouch. Oxford: Oxford University Press.

Taylor, R. 2009. *The State in Myanmar*. London: Hurst.

Teets, J. C. 2014. *Civil Society under Authoritarianism: The China Model*. New York: Cambridge University Press.

Than Tun. 1938. "Race Riots in Burma." *Workers' International News* 1 (9): 810.

Thant Myint-U. 2001. *The Making of Modern Burma*. New York: Cambridge University Press.

Tharaphi Than. 2013. "The Languages of Pyidawtha and the Burmese Approach to National Development." *South East Asia Research* 21 (4): 639–654.

Thawnghmung, A. M. 2001. "Paddy Farmers and the State: Agricultural Policies and Legitimacy in Rural Myanmar." PhD diss., Department of Political Science, University of Wisconsin-Madison.

Thawnghmung, A. M. 2003. "Rural Perceptions of State Legitimacy in Burma/Myanmar." *Journal of Peasant Studies* 30 (2): 140.

Thawnghmung, A. M. 2004. *Behind the Teak Curtain: Authoritarianism, Agricultural Policies and Political Legitimacy in Rural Burma/Myanmar*. London: Kegan Paul.

Thawnghmung, A. M. 2019. *Everyday Economic Survival in Myanmar*. Madison: University of Wisconsin Press.

Thawnghmung, A. M., and K. Noah. 2021. "Myanmar's Military Coup and the Elevation of the Minority Agenda?" *Critical Asian Studies* 53 (2): 297–309.

Thelen, K. 1999. "Historical Institutionalism in Comparative Politics." *Annual Review of Political Science* 2(1): 369–404.

Thompson, J. S. 1959. "Marxism in Burma." In *Marxism in Southeast Asia: A Study of Four Countries*, edited by F. N. Trager, 14–57. Stanford, CA: Stanford University Press.

Thorndike, J. J. 2009. "'The Unfair Advantage of the Few': The New Deal Origins of 'Soak the Rich' Taxation." In *The New Fiscal Sociology: Taxation in Comparative and*

Historical Perspective, edited by I. W. Martin, A. K. Mehrotra, and M. Prasad, 29–47. New York: Cambridge University Press.

Tin Maung Maung Than. 1993. "Sangha Reforms and Renewal of Sasana in Myanmar: Historical Trends and Contemporary Practices." In *Buddhist Trends in Southeast Asia*, edited by T. Ling, 7–63. Singapore: Institute of Southeast Asian Studies.

Tin Maung Maung Than. 2007. *State Dominance in Myanmar: The Political Economy of Industrialization*. Singapore: Institute of Southeast Asian Studies.

Tinker, H. 1957. "Nu, the Serene Statesman." *Pacific Affairs* 30 (2): 120–137.

Tinker, H. 1967. *The Union of Burma: A Study of the First Years of Independence*. Oxford: Oxford University Press and Royal Institute of International Affairs.

Tinker, H. 1984. *Burma: The Struggle for Independence 1944–1948, vol. 1*. London, Her Majesty's Stationery Office.

Tosa, K. 2018. "Transformation of Buddhist Associations into Non-Governmental Organizations in Myanmar." Paper presented at the Thirteenth International Burma Studies Conference, Bangkok, 3–5 August.

Townsend, L., and C. Wallace. 2016. *Social Media Research: A Guide to Ethics*. Aberdeen: University of Aberdeen Press.

Trickett, E. J., and M. E. Oliveri. 1997. "Ethnography and Sociocultural Processes: Introductory Comments." *Ethos* 25 (2): 146–151.

Tripartite Core Group. 2008. *Post-Nargis Joint Assessment*. Yangon: TCG. https://reliefweb.int/sites/reliefweb.int/files/resources/C675C571D9F845A7C125748D0046C5A3-Full_Report.pdf.

Trocaire. 2011. "Private Sector and Humanitarian Relief in Myanmar." Myanmar Marketing Research and Development, October. http://www.burmalibrary.org/docs13/Private_Sector+Humanitarian_Response.pdf.

Turnell, S. 2009. *Fiery Dragons: Banks, Moneylenders and Microfinance in Burma*. Copenhagen: Nordic Institute of Asian Studies Press.

Turnell, S. 2011. "Fundamentals of Myanmar's Macroeconomy: A Political Economy Perspective." *Asian Economic Policy Review* 6 (1): 136–153.

Turner, A. 2009. "Buddhism, Colonialism and the Boundaries of Religion: Theravada Buddhism in Burma, 1885–1920.". PhD diss., Divinity School, University of Chicago.

Turner, A. 2011. "Religion-Making and Its Failures: Turning Monasteries into Schools and Buddhism into a Religion in Colonial Burma," 226–242. In *Secularism and religion-making*.

Turner, A. 2014. *Saving Buddhism: The Impermanence of Religion in Colonial Burma*. Honolulu: University of Hawai'i Press.

U San Thein, J.-C. Diepart, U Hlwan Moe, and C. Allaverdian. 2018. *Large-Scale Land Acquisitions for Agricultural Development in Myanmar: A Review of Past and Current Processes*. Vientiane: Mekong Region Land Governance.

UNICEF. 2020. *Using Myanmar's Supplementary Budget to Respond to and Recover from COVID-19, and Reimagine a Better Future for Children*. Yangon: United Nations Children's Fund.

Union of Burma. 1954. *Pyidawtha: The New Burma*. London: Hazell, Watson and Viney and Economic and Social Board of Burma.

Van Klinken, G. 2007. "Return of the Sultans: The Communitarian Turn in Local Politics." In *The Revival of Tradition in Indonesian Politics: The Deployment of Adat from Colonialism to Indigenism*, edited by J. Davidson and D. Henley, 149–160. London: Routledge.

Vandergeest, P. 1991. "Gifts and Rights: Cautionary Notes on Community Self-Help in Thailand." *Development and Change* 22 (3): 421–443.

Vatikiotis, M. 1996. "Grim Reaping: Strong-Arm Policies Help Spur Burma's Growth." *Far Eastern Economic Review* 159 (6): 48.

Vatikiotis, M. R. J. 1998. *Indonesian Politics under Suharto: The Rise and Fall of the New Order*. New York: Taylor & Francis.

Vicary, A. 2010. *The Hidden Impact of Burma's Arbitrary and Corrupt Taxation*. Chiang Mai: Network for Human Rights Documentation, Burma.

Walinsky, L. J. 1962. *Economic Development in Burma, 1951–60*. New York: Twentieth Century Fund.

Walker, A. 2012. *Thailand's Political Peasants: Power in the Modern Rural Economy*. Madison: University of Wisconsin Press.

Walton, M. 2012. "Politics in the Moral Universe: Burmese Buddhist Political Thought." PhD diss., Department of Political Science, University of Washington.

Walton, M. 2014. "What Are Myanmar's Buddhist Sunday Schools Teaching?" *East Asia Forum*, 16 December.

Walton, M. 2016. *Buddhism, Politics and Political Thought in Myanmar*. Cambridge: Cambridge University Press.

Walton, M. 2018. "Nation-Building." In *Routledge Handbook of Contemporary Myanmar*, edited by A. Simpson, N. Farrelly, and I. Holliday, 393–403. New York: Routledge.

Walton, M. 2008. "Ethnicity, Conflict, and History in Burma: The Myths of Panglong." *Asian Survey* 48 (6): 889–910.

Walton, M. 2015. "The Disciplining Discourse of Unity in Burmese Politics." *Journal of Burma Studies* 19 (1): 1–26.

Wedeen, L. 2010. "Reflections on Ethnographic Work in Political Science." *Annual Review of Political Science* 13:255–272.

Wells, T. 2016. "Myanmar's Other Struggles for Democracy: Narratives and Conceptual Contest in the Burmese Democracy Movement." PhD diss., University of Melbourne.

Wells, T. 2018. "Democratic 'Freedom' in Myanmar." *Asian Journal of Political Science* 26 (1): 1–15.

Wells, T. 2021. *Narrating Democracy in Myanmar: The Struggle between Activists, Democratic Leaders and Aid Workers*. Amsterdam: Amsterdam University Press.

Widger, T. 2016. "Philanthronationalism: Junctures at the Business–Charity Nexus in Post-War Sri Lanka." *Development and Change* 47 (1): 29–50.

Wilson, J. H. 1975. *Herbert Hoover: Forgotten Progressive*. Boston: Little, Brown.

Winters, J. A. 2011. *Oligarchy*. New York: Cambridge University Press.

Wittekind, C. T. 2021. "Crisis upon Crisis: Fighting COVID-19 Becomes a Political Struggle after Myanmar's Military Coup." *ISEAS-Yusof Ishak Institute Perspective*, 11 May.

Wong, J. 2006. *Healthy Democracies: Welfare Politics in Taiwan and South Korea*. Ithaca, NY: Cornell University Press.

Wood, G. 2003. "Staying Secure, Staying Poor: The Faustian Bargain." *World Development* 31 (3): 455–471.

Wood, G., and I. Gough. 2006. "A Comparative Welfare Regime Approach to Global Social Policy." *World Development* 34 (10): 1696–1712.

Woods, K. 2011. "Ceasefire Capitalism: Military–Private Partnerships, Resource Concessions and Military–State Building in the Burma–China Borderlands." *Journal of Peasant Studies* 38 (4): 747–770.

Woods, K. 2015. *Intersections of Land Grabs and Climate Change Mitigation Strategies in Myanmar as a (Post-)War State of Conflict*. The Hague: International Institute of Social Studies.

Zieger, R. H. 1977. "Herbert Hoover, the Wage-Earner, and the 'New Economic System,' 1919–1929." *Business History Review* 51 (2): 161–189.

Index

Figures are indicated by f.

abbot (*sayadaw*): aid dispersion and, 111; Byama-so chapter establishment and, 75; at flood site, 94–95

activists: Bamar Buddhist political, 124; at betel-nut shop, 139; Constitution (2008) and, 204; grassroots, 159, 204; NLD, 143, 172; in non-state welfare efforts, 6, 85; welfare groups of, 85, 92

a-dhamma (against the teachings of Buddha), 127

advisory roles, for rebel leaders, 63

Affordable Care Act, US, 14

AFO. *See* Anti-Fascist Organisation

AFPFL. *See* Anti-Fascist People's Freedom League

agribusiness, 65

a-hlubwe (ritual of giving), 59–60

aid: charitable, 130; customization of, 113; delivered to flood victims, 110–111, 114f; directness of/avoidance of state intermediation, 112–113; distribution of from pagoda, 112–113; freely given, 86; junta restrictions on, 99, 226n6; lack of customization, 113; non-state, 117–119, 124, 149; practical practices of delivering, 124–125, 132–133; residency requirement for, 88–89. *See also* state aid

aid packages, labeling of, 111–112

Allied advances, 34

American welfare capitalism, 39–40

amyo. *See* kin

amyo batha thathana (national religion), 141

amyotha. *See* sons of the nation

Anglo-Burmese War, 115

anti-colonial sentiment, rise in, 33

Anti-Fascist Organisation (AFO), 34

Anti-Fascist People's Freedom League (AFPFL), 35, 36, 42, 43

anti-Japanese propaganda, 34

anti-tax sentiment, 40, 201

anxiety, 140, 221n20, 229n14

Arakan Rohingya Salvation Army (ARSA), 148

Argentina, 130

ARSA. *See* Arakan Rohingya Salvation Army

Ashin Eindaga, 127

Association of Southeast Asian Nations (ASEAN), 100

associative state, 39

Attlee, Clement, 35

Aung Ko Win, 110

Aung San, 34–36, 44, 142

Aung San–Attlee Agreement, 35, 44

Aung San Suu Kyi, 4–5, 8, 54, 61, 84, 104–105; Arakan Rohingya Salvation Army and, 148–149; donations through, 175, 230n1, 231n24; foreign investment and, 209; freedom and, 126; MaBaTha on treatment of Muslims, 136; philosophy of self and democracy, 126–127; relations with tycoons, 173–174, 174f; Rule of Law and Tranquility Committee and, 235n21; on self-reliance, 193–194; viral Facebook photo of, 123–124

Aung Tun Thet, 149

austerity, 16, 206, 212n11; post-1988, 5, 8, 63–65, 113, 132, 136–138, 178, 197–198. *See also* market liberalization and reform; social outsourcing

autarkic socialist dictatorship, 25

autocratic austerity, 5, 113

autocratic leaders, 11–12

autocratic welfare capitalism, 80–81, 89, 146, 202–203, 209–210

Auyero, Javier, 130

Ayeyarwaddy Delta, 26, 94, 98

Ayuthaya, sacking reenactment, 161, 161f

Bago Region, 1, 166, 171

Bamar Buddhist political activists, 124

Bamar soldiers, 42

banking sector, privatization of, 79, 155–156

Bayinnaung (king), 160–161

Best Village awards, 191

"big people." *See lu gyi*

bilateral ceasefire, between KNU and Myanmar military, 21

black market: blossoming during BSPP period, 50–52; BSPP attempted control of, 53–55; SLORC/SPDC attempted revenue raising from, 62–63, 219n6; smuggling of commodities via, 44. *See also hmaung-kho*
blood centrifuge machinery, 134–136, 139
BNA. *See* Burma National Army
Border Areas Development programs, 63
Bornstein, Erica, 85, 107–108, 111
Bourdieu, Pierre, 152–153
Brac de la Perriere, Benedicte, 226n8
British: administrative limits of colonial Burma, 29f; chiefs acknowledged by, 28; colonial rulers, 25; insufficient pay to Burmese state employees, 35; railroad construction, 27; soldiers, 30; struggle for independence from, 28
British Burma Army, 42
British House of Commons special committee, 36
Brubaker, Rogers, 97
BSPP. *See* Burma Socialist Programme Party
Buddha, 95, 112; Dhamma school and, 140–141; doctrine of, 127; Mangala Sutta sermon, 71–72, 222n24; parade floats depicting life of, 162; water pouring ritual, 115
Buddha Dhamma Parahita Foundation, 229n16. *See also* MaBaTha
Buddhism: charitable giving *(dana)* and, 41, 51, 83–87, 92, 184, 234n13; consensus on unregulated capitalism and, 25–26, 202; ethics, 71; Five Jewels of, 224n50; meditation, action contrasted with, 101; notions of just rule (post-1988) and, 137; obligations of activism, 85; politics, citizenship and, 229n15; quasi-voluntary compliance and, 82, 85, 118; social welfare groups after 1988 and, 21; social welfare groups during BSPP and, 51–52; as state religion, 46, 235n20; unregulated capitalism and, 25–26, 202. *See also* charity; social work *(parahita)*
Bulloch, Hannah, 192–193
bureaucracy, of Myanmar, 132–133
Burma Corporation, 39
Burma National Army (BNA), 34, 42
Burma Rebellion, 24–25. *See also* Saya San
Burma Socialist Programme Party (BSPP), 47, 49, 55, 61, 83; autarky and, 51; *The Burmese Way to Socialism*, 46–47; central committee, 53; forced labor and, 179; military-laid path to socialist dictatorship and, 42–43; self-reliance and, 188. *See also* black market; import-substitution industrialization

The Burmese Way to Socialism (BSPP document), 46–47
businesses, disaster relief from, 103–104
Business for Peace scheme, of NLD, 236n2
businesspeople: behavior regulation of, 124–125; junta-linked, 183; land transactions with, 170; loans and regime-linked, 78, 155–156; obligations of, 145–147, 183; as "stingy," 144; wealth redistribution and, 82, 103–104. *See also* autocratic welfare capitalism; democratic welfare capitalism; philanthropy; social outsourcing; tycoons
Byama-so (charitable organization), 75–76, 79–80, 86
byama-so taya (meritorious practices of moral conduct), 84

Calcutta, India, 28
Callahan, Mary, 28, 49
campaigning, 129–130
capitalism: American welfare, 39–40; autocratic welfare, 80–81, 89, 202–203, 209–210; Buddhist consensus on unregulated, 25–26, 202; ceasefire, 63; collaborative industrial democracy and, 39; crony, 61, 92, 152; expectations of democratic welfare, 165; imperial, 28; inequities created by, 230n7; interventionist welfare, 37–38; morally respectable, 146; socialism fused with urban welfare, 37; transition to post-socialist, 67–68; welfare, 26, 40, 48, 85, 103. *See also* philanthropy; social work *(parahita)*; welfare capitalism
capitalist: democratic polity, 152; junta, 54; social aid, 14
CB. *See* Cooperative Bank
ceasefire capitalism, 63
cedana. See goodwill
Center for Peace and Conflict Studies (CPCS), 100
Central Cooperative Society, 79
central-east Myanmar, 18–19
ceremonies, public, 73, 163, 230n7, 231n15
charity: after 1988, 82; as critique of dictatorship after 1988, 130; expanding scope of, after 1988, 82; selflessness of, 143; social role of philanthropy after 1988 and, 23, 70–81; as spiritual practice, 87; USDP initiatives and, 131. *See also* Buddhism; non-state welfare; social work *(parahita)*
Chatterjee, Partha, 191
chaw swe. See enlistment by state officials
Cheesman, Nick, 188–189

chettiars (South Indian merchants), 27, 31
Chin State, 108, 117
Christians, 234n12; social capital and, 230n23
citizens, social ties between, 98
citizenship: BSPP revision of laws regarding, 50; as described by Myanmar's 2008 Constitution, 115–116; duties/obligations to collective and, 187, 188–192, 207; informal and moral notions of, 97, 104, 113–117; nationalist Buddhist ethics and, 71; social *vs* ethical citizenship, 16, 104. *See also* disasters; national races (*taingyintha*) ideology; political community; polity; rights; self-reliance
civil disobedience: against militarization of bureaucracy (2015), 135, 228n10; movement after 2021 coup, 198, 209–210, 228n10
clientelism, 151; electoral failure of, 132. *See also* patronage
colonial Burma, 22, 26–27, 29f; direct rule, in lowland areas, 28; extractive model of, 28; foreign economic interests in, 30–31; indirect rule, in periphery, 28; legal system of, 30; period, 22, 26–27; post-independence legacies of, 42; rule, 42; strikes by Indian and Burmese dockworkers during, 32; system of rice cultivation, 26; taxation system of, 30, 32; teak and oil industries of, 31; underpayment of Burmese state employees during, 35; use of Indian laborers and soldiers during, 30, 31
command-and-control economy, 50
commercial elites: donations after 1988 and, 69, 74, 153; informal administration and, 78, 97–98; public goods and, 166–167, 201; state aid and, 190–91
Communist China, 44
Communist Party of Burma, 42–43, 50, 54; White Flag faction, 42–43
community, 92–93; contributions of, 180f; informal arrangements, 8–9, 77–78
competition for state aid, 183–184
Constitution (2008), 5, 104, 115–116, 204; amendment to, 138–139
Constitution of the Burma Socialist Programme Party (Revolutionary Council), 47
Constitution of the Union of Burma (1947), 36–38, 50
construction, 76–77, 156; British railroad, 27. *See also* road construction
Cooperative Bank (CB), 79, 154–155. *See also* Kaung Myanmar Aung Group; Khin Maung Aye

cooperative movement, 49
coproducing development, 192–193
corporate leaders, 6–7, 103, 154
corporate measures, for welfare of workers, 39. *See also* labor; welfare capitalism
corporate social responsibility, 154, 226n14
corruption, as individual moral failing, 125, 127
counterinsurgency, 43
coup of 1962, 48, 55, 137, 180, 202; socialist and anti-capitalist justification for, 46–47. *See also* BSPP; nationalist socialism; Ne Win; welfare capitalism
coup of 2021, 5–6, 8, 61, 198–199, 209–210
COVID-19, 5, 8, 119, 176, 209, 212nn7–8
CPCS. *See* Center for Peace and Conflict Studies
credit: anti-colonial sentiment/Burma Rebellion and, 32–33; anti-Muslim sentiment (post-2011), 145; BSPP inability to repay foreign debt and, 49, 52–53; colonial credit regulations and *chettiars* (money-lenders), 3, 27, 31, 38; enabling philanthropy by tycoons, 163; Green Emerald loans scheme (2011–2021), 190, 233n7, 235nn22–23; individual/household indebtedness and foreclosure and, 31, 32, 65, 201, 225–226n53; patronage structures and, 230n3; privatization of banking sector (post-1988), 62, 79, 155; provided by regime-linked businesspeople, 65, 78, 155–156; public debt and COVID-19, 176; SLORC/SPDC inability to repay foreign debt and, 65; State Agricultural Bank and, 38. *See also* autocratic welfare capitalism; businesspeople; democratic welfare capitalism; formal taxation; informal taxation; tycoons
cronies, 2, 8, 61, 78, 80–81, 92, 152, 157, 160, 169, 173–177, 189
crony capitalism, 61, 92, 152
cultivation under colonial rule, intense system of, 26
cultural insensitivities, 31
Cyclone Komen (2015), 93–94, 96, 104–106, 202
Cyclone Nargis (2008), 93–94, 96, 98–104, 106, 202
cyclone victims, songs for, 106–107, 107f

dana. See Buddhism
Daw Aung San Suu Kyi. *See* Aung San Suu Kyi
Daw Khin Kyi Foundation, 130
Daw Khin Nwe, 86–87

debt: of individuals and households, 31–32, 65, 201, 225–226n53; patronage and, 230n3; of public/sovereign, 53, 176. *See also* credit

Defence Services Institute (DSI), 45

democracy: citizenship and, 139, 143; collaborative industrial, 39; differing ideas of, 126; enlightened mind and, 125; ideals of, 124, 131, 136, 140; moral notion of, 125–128, 139; social licensing and, 163; vernacular notions of, 125, 143. *See also* Aung San Suu Kyi; citizenship; oligarchy; polity; rights

democratic welfare capitalism, 136, 165

democratization, in East and Southeast Asia, 11, 135

demonetization, 53

dengue fever, 134–135

Department for Promotion and Propagation of the Sasana, 71

Department of Rural Development (DRD), 190

deservingness: exclusion and, 188–189; of the needy, 96–97, 193–194

dhamma seh gya (female chanting groups), 224n51

dhamma (the Budha's teachings), 228n12

Dhamma School Foundation: Buddhism in politics, citizenship and, 229n15; Buddhist ethics teaching at, 140–141; recitation competition, 162

dimensions of philanthropy, 152

direct rule, in lowland areas, 28

direct state social action, absence of, 6

disasters: belonging and, 95–96; business response to, 103–104; government response to, 96–100, 108; relief efforts and, 95–97, 157–158; welfare groups and, 100. *See also* charity; citizenship; Cyclone Komen (2015); Cyclone Nargis (2008); informal taxation; political community; social imaginaries; social work (*parahita*)

dissolution, of socialism (1988), 25

distant others, social duty to, 119

distributive politics, ideals of, 6, 7, 13, 17, 22, 124–125

distrust, of government-purchased centrifuge machine, 135–136

Dobama Asiayone (Our Burmese), 33

do it yourself local improvement projects (*kothu kotha*), 178, 179, 182. *See also* self-reliance

dominance, of elites, 12, 163–164. *See also* oligarchy

donations, 41, 70, 84, 174, 230n2; through Aung San Suu Kyi, 175, 231n1, 231n24; coerced solicitation of by SLORC/SPDC, 74–75, 82, 84; as form of taxation, 73–74, 225n57; of household relative to income and expenditure, 87–88, 184–185; imbalances of taxes *versus*, 176; media coverage of, 73; Muslim rate of, 146; to non-Buddhist areas, 117; private, as crucial to public welfare, 152; public trust in (compared with taxation), 133, 134f; pyramids, 73, 151f; quasi-voluntary compliance and, 82, 85, 118. *See also* charity; informal taxation; social work (*parahita*)

DRD. *See* Department of Rural Development

DSI. *See* Defence Services Institute

dukkha-theh (victim), 107, 135

dumpster project, of Khin Maung Aye, 167–168, 168f

Dun, Smith, 44

dyadic relations, 151

East and Southeast Asia, 11

economic elites, 139–140

economic inequality, 10, 17, 198

economic reforms, 52, 53

88 Generation Peace and Open Society, 127

elected officials, policy change and, 5

elections: 1990, 126, 180f, 219n1; 2015, 123, 131–132, 167

Eleven Media, 172

elite dominance, 12, 163–164

elite philanthropy, 152, 166–67, 176–177

emotive engagement, 105–108, 119–120

endorsement letters, 77

enlistment, of resources by civil servants (*chaw swe*), 71

entitlement. *See* citizenship; rights

entrepreneurs, 69

Esping-Andersen, Gøsta, 10

ethnic cleansing, by Tatmadaw, 231n24

ethnic minority areas, 49

ethnography, in Myanmar, 19, 20

ethno-nationalist struggles, 52

eviction, of families, 170

excluded areas, 28

exclusion: of minorities, 23, 117–118, 195–196, 203, 208; from welfare regime, 118–120

expansion: of 3G cellular network, 105–106; of state social spending (after 2011), 184–185

expectations: of democratic welfare capitalism, 165; for economic elites to substitute for state, 169–170

expenditures (social): by non-state actors, 13; by state actors, 96–98, 99, 110
extension, of state-led schemes, 11–12
extraction, of resources, 28

Facebook: Aung San Suu Kyi and, 123–124, 148–149; ethical and methodological approach to use of, 22, 135
family members: strangers as reincarnated, 95; working abroad, 65
February 2021 coup, 5–6, 198–199, 209–210
female chanting groups (*dhamlseh gya*), 224n51
flat-rate taxes, 30
floods, following cyclones, 94, 105
flood victims: aid delivered to, 110–111, 114f; fundraising for, 107f
food rations, from BSPP regime, 49
food supply, BSPP attempt to control, 51
forced labor and contributions to state, 179–180, 233n11, 233nn5–6
foreigners in law enforcement, 30
foreign investment, 62
formal institutional constraints to state redistribution, 138
formal lending, barriers to, 155
formal taxation, 68, 77, 90, 174. *See also* informal taxation
four corruptions, of Buddhism, 126
Four Year Plan (1960), 46
freedom: Aung San Suu Kyi on, 126; of expression, 172; non-state welfare and, 124
Freedom from Fear (Aung San Suu Kyi), 126–127
Free Funeral Service Society, 81, 84
fundraising: for families in crisis, 88, 92–93; for flood victims, 107f; government funding limitations and, 235n26; inefficient efforts of, 109–110
funeral and ambulance services, 76
funeral costs, 74–75, 87–88, 130

GAD. *See* General Administration Department
garbage cleanups, 123–124
Geertz, Clifford, 161
General Administration Department (GAD), 235n28, 236n28
giving ceremonies, 175
GONGOs. *See* government-organized, nongovernmental organizations
goodwill (*cedana*), 82, 168
Gordian knot (*thabu-oo*), 132

Gough, Ian, 9
government: disaster relief of, 96–100, 108; efforts to take credit for non-state aid, 111; food rations during BSPP, 49; newly elected, 3; outsourcing welfare obligations of, 40; response to Cyclone Komen (2015), 105; response to Cyclone Nargis (2008), 98–99; social outlays, 178; social role of, 11, 12–13, 21; wartime social expenditure, drop in, 34. *See also* social outsourcing
government-declared revenue, by SLORC/SPDC, 65
government-organized, nongovernmental organizations (GONGOs), 72–74, 81; moral scrutiny of donations to, 82
grace, Christian concept of, 102
grassroots: activists, on campaign manager, 159; democracy activists, 204; ideals of democracy, 136, 140
Gravers, Mikael, 126–127
the Great Depression, 14, 24, 31–33, 201
Green Emerald loans scheme (2011–2021), 190, 233n7, 235n22, 235nn22–23. *See also* credit

Haggard, Stephan, 11
health care, 14, 83, 230n9
health facilities, of Sitagu Sayadaw, 83
health insurance, private, 14
hidden welfare state, 91
Hinthada, 114
hmaung-kho. See illegal traders
home for aged, in Taungoo, 59–60, 76, 131
Hoover, Herbert, 39
horizontal solidarity, 67, 100
hospitals, 230n9; Kyaw Thu charitable, 156
household: debt, 65; donations, 87–88, 184–185; expenditures, 91, 230n9
housing project, 123–124
human development indicators, 66f
hybrid rule, 28

idealization, of precolonial period, 137
ideals and practices: of democracy, 124, 131, 136, 140; of non-state welfare, 7–8, 16, 19, 105, 119, 124; of reciprocity, 92, 105, 209; of redistribution, 6, 13, 17, 22, 124–125; self-reliance, 181–182
idioms, of nationhood, 97
Illegal traders (*hmaung-kho*), 51–52, 54
ILO. *See* International Labour Organization Forced Labour Convention
independence from British, struggle for, 28

Indian labor. *See* colonial period
indirect expenditures (social): funded by tax,
    89–91; by state, 15
indirect rule, in periphery, 28
individual moral failing, corruption as, 125
Indonesia, 163, 191–192, 235n27
industrialization: import-substitution
    industrialization (ISI), 48; post-autocratic
    strategies for, 11
industrialized democracies, 14, 149, 205,
    213n19
inequality, economic, 10, 17, 198
inequity, capitalism causing, 230n7
informal community arrangements, 8–9, 77–78
informal institutions, 12–13, 61, 67; practical
    vs normative appeal of, 3, 6, 14–15, 23, 68,
    110–111, 124, 132–147, 169, 176–177, 182,
    194–197, 204–208. *See also* charity;
    philanthropy; social licensing; social
    outsourcing; social work (*parahita*)
informal taxation, 53, 70, 132, 225n58; implicit
    taxes as, 90–91; in-kind contributions, 180,
    225n56; quasi-voluntary compliance and,
    82, 85, 118. *See also* donations; formal
    taxation
INGOs. *See* international nongovernmental
    organizations
International Labour Organization (ILO),
    Forced Labour Convention, 179–180
international nongovernmental organizations
    (INGOs), 100
interventionist welfare capitalism, under
    U Nu, 37–38
The Irrawaddy (newspaper), 79
Irrawaddy Delta, 24
Irrawaddy Flotilla Company, 31
irrigation infrastructure development, 179,
    232n3, 233n4, 233n11
ISI. *See* import-substitution industrialization

Jordt, Ingrid, 73
Junta, SLORC/SPDC. *See* State Law and Order
    Restoration Council/State Peace and
    Development Council
junta-linked businesspeople, 183. *See also*
    businesspeople; cronies; crony capitalism;
    tycoons

Kachin Independence Army (KIA), 63
Kanbawza Bank, 176, 231n24
Karen Baptist leaders, 75–76
Karen National Defense Organization
    (KNDO), 42, 43

Karen National Union (KNU), 19, 21, 196,
    236n30
Karen State, 17–19, 21, 171, 192, 196–197,
    236n30, 236nn30–31
Kaufman, Robert, 11
Kaung Myanmar Aung Group (KMA), 79,
    154, 171. *See also* Khin Maung Aye
Kayah State, 117
Khin Maung Aye, 75, 78–80, 81, 128, 142, 160;
    clients of, 155; employees of, 154–155; 500th
    Kaytumadi festival and, 164–165, 231n11;
    industrial zone of, 157; infrastructure
    projects of, 167; land disputes and, 171–173;
    legal and social licensing of, 21, 91; loans
    provided by, 155; municipal officials and,
    165; neighborhood level financial ties of,
    162–163; NLD and, 158–159; pagoda festival
    of, 161–162; philanthropy of, 154–164
Khin Nyunt, 98, 230n5
Khin Swe, 232n6
KIA. *See* Kachin Independence Army
kin (*amyo*), 135, 141
kindness (*myitta*), 84, 102, 131
kinship, 85, 106–108, 226n4. *See also* social
    imaginaries
KMA. *See* Kaung Myanmar Aung Group
KMT. *See* Kuomintang
KNDO. *See* Karen National Defense
    Organization
KNU. *See* Karen National Union
kothu kotha (do it yourself local improvement
    projects), 178, 179, 182. *See also* self-reliance
Kumada, Naoko, 152–153
Kuomintang (KMT), 44
Kyaw Naing, 185–188, 189–190
Kyaw Thu, 80, 81, 84, 145, 156–158
Kyaw Tu, 2–3, 156–158
Kyaw Yin Hlaing, 51, 70

labeling, of aid packages, 111–112
labor: activism after post-2021 coup, 198, 210;
    in colonial era, 27, 31–33, 35; contributions
    (unpaid) to development, 192, 234n13;
    forced (SLORC/SPDC), 179–180, 233n11,
    233nn5–6; trade unions and mobilization
    of, 10–11, 54, 180; welfare schemes and, 12,
    16, 38–41, 48, 52–53, 202, 217n24, 217n26,
    218n35, 218n45. *See also* self-reliance; Social
    Security Board; welfare capitalism
land: inheritance of, 80–81; nationalizations,
    demands for attempts at, 37–39; taxes, 32;
    transfer to nonagricultural interests, 27,
    170–171

land grabs, 65, 70, 170–173, 175, 189, 206. *See also* military (Tatmadaw); tycoons
landslides, 117
large-scale agribusiness, 65
late-developing countries, social protection in, 8–9
Latin America, 12–13
leftist ideology, 33
legibility, to authority, 191, 235n25
liberal altruism, 107
liberty, notion of, 127
Lieberman, Evan, 118
limited capacity, to tax populations, 10
local entrepreneurs, support from, 71
local hospital, Byama-So and, 76
local infrastructure, "big people" and, 76–77
local reciprocity and mutuality, 51, 95, 100–102, 115, 116, 204
local relief efforts, following cyclone, 99–100
lowland areas, 26; political leaders and ethnic minority populations in, 33; Taungoo, topographical map of, 20f; upland contrasted with, 18–19
low tax revenues, of Myanmar, 6. *See also* formal and informal taxation; social outsourcing; state-capacity
lugyi, secretary of township funeral group on, 76–77
lu-mu-yay (social affairs), 76, 84

MaBaTha, 129, 135–136, 144–145, 229n16. *See also* Buddha Dhamma Parahita Foundation; Sitagu Sayadaw; Wirathu
Magway Region, 105, 108
Malaysia, 27
Mandalay Region, 164
Mandalay University, 73
Mangala Sutta (Buddha sermon), 71–72, 222n24
manufacturing sector, 51
market liberalization and reform, 7, 16, 26, 67–68; after 1988, 61, 155–156, 234n19; after 2011, 104–105, 151–153; role of regional military commanders in (post-1988), 67–75, 221n17. *See also* autocratic welfare capitalism; democratic welfare capitalism; social licensing; social outsourcing
Martyr's Day, 142
Martyr's Road, 114–115
Marxist thought, 33
The Meltzer-Richard model, 10
memorialization, of Taungoo dynasty, 162
meritorious giving (*hlu dan*), 101, 111–112

meritorious practices of moral conduct (*byama-so taya*), 84
military (Tatmadaw): 62–63, 67–68, 76–77, 148–149, 236n30; administrators, road resurfacing and (SLORC/SPDC), 76–77; business conglomerates of, 45; donations to welfare groups and, 75; ethnic cleansing of Rohingya by, 116, 148–149, 157, 231n24; installations around Myanmar by 2012, 64f; officials, at charity event, 60; post-1988 battalion self-financing and, 65; regional commanders and post-1988 commercial licensing, 67–75, 77, 221n17; role in exclusion and expulsion of Rohingya, 116, 148–149, 157; state-building, 63
military-drafted constitution, 98
military rule, 4–5, 211n3; BSPP, 42–43; morality and, 140; SLORC/SPDC, 92, 127
Min Aung Hlaing, 98, 105
Ministry of Agriculture, Livestock, and Irrigation, 171–172, 181, 190, 211n6, 233n7
Ministry of Cooperatives, 79
Ministry of Defence, 5, 211n5
Ministry of Finance, 99
Ministry of Health, 135–136
Ministry of National Planning and Economic Development, 180
Ministry of Social Welfare, Relief, and Resettlement (MoSWRR), 62, 76, 99, 103
Min Ko Naing, 127
mixed-method research, 19
MMCWA. *See* Myanmar Maternal and Child Welfare Association
mobilize, capacity to, 11
monastic authorities, 83
moneylending, in colonial Burma, 27. *See also chettiars*; credit
monks, 127, 140, 223n40, 223n42; Byama-so funeral organization formed by, 75–76, 79–80, 86; merit-making ceremony for, 161–62; "rules of ideal conduct," 228n12; scope of charity and, 83–84; Sitagu Sayadaw, 83–84, 101, 223n43, 226n13; *Thadu Thadu Thadu* (phrase of gratitude), 60, 95; wealth redistribution and, 101; Wirathu, Buddhist, 136, 228n5
moral community. *See* political community; polity; social imaginaries
moral conduct, Buddhism and, 127
moral democracy, 125–128, 139
moral obligations, 103, 111, 119, 147
moral order, 97
moral value, of unity, 139

MoSWRR. *See* Ministry of Social Welfare, Relief, and Resettlement
Moulmein, 27
Mountbatten, Louis, 34
Muehlebach, Andrea, 16, 138
Muslims, 144–146, 234n12; laws restricting reproductive rights of, 229n19; MaBaTha on treatment of, 136; oppression under SLORC/SPDC junta, 145; sexually aggressive stereotype of, 145, 229n22; social capital index of, 230n23. *See also* Rohingya
Myanmar Airways International, 79
Myanmar Maternal and Child Welfare Association (MMCWA), 69–70
myitta (kindness), 84, 102, 131
myo mi myo pah (town "elders"), 77–78, 156–157

National Community Driven Development Project (NCDDP), 191
nationalist groups (*wunthanu athins*), 32–33
nationalist interpretation, of Buddhist ethics, 71
nationalist socialism, 54–55. *See also* coup of 1962
nationalization, of export trade, 47–48
National League for Democracy (NLD), 2, 79, 104–105, 109, 123, 231n22; activists, 143, 172; Business for Peace scheme, 236n2; campaign manager, 158, 159; candidate on democratic reform, 137; formation of, 126; support for, 129–132; tycoon funding of, 158–159. *See also* social welfare; democratic welfare capitalism
national races (*taingyintha*) ideology: hierarchy of belonging and, 115–16; legitimizing exclusion of Rohingya, 118; MaBaTha and, 135–136; role in state-building, 227; zero-sum logic of rights and, 195–196, 207–208. *See also* citizenship; MaBaTha; Muslims; political community
national religion (*amyo batha thathana*), 141
Nationwide Ceasefire Agreement of 2015, 19, 21
natural catastrophes, in post-1988 Myanmar, 95
Naypyitaw, 62–63, 69, 79, 149
NCDDP. *See* National Community Driven Development Project
neighborhood welfare groups, 76, 87, 89, 225n54
neikban. See Nibbana

networks, connecting political elites to welfare groups, 21
New Deal welfare initiatives, 14, 40, 225n3
Ne Win, 24, 25, 34, 43–46, 47; Khin Maung Aye and, 78–79; socialism of, 181–182, 194, 202. *See also* nationalist socialism
NGOs. *See* nongovernmental organizations
Nibbana (*neikban*), 41, 71, 83
Nishizaki, Yoshihiro, 163
NLD. *See* National League for Democracy
nongovernmental organizations (NGOs), 8–9, 102
non-state actors, 3–4, 11, 55, 67
non-state aid: necessity of, 124; problems with reliance on, 117–119, 149
non-state social provision, 13–14
non-state welfare: distribution, 7–8, 16, 22, 124; expansion from local to translocal focus, 100–109; ideals and practices of, 7–8, 16, 19, 105, 119, 124, 132, 196, 210; influence on politics, 125, 128, 146–147, 200–218; material and identity-based limits of, 84–89, 113, 116–118; normative support for, 12–13, 136–137; perceived as morally superior to government aid, 134–135

Obama, Barack, 14
obligation: of businesspeople, 145–147, 202; toward needy, 82, 97–98; to others, 85, 208
OECD. *See* Organization for Economic Cooperation and Development
oligarchy: elite dominance and, 12, 163–164; entrenchment, of elite economic interests and, 12, 16, 177; incubation of political elites and, 152; philanthropy and, 16–17; rigged laws and, 12–13, 17, 104, 146, 173, 176, 204–207. *See also* cronies; crony capitalism; philanthropy; polity; social outsourcing; tycoons
Organization for Economic Cooperation and Development (OECD), 10, 203
Our Burmese (*Dobama Asiayone*), 33
Outsourcing. *See* Social outsourcing

pagoda (Shwe San Daw), 78–79; construction of, 83; parade, 162; removal of shoes at, 31
Panglong Conference (1947), 35–36
parahita. See social work
parahita seit. See social consciousness
partial civilian rule (2011–2021), 19, 25, 61, 211n3; changes to constitution during, 138; philanthropy and, 153; social rights and,

178; transition to, 5, 166, 170–171. *See also* hybrid rule

participant observation, 21

partisan affiliations, welfare work and, 128–130

path dependence, 6, 9, 12–13, 17, 22–23

patronage: of Buddhist structures, 41; civilian politicians (2011–2021) and, 151–152; of collective identity, 163; commercial licensing (post-1988), 67–71, 77; philanthropy and, 150; pyramid of, 78

patron-client relations, 151, 151f, 230n3; between businesspeople and regional military commanders (post-1988), 67–71, 73–78. *See also* autocratic welfare capitalism; social outsourcing

peer pressure, 69–70

"people's contributions," labeling by state, 182

People's Stores, 48–49

People's Volunteer Organisation (PVO), 35, 43, 44

perfunctory donations, 74

personal virtue, 108–109

philanthronationalism, 80

philanthropy: civic, 143; civilizational, 165; collective identity and public, 160–161; elite, 152, 166–167, 176–177; in Europe, Myanmar compared with, 149; of Khin Maung Aye, 154–164; magnitude of giving and, 153; network evolution of, 150; normative support for, 12–13, 136–137; partial civilian rule and, 153; as path to capital accumulation (post-1988), 78–80; patronage structures and, 150; personal and public dimensions of, 152; provision of public goods, 207; public dimensions of (post-2011), 150–151, 153–154, 158–159, 177, 204–205; role of charity and, 23, 70–81

Phyo Win Latt, 189, 230n2

pioneer agriculturalists, 26

policy feedback, 6, 9, 12–13. *See also* path dependence

political autonomy, for minority populations, 63

political change, periods of, 17

political coalitions, 11

political community, 7, 118–119, 208; 2008 Constitution and, 95, 115–116, 118; inclusion in and exclusion from, 23, 49, 93–97, 105, 116, 118, 135–136, 189, 194–195, 208; provincial form of moral and, 161, 164; role of state vs non-state redistribution within, 115, 118, 132, 136, 139, 146–147. *See also*

citizenship; disasters; kin; national races (*taingyintha*) ideology; polity; social imaginaries

political contestation, 49

political discussions, welfare groups and, 128–129

political liberalization (2011), 124, 129

political loyalty, 130

political reform, moral conduct and, 127

political theater, 161

polity: austerity and, 16, 212n11; bonds of and hierarchies of belonging within, 93–97, 116–119, 141; democratic form of, 152; democratic ideal of, 139, 141; potential for redistributive form of, 208–210; privatized form of (post-1988), 7, 97, 109–110, 116–119, 139, 163; social outsourcing and, 206–208. *See also* blood-based theories of belonging; citizenship; national races (*taingyintha*) ideology; political community; social imaginaries; social outsourcing; welfare capitalism

post-authoritarian contexts, 125–126

poverty, 65–66

Poverty Reduction Fund, 233n7

practical practices, of delivering aid, 124–125, 132–133

practices, of non-state welfare, 124

Prasse-Freeman, Elliott, 189, 230n2, 235n20

precolonial period, idealization of, 137

price: of land in colonial-era delta, 27; of rice, 24, 32, 41–42; setting during BSPP, 50–51

private donations, as crucial to public welfare, 152

private health insurance, 14

private imports, BSPP ban of, 47–48

private manufacturing, BSPP decline in, 52–53

private redistribution, 194–195

productivist welfare capitalist regimes, 11, 91

Progressive reformers, 39

protection, offered by state, 96–97

protective areas, of social policy, 11

Psychological Warfare Unit, 44–45. *See also* Tatmadaw

public ceremonies, 73, 163, 230n7, 231n15

public gifting, as source of social hierarchy, 152–153

public goods: coproduced, 183, 201; tycoons as crucial to, 150, 153

public health expenditure, 66f

public-private partnership, Aung San Suu Kyi, 173–174, 174f; donations and, 230n1 punishments, for going against junta officials, 68

PVO. *See* People's Volunteer Organisation

The Pyidawtha Plan, 25, 37–38, 40–41, 44, 48; fusing urban welfare capitalism with socialism, 37; junta and, 72; vision of, 201–202.

pyramid of patronage, 78

quid pro quo, of SLORC/SPDC commercial deals, 60–61. *See also* social outsourcing

Rakhine State, 117–118, 148–149, 174; Khin Swe, 232n26; public-private partnership of, 230n1. *See also* Rohingya

Rangoon, 25, 27

RC. *See* Revolutionary Council

reallocation of government funds, to military portfolios, 62. *See also* autocratic welfare capitalism

rebel leaders, advisory roles for, 63

reciprocity, 5, 74, 125, 208; ideals and practices of, 92, 105, 209; localized, 51, 95, 102, 115, 116, 204; transactional, 69

redistribution: Communist Party of Burma demands of, 40; models, 87–88; politics of, 4, 36–37; private, 194–195; without taxation (welfare capitalism), 26; of unused land, 231n22; in wake of disasters, 92–93; wealth, 82, 101, 103–104; welfare regime, 54

referendum, to approve 2008 Constitution, 99

reform *(pyu pyin)*, 137

regulation, of businesspeople behavior, 124–125

relational labor, of volunteers, 16

relief efforts: local following cyclone, 99–100; in Taungoo, 106–108. *See also* disaster relief

religious actors, involvement of, 74, 101–104, 133, 226n13

religious instruction *(sasana)*, 84

religious intermediaries, 110–111

religious minorities, as scapegoats, 143–147

repatriation, of Rohingya Muslims, 148–149, 174, 175, 195, 232n25

research methods, 17–18

research site, Myanmar as, 4–5

residency within community, as requirement for aid, 88–89

resistance efforts (post-2021 coup), 8, 209–210; role of charity and welfare groups in sustaining, 133, 209

resource extraction, 28

resources, inheritance of, 80–81

Revolutionary Council (RC), 47

"revolution of the spirit," 126

rice: on black market, 50–52; boost in crop yield of, 52; prices, 24, 32; quotas, 51

rice merchant, on permit donations and, 72–73

Rice Traders Association, 75

rigging, of regimes, 10

rights: eligibility, legibility and exclusion, 188–193; legibility and legitimate exclusion, 188–192; moral order (Charles Taylor) and, 97; Muslim restriction to reproduction, 229n19; one-way flow of, 235n20; politics of entitlement and, 19; relationality after social outsourcing and, 137–139; relative to duties, 8; restriction of reproductive (of Muslims), 229n19; right to have, 188; zero-sum logic of, 191–193, 195–197, 208. *See also* deservingness; land grabs; polity; self-reliance; social outsourcing

riots, in Rangoon, 50

ritual of giving *(a-hlubwe)*, 59–60

road construction, 71, 76–77, 183; abrupt end of self-reliant projects, 187; contributions to, 185f, 233n8, 234n14, 234nn16–17, 236n31; "doing it yourself" repair, 186–187; endorsement letters and, 77; perception of, 181f

Rohingya, 116, 118; exclusion, expulsion and NLD plans for repatriation of, 148–149, 174, 175, 195, 208, 232n25. *See also* national races *(taingyintha)* ideology

Roosevelt, Franklin D., 14, 40

Rose, Nikolas, 188

Royal Kaytumadi hotel, 161

Rule of Law and Tranquility Committee, 235n21

rural development initiatives, 180, 180f, 236n29

rural villages, in Taungoo, 18

Saffron Revolution (2007), 126–127, 223n40

sasana (religious instruction), 84

sawbwa (Shan dynasties), 28

sayadaw. See abbot

Saya San, 24–25, 32

scapegoats, religious minorities as, 143–147

Schaffer, Frederick, 125

schemes, of social insurance, 11

scorched earth policy, 42–43

Scott, James C., 32, 151, 230n4

second-tier cluster clients, 151

Second World War, 33–34

security councils, 45
Seekins, Donald, 100
self-help outlook, as idea, 182
self-reliance, 232n1, 234nn14–15; as criteria for state aid, 187, 188–192, 207; as ideal, 181–182, 234n15; normative outlook of, 14–15, 23, 178–179, 205–206; post-1988 Tatmadaw self-financing, 65; projects, 182, 234n14
Senegal, 125
separation, of Burma from India, 33
services, provided without tax increase, 41
Seven Step Roadmap to Discipline-Flourishing Democracy, 98
Sgaw Karen, 22
Shan dynasties (*sawbwa*), 28
shopkeepers, 1–2
shopping mall proposal, 1–3, 158
Shwedagon pagoda, 114
Shwe Linn, 168–169
Shwe San Daw (pagoda), 78–79
Silber, Illana, 152
Silpa-archa, Barnharn, 163
Sitagu Sayadaw (U Nyanissara), 83–84, 101, 223n43, 226n13. *See also* MaBaTha
the Sitwundan, 43
SLORC. *See* State Law and Order Restoration Council
social affairs (*lu-mu-yay*), 76, 84
social austerity, 5, 8, 16, 65
social capital index, 230n23
social consciousness (*parahita seit*), 86, 108, 135, 141–142. *See also* citizenship; polity; social imaginaries
social contract: conception of pre *vs.* post-1988, 137, 188, 206
social discipline, 140
social duty, to distant others, 119
social imaginaries, 96–97; blood and kin-based notions of, 95, 106–108, 118, 135–136; moral bonds of and exclusion from, 86, 104, 115–118, 146, 194, 195; provincial form of, 161–164. *See also* disasters; kin; political community; polity; social consciousness; social work
social intimacy, between patron and client, 151
socialism: dissolution of, 25; fusion with urban welfare capitalism of, 37; late colonial consensus in favour of, 36
Socialist Economy Construction Committee, 47
Socialist Party politicians, 50–51, 54

social licensing, 7, 69, 77–78, 110, 150; dispute, between junta officials and civilian clients, 79; tycoons and, 165–166. *See also* autocratic welfare capitalism; market liberalization and reform; tycoons
social obligation: ethos of, 138; outsourcing of, 137–138; of state, 71; of wealthy, 109–110
social outsourcing, 3–4, 26, 54–55, 61, 146–147; business expansion and, 78–79; developmental tradeoffs of, 6, 63–67; diverse and enduring appeal of, 23, 200–201, 203–204; enduring appeal of, 23, 200–201, 203–204; entitlement and, 16; ideology and logics of, 71–72, 158; inequality and, 200–201; post-1988 austerity and, 16, 63–65, 206, 210, 212n11; reimagined role of Buddhist sovereign and, 137; social progress and, 206; state encouragement of nongovernmental actors and, 67; state welfare and, 6; trust in state social action and, 176–177. *See also* cronies; market liberalization and reform; social licensing; Social Security Board; tycoons; welfare capitalism
social protection, in late-developing countries, 8–9
social reputation, of donors, 152
social rights, 14, 178–179
social sectors, allocations to, 211n4
Social Security Board (SSB), 40, 42, 48, 218n46
social ties, between citizens, 98
social welfare: gaps, 5; spending on after 2011, 211n6, 232n1
social work (*parahita*), 82–84, 101, 112, 115, 141; expansion of focus from local to translocal needy, 100–109. *See also* disaster relief
socioeconomic vulnerability, 5–6
solicitation, for donations to state initiatives, 174
solidarity, political loyalty and, 130
sons of the nation (*amyotha*), 143
sons of the soil, 227n25
South Indian merchants (*chettiars*), 27, 31
SPDC. *See* State Peace and Development Council
Special Rebellion Commission, 32
spiritual merit, donations and, 73
Spiro, Melford, 41, 83, 234n13
SSB. *See* Social Security Board
stable government, effectiveness of non-state aid and, 119
state, welfare provision and, 5
state aid: access to, 14–15, 179, 185–186; inefficiency of, 97–108; seeking of, 185–186

state-building, 61–63, 91, 194, 227n25; colonial institutional inheritances and, 28–29; role of national races ideology in, 227; role of PVO in post-independence, 35; SLORC/SPDC attempts at, 62–63, 91. *See also* autocratic welfare capitalism; ceasefire capitalism; social outsourcing

state-business relations: post-1988 non-state welfare provision and, 87; under SLORC/SPDC, 69, 82. *See also* autocratic welfare capitalism; democratic welfare capitalism; market liberalization and reform; oligarchy; social licensing; social outsourcing

state capacity: to deliver services with limited resources, 169, 200; for redistribution, 17; to repay loans, 49; to tax population, 10, 91–92, 120

state-coordinated donation rituals, 82

state involvement, in "self-reliance" projects, 184

State Law and Order Restoration Council (SLORC)/State Peace and Development Council (SPDC), 54, 60–61, 73, 92, 126, 230n5; allocation of disaster relief responsibilities to businesses and, 103; awards for contributions to social causes, 72; coerced solicitation of donations by, 82–84; donations and, 70, 73; forced labor and, 179–180, 233n11, 233nn5–6; headmen managing, 234n15; land transactions with business-people by, 170; legacies of Pyidawtha Plan, 72; market reform by, 54; Muslim suffering under, 145; patron-client relations and, 151, 230n5; punishments for going against, 68; restrictions on aid following Cyclone Nargis (2008), 99, 226n6. *See also* autocratic welfare capitalism; market liberalization and reform; military (Tatmadaw); social outsourcing

state-led schemes, extension of, 11–12, 13

state-mediated social safety net, as gift, 198

State Peace and Development Council (SPDC). *See* State Law and Order Restoration Council (SLORC)

state policies, 13, 16, 96–97

state redistributive capacity, 17. *See also* state capacity

state social responsibility, 22, 69

state social retrenchment, 67. *See also* austerity; social outsourcing

state-society relations, 96–97

state spending, in the United States, 15

state tax revenue, 90–91, 91f

strangers, as reincarnated family members, 95

students giving blood, at Taungoo general hospital, 86

subnational patronage, 164

sufferer (*dukkha-theh*), 107, 135

suffering of Muslims under junta, 145

Suharto (president), 175

Sunday Dhamma schools, 140–141, 229n15

support: for charitable works and tax evasion, 144; from local entrepreneurs, 71

symbolic capital, 152–153, 206

System of Correlation of Man and His Environment (BSPP document), 46–47

Tabinshwehti (king), 160

tageh demokrasi (true democracy), 135

Tatmadaw:*See* military (Tatmadaw).

Taungoo, Myanmar, 1, 3, 18–19, 79–80; demographic of, 18; home for aged in, 59–60, 76, 131; Khin Maung Aye and, 154; lowland areas topographical map, 20f; relief effort in, 106–108; rural villages in, 18; urban population of, 15

Taungoo dynasty, 160–161, 162, 163–164; memorialization of 500th anniversary, 164–165, 231n11

Taungoo General Hospital, 76, 86, 134–136, 139

taxation, 53; attempt to provide services without increasing, 41; capacity to levy, 10; colonial, 30, 32; donations as form of, 73–74, 225n57; evasion, 144, 206–207; formal, 68, 77, 90, 174; of indirect expenditures, 89–91; informal, 53, 70, 132, 225n58; informal and implicit, 90–91; land, 32; limited capacity, to tax populations, 10; low-income population flat-rate, 30; opposition towards, 40, 201; quasi-voluntary compliance and, 82, 85, 118; redistribution without, 26; revenue, 6, 90–91, 91f, 175–176; spending, 91, 133, 133f; trust in relative to donations, 176; trust lacking in, 133, 133f. *See also* autocratic welfare capitalism; democratic welfare capitalism

tax concessions, 15, 90, 132–133, 202, 207; for private donations, 15–16, 118–119, 225n57; untaxed economy, 53. *See also* social outsourcing; state

Taylor, Charles, 97

thabu-oo (Gordian knot), 132

Thailand, 191, 236n29

Thamanya Sayadaw, 83

Thandaungyi (Karen State), 196

Tharrawaddy, 25

Thein Stein, 79, 105, 128–129

Thingyan, 59–60
3G cellular network, expansion of, 105–106
Three Worlds of Welfare Capitalism (Esping-Anderson), 10
Tibetan Buddhism, 125
town "elders" (*myo mi myo pah*), 77–78, 156–157
town-hall meeting, about shopping complex, 1–3, 165
trade unions. *See* labor
transactional reciprocity, 69
transitionary elites, 12
translocal needy, 105–106
trash collection, 141–142, 143, 167
Tripartite Core Group, 100, 226n5
Trocaire, 103
true democracy (*tageh demokrasi*), 135
trust: donation confidence and, 133, 134f; taxation spending and, 133, 133f
Turnell, Sean, 90
Turner, Alicia, 229n14
tycoons, 23, 150, 152, 153–156, 204; Aung San Suu Kyi relations with, 173–174, 174f; competition between, 166; critiques of, 169–170; organizational affiliation, with NLD, 128; past injustices and, 170–173; shakedown of, 175; tax evasion and, 206–207; tensions with shopkeepers, 3. *See also* cronies; crony capitalism; Khin Maung Aye; oligarchy; philanthropy

UEHRD. *See* Union Enterprise for Humanitarian Assistance, Resettlement, and Development
uncertainty, about tax spending, 133, 133f
undeserving poor, deserving poor *versus*, 193–194
unemployment, 234n19
Unilever, 42
Union Enterprise for Humanitarian Assistance, Resettlement, and Development (UEHRD), 149, 230n1. *See also* Muslims; Rohingya
Union of Burma Parliament, 45
Union of Myanmar, 5
Union Solidarity and Development Association (USDA), 69–70, 82
Union Solidarity and Development Party (USDP), 79, 128, 131–132, 158, 186
"Union Solidarity and Development Party village," 123
United Nations Security Council, 148
United States (US), 203, 205; Affordable Care Act, 14; state spending in, 15

untaxed economy, 53
U Nu, 25, 45–46, 54–55; embrace of capitalism by, 37–38, 40–41; perceived denial of Burmese grievances by, 43; rejuvenation of Buddhist customs and, 41; vision of self-reliant development and, 182. *See also* Pyidawtha Plan
U Nyanissara. *See* Sitagu Sayadaw
upland Myanmar, 117
upward mobility, 27, 78
USDA. *See* Union Solidarity and Development Association
USDP. *See* Union Solidarity and Development Party
U Win Thein, 2

Walinsky, Louis, 40
Walker, Andrew, 191, 235n25
Walton, Matthew, 102, 127
waste management, 168–169
water ritual, pouring over Buddha, 115
wealth defense. *See* democratic welfare capitalism; oligarchy; philanthropy
welfare: parastate, 90; work and partisan affiliations, 128–130; of workers, 39
welfare capitalism, 26, 48, 85, 103, 109–110, 146; American, 39–40; autocratic, 72–73, 80–81, 89, 202–203, 209–210; democratic form of, 136, 165; interventionist, 37–38; productivity benefits of, 39; socialism fused with urban, 37; U Nu's Pyidawtha Vision of, 40–42, 54
welfare groups: of activists, 85, 92; disaster relief leader, 100; organization of, 110–11
welfare regime(s), 9–10, 17, 48, 90, 97; BSPP model of, 50–55, 61, 68; development and, 13–14, 67; insecure, post-1988 model of, 65–67, 68, 71–72, 74, 90–92, 105, 115, 118–120, 169, 185, 197–198; post-independence model of, 40–42, 54; types of state, 10–11. *See also* autocratic welfare capitalism; Burma Socialist Programme Party; democratic welfare capitalism; The Pyidawtha Plan; social outsourcing
Wells, Tamas, 127, 138–139
Western companies, 47
Wirathu (Buddhist monk), 136, 228n5
Wood, Geof, 9
worker-oriented social citizenship, 16
World Bank, 18, 191, 235n23
wunthanu athins (nationalist groups), 32–33

Yangon, 101, 106, 226nn8–9
Yangon School of Political Science, 22
Ye Htut, 106

www.ingramcontent.com/pod-product-compliance
Lightning Source LLC
Chambersburg PA
CBHW030348270326
41926CB00009B/1003